# ANTONI GAUDÍ

**1852  1926**
**architecture, ideology and politics**

**juan josé lahuerta**

**Electa**architecture

*Editor*
Giovanna Crespi

*Page Layout*
Lucia Vigo

*Translation*
Graham Thompson

*Copy Editor*
Gail Swerling

*Technical Coordinators*
Paolo Verri
Andrea Panozzo

Distributed by Phaidon Press
ISBN 1-904313-20-5

www.phaidon.com

www.electaweb.it

Printed in China

# Contents

In 1930 Salvador Dalí wrote
in *L'âne pourri:* "This pleases
us today; this impressive number
of delirious buildings
disseminated all over Europe,
scorned and ignored in the
anthologies and the studies."
Walter Benjamin observed
the same thing in his notes
for the book he planned
to write on the arcades,
and added: "Perhaps Barcelona
is the city that, with
the buildings of the architect
who designed the Sagrada
Família, can offer the most
perfect examples of this
Jugendstil."

## Bourgeoisie and Nobility
Verdaguer, Gaudí and the Symbolic Production
of the Barcelona *Haute Bourgeoisie*, 1878–88

*"Modern Advances, Modern Magnificence"*
The almost always enthusiastic comments that
Josep Yxart devoted to the Barcelona International Exhibition, which officially opened at four o'clock
on the afternoon of May 20, 1888, are eloquent
testimony not only to the way those Barcelona intellectuals who were in favor of the Exhibition
saw it, in its spectacularity, as the culmination of
the processes that had radically transformed the
city over the previous twenty years, but above all
how they regarded that transformation; what they
understood and what they did not understand; how
they interpreted it.[1]
Yxart reflected optimistically on the need for the
Exhibition. This was "of necessity" to be held in
Barcelona, a city that, "with the black chimneys of
an English suburb, with the restaurants and the
bookshops of a Parisian boulevard, with the gardens and sails on the sea of an Italian port," was
already, in relation to the rest of Spain, "something
different, something continental rather than
peninsular," and a city that, in contrast to the other major cities of the State, "with their backs to
the world, looking to the Court, turns towards the
Pyrenees and peers over them at Europe."[2]
Cosmopolitanism, modernity: above all, those two
things signify for Yxart the "European spirit" he
finds in Barcelona. And those are precisely the
words with which he most frequently characterizes
his impressions of the new city.
A *new* city, certainly, but not astonishingly new.
We have already seen that Yxart felt the Exhibition to be a necessity. But what kind of necessity
was it? Barcelona, he writes, "has in a very few
years seen its perimeter enlarged with its new expansion, to the extent that today, on the point of
absorbing the industrial towns around it, it is
poised to become a vast center with a very dense
population extending between the two rivers that
delimit its boundary." Properly integrated into
these processes, the Exhibition could not be anything other than their result, or better still, an
exemplary moment, their provisional corollary.
With regard to this, Yxart writes: "Barcelona
has indefatigably planned and carried out various

improvements that have entirely altered its appearance; it is at present completing others …
And he adds with clarity: "This urge, this delirium, this vertigo for construction … has certainly
not been the least important inspiration for the
idea of an Exhibition, nor the least important element in fueling the expectation of seeing it."[3]
The Exhibition, then, in the eyes of its contemporaries, was not so much intended to intervene in
the processes of transformation of the city—stimulating or correcting them, for example—as to be
their privileged shop window; in other words, to
put them on display. Is it so strange, then, that in
spite of the spectacularity it was perceived as having at the time it did not effect any change in the
natural tendency of that development but, on the
contrary, served to confirm it and sought to ensure
its continuity?[4] Indeed Yxart finds nothing odd in
the new scale of Barcelona, its dynamism, its power. From this point of view, the Exhibition cannot
surprise him. There were only half innovations:
this was an anticipated spectacle.
And he can also write that "Barcelona … was at
once theater and spectator and a grandiose event."[5]
The city, then, exhibited itself looking at itself, and
at the same time recognizing itself: the mannered
symmetry of that phrase is certainly highly significant. The need for the Exhibition was therefore
symbolic.
Yxart's account, then, moves freely when he is describing—and justifying—quantitative changes in
Barcelona as an organism. The reason is immediately apparent: a conventional—and exalted—idea
of progress serves him as a pattern to which to
assimilate in linear sequence all of the forms of that
growth, industrial, commercial, physical and spiritual, in this way avoiding surprises and escaping
contradictions. But in projecting rigidly that
schema on to the complexity of the city, what is
Yxart doing but proposing another reality? The
vehemence with which he sets out his impressions
and the exaggeration with which on more than one
occasion he calibrates the situation he describes
are not effects of the obfuscation caused by the
enthusiasm and euphoria always present in the

excerpts quoted above, but essentially a form of *amplificatio*, the *medium* of a proposal.

Yxart is, as we have said, projecting. But projecting what? Simply what he regards as *normality*. When he speaks of the cosmopolitanism of Barcelona, its modernity, its Europeanism, he is manifesting something that, if it were not taking place in "the capital of a province of Spain, of an utterly feeble nation, unfortunately for us,"[6] would be absolutely normal, undeserving of special attention. Of course Yxart is not very ambitious: his euphoria and his exaggerations serve as an inverse reflection or negative image of what the people at whom he directs his projection are lacking.

The Exhibition is both result and image of the power of Barcelona, but that "majestic display of grandeur and might that only the great capitals of the great nations have attempted"[7] has been made possible solely and exclusively by the city's bourgeoisie: something else that would be absolutely normal if it were not taking place in Spain—a Spain that, Yxart writes, 'is almost alien to us.'"[8] It is at that bourgeoisie, and not at the "classical Spain" so well represented in Barcelona itself in those days by the presence of the Royal Court, that Yxart directs his projection: his proposals of modernity and cosmopolitism are aimed at them.

Yxart is quite clear that it is the industry of that bourgeoisie that has made the Exhibition possible, but its success clearly demonstrates that that bourgeoisie is no longer content to be simply industrious. Commenting on the official speeches delivered by the Spanish authorities at the ceremonial closing of the event, Yxart writes with barely controlled rage: "We beseech our illustrious guests, with the greatest courtesy, to desist, by the five wounds of Christ, from calling us either *industrious*, or *active*, or *industrial*."[9] In contrast to what had happened with the processes of Barcelona's transformation, for Yxart the difference on this occasion—far more important than the other—is qualitative. This is how he describes that middle class: "Our bourgeois likes to live in a comfortable, luxurious house, constructed on modern principles, he embellishes it with paintings, adorns it with the gewgaws of modern magnificence, and takes diversion from his daily prose in artistic pastimes formerly denied to the *épicier* by the long-haired Romantics. And when he leaves his house he craves his city statues and monuments, he dreams of Versailles-like parks, and scrutinizes and judges the municipal public works as something that concerns him directly." Yxart's description of the Barcelona bourgeoisie might seem, like his comments on the city, exaggerated. Nevertheless, he notes that the homes of that bourgeoisie "of the Stock Exchange and the cashbook" still have "that visible but indefinable varnish that adheres to everything connected with the nouveau riche."[10] This prejudice, perfectly clear and repeated on several occasions, enables us to understand Yxart's comment not as a description of reality but, once again, as the projection of an idea onto that reality. Like his comments on the growth of the city, his description of the customs of its bourgeoisie are not intended as anything but an extended observation of things as they are: it is in that critique that we find Yxart's proposal, his project.

Coinciding approximately with the period of political stability that followed the restoration of the monarchy in 1875, the Barcelona bourgeoisie enjoyed a major expansion of business and a great accumulation of wealth that was interrupted by the stock-market crash of 1882, the consequences of which were still very much in evidence in 1888, the year of the Exhibition.[11] In a novel published in two parts in 1890 and 1892 entitled *La febra d'or*, "Gold Fever," Narcis Oller narrates, with moralizing overtones, the rise and fall of an example of the new bourgeoisie, Gil Foix, a tradesman who suddenly finds himself spectacularly rich thanks to his investments in the Stock Exchange, only to be ruined in the crash of '82.[12] Fever, delirium and madness are the words Oller uses most frequently to characterize the situation: "Gil Foix was not wrong: gold fever, spread all over Europe, was growing without respite in Barcelona. All of the money emerged from the hiding places where prudence had salted it away and passed crazily from hand to hand. Once again there had sounded the clarion

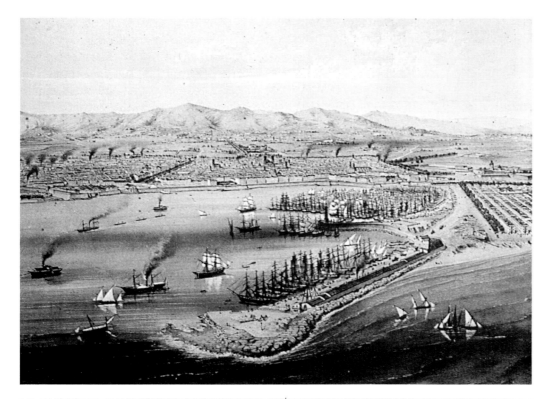

calls that awaken the covetousness of the humble and unleash, from time to time, these great crusades to conquer the golden calf."[13] Oller centered his novel on the Stock Exchange boom that immediately preceded the crash precisely because what most impressed him about the situation was the incredible abundance of money; money—and hence the come-uppance suffered by the protagonist at the end of the novel—that is not the fruit of hard work and effort, and is therefore linked not to real things and their value but to pure speculation: "The atmosphere of well-being that was breathed on all sides led even the most austere to spend and exchange the gold that had been amassed with sweat and privations for those scraps of paper, printed in half tones, that credit was distributing by the cartload."[14] Money presented itself, then, in its most radically abstract aspect—credit, paper— and was thus converted, in the eyes of a traditionalist such as Oller, into something almost incomprehensible: enchanted money that circulated in the air, without touching things. The social consequences of that circulation are also characterized by madness and fever: "The theaters, always packed, were dazzling. The ironmongers and carpenters struggled to make ends meet while the demand for jewelry and fine furniture kept growing. The number of confectioners, glove makers, fancy bakers and luxury restaurants multiplied as if by magic … and while construction in the industrial districts declined, to right and left there sprang up magnificent houses, villas and authentic palaces."[15] Alluding, in the midst of all this wealth, to a very real industrial recession, Oller moralistically contrasts the traditional work ethic to the new aesthetic of consumption. But what was this consumerism that possessed the Barcelona bourgeoisie with a fury never seen before, other than the clearest and most specific sign of its access to modernity; in other words, the equating of its way of life with that of the middle classes of the advanced societies of Europe?[16]

Like Yxart, Oller consciously exaggerated—and along the same lines—the consumerist tendencies of the bourgeoisie, but the intentions of the two

*A. Gaudí, the Transatlántica
company pavilion at the Barcelona
International Exhibition of 1888.*

*Castelucho, "Barcelona. View
from the fort of D. Carlos, at 380 m
distance and 350 m height above
sea level." In the foreground
is the Ciutadella park as laid out
in Fontseré's project of 1872.*

writers were very different. We have seen how Yxart's depiction of the new way of life of the Barcelona bourgeois centered on the description of his home and of his city: a comfortable, luxurious, beautiful house that had its continuation in a city of statues, monuments and parks. Oller, referring to the delusions of grandeur of the nouveau riche Gil Foix, takes the same line. This is his new house: "A shopkeeper, also improvised, who did out everything in the *boudoir de cocotte* style had decorated that house for them in such a way as to make it a torment. The family was suffocated, there was no air; with so many curtains, hangings, carpets … so many pouffes, little tables, chairs, so many pedestals to trip over; he detested that profusion of porcelain flowers, little pictures and fragile *bibelots* that, scattered all around, repressed the most natural movements and were a daily source of vexation and the cause of reproaches and tears for the servants."[17] But the worst thing, for Oller, is that all memory, every trace of the past, has disappeared from this house so absolutely packed with con-

tents: the time of concrete things, of life itself, has been erased. He writes: "The old furniture had been banished, regardless of whether or not it held family memories."[18] Oller cannot prevent his traditionalism from tingeing his caricatured description with bitterness. But, as in Yxart's case, that house so cherished by Gil Foix has its continuation in his dreams for the city: "Gil Foix … had proposed various projects of this kind. One of these consisted in moving the Santa Creu hospital, and installing on the space this would leave vacant the market of San José, thus completing the plaza occupied by the market, in the center of which there would be an equestrian statue, and at its feet, gardens and great streetlamps."[19] The urban reforms Oller is alluding to here are no mere fanciful invention: this was a plan that had been tabled for discussion on more than one occasion by Barcelona's municipal authorities, and was to be proposed again on many more occasions, the last quite recently.[20] What is grotesque about the situation, then, is the megalomania of the nouveau riche prepared to pay the

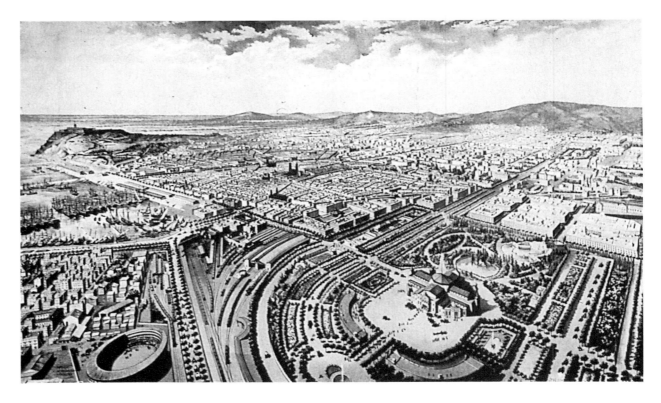

"*Plan of Barcelona with the part of the Ensanche [Eixample] currently under construction,*" 1894.

"*Plan of the municipal area of Barcelona,*" 1891.

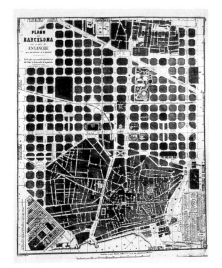

cost of the whole operation out of his own pocket. But it does not end there. On this occasion, too, Oller intervenes in the narrative with a moralizing reflection: "Every day the authorities received more and more plans for new projects, with their corresponding reports, in which the hypocritical motive of speculation was dressed up in an impassioned patriotism, zealously forward-looking and paternal."[21]

Is it really, in Oller's view, only speculation that drives the projects for the rebuilding of Barcelona? Perhaps not, but the *ethical* radicalism of the novel has no place for anything else. Yxart and Oller, then, are not only speaking about the same thing, they use almost identical words—and, of course, the same images. Both writers schematize and exaggerate the same kinds of behavior in the same way, and both have an exemplary end in view: the latter's aim is quite clearly moralistic while the former's purpose might be best described as educational. In the forms of conduct engendered by the new wealth Oller sees an opportunity to ridicule a

certain section of the bourgeoisie and to reproach it for the excessive ease with which it has acquired its money and its position; in those same behaviors Yxart perceives the changes that will lead that Barcelona bourgeoisie—which he regarded as far more generic, more indistinct—to throw off its old crafts-based mentality and become totally incorporated into the advanced societies of Europe. Gil Foix's house, as Oller describes it, is very little different from Yxart's picture of the bourgeois home, but if in Oller the consumerism represented by the plethora of useless objects that cram the house is an occasion for caricature, in Yxart that accumulation is synonymous with modernity. In his three-line description, in fact, Yxart uses the word "modern" twice: "modern advances" and "modern magnificence."[22] For Yxart, then, the relation between modernity and consumption is very clear. If, as we noted above, Yxart's projection consists in proposing to the bourgeoisie of Barcelona a modern, cosmopolitan attitude—in other words, assimilation into the advanced European middle

classes—we now find that the means of achieving this involves increasing its habits of consumption. But consumption of what? Once again with reference to the Barcelona bourgeoisie, Yxart writes: "Its intellectual movement ... is not in due proportion to its material advances."[23] This is evidently not a criticism of the intellectuals but a call for the bourgeoisie to support them financially. The answer to the question is thus perfectly clear: the consumption, above all, of culture, of art.

It is easy enough to deduce from all of this that the relationship between art and society is the central theme of almost all of Yxart's reports on the Exhibition. "This," he writes, "amounts to very much more than a show of manufactures, and implies a powerful artistic movement."[24] Or, in an excerpt to which we referred above, with regard to the transformations that have led to the Exhibition: "This delirium for constructions, developing the aptitudes, tempering the muscles, stimulating the interest of all the artists and all the craftsmen employed in them, has certainly not been the least important inspiration of the idea of an Exhibition."[25] The Exhibition thus presents itself to Yxart as a privileged moment in the relations between the public authorities, the industrial and commercial interests of the bourgeoisie and the interests of artists and craftsmen: it is, above all, from this point of view that it assumes, for Yxart, that symbolic value we have already seen it as having for him. When Yxart strolls through the galleries of paintings and sculptures in the Palace of Fine Arts, when he describes in minute detail buildings and pavilions, when he paces inquisitorially the streets of the city speaking of its new monuments, he is not only generous in his praise of the flashes of modernity he discovers there; above all, he is fiercely critical of every instance of bad taste or provincialism. It is significant, for example, how he comments the new constructions. He recognizes in them "solidity and even daring and innovation," but laments the poverty of "their decoration," and concludes: "The pity is that it has not been possible to seize this great opportunity to show outsiders the very newest architectural tendencies, and pre-

pare the taste of our public in general!"[26] To prepare people's taste, to educate ... for consumption: that, as we have said, is the keynote of Yxart's text. But in urging them to consume more and to consume a thoroughly new art, what is Yxart doing if not proposing to that Barcelona bourgeoisie the creation of an art of their own? And, consequently, what is he doing but calling for a new kind of artist, a liberal artist, supported not by the institutions and the academies, but by a market: the market created by that same bourgeoisie?

Yxart, however, speaks always in generic terms—"our bourgeois," "our public in general"—and with the aristocratic distancing of the old-style intellectual. The result is that his proposal has to be deduced from the euphemisms and the contradictions that fill his articles. In fact it was not until Raimon Casellas joined the magazine *L'Avenç* in 1891 that a consciously and systematically *Modernista* art criticism came to be developed.[27] But alongside the highly significant generalizations of Yxart's critique we can set other factors: between 1883 and 1888, the year of the Exhibition, Antoni Gaudí had already constructed such works as the Casa Vicens, the stables and boundary walls on the Güell estate, the Palau Güell ... Without a doubt it is this architecture that Yxart has in mind in lamenting the absence of the "very newest tendencies" in the Exhibition.[28] But there is more: in every case these are houses commissioned by individual clients, members of the bourgeoisie. Wealth plus great consumption equals modernity: the equation that we have discerned in Yxart's articles *seems to present itself* for the first time in Barcelona in those three works, and perhaps Gaudí is, in this respect, the first modern artist of a bourgeoisie capable of making that equation.[29] Let me insist: not "our bourgeois," but a bourgeoisie. But, as we shall see, perhaps this is mere appearance, and the factors of that equation, although real enough, may have surprises in store.

It was above all in the specular character of the Barcelona Exhibition—at once "theater and spectator," as Yxart said—that its symbolic value was contained: the city was beginning to be a place not

only to be seen in, but also to look out from. There was, without a doubt, a bourgeoisie that was very far from generic, a bourgeoisie that had understood very well—and not necessarily in Yxart's terms—the value of that new city and with it the value of its new habits, of its newest art. A stroll around that new city would suffice to show that there was nothing generic about that value, either; it was thoroughly concrete, both politically and ideologically.

*The Perplexed City*

In 1881 and 1882, the years of the Stock Exchange boom that provides the background to *La febra d'or*, twenty-seven new banks were founded in Barcelona, more than half of which went under in the crash of 1882, when the Stock Exchange fell by over 50% in only two months. At the same time the principal Catalan manufacture, textiles, was suffering from a slump in the domestic market and increasing foreign competition, with a notable curtailing of its growth from 1878. There was serious overproduction in 1884, followed in 1888 by a restructuring that affected even major firms such as La España Industrial and the Güell factories. And on top of all this, Catalonia's most important agricultural activity in the 1870s, wine production, went from a period of euphoria in which it accounted for 63% of Spain's total wine exports to the crisis occasioned by the penetration of the phylloxera plague: by 1888 the blight had already destroyed over 30% of Catalonia's vines. The International Exhibition took place, then, at a time of major crisis—financial, industrial and agricultural—and in the midst of the acute social conflict that Barcelona experienced as a consequence of this crisis.[30]

But that is not the whole story. As we have seen, the transformations to which Yxart refers are for the most part changes in the appearance of the city, since this is obviously where they are most evident. These are transformations that are resolved in quantitative terms and for which the idea of progress, as we have said, always offers plausible explanations. But were there not other changes taking place in Barcelona that were more difficult

to understand, harder to explain in terms of the conventional image of the city that grows naturally? Oller perceived a hypocritically speculative intent behind the projects for the embellishment of Barcelona: we have already noted the moralism of his reaction, but we should not find it too surprising, bearing in mind that the removal of the old city walls and the occupation of the plain of Barcelona from 1860 on with the project for the Eixample had provided the upper middle class with an opportunity for profit on a scale that was unimaginable in the densely packed old town. The 1870s and the early 1880s saw a volume of capital investment in the central sector of the Eixample greater than that invested during the same period in the whole of industry, services and consumption, with profits of up to 300% in only four years.[31] All at once, and in a totally unexpected dimension, the city had been literally transformed into a commodity. Thus, in the proper sense of the word—which has nothing to do with size—Barcelona had become a metropolis. Both Yxart and Oller detect this in its most evident forms, those in which change presents itself as the sole, the absolute value: new shops with brilliant window displays, new restaurants, new cafés, new theaters and new amusements—we might think here of the excellent chapter in *La febra d'or* describing the opening of the Hipódromo race track.[32] Where else but in that city transformed into a commodity could there occur the astonishing growth that Oller ridiculed and Yxart hailed as a sign of modernity? But if Oller clearly found those transformations incomprehensible, for Yxart they were in many ways at least paradoxical. Especially meaningful here is Yxart's sense of disorientation when confronted with another of the emblems of the new city: the crowd. Yxart speaks on more than one occasion of the "wide-eyed pedestrian, dazed, dizzy, stunned"[33]; of the nameless passer-by; of the "man" who walks amid panoramas and shops, who attaches himself to groups of strangers, who crosses streets that are rivers of human beings and is constantly led on by the spectacle of the merchandise inside and outside of the Exhibition precincts. In his description of

one of the most multitudinous events of those days, the cavalcade,[34] Yxart even adopts a different and for him unaccustomed narrative technique: he abandons the first person voice he has used up to that point and describes what is seen by the eyes of one of those disoriented individuals in the third person. "My man let himself be carried by the current, wherever it willed," Yxart writes. This little story is simply the man's itinerary through streets "full of inexpert outsiders spilling over the pavements,"[35] as he tries to find the place where the cavalcade is to ride past: everything he sees is fragmented, he can never form an idea of the street as a whole, of the relationship between the groups that throng it, and even the cavalcade—when after a considerable effort he manages to reach it—appears to him not as a unitary comprehensible spectacle but in snatches, and often simply as a reflection, as something intuited from the movements it provokes in the crowd. Yxart's "man" knows he is there where the event that will be written about in the next day's newspapers is taking place, but he has lost the natural capacity of seeing it. The brief account is full of anecdotes and ironies on the misadventures of the man, to the point of rendering him ridiculous. Nevertheless, this does not help Yxart give us a better description of the cavalcade: that suddenly disproportionate and, above all, abstract multitude—Yxart speaks time and again of "outsiders" and "the curious"—cannot be compared to anything known, it is not comprehensible. And what is more, by turning the city into a flux, a current, it makes its physical recognition impossible. The great speculative processes, the dazzling new shops, the anonymous multitudes, are simply different aspects of the same thing. Oller's ethical response and the disorientation of Yxart's man have the same origin: their city, transformed into a commodity, no longer has a form, is no longer familiar. On the one hand, then, a severe financial, industrial and agricultural crisis, and on the other, acute social conflict, a new city in the less optimistic sense; in other words, an abstract city. Against a backdrop of this kind, Yxart's enthusiasm for the transformations being undergone by Barcelona

inevitably takes on new shades of meaning. The display of "wealth and power" that was the Exhibition becomes, in the context of that real weakness, in something much more interested, more purposive; the symbolism attached to it becomes more loaded and the need for it is, without a doubt, all the greater.

*The Eloquent City*
The opposition of the Barcelona bourgeoisie to the project for the Cerdà Eixample, which was imposed on the city by the Spanish government, had a twofold basis. On the one hand, Cerdà had not taken due account of the expectations of profit that had for some time past accompanied the possession of real estate when he privileged, by means of various partial operations, the area around the future Passeig de Gràcia, where the principal thoroughfares of the old town—the Rambla, the Porta de l'Ángel—were to converge; on the other hand, he was indifferent to that bourgeoisie's desire to construct a city that would satisfy its new need for representative status. Barcelona was no longer merely an industrial and commercial city but the financial capital of the Spanish State, and as such it considered itself entitled to the great symbolic set-piece that the isotropy of the Cerdà Plan denied it.[36] Commodity city, capital city: the two identities came into conflict in the same place. However, that contradiction, although real enough, is too generic. In the case of Barcelona, the exceptionally intense property speculation that took place in the Eixample, to which we have already referred, must be contrasted with the contingency and the timidity of the prestige interventions carried out in the same period, including the Exhibition itself. This seems to show not only a Barcelona that was less modern and cosmopolitan a city than Yxart chooses to depict but, above all, the debility of its generic bourgeoisie. But here we need to narrow our focus a little and look more closely at the form taken by one or two of those operations: perhaps in this way we can engage, as we set out to do, with a bourgeoisie and an ideological program.

The itineraries described by Yxart in the chronicle

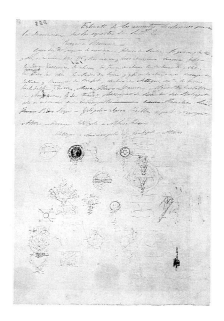

entitled *Panoramas* and those recommended in the guides to the Exhibition—the one by Artigas, for example, or the even better one by Juan Valero de Tornos[37]—traced a very precise rectangle that covered the old town—traversing it by way of the Ramblas—and a small part of the new Eixample. Within that circuit were concentrated not only the principal infrastructural operations—new paving and gas and electric streetlighting—but also the principal monuments. Some of these, such as the monument to the Catalan spirit, *El Geni Català*, in the Plà del Palau had already been there for many years; others were temporary, such as the triumphal arches erected in the Ramblas and the Gran Vía that Yxart criticized as being in bad taste: "they belong to the number of those absurdities whose presence we deplore."[38] Only three of the monuments that the visitor would encounter on this itinerary were regarded by Yxart and the authors of the guidebooks as new, and although all three had been commenced before the Exhibition, they were completed or remodeled for the great occasion. On the one hand there was the monument to Columbus, rising above the port in the virtual right angle formed by the new Passeig de Colom and the Ramblas, and, on the other, at the opposite ends of these two thoroughfares, the monuments to Antonio López and to Joan Güell, respectively.[39] In other words, the Great Discoverer found himself in the company of two burghers who had died only a few years before the Exhibition at the focal points that articulated and delimited the most prestigious stretch of the circuit we referred to above. As we shall see, however, and despite appearances to the contrary, this was not so disproportionate a state of affairs.

Back in 1881 Barcelona City Council had announced a competition for a monument to Christopher Columbus to preside over the port, at the opening in the seaward side of the old city wall at the bottom end of the Ramblas. Officially the reason for constructing the monument was that, on his return from his first voyage to the Americas, the "Admiral of the Ocean Sea" had been received by the Catholic Monarchs in Barcelona. But this hard-ly explains the fact that the monument should be not only the most important in Barcelona, both in height and in terms of its urbanistic impact but (as contemporary chroniclers repeated with pride) the tallest monument to Columbus anywhere in the world. No doubt the report published in 1882 by Gaietà Buigas, who won the competition, affords us a clearer understanding of its significance. Buigas' theme was: "In honoring Columbus, Catalonia honors her favorite sons."[40] And indeed, at the foot of the column on which Columbus stands are the statues of four Catalans who were connected with the American voyages in one way or other: Bernat de Boïl, appointed by the Borgia Pope Alexander VI first vicar apostolic of the West Indies; Pere Margarit and Jaume Ferrer of Blanes, who sailed with Columbus on his second expedition and, finally, the Valencian Jew Lluís Santangel, who in large part financed the first voyage. The symbolic intention of the monument was thus quite explicit: to vaunt the part played by Catalonia in the adventure of the Discovery, a contribution that the official history of Spain, with its tale of Isabel and her jewels, had always denied. There is no doubt that this proud claim reflected an entirely conscious ideological plan: that much is evident from the meticulous care with which the *image* was chosen. It is worth comparing the monument to Columbus with another project carried out only a year before, in 1880, for the same site: Antoni Gaudí's design for the streetlamps to be placed along the seafront promenade created by the demolition of the old Muralla de Mar wall.[41] A tall metal column standing on a base of four schematic keels topped by a system of masts and cables in allusion to a ship's rigging are the elements of Gaudí's proposal. Hanging from this structure like filled sails are the coats of arms of the realms that had come under Catalonia's medieval expansion and the names of its greatest seafarers: Bernat de Rocafort, Roger de Llúria, Bernat Marquet, Ramón Cortada … An autograph folio in Gaudí's hand, now in the Museu Municipal in Reus,[42] contains brief notes—probably taken from an article by Ramón Muntaner describing Roger de Flor's mythic expedition to the

Orient—and a few preparatory sketches for the project. Below the notes, a number of shields bear the names of some of the places that had been the scene of Catalan adventures: Adrianopolis, Gallipoli, Athens ... Gaudí's streetlamps were conceived, then, as a monument to the mariners of medieval Catalonia and, through them, to the mercantile and commercial spirit of modern Barcelona. But symbolism of this kind was an established convention in 1880: the names of the streets of the orthogonal Eixample grid make reference to the history of Catalonia, essentially to its past as a Mediterranean power, with lands and kingdoms on the one hand—Valencia, Mallorca, Sicily, Naples, Corsica—and sea-captains on the other—Rocafort, Muntaner, Entença, Roger de Llúria, Roger de Flor ... Indeed Gaudí himself, in a report presented to Barcelona City Council outlining the symbolism of an earlier project for streetlamps two years previously (a project that was actually constructed), recalled "the continual traffic carried out by the Catalans with the Orient, the domination of Italy and Sicily and the epic expedition to the Greek empire" concluding that once again "Barcelona is summoned to play a great part in the commerce of the Mediterranean."[43] The epic poems, songs and plays of the Catalan Romantic writers, so many of them centered on the country's medieval past as a great maritime power and especially on that expedition to the Orient that inspired Gaudí, had reduced that history to a commonplace: even a number of Spanish writers took it up as a theme in their patriotic poems.[44] Who could possibly identify with such a generic patriotism?

Gaudí's project was evidently commissioned by the City Council—this was the period when the streetlamps in the Plaça Reial and the Plà dei Palau were erected—and its object was, as we have said, to monumentalize the new seafront promenade. Within a year, however, the same City Council decided to change the project without changing the site or the original monumental intention. The maritime allusions were retained, and with them the reference to the commercial and mercantile character of Barcelona, but the symbolic program was now much more concrete. In place of Mediterranean adventures and sea-captains shrouded in legend there was Christopher Columbus and the participation of the Catalans in the discovery of America, and above all, in place of a Romantic history and evocations of generic patriotism, a history of Spain that clearly vaunted its imperial past. From the formal standpoint there is not the slightest doubt that Buigas' project was derived from Gaudí's: the elements employed—pyramidal base, metal column—are exactly the same, as is the organization of its outline. However, the four ship's keels in the first project have been converted, in the second, into four statues of illustrious Catalans; the mast has become a commemorative column, and the rigging a hieratic figure of Columbus. In fact, in the course of the monument's construction, Columbus was to undergo another important change: in the final version his arm is extended to point, ideally, from Barcelona to America. It has gone, then, and by no means subtly, from a generic project for the monumentalizing of the new boulevard to a very concrete symbolic project: the clamor with which one program has taken the place of the other could hardly be more significant. The monument had a very clear mission: to resolve and do away with the contradictions of the abstract city; to symbolize it, then, making it eloquent. The city speaks: in this case, by way of its first great modern monument, Barcelona petitions for a new history of Spain that will recall—and amplify—the important part played by the Catalans in the very origins of the Empire. What interest could the Barcelona bourgeoisie of the early 1880s—when the great crisis to which we have already referred was just beginning—have in making the new symbolic image of the city coincide with such a demand?

But perhaps now we might start to be more concrete, too, with reference to that bourgeoisie, and look at specific sectors or families. As we have already said, in 1888 the monument to Columbus was seen by Yxart as the point at which Barcelona's two most prestigious avenues articulated with one another: the old Ramblas threading

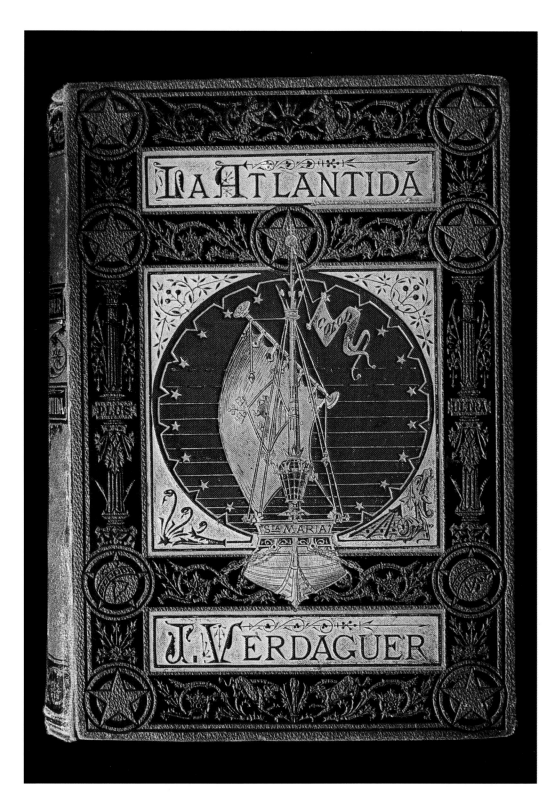

*J. Verdaguer, L'Atlàntida. Cover of the first edition, designed by Lluís Domènech i Montaner, and emblem on the frontispiece.*

through the old town, and the new Passeig de Colom, with its brand-new electric streetlighting, "parallel to the sea and the harbor, animated by its traffic."[45] We also noted that at the far end of each of these streets there stood a monument: the statue of Antonio López, erected a few years before, in 1884, but extensively remodeled for the Exhibition, and the statue of Joan Güell, the idea for which went back as far as 1878, begun in 1886 and actually unveiled in 1888.

Güell had died in 1872; López in 1883.[46] The former had been first and foremost an industrialist, as well as an economist who wielded great influence on the thinking of the Catalan bourgeoisie, the latter a merchant and financier, but the two shared powerful economic interests. In addition, both were of humble origins (their hagiographers constantly refer to them as the outstanding examples of the self-made man) and their very considerable fortunes came from a common source: both had been amassed in Cuba in a short period of time— López's thanks, fundamentally, to the slave trade. As we shall see, Güell and López had many other things in common, but for now it is worth looking more closely at the last of these points: the Cuban origins of their fortunes.

Of course, there is nothing extraordinary about this; on the contrary, it was very frequent. In fact, most of the successful entrepreneurs of nineteenth-century Barcelona had made their money in the Americas (such men were known as "indianos"). Naturally this resulted in a network of economic interests in Cuba and Puerto Rico that was shared in by most of the other wealthy families (almost all of them related to one another by marriage) and staffed by a whole host of small merchants, shopkeepers and employees who depended directly or indirectly on these great business empires, and who in turn managed to save enough money to retire in due course to their native land.[47] The extraordinary importance of Catalan interests in Cuba is well documented. J.G.F. Wurdermann, a North American traveler who published his *Notes on Cuba* in 1844, wrote: "A large part of the trade of the island is in (Catalan) hands, as is a consider-

*Excursionists from Catalonia
and the Roussillon in the cloisters
of Elna Cathedral, in 1883.
Among them, in addition to Gaudí
(in profile, the fifth from the right),
are J. Verdaguer, N. Oller
and Á. Guimerà.*

able part of its wealth. In the interior they appear to monopolize all branches of commerce, from the humble tinker to the well-stocked village shop; and in the coastal towns, many commercial houses, whose ships cover the sea, also belong to them ... Much of the interchange with Spain is in their hands, and lately they have extended their contacts to other countries, entering into active competition with foreign merchants." He concluded by wondering how long it would be before the Catalans were really the proprietors of the whole island. And John Granville Taylor, an English settler, wrote in 1851: "They have in their hands almost all the trade of Cuba and, I believe, also that of Spain."[48] We could cite many more observations of this kind, and complement them with references to the cohesion with which the Catalan community fought for and defended its business. But for now let us interest ourselves in a quotation of a different kind: "Catalonia, with the impetus of capital from overseas, has seen its machines set in motion, its towns beautified, its formerly arid plains irrigated, and

formed in its blue skies that aureole of fame and renown that place it at the head of the modern movement in Spain."[49] These words, which appeared in *Las Antillas* in 1866, describe with perfect clarity a typical colonial situation: the fortunes acquired in the colony and invested in the mother country provide the impetus for its economy and its processes of production. But in the case that concerns us here, the situation is colored with tonalities of evident exasperation. Spain had in effect been completely excluded from the sharing out of imperial spoils overseen by the great European powers. Among the remnants of its old colonial empire, Spain still had small enclaves in North Africa, on the coast of Guinea and in the far-off Philippines, but Cuba and Puerto Rico were the only profitable colonies, and meager enough the profits would have been if it were not for the islands' special economic system, which was still slave-based. The continuation of this system was bound up with the existence of an anachronistic class of great landholders and slave-owners that thwarted any possi-

*The main salon of the Palau Moja, with frescos by "el Vigatà."*

bility of an autoctonous modern middle class emerging and was the basic condition for the concentration of all political and economic power exclusively in the hands of foreign colonists—British, North American or Spanish, but above all, as we have said, Catalans. That was the island's only bourgeoisie.[50] However, the profits of these modern capitalists were invested far from Cuba, to provide the "impetus" for the machines of Catalonia.

The maintenance of their pre-capitalist reserve in Cuba was, then, essential for the productive processes of the Catalan bourgeoisie. It was therefore inevitable that it was precisely the Catalan middle classes who were most energetic in suppressing the risings of the Cuban independence movement from 1868 on, with the outbreak in Cuba of what is known as the "ten years' war" which subsequently continued from 1878 as the "chiquita war," culminating in the definitive war of independence from 1895 until 1898. The reaction of the Catalan industrial and commercial élite was immediate: they set up a private commission to petition the *Diputación* (Barcelona County Council) to take urgent measures, and the *Diputación* duly proposed to the Spanish government the formation of a batallion of exclusively Catalan "volunteers," financed in part by a private cartel composed of Barcelona's most powerful merchants, industrialists and bankers, among them Antonio López. Early in 1869 the government accepted the proposal and in April the batallion set sail for Havana. The Barcelona bourgeoisie thus killed two birds with one stone: on the one hand it was defending its colonial interests; on the other, by recruiting an exclusively Catalan expeditionary force, it sought to palliate the high level of industrial unemployment created by the crash of 1867 and the social conflict that this generated.[51] And, inevitably, this kind of two-or three-pronged operation also demanded the construction of an ideological discourse with different intentions. In one of the rhetorical poems dedicated to the batallion of "volunteers"—whose uniforms had special insignia to distinguish them from the rest of the Spanish troops garrisoned in Cuba—the poet re-

calls the adventures of medieval Catalans in the Mediterranean ("one day they sail to Orient, another to Moorish lands"), with enthusiastic references to their age-old symbols ("they have but one cry: Saint George and hurray for the stripes of the Catalan flag!"), before claiming for Catalonia an essential place in the history of Spain ("The stripes of old history that in every mortal struggle have always been the support of the towers of Castile") and in the vanguard of modern-day Spain ("now we are / more Spanish than ever").[52] The poem is simply one of the range of possible reflections in ideological terms—crudely patriotic in this case—of the *fact* that Catalonia was "the head of the modern movement in Spain."

That, in outline, is the schema of the ideological discourse deployed by the Barcelona bourgeoisie in attempting to justify itself as a new class and to underpin its colonialist demands and, a little later, its new imperialist projects. For a Catalan audience, the progress of industry and trade was Romantically identified with the evocation of Catalonia's medieval past, and was at the same time the motif and symbol of the restoration of the country's greatness. Outside of Catalonia that progress was converted into the role as *head* of Spain and embodied in a much more operative patriotism, as the true continuation of the Spanish empire itself. At the same time this was an ideological operation of commitment that was perfectly tailored to the strongly protectionist interests of Catalan industry, whose greatest exponent was Joan Güell.[53] An ideology of commitment, then, but not only an ideology: there was action, too. Following the revolutionary period of 1868 and the First Republic, the Barcelona bourgeoisie emerged as one of the principal defenders of the Bourbon Restoration in the person of Alfonso XII, who, not surprisingly, chose the port of Barcelona for his arrival in Spain in 1875.[54] The elaborations of that ideological discourse down to the monument to Columbus, and even beyond, became increasingly subtle and brilliant, and other circumstances and elements subsequently served to reinforce it.

As we have seen, Antonio López was a member of the unofficial committee that raised the batallion of "volunteers" in 1868. In 1876 he went on to found, with other Catalan financiers, the Banco Hispano-Colonial, essentially in order to pay for the war in Cuba. Meanwhile, in 1871, the Foment de la Producció Nacional—the most important Catalan business association—set up the Círculo Hispano Ultramarino de Barcelona for the purpose of defending slavery from its abolitionist opponents. The Círculo's president was Joan Güell, and Antonio López was vice-president. Joan Güell—the champion of economic protectionism, as we have said—had also in 1871 published the pamphlet *Rebelión Cubana*, in which he clearly advocated Spanish domination in Cuba, expounding the terms in which that domination benefited the Catalan bourgeoisie; in other words, presenting slavery as the only means of holding back the rise of a Cuban consciousness and thus of a native middle class. The López business empire controlled, practically single-handed, all the major interests of the dwindling Spanish colonial system: Compañía Transatlántica, Banco Hispano-Colonial, Compañía de Tabacos de Filipinas, Compañía de Minas del Rif ...[55] In 1871, Güell's son Joan married Isabel López, daughter of Antonio, and gradually became involved in those businesses, while at the same time developing others of his own. The Güells and the Lópezs are a paradigmatic case of the endogamic process that, above all in the 1870s, formed the core of of the select group of families of Barcelona's haute bourgeoisie, now definitively differentiated from the petty bourgeoisie and the lower classes.[56]

The reliefs at the foot of the statue of Antonio López featured, among other things, the coats of arms of Barcelona, Cuba and the Philippines. The statue of Joan Güell was raised up on figures representing the arts, industry, agriculture and shipping.[57] The meaning of the circuit that linked these two monuments, by way of the monument to Columbus, is quite clear: in contrast to the contradictions and uncertainties of the crisis that followed the business boom of the 1870s, and at the same time in contrast to the absence of form of the

commodity city, the public value of that itinerary—founder of a new city, legitimation of its new élites, ideological expression of its political and economic strategies—is unmistakable. But, does it not seem imprudent for a bourgeoisie that was at precisely that time starting definitively to close its ranks, just as it wove a dense network of family economic interests that effectively denied access to new members, to identify itself so blatantly with two of its representative figures, with two specific individuals? Imprudent, yes; but, for a bourgeoisie so uneasy about its own weakness, no doubt necessary. In 1888, in fact, the Güells and the Lópezs were unique in having disseminated a complex and powerful ideological discourse directed at promoting their own greater glory. In times of fast-made fortunes, of *febre d'or*, when money seemed capable of achieving everything, they were not bourgeoisie, but lords and ladies; in times of crisis, when everything seemed to be alienated by the new condition being adopted by a city converted into a commodity, they owned not only things, but time itself. Poets, painters and architects were set to work to give form to this mystery—in a way that leaves Yxart looking naïve for reproaching the timid Barcelona bourgeoisie because they were incapable of imitating it.

### New Wealth, New Tradition

On May 6, 1877, the special prize at the Jocs Florals literary awards in the Teatre Principal in Barcelona was bestowed on the priest Jacint Verdaguer for his vast epic poem *L'Atlàntida* (a few years later Verdaguer was to receive from the hands of Bishop Morgades the crown of bay proclaiming him poet laureate of Catalonia, at the official inauguration of the restored monastery in Ripoll before the highest ecclesiastic and civil authorities of Catalonia, in a truly extraordinary ceremony that he later recalled with bitterness in his *Llorers espinosos*).[58] In those same Jocs Florals of 1877 the three ordinary prizes were awarded to Ángel Guimerà, who was also granted the title of *mestre en Gai Saber*—"master in the Art of Poetry."[59] The remarkable triumph of Guimerà's poem *L'any mil* did not,

however, bring him the fame that immediately attached to Verdaguer, a fame attested to by the fact that by the turn of the century *L'Atlàntida* [*Atlantis*] had been translated into seven languages; but rather than these material indices of its success, we need to consider now others that are more difficult to quantify. In effect, *L'Atlàntida* was from the first moment surrounded by a strange aura of admiration, a veneration that made of the poem, and its author, a kind of living legend.[60] Contemporary accounts describe the almost idolatrous enthusiasm manifested by the public at the reading of excerpts from the work,[61] both on the day of the Jocs Florals awards themselves (which Verdaguer did not attend, excusing himself on the grounds that he was a priest) and the following day, at the ceremony in honor of the prize-winners. Verdaguer, thirty-two years old at the time, was to be known from then on as "the poet of *L'Atlàntida*," and in the dramatic letters later published in *En defensa propia*, written in the late 1890s, he referred to the poem as "the flower of [his] existence."[62] Indeed, Catalan literary historians and critics have been virtually unanimous in considering *L'Atlàntida* as the work that gained Catalan a place among the modern literary languages.

Certainly, the expectation that Verdaguer had built up for the poem in advance helps to explain its reception: during the prolonged period of its composition he had showed constantly changing excerpts, drafts and provisional versions to some of the most influential figures on the Catalan literary scene—Milá i Fontanals and Jaume Collell, for example—and in the latter stage of its coming to fruition the poem, with its progress and its setbacks, became one of the major themes of their correspondence during the long ocean voyages to which we shall refer in due course.[63] There was, then, a small number of people who, with their advice and suggestions, found themselves involved in the poem's evolution, while at the same time the public who were to be its readership—also small in number, of course—was being prepared in advance, occasionally hearing news or reading fragments of a work whose whole evolution—lengthy,

complex, shrouded in the mystery of things half glimpsed—necessarily announced it as something extraordinary. So it is hardly surprising that in the foreword to the definitive edition of 1878—which is in places significantly different from the prize-winning poem of less than a year before—Verdaguer should give a decidedly autobiographical account of the origins of *L'Atlàntida*, tracing its first inspiration to childhood impressions and his early reading, or that with the passing years he should allude to the poem in heroic terms: "… the sea, from which, in perilous and terrible struggle, I had just wrested the poem *L'Atlàntida* ready for printing."[64] *L'Atlàntida* was, then, more than a mere poem. From the very outset, from its first conception, there had been invested in it a transcendent will, the desire to construct a legend.

Nevertheless, it is evident that the process of elaboration of *L'Atlàntida* was unusually complex. Between 1865 and 1867, Jacint Verdaguer began working on the poem that is now known as *Colom.*[65] This was no less than an account of Columbus' voyage across the Ocean and the discovery of America, and among its episodes was one in which the Devil takes Columbus to the top of a mountain to show him the Atlantic and, to dissuade him from his voyage, describes to him the terrible disappearance there, in ancient times, of a continent. The ideological burden of the poem, then, could hardly be clearer: by alluding to innumerable catastrophes the Devil had tried to prevent the Discovery because it would lead to the evangelization of the New World. At this time Verdaguer was a humble seminarist whose thinking, when it came to conceiving great projects, was inevitably constrained by the ingenuous forms of scholastic doctrine. And yet the poet did not abandon his underlying idea. At the beginning of 1868 Verdaguer decided to develop just one of the episodes of his *Colom*, the part describing the destruction of Atlantis. He went on to compose a poem in five cantos of alexandrine quatrains based on a highly individual interpretation of the tenth and twelfth labors of Heracles. The Greek hero saves Pyrene, queen of Spain, from fire in the Pyrenees, proclaim-

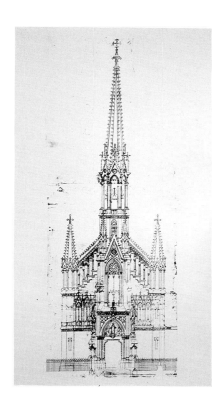

ing himself her heir as he does so. He then sets off in search of the Garden of the Hesperides, which Verdaguer situates in Atlantis, founding a number of cities on his way, including—amid premonitions of its future greatness—Barcelona. Having slain Ladon, the guardian of the Garden, Heracles takes the golden fruit from the branch of the orange tree; in response to the anger of the children of Hesper, Heracles provokes a great cataclysm that submerges the continent, while at the same time, on the other side of the Mediterranean opened by the hero, a new land emerges. Finally, Heracles returns to Spain (to plant the branch of the orange tree and leave with it the lyre of Hesper, who has now borne him children, his heirs). Verdaguer gave his poem a highly significant title: *L'Espanya Naixent*—Spain Nascent.[66] It is evident that the fragment of the earlier *Colom* has here been converted into a mythological account of the origins of Spain: heroic origins in which Spain not only inherits the orange branch and the lyre, the treasures of Atlantis, but, with the Pyrenees in flames, with the Mediterranean pouring into the Ocean through the opening in the Calpe massif, with the sinking of Atlantis itself, is left on its own, separated from the three continents and thus ideally equidistant from all three; in other words, in the center.

In spite of Heracles, then, the real protagonists of the poem are the mountains and the seas, those masses that break away, sink, emerge or are moved by gigantic forces in order that a privileged land may take shape and be born between the three parts of the world. But this was rather a strange patriotic poem: Spain is not represented here as *patria* or mother country, but as a land or, indeed, as geography. What kind of reality, what kind of present could engage a fable such as this? Who could have an interest—in the dual senses of feeling curious and having a stake—in a story that was certainly charged with feeling, but so remote as to be impossible to translate into the reader's own place and time; in other words, to understand? And indeed the impression that this was a fable without a meaning was clearly reflected in the indifference of both the jury and the public at

the Jocs Florals of 1868, to whom Verdaguer presented his poem without the least success.[67]
*Colom* and *L'Espanya Naixent* after doubts and failures, those are the two themes that Verdaguer set out to unite in a new version of the poem, to a new plan that was to culminate ten years later in *L'Atlàntida*. It was the bringing together of the two themes that was to give them a new and definitive meaning and significance. The poem that took the prize at the Jocs Florals in 1877 consists of ten cantos that explore in more extended form the same theme of the labors of Heracles and the disappearance of Atlantis found in *L'Espanya Naixent*, but now with a prologue and an epilogue that develop the Columbus theme. The story of the destruction of Atlantis and the mythic birth of Spain is told to the young Columbus, shipwrecked on the coast of Portugal by a mysterious old hermit, not to dissuade him from the enterprise for which Providence had intended him, as the Devil did in the first version, but to inspire him with a sense of his special destiny. Finally, in the epilogue, Columbus is received by Isabella in a newly reconquered Granada. In a premonitory dream the Catholic Queen has seen the Genoan bring her new worlds. When Columbus obtains the ships he needs thanks to her jewels, the old hermit in his lookout knows that his mission is fulfilled. His "Speed on, Columbus … now I can die!," are the final words of the poem, and an explicit declaration that the circle of the old and the new, of myth and history, has been closed. These, then, are the two levels on which *L'Atlàntida* is developed: on the one hand the legend of the origin of the land of Spain as a particular orographic configuration whose singularity presages its destiny, described in the gigantic movements of rivers, mountains and seas; on the other, the patriotic narrative of the political origin of Spain and its world empire centered on historical personages—Columbus, Isabella—who are obviously the heirs of the mythical hero. In this way Europe and America, separated by the action of Heracles, King of Spain and heir of Atlantis, are united once again by Columbus and Isabella.[68] The earlier version, in which the discovery of America

*The Salesas church as it is today and a detail.*

is seen as the beginning of the evangelization of the whole world, has here been made far more complex: this is something more than conversion, it is the very order of the continents that has been restored, with Spain thus fulfilling the destiny for which, amid so much destruction, she was born. The myth and the history perfectly fuse their meanings in a process characteristic of Romantic culture: by historicizing the myth, history and the present are made mythic. This, then, was the poem that fired so much patriotic enthusiasm in 1877.

Out of the ideological ingenuousness of that first *Colom*, and the vagueness of the myth of *L'Espanya Naixent*, Verdaguer gradually defined a project and gave form to a poem that now reflected, in its *almost* perfect circularity, ideas and sentiments that were very concrete and very much present. There is no need to repeat what we said above about Spain's colonial insecurity, especially with regard to the Cuban wars of independence throughout the course of the 1870s; about the patriotic fervor that these aroused, exalting the country's imperial destiny, past and present, and about the two-pronged ideological discourse, both Catalan and Spanish, fashioned by the Barcelona bourgeoisie to justify its interests.[69] Verdaguer's poem began to take shape in the midst of that historical juncture, and there can be little doubt about the ideological connections between the two. The years when he was completing his poem, on the other hand, were the years of the Bourbon Restoration, of the arrival of Alfonso XII in Barcelona, of the start of a great upswing in the business cycle, as we noted above. In a period of accumulation and concentration of wealth in the hands of a small élite, what better than the great fable narrated in *L'Atlàntida*, not only to sublimate a patriotism that was far from disinterested but to exorcize the idea that there might be anything excessively sudden or *parvenu* about this recently acquired wealth?

Verdaguer's poem, as we have said, immediately took on the status of myth and symbol, and—undisputed though its extraordinary literary qual-

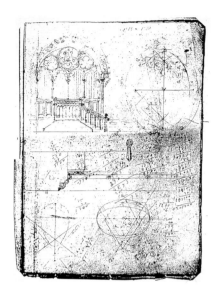

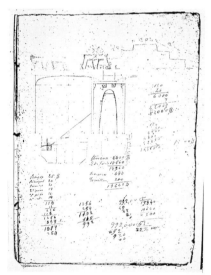

ity is—not only in literary terms. As we have seen, a number of important changes were made to the text between the version of *L'Atlàntida* that took the special prize at the Jocs Florals of 1877 and the definitive version published a year later, one of these being the inclusion of a new canto (Canto VII), entitled *Chor de les illes gregues*, apparently tangential in respect to the main plot, with a description of the emergence of Greece thanks to a fall in the level of the Mediterranean; there is an evident relation to the muted lyre of Hesper, left hanging from a willow after the irruption of Heracles, taken by Hesper to Spain with a single string, the string of pain, but restrung by Heracles with strings of gold. This lyre, the ancient poetry of Atlantis, is then inherited by a Spain that comes into being at the same time as the Greek islands, which now sing—with an allusion here to the lyre of Orpheus—a new poetry. The fusion between the mythic and the historical produce this time, on a new plane, the literature, merging the origin of Spain with that of the lyre, which is literally planted in the new land and reborn with it. But we shall consider this more closely in due course. But it is another of the new elements in the definitive edition in relation to the manuscript presented to the competition (although present in the publication of the winning compositions at the Jocs Florals themselves) that is of greatest interest: the inclusion of a prologue and a dedication to Antonio López. Dated November 18, 1876, this dedication reads: "Riding on the blessed wing of your ships / I sought the flowering orange tree of the Hesperides; / But alas! It is long despoiled / By the wave that, many centuries past, overtook it, / And I can only offer you, if it please you, these leaves / Of the tree of the golden fruit."

Antonio López had paid for the definitive edition of *L'Atlàntida* in 1878 from his own pocket. At the same time it is important to remember that in the winter of 1877, just a few months after winning the special prize at the Jocs Florals, Verdaguer took up residence in the López's town house on the Ramblas in Barcelona, acting as chaplain and later as almoner to the family, whose service he had

entered in 1874 as priest on the Compañía Transatlántica ships that plied the route between Spain and Cuba. Between 1874 and 1876 Verdaguer made a total of nine voyages to and fro across the Atlantic in Antonio López's ships, and makes specific reference to this not only in the dedication we have transcribed here, but also in the foreword to the poem: "In bidding farewell, not long ago, to the sea, cradle of my latest aspirations, with my feet already firmly on the steps of Barcelona harbor, I did not expect to have so cordial and pleasing a welcome for the poem that, in disordered manuscript, I carried under my arm, still salty and smelling of tar and marine algae."[70] From the outset, then, and in a clearly intentional way—because it did not correspond to the facts—Verdaguer identified much of the theme and the writing of his poem with his experience on the ships of the Compañía. With all of this in mind, we should not be too surprised at the generosity of Antonio López in financing the publication of *L'Atlàntida*, which, significantly, appeared together with a Spanish translation by Melcior de Palau, also commissioned by López. The proprietor of the Transatlántica, and of so many other businesses overseas, had very good reasons for wishing at that particular moment to associate his name with the extraordinary poem, and Verdaguer, it must be said, was quite happy for this to be so. By this gesture, López offered Catalan culture the definitive version of a work that had, from the very moment it won the poetry prize, assumed a symbolic value as a point of reference for that culture, and with the Spanish translation he made sure it would be known in the rest of Spain, where it was also a great success. What is more, the work now commenced with his name, with the poet's explicit acknowledgment of the man who had made possible not only its publication, but the very poem itself. López thus effectively appropriated—in the widest sense of the word—the symbol and made it his own. The disinterested action of the great patron of the arts was in reality, then, a naked demostration of distinction and power, and in time Verdaguer was to become bitterly aware of how

that same power could turn against him, gathering around itself the very forces of the culture, the bourgeoisie and the Church among which the symbol had been raised.[71] The generous act in favor of Catalan literary culture revealed itself (bearing in mind the transcendent resonances of *L'Atlàntida*) as an aggressive act. By setting his name and the name of his ships on the first page of the book, making himself the *first* recipient of Verdaguer's offering (those "leaves of the tree of the golden fruit"; in other words, the poem itself), López unashamedly reserved for himself the right of give it to the world and, in thus setting himself above his peers, effectively eradicated all competition. The great epic construction of *L'Atlàntida*, gigantically abounding in a sense of community, had to a great extent been privatized. And it is relevant to recall here that the fortune of Antonio López ("the greatest fortune in Spain,"[72] as Verdaguer described it to his son when, almost twenty years later, friendless and alone, he had to defend himself against his former "protectors"), much of it amassed in Cuba, as we have seen, was new—he started relocating it in great limited companies in 1875[73]—and, above all, that it was founded on the slave trade; or to add that although his wife was Catalan and he had lived in Barcelona since 1858, López was not from Catalonia, but from the small town of Comillas in Cantabria. His need for social legitimation among the Catalan bourgeoisie—whose endogamy we have already noted—was great, as urgent as the need to exorcize the bad name that had attached to him on account of the shadowy origins of his business. In 1878, the same year in which he financed *L'Atlàntida*, the title of marquis of Comillas was created for López: these are merely two facets of a many-sided prism.[74] With *L'Atlàntida* Antonio López took possession of myth and history, and this was also exactly the effect of his noble title, investing him with both new and old power. López's action thus had a very clear purpose: to take possession of time, of the past and the present, of its value as continuity, of its value as memory. Seen in this light, his is not an unusual ambition, but one common to all new élites. Pierre Bourdieu has described how such

new élites, which can come to exercise an economic or social power as great as or greater than that of the old nobility, cannot, however, attain its "social power over time." As Bourdieu says: "To possess what is old and ancient ... those things that come from the past, that accumulated history, stored away as a treasure, crystallized, to possess aristocratic titles or noble names, castles or historic houses, paintings and collections, to have still those old wines and old furniture, is to dominate time ... thanks to all those objects and possessions that have in common the fact that they can only be achieved with time, *with time*, against time."[75] With the inspiration of *L'Atlàntida* voyaging in his ships, Antonio López not only sought, distinguishing himself aggressively, to achieve power over time—mythical, historical—but to imbue with that transcendent time—above all on the basis of the communal dimension of the poem—his colonial interests.

We shall return in due course to *L'Atlàntida* and the part played by Verdaguer in the ideological discourse that López wove around himself. First, however, it is worth looking, however briefly, at two more of the many aspects that, fitting together like the pieces of a jigsaw puzzle, made up that operation of social legitimation. Thus, for example, in 1870 Antonio López took as his Barcelona residence the Palau Moja.[76] The choice was not entirely fortuitous. This grand old *palau* or mansion is not only situated in the finest part of old Barcelona, near the top of the Rambla, it is also, by virtue of its architectural singularity within the prevailing typology of Barcelona town houses and its decoration—especially the series of paintings by Francesc Plà, "el Vigatà," that adorned both interior and exterior—was without a doubt the most prestigious eighteenth-century mansion in the city. At the same time the *palau*, with its architecture, its paintings and frescos, was in its way one of the symbols of the social and physical renovation of Barcelona that had begun in the 1700s, when, after a period considered in official circles and by Romantic patriotism as decadent, in which the city had remained virtually unchanged, the city began to open up new avenues and construct new public

C. Oliveras, the Casa Provincial
de Maternidad y Expósitos
in Barcelona, commenced in 1889.
Contemporary photograph of the
entrance hall of one of the pavilions
and details of the crown.

and private buildings.[77] López, then, bought more than just a mansion, and we need only read the descriptions of the deliberately anachronistic ceremonial he imposed on the parties and receptions he held there to see that this was also part of a perfectly orchestrated campaign against the new.[78]

Comillas, the birthplace of Antonio López, is the next aspect for us to consider. In that small costal town in the north of Spain, López—in an operation subsequently continued and enhanced with new tonalities by his son Claudio—began in 1878 to construct a mansion and a pantheon, as well as other buildings, such as a new cemetery, a seminary, etc. The aim, then, was not only to monumentalize and give importance to a small and unknown village, but to embody an ideal genealogy of the family. The virtual signification that pervades and unites mansion and pantheon, in which past generations, the present and those to come are united in a single time and a single soil, is inescapable. But the operation at Comillas was more than that: in 1881 the Spanish royal family spent part of the summer as guests in the mansion. In their honor López staged an impressive display of his ships off the coast, as well as organizing excursions, concerts by Chapí in the park, bathing in the sea (from a kiosk that ran on rails) and fitting the house with electric light.[79] Antonio López thus scored a great diplomatic *coup* and, thanks to the prestige he had won, established Comillas as a fashionable place to spend the summer. This was essential as a means of projecting and consolidating the cohesion of certain élites, but it was also a form of selection, of distinction: Comillas was the property of Antonio López, and this was true in both the symbolic and the strictly material senses of the term: there was the pantheon to demonstrate that this was his land. It was he, the marquis of Comillas, who made the place available and *wove* the relationships: here once again, an apparently conciliatory action was in reality aggressive. Many of the families who were connected by economic interests or marriage—or in most cases, both—to López and his business empire (or in pursuit of that connection) visited Comillas at one

time or another, and many also built villas or country houses of their own. There, too, Verdaguer spent the summer, accompanying the family; there the Güells were regular guests.

If in Barcelona Antonio López had managed to buy the time, the wealth and the prestige of the Palau Moja, in Comillas he discovered and immediately understood the social and political advantages that could be derived from patronizing the forms of modern art. Antonio López—and even more so, after his death in 1883, his son and heir Claudio—brought to Comillas many of the artists and architects most active in advanced Barcelona circles. Sculptors such as Llimona and Eusebi Arnau, but most importantly the architect Joan Martorell and, around him, the young Lluís Domènech i Montaner, Cristóbal Cascante, Camil Oliveras and Antoni Gaudí himself, all worked in Comillas at different times on a variety of projects.[80]

We have said "around" Joan Martorell.[81] A closer look at this key figure here may provide us with a clearer view of certain things in due course. Martorell, born in 1833, was without a doubt the most cultivated and the most internationally-aware of the Barcelona architects of his generation. His Neo-Gothicism, deriving not so much from the books of Viollet-le-Duc as from his actual buildings, principally in the south of France and especially in Toulouse, was deployed in small decorative details drawn from a wide variety of languages and brought together in a strange collage whose effect was to dispel any sense of "archaeological" rigidity. Things that from an academic point of view might be seen as deficiencies appeared to the eyes of his young followers as advantages. His church of Las Salesas, in particular, constructed in Barcelona between 1882 and 1885—on which his assistant was Antoni Gaudí[82]—served as a model and inspiration for the most progressive young architects newly graduated from the School of Architecture. It is significant that the jury's rejection of the project he presented to the 1882 competition for the completion of the façade of Barcelona cathedral generated a great polemic in the city's cultural and artistic circles, where Martorell was defended not

only as the outstanding exponent of a "modern Gothic"—as opposed to the archaeologism of the winning project—but above all, in a series of comments very much in line with the spirit of modernization that Yxart was preaching to the bourgeoisie, for the "grandeur and breadth" of his plan. Even more noteworthy for our interests is that the beautiful drawing used to present Martorell's cathedral project was drawn by Gaudí and inked by Domènech i Montaner.[83] The fact is that, perhaps even more than his architecture, always of the highest intrinsic quality, Martorell himself was of the greatest significance, gathering around him architects such as these—precisely the ones who, explicitly or by omission, were most fiercely critical of the rigidity and academicism of the teaching at the School of Architecture, whose director was Elías Rogent.[84] Cristóbal Cascante, Camil Oliveras—both dead by the end of the century—and Antoni Gaudí constituted the inner circle closest to Martorell.[85] In the works they produced in the 1880s these three architects developed a

singular formal language with very striking characteristics (many of which were taken by Gaudí in the course of his career to almost unrecognizable extremes) that range from the constant use, with a truly signature status, of the parabolic vault, to subtler features such as the obsessive dissolution of the walls in the corners. All of this is clear proof of the fruitfulness of the exchanges that took place within the small group. And it was precisely that architecture, so highly signified, so recognizable (especially Gaudí's, without a doubt the most uninhibited) to which such perceptive and interested critics as Yxart were to refer—as we have seen—as "the very latest tendencies."

In that same remarkable year of 1878, Martorell received the commission to design the mansion and the pantheon in Comillas. Some time later, it would seem, he was also commissioned to design the seminary. Alongside Martorell, the whole group was involved in the construction of Comillas. For example, Gaudí designed the furniture for the pantheon, a somewhat eccentric kiosk erected in honor of the

*A. Gaudí, fountain in the gardens of the Güell estate in Pedralbes. Present state.*

*A. Gaudí, entrance pavilions
to the Güell estate in Pedralbes.
Photographs from 1893,
the first taken by the architect
A. Casademunt.*

visit by the Spanish royal family in 1881, and later, in 1883 and 1884, the famous villa El Capricho for Máximo Díaz de Quijano, brother-in-law of the marquis. Oliveras' responsibilities included site direction of the building of the mansion, while Cascante not only supervised the construction of El Capricho but—as of 1883—took over from Martorell on the seminary project (finally decorated by Domènech i Montaner) and in 1885 designed the monument to the marquis.[86] The fact that these works could be designed by one member of the group and supervised by others without apparent conflict, being passed from hand to hand at different stages in their evolution, is clear testimony to the high degree of mutual understanding that the group had established.

In Comillas there was none of that accumulated time that López had acquired in the Palau Moja along with the architecture and the frescos. The place was new, and so the embodiment of distinction constructed there would also, by necessity, be new. The "very latest tendencies" were also acquired by the Lópezs, but they were *utilized* to construct a mansion and a pantheon: the heritage accumulated there, in those buildings, was to be the most transcendent; successive generations of the family, real or invented, would be eloquently represented in those constructions that speak in the language of the time—or rather, of the moment—in which the marquis commissioned them: in their own language. The whole town was to become a celebration of his power over an invented history transformed into heritage. It is hardly surprising that the architects we have mentioned should be the ones chosen to give form to this symbolic project. As we have said, they were modern architects; undoubtedly the *most* modern Barcelona architects of the day: the most openly committed opponents of the academicism and archaeologism of the official culture so well represented by Rogent; the ones who created a less hidebound, less inhibited architecture that constantly renewed both its own codes and the prevailing typologies. The most modern, too, in Yxart's sense of the term: the richest. Nevertheless, we

must be prudent and try to appreciate in just measure what we are dealing with here: architects who represent a break with tradition, not to cancel it out but, on the contrary, to invent it anew. It was, in a sense, a question of moving on from historicism and archaeologism on the basis of its own rules, in order to establish these afresh. For example: the parabolic vault, used systematically in these architects' early works as a formal sign of innovation, was always explained by Gaudí as a correction of the imperfect system of equilibrium of the pointed Gothic arch.[87] This explanation is not as linear or as innocent as it seems; in fact, it perfectly expresses that desire to improve on history without diverging from its path, helping it take the next step forward, as an inseparable continuation of its first steps. There is in this approach an evident spirit of regeneration, and regeneration is surely dependent on the traditions it seeks to put in order, to correct, to restore to their pure state. It was the tradition itself that interested those architects, but, as I have said, a restored tradition: a new tradition, invented, made useful again. We might speak here—in a paradox that is only apparent—of modern architects who were at the same time anti-*Modernista*. In due course we shall clarify this point by analyzing various aspects of the work of the only one of these architects who went on to achieve authentic development: Gaudí.

A *new* tradition: this is not so very different what is projected and constructed in *L'Atlàntida*. Is there any better form of power over time? These had to be the architects of the marquises of Comillas. But not only theirs: there would be one who would touch still subtler chords.

*Mythical Garden, Mystical Garden*

On the boundary of the districts of Les Corts de Sarrià and Pedralbes, in what now is the upper part of Barcelona, Joan Güell had acquired around 1860 a couple of large plots of agricultural land amounting in total to almost thirty hectares. On the highest part of the property there was a large farmhouse that Güell thoroughly refurbished and surrounded with gardens to convert it into in a

*Detail of the antimony orange tree as a decorative motif.*

*Details of the decoration featuring
the rose as a dominant motif,
Güell estate.*

grand country house. Joan Martorell decorated it in a pompous Second Empire style and built next to it a small Neo-Gothic chapel for semi-public use. In 1883, Eusebi Güell extended the estate with the purchase of adjoining properties and almost immediately decided to undertake not only a series of refurbishments and improvements to the house and garden but also—probably with a view to subsequent residential development of the estate—the construction of a boundary wall with belvederes, stables, a lodge and several gates, one of which (the one closest to the house, at the end of the private road that led to the estate) was to have a monumental character. This series of commissions was entrusted to Antoni Gaudí, and work commenced in 1884.[88]

This house, which had been the favorite summer residence of Joan Güell, became, after his death in 1872, the retreat of his son Eusebi and of the family of Eusebi's wife, the Lópezs. In fact Antonio López stayed there for long periods in the last years of its life, after the death of his eldest son in 1876. There too, in that same year, Jacint Verdaguer, recently released from his duties as chaplain on the ships of the Transatlántica, was officially presented to the Lópezs—and was taken into their household with the specific duty of celebrating a daily mass for their dead son—and the Güells, with whom he also developed a close relationship. That relationship, formed during Verdaguer's stays on the estate, is evidenced by references in the articles *En defensa propia*,[89] and by dedications in his own hand in copies of books such as *Lo somni de Sant Joan* and *Canigó*, in a copy of which he wrote: "To Sra. doña Isabella López de Güell, kind mistress of the villa Satalia, where some of these pages were written; yours truly in Christ, Jacinto Verdaguer, priest."[90] Verdaguer's new epic poem (perhaps begun as early as 1880 but not published until 1885), which centered on the medieval legends of the origin of Catalonia and very different both in form and ideological intent from *L'Atlàntida*, was explicitly linked by the poet himself—albeit in a private dedication—to the estate that he had dubbed Torre Satalia. Meanwhile, in May 1884 Verdaguer accom-

panied Güell on a tour of central and northern Europe.[91] This experience was to have a profound, and in some ways complementary, influence on both men. In his account of his impressions Verdaguer seems obsessed by the presence and the situation of the Catholic faith in the countries they visited (France, Germany, Russia and Switzerland), and at times his comments, colored by the prejudices of his traditionalism, appear grotesquely distorted: for example, he has no hesitation in referring to Paris—where he met Mistral, then at the height of his success, and as a token of friendship offered to translate his recently published *Nerto*—as "Babylon of the Apocalypse."[92] But there are also beautiful moments, such as the passage in which the sight of the Swiss mountains prompts a nostalgic recollection of the mountains of Catalonia. However, it was probably not only the mountains that filled the poet's heart with yearning: the fact that Switzerland was a confederation of cantons in which different peoples and languages could coexist in peace may also have had something to do with it. Indeed, a number of years later, in 1900, Eusebi Güell was to indulge one of his most interesting facets—that of the dilettant scientist—by writing a treatise on the similarities between Catalan and the language of Rhaetia, in the Swiss Alps, referring expressly to that 1884 journey. The thesis advanced by Güell, that both languages are older than Latin, may well be eccentric from a philological point of view, but it has a closely thought-out ideological intention. However, we must not run ahead of events.[93] First it is worth considering how Verdaguer's nostalgic yearning and Güell's political interests coincided in that Alpine landscape: a coincidence with overtones very different from those that gave the world *L'Atlantida*, and perhaps it is relevant to note here that, as if history were repeating itself with a variation, the publication of *Canigó* was personally financed by Eusebi Güell.[94] But in order to understand how this came about and what it means, we may as well begin in the place where the *remains* of the poem Verdaguer dedicated to Antonio López seem definitively to come apart: on the Güell estate, in Gaudí's architecture—the first works he

designed for the man who was, all through his career, his principal client.

We have seen that in 1883 and 1884 Eusebi Güell extended the estate and commissioned Gaudí to design the architecture: 1883 was the year of Antonio López's death, and 1884 the year of the closest rapport between Verdaguer and Güell. We have also noted in passing that it was Verdaguer who gave the Güell estate the name Torre Satalia, an allusion not to the city in Asia Minor famous for its groves of orange trees, as has been suggested, but to the variety of white rose known as Satalia in Catalan.[95] As we shall see in due course, the point is not without its significance, but what interests us now is to note how Verdaguer appears here right at the outset, giving a symbolic name to the estate that Güell was to transform so profoundly. Among the elements constructed by Gaudí in the gardens we shall now focus on a small fountain not far from the house.[96] This is a semicircular stone bench backed by a wall, from the center of which there emerges a wrought iron spout in the form of a dragon. On top of the wall stands the pedestal of a bust in old marble, which in a period photograph appears as a man with a beard and a great helmet. The water from the dragon's jaws pours into a basin whose overflow is channeled down the four stripes of the flag of Catalonia so that the water falls into the drain below. It has been supposed—rightly, in my opinion—that the bust represented Heracles clothed in the skin of the Nemean Lion; Heracles atop a Ladon converted into a water spout, a prisoner for ever more. The allusion to *L'Atlàntida* could hardly be more direct. But Gaudí's fountain is not only a representation of Verdaguer's poem: there are also other interpretations superimposed here, subtly drawing out new tonalities, the ones that are least apparent in a literal reading of the work dedicated to Antonio López. The dragon is, in effect, condemned eternally to water the shield of Catalonia, turning its stripes into streams, and thus Ladon and Heracles are imbued with the spirit of what is without a doubt the most common motif in the patriotic imaginary of the *Renaixença*: St. George and the drag-

*Examples of the Mudéjar style*
*in the San Pedro church*
*and the Torre de San Martín*
*in Teruel, early fourteenth century.*

*J. Martorell, Salesas church. Detail.*

on. That emblematic transposition of figures that reflexively enhance and extend each other's necessarily complementary symbolism—a symbolism that is Christian even before its time—is an essential aspect of *L'Atlantida*. There the hero of Greek mythology becomes an instrument of Providence, just as the gods of Mt. Olympus are replaced by Jehovah. Given the great length of the poem, this inevitably gave rise to a series of technical difficulties and almost insuperable discontinuities that, as has been rightly remarked, Verdaguer did not entirely resolve.[97] Nevertheless, what is interesting here is to note how *L'Atlantida* can shift from the very large scale of the community to the very small scale of the private fountain without the slightest change in the technique of symbolic representation. Although, certainly, in the shady corner of the garden of the Güell estate there are no difficulties to overcome. The figures resonate here almost imperceptibly, following the flow of the water, without either figure ceasing to be itself. Heracles and Ladon or the dragon of St. George: everything has become smaller and more familiar. Native land and devotion are here, like the place, more recognizable, more intimate, but also, for that very reason, everything is essentially different. Gaudí carried that form of bestowing value on things by loading them with superposed and mutually enhancing symbolic explications that complement or contrast with one another without ceasing to apply to the same site to obsessive extremes in his work, but without a doubt its origin is in Verdaguer. Not only because Gaudí and Verdaguer, as we know from so many reliable accounts, developed a fairly intense friendship in those years,[98] but above all because, as we shall see, Gaudí learned to work with Verdaguer's technique, embodying his programs. In a letter to Collell in December 1884, Verdaguer wrote: "In the house of Mr. Güell there is a spring of abundant water beneath a Roman bust. You must find it a beautiful Latin name! Gaudí has asked me and nothing interesting has come out of my head for some time."[99] Verdaguer was in the habit of bemoaning his lack of inspiration; his modesty was equally proverbial. But what the letter to

Collell clearly reveals is that the man who gave the estate its name also gave the fountain its *theme*. Nevertheless, the pedestal remained without a Latin inscription: a word would have broken the smooth flow of the symbols. That, as we shall see, is something Gaudí was never to understand.

But the charming fountain we have just described is merely a small essay of what would be the main gate of the estate, between the lodge and the stables, also built, as we have said, by Gaudí. This very wide single gate for vehicles, of wrought iron and industrial elements, is in the form of a great dragon with open jaws and claws outstretched that, although held captive in chains and fetters, seems to move menacingly as the gate was opened and closed. The gate hangs from a tall pillar of red brick crowned with a capital of stone and an orange tree of antimony. Here again the dragon in chains and the orange tree are a literal representation of a passage from *L'Atlàntida*, from the tenth canto. The Güell estate, then, has been transformed into the Garden of the Hesperides, just at the moment when Heracles has vanquished Ladon and the daughters of Hesper have been turned into trees: willows, poplars and elms, the species of their metamorphosis, were planted in the garden. And even more: in the forms of Ladon, looking to the North, we can see the constellations of Hercules and Draco. Finally, the lyre hangs on the little side gate for pedestrians.

There can be little doubt that Verdaguer came up with the symbolic program for the gate, bearing in mind that when it was designed in 1884, he was accompanying Eusebi Güell on his trips around Europe. And little doubt, either, that the gate is a monument; a monument in which Güell paid tribute to his brother-in-law, who died the year before. 1884 also saw the construction of the monument on the Passeig de Colom that was subsequently remodeled for the Exhibition. The coincidence is striking, but the two monuments are obviously very different: all that in the one is public and apparent, in the other is private and hidden; all that in the one is elementary and direct, in the other is complex and veiled. Not in the theme—it is ab-

solutely clear, for all the many subtleties, that this is *L'Atlàntida*, although no contemporary source makes the slightest reference to the fact—but in the action. The ideological import of the poem dedicated to Antonio López is in effect profoundly transformed by Eusebi Güell's representation of it. This is a monument, without a doubt, but a monument that memorializes its subject in and for the family, among friends, and only they would be capable of understanding the theme in full. The significance of the subtler details would be lost on an outsider: not only would the gate of the garden, with its poplars, willows and elms, be closed to them but they would find it very difficult, if not impossible, to discern the lyre on the gate or the constellations represented by the claws, tongue and tail of the dragon.[100] In the great tradition of hermeneutics and the language of emblems, the dragon gate reveals certain things on a more immediate level, but conceals or veils others: the pleasure of recognizing these, of possessing what is not explicit, effectively excluding the uninitiated, is what unites the family and determines its distinction. And that pleasure is, of course, one that is not revealed: as far as we know Güell never disclosed the significance of the gate, and, as we have said, no contemporary commentator ever offered the most tentative interpretation in such a light, or the slightest indication that they were aware of it. This was, for Güell and those closest to him, a private, secret tribute: a mechanism of exclusion. Thus veiled, basic elements of the common culture are made more private, radically personal and autobiographical. A form of possession, then, that goes beyond the things themselves to take on an inner meaning of its own, a meaning that is not revealed. If *L'Atlàntida* can be read at face value, the dragon gate cannot, and there lies the greater pleasure of inventing it, of possessing it. And here too, as we saw in the little Heracles fountain, other meanings are lightly overlaid on the ones we have already noted: embossed in the sheet iron of the gate, worked in the stone crests, represented in the ceramic, we find a multitude of roses, evidently the *satalia* that gave the estate its name. The

44

*Ll. Domènech i Montaner,
Montaner i Simon publishing
house, Barcelona, 1881–86.
Detail of the façade.*

rose, especially the white rose (and quite explicitly on many occasions the *satalia)*, is the symbolic image Verdaguer uses most frequently to refer to the Virgin, who in his poetry can only be the Virgin of Montserrat. The celebrations for the Millennium of Montserrat in 1881 mark one of the supreme moments in the strategy of political restoration pursued by the Catalan church at the end of the nineteenth century.[101]

If Eusebi Güell played an active part in the organization of the great celebration, Verdaguer was one of its *inventors* and, of course, its greatest propagandist. The two books of poems he published for the occasion—*Cançons de Montserrat* and *Llegendes de Montserrat*, reissued together in 1889 under the simple title *Montserrat*—were of key impor-

tance (without a doubt the most effective from point of view popular) in forging the now habitual identification between Montserrat and Catalonia. "The white satalia / Says smiling / It is the Virgin Mary / Who is her Gardener," writes Verdaguer, and also: "Like a rose / My homeland / Places you / Over its heart."[102] As with the dragon that watered the stripes of the Catalan flag, the roses intertwined on the gate overlay it with other meanings, patriotic and devotional, and breathe life into the very name of the estate, at once the Garden of the Hesperides and the garden of Mary.

But, in any case, a garden. If *L'Atlantida,* so ideologically charged, so impassioned, has been converted into a veiled monument, the secret emblem of private sentiments, there is nothing strange in

*A. Gaudí, entrance pavilions*
*on the Güell estate in Pedralbes.*
*Plan, elevation and section.*

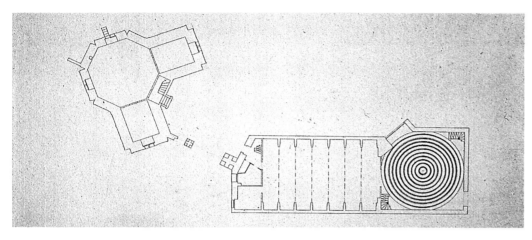

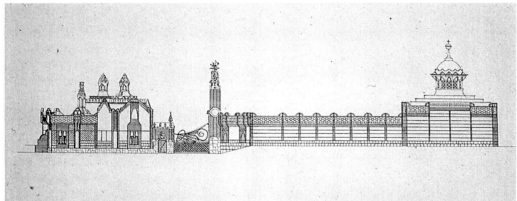

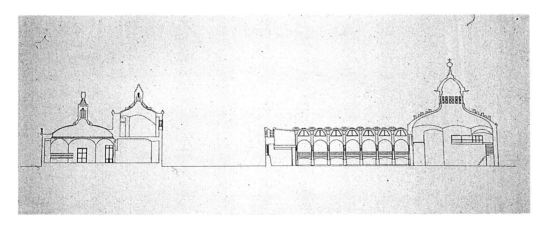

Güell's choice of canto for this demonstration of his culture to himself and his circle: what else should it be but the Garden of the Hesperides? From the *hortus conclusus* of classical tradition on, the garden has been the place closed to the passing of time, outside of history: the place always in flower. And the Güell garden is mythological and mystical, both at once and both in secret. It seems, then, that Eusebi Güell is perverting here the symbols that Antonio López had possessed directly, and in a sense this is so. The garden is a closed retreat, the gate a veiled emblem. Everything that in López had been explicit and aggressive, in Güell seems to become hermetic and interior. Güell also seems, here at least, to have escaped the burden of needing to manifest his interests, both personal and general: but those interests are now static, and the distinction—his own and that of the initiated—is more radical, but consolatory. Güell's aristocracy without a title (as yet) was clearly of a very different kind from that of the marquis of Comillas, and so too was his understanding of what was to constitute *pouvoir social sur le temps*.

### "The Very Latest Tendencies"

But there are other things that bear witness to all of this, and eloquently; for example, the style not only of the gate but of the other elements of Gaudí's intervention in the estate. Scholars have always spoken of Gaudí's early works in terms of an eclectic period. Thus, the villa El Capricho, Casa Vicens and, above all, the actuations on the Güell estate have commonly been categorized, with all the caveats required by Gaudí's *genius*, as neo-Mudéjar.[103] Certainly, ever since in 1859 José Amador de los Ríos took his place in the Real Academia de Bellas Artes de San Fernando with a paper entitled "The Mudéjar Style in Architecture," Mudéjar has been regarded as a "characteristic creation of Spanish culture,"[104] a style in which the historical synthesis of the Christian and Muslim civilizations that combine in the very origins of Spanish culture finds one of its most privileged expressions. There is nothing strange in this dis-

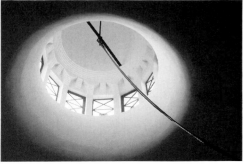

covery at a time when all over Europe—and in Spain, obviously, with the very special characteristics of the country's specific history—a philological and archaeological Arabism was beginning to take shape. In fact the debate engendered by Amador de los Ríos' paper, and especially Pedro de Madrazo's response to it, was always scientific and scholarly. Nor was it strange that it should emerge at a time of heated discussion in magazines and congresses about the need for modern art to manifest, before all else, a national character.[105] Mudéjar, regarded from its first invention as the most authentic and original Spanish contribution to Western art, inevitably assumed the status of the Spanish style *par excellence*. Thus, for example, the Spanish pavilions at a series of International Exhibitions—from Vienna in 1873 to Paris in 1878 and 1889—were in a neo-Mudéjar style, as were many of the constructions for the Exhibition in Barcelona in 1888, not least among them the Arch of Triumph that was its gateway.[106] But Mudéjar was not only that: the polemics pursued by the most perceptive architects and critics of the last quarter of the nineteenth century also centered on Mudéjar's potential to serve as model and inspiration for a new Spanish architecture, a regenerated architecture. From a very early date—1878, the year that Gaudí graduated from the School of Architecture—Lluís Domènech i Montaner (one of Gaudí's closest acquaintances) addressed the question directly in his highly influential *En busca de una arquitectura nacional* [*In search of a national architecture*],[107] in which he argued lucidly in favor of an erudite and uninhibited eclecticism; and as late as 1899, in a treatise significantly entitled *Causas de la decadencia de la arquitectura* [*Causes of the decadence of architecture*], Mélida was still pinning his hopes of regeneration on the Mudéjar style.[108] Certainly, neo-Mudéjar—from archaeological discourse, to polemic, to built work—was the form of historicism most widely accepted all over Spain by the architects of the Restoration. Nevertheless, to relate Gaudí's exoticism to this is simply to surrender to historiographical prejudice.

Let us focus in greater detail on the group of ele-

ments that configure the main entrance to the Güell estate. The lodge, to the left of dragon gate, is an octagonal volume with a circular domed roof topped by a small cupola. The two-story wings that extend from two sides of the octagon are rectangular in plan, with the door set between them. Access to the stables on the other side of the gate is by way of a small vestibule. In the interior, the slender parabolic vaults of the structure—with the feeding stalls between them—divide the space diaphragmatically, and the diffuse light that enters through the trapezoidal windows between the arches is diffuse and atmospheric. Finally, the riding area at the end of the stables, square in plan, is roofed with a circular dome that opens into a wide lantern. We have here, then, a series of spaces each with its own individual character that have nevertheless renounced a truly separate articulation. In effect, the process of addition adopted by Gaudí here is clearly manifested in the elementary form in which the cuboid volumes of the lodge are simply abutted onto the central octagon, and even more so in the juxtaposition, by way of a simple door, effected between the parallel sequence of arches of the stables and the centralized volume of the riding area and in the far from explicit way that each of the volumes modulates from the polygonal form of the base to the circular form of the dome topped by its lantern. At the same time, the treatment of the exterior, although unitary in the different parts of the whole, is also based on fragmentation and juxtaposition. Rising up from a socle of stone, the walls are decorated with interwoven geometric reliefs, while the parabolic or rectangular doors and windows are framed in red brick and protected by grilles, blinds and wooden lattices in a great variety of forms. There are also lattices on the crest of the walls, this time of fair-faced brick, and, finally, domes and the lanterns are finished with colored ceramic tiles that in some cases, and for the first time in Gaudí's work, have been fragmented using the technique he was to make famous, *trencadís*. But this heterogeneity, extending from the greater to the smaller scale and from one end of the complex the other, is even more surprising if we think of

the specific models Gaudí drew on in resolving each of its parts, each separate element. Thus, the larger sections of the lodge and the riding area, each with its dome that seems to narrow into the neck of the lantern above, are directly derived from the medieval French kitchens illustrated by Viollet-le-Duc in volume IV of his dictionary.[109] And Gaudí had previously used parabolic vaults such as those in the stables, albeit of wood, in 1883 for the laundry in his project for the Sociedad Obrera Mataronense, following the models and procedures described by Rondelet and Emy, whose treatises were available to Gaudí in the library of the School of Architecture. What is more, the diaphragmatic succession of those arches derives from one of the essential structural characteristics of Catalan Gothic. In the monastery of Poblet, a building for which Gaudí had a great admiration (in May 1882 he had organized for the Asociació d'Excursions Catalana, of which he was himself a member, a fantastic nocturnal illumination of the monastery, with torches and fireworks),[110] the very long bays of the dormitories are a paradigm of this type of spatial organization. But if this is true of the definition of the interiors, it is no less true of the forms and decoration of the exteriors. The little cupolas and lanterns—like the crests of the Casa Vicens or the tower of El Capricho—are taken directly from the minarets of Cairo that Gaudí had seen illustrated in the books of Pascal Cost, Prisse D'Avennes and in the collection of photographs of Egyptian monuments in the library of the School of Architecture, acquired when he was a student there.[111] From those minarets—or rather, from the prints depicting them—Gaudí isolated and selected certain parts—a cornice, a projection, a dome—to be incorporated into his project, interpreting and assembling them in a new order. For example, it is not hard to see in the lantern of the riding area certain sections of the crest of the minaret of Qala'un or of the corbels of the balconies of al-Azhar. Indeed, is this not precisely the way that, in the notes on ornamentation he compiled in 1878 for a purely operative purpose, Gaudí focused on the objects he was studying?

"Examination of the photographs of the Alhambra, observing that the columns, which are small in diameter, are shortened, elongating the capital by means of moldings in the shaft; I believe in the application of colors especially on the base in order to leave a short length of shaft. *Idem* in the different rooms to support vaults, small columns that enlarge the room or member affording play for the imagination as in Gothic dosserets. *Idem* the bands that are superimposed, whose lines are inverse directions, so that if the interior follows the motif or pattern in the direction of longitude, the exterior follows the latitude; this latter done by the Arabic inscriptions."[112] So runs the first paragraph of Gaudí's notes. The repetition of the Latin *idem* indicates that these observations are not organized as a discourse: these are scattered visions, wondering at this thing or that (a band of color, a molding, a decorative motif), which automatically, unexpectedly invoke others: from the small columns of the Alhambra to Gothic dosserets, from a geometric motif to an Arabic inscription. In the long pages of his manuscript, among reflections on color, light, decoration or the liturgy, Gaudí ranged far and wide, from the abacus to an Ictinus capital on a stairway he saw in a house in Reus to the details of his own desk, and could write (with eccentric syntax) that "the cathedrals have the arc of the circle in almost parabolic vaults."[113] But this continual to and fro does not, as has often been said, stem from the inherent disorder of a set of personal notes that make no claim to theoretical originality, but is quite simply a consequence of Gaudí's culture, of his method of acquiring that culture and the mechanisms through which he interprets it. Gaudí's culture is uniquely and exclusively visual, and his procedure is one of automatic shifts, the successive illuminations one vision casts on the next: is it not significant that the manuscript should begin with the "examination" of a photograph that has been forgotten by the next line? From the time Gaudí made those notes in 1878 to his first works of genuine importance, four or five years later, few things in that culture and that procedure seem to have changed. We have seen the variety of sources for

*Poblet Monastery. Novices'*
*dormitory, thirteenth century,*
*and monks' dormitory,*
*early fifteenth century, in two*
*photographs from 1908.*

*A. Gaudí, entrance pavilions
on the Güell estate in Pedralbes.
Domes and lanterns.*

52

*Details of the lanterns, the façades
and the "voided" corners
of the Pedralbes entrance pavilions.*

the models that serve to structure the different spaces, the montage used to recompose the sections of domes and lanterns, and we could carry on down to the most detailed decorative solutions and find the same procedure time and again: interweaving geometric motif on the walls taken directly from the plates of the D'Avennes book we mentioned earlier,[114] Japanese blinds like the ones in the Casa Vicens,[115] Arab-style ceramic tiles; a colorist obsession that, in the long paragraphs he devotes to the subject in his manuscript, draw on sources that extend as far as Hittorf,[116] and popular techniques such as the *trencadís*. And all of this without forgetting that between the two volumes we are describing here we have the great dragon of wrought iron, the orange tree of antimony, the pillar of brick and stone.[117]

From the structure to the fine detail of the decoration, the whole is thus thoroughly heterogeneous, as if variety, understood as abundance, as excess, had been the basic premise of the project. In every one of the spaces, in each of the parts of the volumes (walls, domes, lanterns), in each element of the decoration and each of the materials he used Gaudí seems to revel in an intrinsic value that, instead of being articulated with others, is isolated, converted into a complete image or sensation, regardless of the unity or otherwise of the result. Variety, we have said, but also innovation: innovation in the elements, in the technique, in the forms of aggregation, in the syntax. Indeed, perhaps variety and innovation are the essential conditions of a project that really aspires to be a project. One supremely important detail here reveals the conscious radicalism with which Gaudí sets out to embody these values: the way he prevents the walls from articulating in the corners. In effect, all the corners of the lodge are *voided* from top to bottom, from the first course of the stone socle to the latticed cornice. Thus the corner, the place where the wall doubles back to expose its greatest tension, is materially absent, it has literally disappeared. The fact that the sharp angle of the first course of the socle at ground level is retained, or that the upper part is virtually reconstituted with a lattice of

brickwork that reveals its empty interior, reflect the absolute consciousness with which Gaudí was working. But that violent voiding of the corners is not the only way in which Gaudí seeks to dematerialize his work. At one of the secondary entrances to the estate, when the brickwork arrives at the two pyramidal turrets that top the gateposts (today much mutilated) this is broken down into low parallel parapets, as if peeled away (exactly as Gaudí had done on a larger scale with the crests of the Casa Vicens, where the parallel walls on corbels project out perpendicular to the house). In one of the corners of the perimeter wall Gaudí constructed a belvedere (since demolished). On top of the parabolic arch was an almost transparent, weightless latticework wall, through which could be seen the section of the stairway that led up to the balcony, below which two low corbeled parapets did no more than allude to an absent element of support. Something similar occurred in the projecting stairway (also no longer extant) that Gaudí constructed on the flat roof of the main house, alongside which

a chimney literally bristling with colored ceramic tiles exhibited its own astonished deconstruction. In the house itself, the Torre Satalia, Gaudí seems to dispel the solemnity of his former master Martorell by setting great shields with the letter G for Güell on the corners. A dematerialization, in short, of all the walls by means of the tiling and the color.

Gaudí's constructions on the Güell estate shed weight, become light, cease, in effect, to be constructions in the tectonic sense of the word. But let us return to the place where this is most in evidence: the pavilions by the main gate. Voiding the corners, Gaudí presents each one of the walls isolated in itself, while the decoration or the openings in the wall are surrounded by frames that separate and distinguish them from the whole, which as a result can only be understood as an aggregate compound. Each wall is thus a panel, and each panel contains a complete image. The whole is the sum of those images: an exhibition or *mise-en-scène*. Gaudí's eclecticism—the automatic de-

*Stairway exit, chimney of the Torre Satalia and belvedere on the perimeter wall of the Güell estate, photographed in 1893 and at the start of the twentieth century. Demolished in 1919.*

tail, the shift, the montage—is a long way from any kind of historicism. Cornices, oriental domes and lanterns, Japanese blinds, popular techniques or formal signs of innovation: the result of this composition could hardly be less concrete. With the loss of material it is the recognizable objects of historicism that absent themselves. Gaudí's work is literally exotic, because its origins are strange. In the first place, Gaudí's visual culture is strange, its primary condition being an avidly excessive accumulation of images and the need to exhibit them all. The second strange thing is his process of composition, that imperfect composition called addition that requires, in the extreme, the elimination of the material, the cancelling of the weight, so as to leave the evocative attributes of the images floating on their own. Non-concretion, evocation: Gaudí here does not refer to historical *styles* but to "le splendeur Orientale,"[118] to that Orient in which the European imaginary of the age of progress locates all the treasures, all the riches, all the passions that have disappeared from the modern West. The excess, the unrestrained abundance concentrated in and overflowing the minor work we are considering here is precisely the compression in images of the consoling irrationalism of that obsessive Orient: "Luxe, calme et volupté."

Clearly, then, it was history as a system of data that had to be eliminated from that vision, and the way that Gaudí symbolically loads all the details of his work with richness could not be more eloquent. A further small illustration of this is the fact that Gaudí had tiny fragments of colored ceramic inserted in the mortar of the joints between the bricks—fragments that are only apparent on the closest inspection. What an excess of effort for a result that is all but invisible, but how much it enriches what in itself was nothing, charging with aristocratic value by virtue of that squandered effort, that work for which there is no quantifiable time! There can be no clearer demonstration of disregard for the utility of the modern world. And it is precisely in demonstrating this that Gaudí evokes a fantastic Orient that is to all intents and purposes the Orient of so many travel books, so

*A. Gaudí, views of Casa Vicens, 1883–85.*

CARRER
DE LES
CAROLINES

59

many tales and so many *fin-de-siècle* novels, that as Lily Litvak has perceptively observed,[119] had replaced the magic carpets and the princesses of other eras with a sense of *decline* that amounts to a total rejection of the modern and a nostalgia for a time without a future, the undaunted time of the *durée.* An Orient synonymous with the remote and the unchanging, impassive before the profane time of Western reason.

Could Eusebi Güell have found a more fitting site for his unique representation of *L'Atlàntida?* The private monument is here the *mîse-en-scène* of the most radical anachronism. If the *Atlàntida* of Antonio López reflected the ideological discourse of an aggressive colonialism, the orientalism of the pavilions on the Güell estate is simply the other side of the same coin: Orient is a place of indifference to progress, the opposite of the West, the extraordinary realm of absence. It was only the crisis of nineteenth-century colonialism—which, as we have seen, was imbued with a particular significance for the Barcelona bourgeoisie—that allowed Europe to embrace such a vision of a fateful Orient outside of time. It was Güell himself, compressing all of *L'Atlàntida* into a veiled image, who chose as *mîse-en-scène* of that image the architecture of a Gaudí who, we should remember, in 1884 had already begun to construct the Casa Vicens and El Capricho. In other words, he had already given the intelligent and sophisticated Güell two examples of his work—and of its meaning. The action of Antonio López, in times of expansion, was unitary: policy and symbolic representation of that policy were enacted, as we have seen, simultaneously, without dissimulation. A directly operative ideological discourse *descended* on those objectives that were actually being achieved, or about to be. Eusebi Güell, in contrast, in a time of crisis, was to change all his strategies, not only economic and political, as we shall see in due course, but ideological, as we have seen. In times of retraction, an operation such as the remodeling of the Güell estate has a very clear purpose: to embody in image all that cannot at present be achieved in reality. The estate is the Garden of the Hesperides, a mystical garden, a rich and

fateful Orient: the Other. In any case, a place outside of any concrete time, closed to the march of history and, above all, to the contingency of the present. In times of real weakness, Güell's possession is sublimated in brilliant images, in names and programs that are veiled, secretly evocative. The old ideology is transformed into a magic powder that falls on his possessions: an aesthetic. The equation between increased consumption and modernity that Yxart outlined to the Barcelona bourgeoisie loses all its meaning in the actuation of Eusebi Güell: he elevates it to the heights of the inimitable. It is not a matter of increasing consumption but quite simply of extravagance, of lavishly squandering the most prized values of bourgeois life: work and quantifiable time. Hyperconsumption, then, precisely because it is not the other factor in the equation that matters here: the object is to be not modern but anachronistic. The most radical anachronism, the time of the *durée:* that and that alone is the possession that his aesthetic sublimates. Where else would Gaudí's reactionary eccentricities have been encouraged? Eusebi Güell sought to be not a bourgeois, but a patrician: for him, Gaudí would construct mansion, city and gardens.

[1] On the Barcelona International Exhibition of 1888 consult the studies published to mark the recent centenary: R. Grau and M. López (eds.), *Exposició Universal de Barcelona. Llibre del Centenari, 1888–1988,* Barcelona, 1988; (various authors), "Barcelona i l'Exposició Universal de 1888," *L'Avenç,* no. 85, Barcelona, September 1988, and in particular: P. Hereu (ed.), *Arquitectura i ciutat a l'Exposició Universal de Barcelona, 1888,* Barcelona, 1988. Josep Yxart (1852–1895), without doubt the first Catalan critic of literature and art deserving of the name, was close to the European and Spanish naturalist school and was its principal theorist in Catalonia. On his work: J. Castellanos, "Próleg," in J. Yxart, *Entorn de la literatura catalana de la Restauració,* Barcelona, 1980; A. Bensoussan, *José Yxart, 1852–1895,* Lille, 1982 (2 vols.); R. Cabre, *Epistolari Josep Yxart-Narcís Oller,* doctoral thesis, Univ. de Barcelona, 1985. For Yxart's comments on the Exhibition, see: J. Yxart, *El año pasado. Letras y artes en Barcelona,* Barcelona, 1889. For further reference see: J. Castellanos, *Raimon Casellas i el Modernisme,* Montserrat, 1983, vol. I, pp. 27–44.

[2] J. Yxart, op. cit., pp. 163–65.

[3] Ibid., p. 166.

[4] For an alternative to the traditional interpretations of the Exhibition as a motor of urban change see the important article by M. Guardia, A. García Espuche, J. Monclus and J.L. Oyon, "La dimensió urbana," in P. Hereu (ed.), *Arquitectura i ciutat a l'Exposició Universal de Barcelona, 1888,* Barcelona, 1988, pp. 129–78.

[5] J. Yxart, op. cit., p. 172.

[6] Ibid., p. 169.

[7] Ibid., p. 169.

[8] Ibid., p. 164.

[9] Ibid., p. 277.

[10] Ibid., p. 167.

[11] On the economic aspects of the Restoration in Catalonia, see the classic overall interpretation in J. Vicens Vives, *Industrials i politics* (1958), Barcelona, 1980, pp. 91–109; another classic, although now appreciably dated, is J. Carrera Pujal, *La economía de Cataluña en el siglo XIX,* Barcelona, 1961 (4 vols.). Especially important is P. Vilar, "La Catalunya industrial: reflexions sobre una arrencada i un desti," *Recerques,* no. 3, 1974, pp. 7–22. See too: M. Izard, *Manufactureros, industriales y revolucionarios,* Barcelona, 1979. Of fundamental importance today are the essays on the subject in (various authors), *Catalunya, la fàbrica d'Espanya. Un segle d'industrialització catalana, 1833–1936* Barcelona, 1985. Another concise study, more centered on the period of the Exhibition, is: B. de Riquer, "La societat catalana dels anys vuitanta," in P. Hereu (ed.), *Arquitectura i ciutat...,* cit., pp. 17–38. And regarding the following section, see: G. Ferré, *La febre d'or a Catalunya,* doctoral thesis, Univ. de Barcelona, 1981.

[12] N. Oller, *La febra d'or (1890–92),* Barcelona, 1980 (2 vols.). Oller (1843–1930), the principal exponent of naturalism in Catalonia, has traditionally been regarded by historians as the creator of the modern Catalan novel. See his own memoirs: N. Oller, *Memòries literàries. Història dels meus llibres,* Barcelona, 1962. On Oller's work in general see A. Tayadella, "Narcís Oller i el naturalisme," *Història de la literatura catalana,* vol. VII, Barcelona, 1986, pp. 605–68. On *La febra d'or* see the contemporary comment by J. Yxart, "*La febra d'or* per Narcís Oller," *Obres catalanes de Josep Yxart,* Barcelona, 1896, pp. 184–91. Fundamental: A. Yates, "The Creation of Narcís Oller's *La febra d'or,*" *Bulletin of Hispanic Studies,* vol. LII, 1975; id., "Narcís Oller i el primer modernisme: a propòsit de *La febre d'or,*" *Actes de colloqui internacional sobre el modernisme,* Montserrat, 1988, pp. 65–78.

[13] N. Oller, op. cit., vol. I, p. 69.

[14] Ibid., p. 70.

[15] Ibid., pp. 69–70.

[16] See: J.Ll. Marfany, "Estetes i menestrals," *L'Avenç,* no. 9, October 1978, pp. 36–41; id., "La cultura de la burgesia barcelonina en la fi de segle," *Serra d'Or,* vol. XX, no. 231, December 1978, pp. 54–63; id., "Modernisme i modernitat: artistes i burgesia," *Actes del colloqui internacional sobre el modernisme,* cit., pp. 9–24.

[17] N. Oller, op. cit., vol. I, p. 73.

[18] Ibid., pp. 72–73.

[19] Ibid., p. 71.

[20] On the reforms in the historic city center, see: M. Torres Capell, J. Puig and J. Llovet, *Inicis de la urbanistica municipal de Barcelona,* Barcelona, 1986, especially pp. 21–26 and 129ff. For a monograph study of a concrete case similar to the one that concerns us here, see A. López de Guereña and I. Solà-Morales, *La Plaça Reial de Barcelona. De la utilidad y ornato público a la reforma urbana,* Barcelona, 1982. More generally: R. Grau and M. López, "Barcelona entre el urbanismo barroco y la revolución industrial," *Cuadernos de Arquitectura y Urbanismo,* no. 80, January–February 1971, pp. 28–40; A. García Espuche and M. Guardia, *Espai i societat a la Barcelona pre-industrial,* Barcelona, 1986, pp. 75ff. On the more re-

cent proposals see: O. Bohigas, *Reconstrucció de Barcelona*, Barcelona, 1985, pp. 207ff.
[21] N. Oller, op. cit., vol. I, p. 71.
[22] On this question, see J. Castellanos, *Raimon Casellas i el Modernisme*, cit., vol. I, pp. 29–30.
[23] J. Yxart, op. cit., p. 165.
[24] Ibid., p. 278.
[25] Ibid., p. 166.
[26] Ibid., p. 197.
[27] J. Castellanos, op. cit., especially vol. I, pp. 101ff. See too: M. McCully, "Impacte d'un critic: Raimon Casellas i els pintors modernistes," *L'Avenç*, no. 23, January 1980, pp. 52–57; J. Castellanos, "Correspondència Rusiñol-Casellas," *Els Marges*, no. 21, January 1981, pp. 85–110. More generally, see: R. Plà i Arxe, "L'Avenç: la modernització de la *Renaixença*," *Els Marges*, no. 4, May 1975, pp. 23–38; F. Fontbona, "La crítica d'art en al modernisme català (primera aproximació)," *Daedalus. Estudis d'art i cultura*, vol. I, no. 1, 1979, pp. 58–85; J.Ll. Marfany, "Assagistes i periodistes," *Història de la literatura catalana*, vol. VIII, Barcelona, 1986, pp. 143–86.
[28] Gaudí was not officially involved in the Exhibition. However, he did receive one commission: the restoration of the Saló de Cent and the grand stairway in Barcelona City Hall, a project finally carried out by Lluís Domènech i Montaner. Nevertheless, at the invitation of the marquis of Comillas, Gaudí remodeled the Compañía Transatlántica Pavilion. On these projects see: J. Bassegoda, *El gran Gaudí*, Sabadell, 1989, pp. 313–17, for the bibliography. In due course we shall attempt to assess Gaudí's "official" absence from the Exhibition. In addition to Gaudí, Yxart must also be referring to architects such as Lluís Domènech i Montaner and Josep Vilaseca, who were nevertheless well represented in the Exhibition, the former with the Café-Restaurant and the Hotel Internacional, the latter with the Arch of Triumph that led in to the Exhibition. Gaudí's innovations have to be contrasted with the highly refined and cultured architecture of his two contemporaries. On Domènech, see: *Cuadernos de Arquitectura*, nos. 52–53, 1963, special monograph issue; (various authors), *Lluís Domènech i Montaner. En el 50 aniversari de la seva mort*, Barcelona, 1973; (various authors), *Lluís Domènech i Montaner i el director d'orquestra*, Barcelona, 1990. On Vilaseca: R. Bletter, *El arquitecto Josep Vilaseca i Casanovas. Sus obras y dibujos*, Barcelona, 1977. In general, on the architec-

ture of the Exhibition: P. Hereu, "L'arquitectura de l'Exposició," *Arquitectura i ciutat a l'Exposició...*, cit., pp. 179ff.
[29] A very eloquent testimony to the perceived innovative value of Gaudí's work is the inclusion (without giving the name of the work or the architect) of a photograph of the gate of the Güell estate in what is perhaps the most interesting guide to the Exhibition: J. Valero de Tornos, *Guide illustrée de l'Exposition Universelle de Barcelone, de la ville, de ses curiosites et de ses environs*, Barcelona, 1888, p. 137.
[30] B. de Riquer, "La societat catalana dels anys vuitanta," *Arquitectura i ciutat a l'Exposició...*, cit., pp. 17–38; also very important for understanding the critical atmosphere in which the Exhibition took place is M. Jove, "Polèmiques, expectatives i valoracions a l'entorn del certamen," id., pp. 41–70.
[31] See: E. Diaz, "La inversió de sol a Barcelona en el procés d'acumulació de capital," and M. Tatjer, "La propietat inmobiliària a Barcelona a mitjans del segle XIX," *Actes del I Congrés d'Història del Plà de Barcelona*, Barcelona, 1984. See, too: X. Tafunell, *La construcción residencial y el crecimiento económico. Barcelona 1854–1897*, doctoral thesis, Univ. de Barcelona, 1988.
[32] N. Oller, op. cit., vol. I, pp. 215ff.
[33] J. Yxart, op. cit., p. 173.
[34] Ibid., pp. 326–34.
[35] Ibid., p. 327.
[36] Much of the debate about the Barcelona Eixample is contained in the re-edition of Cerdà's own book, *Teoría general de la urbanización. Reforma y ensanche de Barcelona (1867)*, Madrid, 1971 (3 vols.), the first two volumes of which are a facsimile edition of the original and the third a study of Cerdà's life and work by F. Estape, together with an important collection of documentary material. On Cerdà and the problems of the Eixample, see, too: F. Puig y Alfonso *Génesis del Ensanche de Barcelona*, Barcelona, 1915; (various authors), *Ildefonso Cerdà. El hombre y su obra*, Barcelona, 1955; A. Soria y Puig, *Ildefonso Cerdà. Hacia una teoria general de la urbanización*, Madrid, 1979, and the monograph issues of various magazines: *Cuadernos de Arquitectura y Urbanismo*, no. 100, January–February 1974; id., no. 101, March–April 1974; *20. Construcción de la Ciudad*, nos. 6–7, January 1977. See, too: M. Torres Capell, J. Puig and J. Llovet, *Inicis de la urbanística municipal de Barcelona*, cit., pp. 61ff.; R. Grau and M. López (eds.), *Exposició Universal de Barcelona. Llibre

del Centenari*, cit., chapters 4, 5 and 6.
[37] J Artigas, *Guía itineraria y descriptiva de Barcelona, de sus alrededores, y de la Exposición Universal*, Barcelona 1888; J. Valero de Tornos, *Guide Illustrée de l'Exposition Universelle de Barcelona...*, cit; J. Yxart, op. cit., pp. 179ff. On the question of the itineraries of the Exhibition and the sense of his prestige, see: M. Guardia, A. García Espuche, J. Monclus and J.L. Oyon, "La dimensió urbana," *Arquitectura i ciutat a l'Exposició Universal de Barcelona*, cit., pp. 160ff.
[38] J. Yxart, op. cit., p. 182.
[39] On the monument to Columbus, designed in 1881 by Gaietà Buigas, winner of the municipal competition, and completed in 1888: G. Buigas Monrava, *Monumento a Cristóbal Colón*, Barcelona, 1882, the official report on the competition scheme. See too: "El monumento a Colón en Barcelona," *La Ilustración Artística*, no. 355, October 15, 1888, pp. 336–44. On Buigas: *Buigas Monravà*, Barcelona, 1973. On the monument to López, designed by J.O. Mestres: *Monumento levantado en esta ciudad y dedicado al Exmo. Sr. D. Antonio López y López*, Barcelona, 1884. And on the Güell monument, designed by J. Martorell and since totally transformed: P.B.T., "Historia de un monumento que renace," *Barcelona Atracción*, no. 306, September 1945, pp. 135–39. See, too: B. Bassegoda Amigo, *Las estatuas de Barcelona*, Barcelona, 1903.
[40] G. Buigas Monrava, *Monumento a Cristóbal Colón*, cit.
[41] This project for illuminating the Muralla de Mar promenade was carried out by Gaudí in collaboration with the engineer José Serramalera. Only three drawings are known, published in J. Ràfols and F. Folguera, *Gaudí*, Barcelona, 1928, pp. 14–16, of which only the original of the third, a general view sketched by Gaudí on the back of one of his own visiting cards, is still extant. On this project see: F. Puig y Alfonso, *Curiositats barcelonines*, Barcelona, 1930, vol. I, pp. 162–63; J. Bassegoda, *El gran Gaudí*, cit., pp. 177–79.
[42] See: C. Martinell, *Gaudí. Su vida, su teoría, su obra*, Barcelona, 1967, pp. 496–98, which reproduces and transcribes the folio that Gaudí entitled: "Extracto de los asuntos históricos para la decoración de los soportes de la I.E." Martinell, I believe correctly, takes this to mean "Iluminación Eléctrica." Collins, on the other hand, from his very North American perspective, considers these to be sketches for a Spanish Pavilion for the Philadelphia Centennial Exhibition that Gaudí never constructed:

G.R. Collins, *Antoni Gaudí*, New York, 1960, pp. 130–31.
[43] On the streetlamps in the Plaça Reial and the Plà de Palau: C. Martinell, "Las farolas de la plaza Real," *Destino*, XXVIII, September 25, 1965, pp. 26–28. Gaudí's report has been reproduced on various occasions: C. Martinell, *Gaudí. Su vida, su teoría, su obra*, cit., pp. 470–74; A. Gaudi, *Manuscritos, artículos, conversaciones y dibujos*, Murcia, 1982, pp. 59–69; J. Bassegoda, *El gran Gaudí*, cit., pp. 132–36. Quoted here from the Murcia edition by M. Codinachis, p. 64.
[44] The work of the Catalan Romantics is exemplified by epic poems such as the *L'Orientada* by F. Pelagi Briz, and tragedies such as *Los Pirineus* by V. Balaguer or the much later *La camí del sol* (1904) by A. Guimerà. Among the Castilians, *Roger de Flor* by J. Quintana or *La Venganza catalana* by A. García Gutiérrez, among many others.
[45] J. Yxart, op. cit., p. 180.
[46] On Joan Güell (1800–1872) it is worth consulting: J. Argullol Serra, *Biografía del Exmo. Sr. D. Juan Güell y Ferrer leída por D ... el 29 de septiembre de 1879*, Barcelona, 1881; P. Estasen, *El economista D. Juan Güell y Ferrer*, Barcelona, 1881; A. del Castillo, *La Maquinista Terrestre y Marítima, personaje histórico*, Barcelona, 1955; J. Vicens Vives and M. Llorens, *Industrials i politics*, cit., pp. 337–44, as well as Güell's own writings, especially those compiled in J. Güell y Ferrer, *Escritos económicos*, 1880. On Antonio López (1817–1884) there are two curious libels against him by his own brother-in-law: F. Brú, *Fortunas improvisadas*, Madrid, 1857; id., *La verdadera vida de Antonio López y López*, Barcelona, 1885, plus such apologies as: *Homenaje nacional a la memoria del Exmo. Sr. D. Antonio López y López, primer marqués de Comillas*, Madrid, 1883, and the Duque de Maura, *Pequeña historia de una grandeza. El marquesado de Comillas*, Barcelona, 1949.
[47] On Catalan trade with the American colonies there is the classic if much manipulated work by C. Martí, *Los catalanes en América*, Barcelona. However, there are also a number of very important published studies: J. Maluquer de Motes, "El problema de la esclavitud y la revolución de 1868," *Hispania*, no. 177, 1971, pp. 55–57; id., "La burgesia catalana i l'esclavitud colonial: modes de producció i pràctica política," *Recerques*, no. 3, 1974, pp. 83–136; id., "El mercado colonial antillano en el siglo XIX," in (various authors) *Agri-

*cultura, comercio colonial y crecimiento económico en la España contemporánea*, Barcelona, 1974, pp. 322–57; M. Izard, *Manufactureros, industriales y revolucionarios*, cit., pp. 163–78; J.M. Fradera, "Catalunya i Cuba en el segle XIX: el comerç d'esclaus," *L'Avenç*, no. 75, October 1984, pp. 42–47; id., "La figura del negre i del negrer en la literatura catalana del segle XIX," id., pp. 56–61. On the architecture of the so-called "indianos" see: *"Americanos." "Indianos." Arquitectura i urbanisme al Garraf, Penedés i Tarragonés (Baix Gaià). Segles XVIII–XX*, Vilanova i la Geltrú, 1990.

[48] Both cit. by J. Maluquer de Motes, "La burgesia catalana i l'esclavitud colonial…," cit., p. 107, with extensive commentary.

[49] Cit. by J. Maluquer de Motes, "La burgesia catalana i l'esclavitud colonial…," cit., p. 112.

[50] J. Maluquer de Motes, "La burgesia catalana i l'esclavitud colonial…," cit., pp. 102ff.

[51] J. Maluquer de Motes, "La burgesia catalana i l'esclavitud colonial…," cit., pp. 113ff.; M. Izard, *Manufactureros, industriales y revolucionarios*, cit., pp. 163–78.

[52] Cit. by M. Izard, *Manufactureros, industriales y revolucionarios*, cit., p. 164.

[53] J. Güell y Ferrer, *Escritos económicos*, cit. On the dispute between free-traders and protectionists: M. Izard, *Manufactureros, industriales y revolucionarios*, cit., pp. 84–141.

[54] On the Revolution and the First Republic: C.A.M. Hennessy, *La República Federal en España. Pi y Margall y el movimiento republicano federal. 1868–1874*, Madrid, 1966; and, although centered on the Revolution, the important: J. Fontana, "Canvi econòmic i actituds polítiques. Reflexió sobre les causes de la Revolució de 1868," *Recerques*, no. 2, 1972, pp. 7–32. See, too: M. Espadas Burgos, *Alfonso XII y los orígenes de la Restauración*, Madrid, 1971. For more specific analysis of the attitude of the conservative Catalan groups to the Restoration, the fundamental: B. de Riquer, "El conservadurisme politic català. Del fracàs del moderantisme al decensís de la Restauració," *Recerques*, no. 11, 1981, pp. 29–71.

[55] See: P. Voltes Bou, *La Banca barcelonesa de 1840 a 1920*, Barcelona, 1963; F. Cabana, *La banca de Catalunya*, Barcelona, 1965; id., *Bancs i banquers a Catalunya*, Barcelona, 1972, and more concretely on the different companies: *Historia del Banco Hispano Colonial*, Barcelona, 1943; id., *Centenario de la Compañía Transatlántica*, Barcelona, 1950. This latter was

the subject of a major exhibition in Barcelona: *La Compañía Transatlántica i el seu temps*, Barcelona, 1988. See: C. Yáñez, "La Compañía Transatlántica," *L'Avenç*, no. 117, July–August 1988, p. 60. And see, above all: M. Izard, "Dependencia y colonialismo: La Compañía General de Tabacos de Filipinas," *Moneda y Crédito*, CXXX, 1974, pp. 47–89.

[56] In general: G.W. McDonogh, *Las buenas familias de Barcelona. Historia social de poder en la era industrial*, Barcelona, 1989.

[57] See: *Monumento levantado en esta ciudad y dedicado al Exmo. Sr. D. Antonio López y López*, cit., and P.B.T., "Historia de un monumento que renace," cit.

[58] On *L'Atlàntida* see: (various authors), *Jacint Verdaguer. En el centenari de L'Atlàntida*, Barcelona, 1977; J. Miracle, *Estudis sobre Jacint Verdaguer*, Barcelona, 1989, pp. 17–104; J. Molas, "Jacint Verdaguer," *Història de la literatura catalana*, vol. VII, cit., pp. 237–50; and the various studies in the *Anuari Verdaguer 1986*, Vic, 1987. See, too, the references to the prize in many biographies, none wholly satisfactory; for example: A. Esclasans, *Jacinto Verdaguer. Un siglo de Barcelona*, Barcelona, 1944, and: J. Torrent i Fàbregas, *Jacint Verdaguer. Resum biogràfic*, Barcelona, 1952. Among the definitive editions of the poem: J. Verdaguer, *La Atlàntida*, Barcelona, 1878, with Castilian translation by Melcior de Palau and a beautiful cover design by Lluís Domènech i Montaner; and the critical edition comparing the manuscripts and the versions of 1877 and 1878 by E. Junyent and M. de Riquer, *L'Atlàntida*, Barcelona, 1946. With regard to Verdaguer's reference to his coronation as national poet of Catalonia: J. Verdaguer, "Llorers espinosos," *En defensa própia (Obres Completes. Edició Popular*, vol. XVII), Barcelona, pp. 44–45.

[59] On the Jocs Florals poetry competition see: J. Miracle, *La restauració dels Jocs Florals*, Barcelona, 1960; M. Jorba, "Els Jocs Florals," *Història de la literatura catalana*, vol. VII, cit., pp. 125–51. On Àngel Guimerà, the most important and influential turn-of-the-century Catalan dramatist: X. Fàbregas, *Àngel Guimerà. Les dimensions d'un mite*, Barcelona, 1971; (various authors), *Àngel Guimerà (1845–1924)*, Barcelona, 1974; X. Fàbregas, "Àngel Guimerà i el teatre del seu temps," *Història de la literatura catalana*, vol. VII, cit., pp. 543–604.

[60] In addition to the Castilian translation that accompanied the first edition, there were translations into French and Italian (1884), Occitan (1888), Czech (1891), Ger-

man (1897) and Portuguese (1909), as well as excerpts in English.

[61] J. Miracle, *Estudis sobre Jacint Verdaguer*, cit., pp. 17–20.

[62] J. Verdaguer, *En defensa pròpia*, cit., p. 9.

[63] E. Junyent and M. de Riquer (eds.), *L'Atlàntida*, cit., pp. XIII–XXII.; J. Miracle, *Estudis sobre Jacint Verdaguer*, cit., pp. 17–104.

[64] Published in 1895 in: J. Verdaguer, *En defensa pròpia*, cit., p. 12. On all this: J. Miracle, *Estudis on Jacint Verdaguer*, cit., pp. 20–84.

[65] See: J.M. Casacuberta, "Sobre la génesi de L'Atlàntida de Jacint Verdaguer," *Estudis Romànics*, vol. III, 1952, pp. 1–56; J.J. Solà i Camps, "Del Colom a l'Atlàntida," *Jacint Verdaguer. En el centenari…*, cit., pp. 40–74; M. Condeminas, *La gènesis de L'Atlàntida*, Barcelona, 1978; id., "Entorn de Colom, poema inacabat de Jacint Verdaguer," *Miscel.lània Pere Bohigas*, vol. II, Montserrat, 1982, pp. 227–52. The edition of *Colom*, by J. Torrent i Fàbregas and J. Verdaguer, *Escrits inèdits. Colom*, vol. II, Barcelona, 1978.

[66] It is generally supposed that *L'Espanya Naixent* corresponds to the so-called *Vic Manuscript*, a facsimile of which is available in E. Junyent, M. de Riquer (eds.), *L'Atlàntida*, cit. See: J. Molas, "Jacint Verdaguer," *Història de la literatura catalana*, vol. VII, cit., pp. 238–41.

[67] J. Miracle, *Estudis sobre Jacint Verdaguer*, cit., pp. 85–104.

[68] It is worth recalling here the illustration that prefaces the first edition of the poem: two rocks rising out of the sea, surmounted by the club of Heracles and the eloquent motto SEPARANDO JUNXIT.

[69] There is nothing strange in the fact that Verdaguer should have reworked the theme in other forms for a less sophisticated public on numerous occasions. For example, we have the very popular book of poems and songs *Montserrat*, an 1889 compendium of two highly successful poems first published in 1880 and reissued separately in 1885. Here, as well as a poem explicitly dedicated to Columbus, there are others such as the "Goigs de Ntra. Sra. de Montserrat," which includes the following lines: "In your holy chapel / Columbus visited you / and perhaps you were the star / that guided him to the New World" (in *Montserrat. Obres completes. Edició Popular*, vol. III, p. 187). There is no need for much comment on this "popular version" of the ideas of *L'Atlàntida*, in which Columbus is associated with the Virgin of Montserrat, patron saint of Catalonia. In the same book there is an eloquent ode

"Als catalans de Filipines."

[70] J. Verdaguer, *L'Atlàntida*, Barcelona, 1878, pp. XVI and XVII. See: J. Miracle, *Estudis sobre Jacint Verdaguer*, cit., pp. 20–84.

[71] On Verdaguer's fall from favor, his dispute with the family at Comillas and the Church hierarchy and the last years of his life there is still no satisfactory in-depth analysis. See, in the first instance, his own letters: J. Verdaguer, *En defensa pròpia*, cit., or the writings of contemporary detractors and supporters of his position, as for example: F. Bru, *El marqués de Comillas, su limosnero y su tío*, Barcelona, 1895; J. Falp i Plana, *Mossèn Verdaguer: el poeta, el sacerdot, l'home, el malalt*, Barcelona, 1903; (R. Turro, *Verdaguer vindicado por un catalan*, 1903; J. Güell, *Vida íntima de mossèn Cinto Verdaguer*, Mexico, 1944; M. Monjas, *Mossèn Jacinto Verdaguer*, Madrid, 1952 (3). Especially beautiful are the recollections in the memoir by J.M. de Segarra, *Verdaguer, poeta de Catalunya*, Barcelona, 1968. There is a good starting point for an analysis in: E. Lluch, "Santa Eulàlia i lo farcell de penes de Mossèn Cinto Verdaguer," *L'Avenç*, no. 117, July–August 1988, pp. 6–12.

[72] J. Verdaguer, *En defensa pròpia*, cit., p. 47. Claudio López is the subject of an extensive bibliography of apologias, still awaiting serious study but very eloquent as a strategy of legitimation; for example: M. Gascón, *Luz sin sombra. El marqués de Comillas*, Comillas, 1925; C. Bayle, *El segundo marqués de Comillas, don Claudio López Brú*, Madrid, 1928; J. Regatillo, *Un marqués modelo: el siervo de Dios Claudio López Brú*, Barcelona, 1948, and even, much later, on the campaign for his beatification: "Hacia la beatificación del segundo marqués de Comillas" *La Vanguardia Española*, May 30, 1969. On this point, see: E. Lluch, "Santa Eulàlia i lo farcell de penes…," cit.

[73] A matter of central importance in the founding of the Banco Hispano-Colonial: F. Cabana, *Bancs i banquers…*, cit, pp. 9–10.

[74] See: *Homenaje nacional…*, cit.; Duque de Maura, *Pequeña historia de una grandeza…*, cit.

[75] P. Bourdieu, *La distinction. Critique du jugement sociale*, Paris, 1979, p. 78, and in G.W. McDonogh, op. cit., p. 145.

[76] On this building: S. Alcolea, *El Palau Moja. Una contribució destacada a l'arquitectura catalana del segle XVIII*, Barcelona, 1987.

[77] On this issue, from classic general interpretations to the more recent and focused,

see for example: J. Carrera Pujal, *La Barcelona del segle XVIII*, Barcelona, 1951; P. Villar, "Transformaciones económicas, impulso urbano y movimiento de los salarios: la Barcelona del siglo XVIII," *Crecimiento y desarrollo*, Barcelona, 1964; R. Grau and M. López, "Barcelona entre el urbanismo barroco y la revolución industrial," *Cuadernos de Arquitectura y Urbanismo*, no. 80, 1971, pp. 18–40; R. Grau, "La metamorfosis de la ciutat emmurallada: Barcelona de Felip V a Ildefons Cerdà," *Cuadernos de Historia Económica de Cataluña*, vol. XX, 1979; and, above all, A. García Espuche and M. Guardia Bassols, *Espai i societat...*, cit., pp. 47–74.

[78] On the solemnity of the mansion see, for example, the memoir: *El poeta Verdaguer (Fragmento de la obra inédita del Conde de Güell y Marqués de Comillas, "Apuntes de recuerdos")*, Barcelona.

[79] See: *La Ilustración Española y Americana*, August 15 and 22 and September 8, 15 and 30, 1881.

[80] On this group of architects see: A. Pabón-Charneco, *The Architectural Collaborators of Antoni Gaudí*, Ann Arbor, Michigan, 1983, pp. 60–72, with bibliography; id., A. Pabón de Rocafot, "Els col·laboradors arquitectònics d'Antoni Gaudí," in J.J. Lahuerta (ed.), *Gaudí i el seu temps*, Barcelona, 1990, pp. 213ff. See also: C. Abad, *El Seminario Pontificio de Comillas. Historia de su fundación y primeros años, 1881–1925*, Madrid, 1928; R.M. de Hornedo, "Algunos datos y consideraciones sobre el edificio del Seminario de Comillas," *Miscelánea Comillas*, nos. 47–48, 1967, pp. 163–202; C. Kent, "Gaudí's Capricho in Context: Barcelona on the Atlantic," *Sites*, no. 20, 1988, pp. 48–56.

[81] Martorell, in spite of his decisive importance in the formation of the distinctive language of the most progressive groups of turn-of-the-century Barcelona architects, has yet to be studied in even a superficial way. See: *Arquitectura y construcción*, no. 172, November 1906, pp. 322–25 and 333–37; B. Bassegoda Amigo, "Juan Martorell y Montells," *Anuario de la Asociación de Arquitectos*, 1909, pp. 138–41. There have, however, been a number of partial studies, such as: J. Aymar, "L'Església dels Jesuites al carrer de Casp. Síntesi de *revivals* i solucions eclèctiques," *Sumari*, no. 59, 1980, pp. 15–20; R. Alcoy, "La arquitectura religiosa de Joan Martorell y el eclecticismo fin de siglo," *D'Art*, no. 10, May 1984, pp. 221–39; J. Bassegoda, "L'arquitectura catalana del segle XIX," *Espais*, no. 18, July–August 1989, pp. 52–56; as well as the short monograph *Butlletí del Col.legi d'Arquitectes de Catalunya. Demarcació de Girona*, no. 12, March 1985. It is worth adding that Joan Martorell's brother Ángel Martorell was manager of the Güell, Ramis y Cía. factory, the most important of Joan Güell's businesses; in all probability the relationship between Martorell and Antonio López was established by way of such links of kinship and friendship. In fact Martorell not only worked directly for both families on a number of occasions (for the Lópezs in Comillas and for the Güells on the Torre Satalia, designing the monument to Joan Güell, etc.), but also received important commissions thanks to their influence: the church and Jesuit college in Barcelona on the recommendation of the Lópezs or, by the Güells, the church of Santa Mònica in Barcelona.

[82] On this and other relations between Martorell and Gaudí: A. Pabón-Charneco, op. cit., chapter 1. For all this plus a basic bibliography: J. Bassegoda, *El gran Gaudí*, cit., pp. 187–89.

[83] The competition was won by Josep O. Mestres and August Font. The drawing was printed in large format in the daily *La Renaixença* and distributed to the paper's subscribers in 1887, the print being paid for by Eusebi Güell. The polemic concerning the façade can be studied in: J. Martorell y Montells, *Anteproyecto de fachada para la catedral de Barcelona. Memoria*, Barcelona, 1882, and the booklet: *Proyecto de fachada de la catedral de Barcelona. Opinión de le prensa reconociendo la superioridad del proyecto del arquitecto Juan Martorell ... seguido de la felicitación que el referido proyecto ha merecido de la mayoría de los arquitectos de Barcelona*, Barcelona, 1882. There is also an interesting study by one of the winners of the competition: A. Font y Carreras, *La catedral de Barcelona*, Barcelona, 1891. See: J. Bassegoda, "La fachada de la catedral de Barcelona," *Memorias de la Real Academia de Ciencias y Artes of Barcelona*, vol. XLV, no. 5, 1981.

[84] Architect of the new Universidad de Barcelona building, first director of its recently founded School of Architecture, director of the International Exhibition of 1888 (from both of which Martorell was excluded), restorer of such essential sites of the Romantic mythology of Catalanism as the monastery of Ripoll, in a way Rogent has been converted by traditional historiography into the forerunner of modern architecture in Catalonia; see, for example, his role in Bohigas' establishment of the supposed chronological limits of *Modernisme*: O. Bohigas, *Reseña y catálogo de la arquitectura modernista*, Barcelona, 1973, chapter 1. At the same time, Rogent is one of the few architects of the period to have been studied in depth. See: B. Bassegoda y Amigo, *El arquitecto Elías Rogent*, Barcelona, 1929, and, above all the works of P. Hereu, *L'arquitectura d'Elías Rogent*, Barcelona, 1986; id., *Vers una arquitectura nacional*, Barcelona, 1987; and his edition of E. Rogent Amat, *Memòries, viatges i lliçons*, Barcelona, 1990. See too: (various authors), *Elías Rogent i la Universitat de Barcelona*, Barcelona, 1988. On the early years of the School of Architecture: *Exposició Conmemorativa del Centenari de l'Escola D'Arquitectura de Barcelona, 1875–76/1975–76*, Barcelona, 1977, pp. 13–91; P. Hereu, "La idea d'arquitectura a l'escola que Gaudí conegué," in J.J. Lahuerta (ed.), *Gaudí i el seu temps*, Barcelona, 1990, pp. 11ff.

[85] On Cascante (1851–1889): B. Bassegoda, "Arquitectos catalanes. Cristóbal Cascante Colom," *La Prensa*, June 22, 1971. On Oliveras (1849–1898): G. Guitart y Lostalo, *La Casa Provincial de Maternidad y Expósitos*, Barcelona, 1904; B. Bassegoda, "Arquitectos catalanes: Camilo Oliveras Gensana," *La Prensa*, May 18, 1971.

[86] A. Pabón-Charneco, *The Architectural Collaborators...*, cit., 1983, pp. 60–72.

[87] This is a theme subsequently mythologized by Gaudí's hagiographers that we shall consider in due course, but see: I. Puig Boada, *El pensament de Gaudí*, Barcelona, 1981, especially many of his "thoughts" on pp. 106–12. But even in Gaudí's youthful notes we find examples of difficult syntax such as: "the cathedrals have the arc of the circle in almost parabolic vaults" (A. Gaudí, *Manuscritos, articulos...*, cit., p. 15).

[88] See data and bibliography in: J. Bassegoda, op. cit., pp. 255–79. See, too, the booklet: *Jardins del Palau de Pedralbes*, Barcelona, 1989.

[89] J. Verdaguer, *En defensa pròpia*, cit., pp. 13–15.

[90] Cit. in: J. Bassegoda, "Verdaguer, els Güell i Gaudí," *Anuari Verdaguer 1986*, Vic, 1987, p. 216.

[91] J. Verdaguer, "A vol d'aucell. Apuntacions d'un viatge al centre i nort d'Europa," *Excursions i viatges. (Obres Completes. Edició popular*, vol. VII), Barcelona, pp. 81–163.

[92] J. Verdaguer, "A vol d'aucell...," cit., p. 158, and, for example, on p. 154: "*La corrompuda i descreguda Paris...*" He speaks about Mistral on these same pages: "*Aquests dies, a Paris, Mistral es lo poeta de moda...*" (p. 152).

[93] See chapter 3.

[94] J. Bassegoda, "Verdaguer, els Güell i Gaudí," cit., p. 216.

[95] For the relationship with that far-off city: J. Bassegoda, "Verdaguer, els Güell i Gaudí," cit., p. 216.

[96] The fountain, concealed under the ivy of the gardens in Pedralbes, was rediscovered in 1983 and restored. See data and bibliography in: J. Bassegoda, *El gran Gaudí*, cit., pp. 275–76.

[97] J. Molas, "Jacint Verdaguer," *Història de la literatura catalana*, cit., pp. 243–44.

[98] A. Boada, "Verdaguer y Gaudí," *Igualada*, 22, June 1968; J. Bassegoda, "Verdaguer, els Güell i Gaudí," cit. Among the very few known photographs of Gaudí there is one, taken in Elna cathedral in 1883, that shows Gaudí and Verdaguer with a large group of Catalanist excursionists: C. Martinell, *Gaudí. Su vida, su teoría, su obra*, cit., pp. 46–47.

[99] Cit. in: J. Bassegoda, "Verdaguer, els Güell i Gaudí," cit., p. 217.

[100] J. Bassegoda, *El gran Gaudí*, cit., p. 273.

[101] On the Millennium of Montserrat see: J. Massot i Muntaner, *Aproximació a la història religiosa de la Catalunya contemporània*, Montserrat, 1973, pp. 35–37; id., *L'Església catalana al segle XX*, Barcelona, 1975, pp. 20–21, id., *Els creadors del Montserrat modern*, Montserrat, 1979, pp. 33–39; M.M. Boix, "Montserrat 1880: la joya del milenario," *Serra d'Or*, no. 265, 1981, pp. 613–37. A spectrum of fundamentalist, regionalist and Catalanist groups took part in the celebration of the Millennium, but the heart and soul of the venture was J. Collell, editor of the newspaper *La Veu del Montserrat* and a central figure in the group of clergy who were active in promoting "vigatanisme," a form of regionalism directed by the institutional Church that was extraordinarily influential in framing the ideology of conservative Catalanism. See: M. Ramisa, *Els orígens del catalanisme conservador i "La Veu del Montserrat." 1878–1900*, Víc, 1985. We shall look more closely at these questions in chapters 5 and 6.

[102] J. Verdaguer, *Montserrat*, cit., pp. 149 and 157. The book also contains the "Virolay," a very popular poem set to music by J. Rodoreda and adopted as the anthem of Montserrat. At the same time we should not forget the impetus given by the Vatican during the second half of the nineteenth century to the devotional use of the Rosary, culminating in a series of encycli-

cals on the subject by Leo XIII: *Supremi Apostolatus* (1883), *Superiori* (1884), *Octobri Mense* (1891). *La Veu del Montserrat* launched a campaign on the basis of the first of these, in issue no. 38 in 1883. See also: J. Torras i Bages, *El Rosario y su mística filosofía*, Barcelona, 1886, and, much later: V. Serra i Boldú, *Llibre popular del Rosari. Folklore del Roser*, Barcelona, 1917. The symbolic association of the Virgin with the rose was enhanced with allusions to the Rosary, a very frequent image in Verdaguer ("Cullím del Rosari / les Roses florides…," op. cit., p. 171) and in Gaudí: we need only recall the allusions in Park Güell and the Pedrera.

[103] This is a question pursued with greater or lesser emphasis by the earliest commentators and the latest and more critical from J.F. Ràfols, *Gaudí*, cit., p. 30 ("the house of Sr. Manuel Vicens … with its Mudéjar recollections…") in I. Solà-Morales, *Gaudí*, Barcelona, 1983, p. 15 (the Güell estate is resolved "on the basis of a free interpretation of the Spanish Mudéjar tradition"). In any case the meaningless "stylistic" division of Gaudí's work never fails to refer to a more or less prolonged early "eclectic" period.

[104] J. Amador de los Ríos, "El estilo mudéjar en arquitectura," *Discursos leídos en las recepciones y actos públicos celebrados por la Real Academia de las tres Nobles Artes de San Fernando*, vol. I, Madrid, 1872, pp. 1–40.

[105] On these discussions, their consequences inside Spain and their repercussions outside of the country, and on the theoretical discussion of architecture in nineteenth-century Spain in general, see: A. Isac, *Eclecticismo y pensamiento arquitectónico en España. Discursos, revistas, congresos, 1846–1919*, Granada, 1987, especially pp. 54–62; J. Arrachea, *Arquitectura y romanticismo. El pensamiento arquitectónico en la España del siglo XIX*, Valladolid, 1989. See also: G. Borras, "El mudéjar como constante artística," *Actas del I Simposio Internacional de Mudejarismo*, Teruel, 1981, pp. 29–39, as well as such dated partial studies as: G. González Amezqueta, "Arquitectura neomudéjar madrileña de los siglos XIX y XX," *Arquitectura*, no. 125, 1969, pp. 3–74, or P. Navascúes, *Arquitectura y arquitectos madrileños del siglo XIX*, Madrid,

1973, pp. 227–37. Finally, for an overall vision: J. Hernando, *Arquitectura en España. 1770–1900*, Madrid, 1989, pp. 231–69.

[106] See: P. Hereu, "L'arquitectura de l'Exposició," *Arquitectura i ciutat…*, cit.; R. Bletter, *El arquitecto Josep Vilaseca* cit.

[107] Ll. Domènech i Montaner, "En busca de una arquitectura nacional," *La Renaixença*, IX, vol. I, 1879, pp. 149–60, reprinted in *Lluís Domènech i Montaner i el director d'orquestra*, cit., pp. 277–88.

[108] A. Melida, *Causas de la decadencia de la arquitectura y medios para su regeneración*, Madrid, 1899. See: A. Isac, op. cit., p. 57.

[109] Noted by T. Torii, *El mundo enigmático de Gaudí*, Madrid, 1983, vol. II, pp. 120–21.

[110] A. Verdaguer, "Reunió Catalanista a Poblet i Santes Creus," *Butlletí de l'Associació d'Excursions Catalana*, vol. IV, 1882, pp. 103–10. On the excursion to Poblet and others see data and bibliography in: J. Bassegoda, *El gran Gaudí*, cit., pp. 167–76.

[111] P. Cost, *Architecture Arabe ou Monuments du Kaire*, Paris, 1839; Prisse D'Avennes, *L'Art Arabe d'aprés les Monuments du Kaire*, Paris, 1877. Noted by T.

Tori, op. cit., vol. II, pp. 10–11.

[112] From Gaudí's manuscripts on ornamentation, now in the Museo Municipal in Reus: A. Gaudí, *Manuscritos, artículos…*, cit., p. 13.

[113] A. Gaudí, op. cit., p. 15.

[114] See: T. Torii, op. cit., vol. II, pp. 78–79.

[115] For an excellent overview of "Japonaiserie" in Spain, and especially in Catalonia, at the end of the nineteenth century, see: L. Litvak, *El sendero del tigre*, Madrid, 1986, pp. 109–45, with specific references to Gaudí on pp. 110 and 126.

[116] Perceptively noted referring to the Casa Vicens in L. Litvak, op. cit., p. 66.

[117] It would of course be possible to cite even more elements, such as the use of pseudo-Ionic capitals, for example, perhaps an echo of the classical decorum that relates this order to the *mediocritas* of life in the country.

[118] Like the lines quoted below, the phrase is from the poem "L'invitation au voyage" in *Les fleurs du mal* by Charles Baudelaire. See: L. Litvak, op. cit., p. 74, and, in general, her very accurate panorama of orientalism in Spain, pp. 55–108.

[119] Ibid., p. 63.

# Un Sobre Tothom
The Town House of Eusebi Güell: Symbol, Myth, Structure

*The "Aristocratic Sense" of Eusebi Güell*

We closed the last chapter by considering Eusebi Güell at some length, and there is no need to return here to the extraordinary importance of his family connections, his industries or his business interests. Nevertheless, his involvement in Catalan public life over the thirty-year period straddling the turn of the century is of sufficient importance for a number of clarifications regarding his personality to be necessary.[1]

In the first place, regarding his political activities. In 1875, the same year in which Alfonso XII's ascension to the throne marked the beginning of the period of the Restoration, Eusebi Güell was appointed to a seat on the Barcelona City Council, and a little later, in 1878, became a provincial deputy and senator.[2] His biographers are unanimous in insisting that those were the only two political posts that Güell held in his life, surpassing themselves in their ecstatic praise of the sense of *service* that accepting these positions implied for a figure of his standing. We should not find the fact surprising: Güell, like other important Barcelona financiers, merchants and industrialists who also occupied posts of this kind, lent the Restoration a certain legitimacy by virtue of his mere presence in its institutions. We must not forget that from the outset the new regime found one of its chief sources of support in the Catalan bourgeoisie—a class in need of a stable political system in the period of flourishing business that followed the revolutionary and republican experiences of the previous years—nor that, in a highly symbolic gesture, Alfonso XII chose Barcelona as his port of entry on his return to Spain.

For Güell, then, as for other members of the Barcelona bourgeoisie, to occupy these quasi-symbolic posts certainly had a very clear significance, and one of service: thanks to such posts, for all that they constituted active support for the regime—and a position from which to make demands on that regime—they could avoid any direct, organized intervention in politics and thus concentrate all their efforts on their business affairs. It is revealing that Güell was to begin in 1875 by accepting a post of immediate legitimation, that of city councilor, and then move on a couple of years later to another post at the national level, and of royal appointment: senator. There were, however, other facets to Güell's political activities. In 1870, along with other leading figures, among them the poet and playwright Àngel Guimerà, he had taken part in the founding of Jove Catalunya [Young Catalonia], a literary association in whose ever-radical Catalanist manifestations it is easy to see a desire to intervene not only in the cultural sphere but, although not openly declared, in politics as well.[3] From a slightly simplified point of view, Güell's position would appear to be grounded in a kind of ramified ambiguity: lending his support to the regime of the Restoration through its institutions and at the same time taking part in a Catalanist group of radical tendencies which although it called itself literary, acted—it could hardly do otherwise—politically. However, it is enough to recall our analyses of the previous chapter regarding the double orientation, internal and external, Spanish and Catalanist, of the ideological program of the Barcelona bourgeoisie to see the relative nature of such ambiguities. It is not insignificant that Güell was the son of the principal theorist of that ideology and the son-in-law of its most physical representative: in Güell, however, it was to be personified in quite a different degree.

Güell's participation in Jove Catalunya was not an isolated event. In 1882 he was involved in the founding of another Catalanist entity, one of much greater influence and consequences: the Centre Català, of which, it would seem, he was to become president.[4] Although founded by a federalist republican politician, Valentí Almirall, the Centre Català set out to create a pressure group integrat-independently of the official parties, both conservative and liberal, which the political system of the Restoration, in order to guarantee its survival, alternated artificially in power. The Centre Català—which declared itself exclusively patriotic and whose statutes expressly prohibited its members from participating in Spanish political parties—achieved a key victory with the presentation to King Alfonso XII of the document known as the *Memorial de Greuges*.[5] In addition to a series of

historically-based demands regarding the Catalan language, culture and rights, the document included other demands of an economic and far more contingent nature—once again calling for a policy of protectionism for Catalan industry—in direct response to the free-trade strategy of the Spanish government and, more specifically, to the trade agreements signed by the latter with Great Britain, which were having a negative impact on the Catalan textile industry. This text—which apart from the various demands we have just mentioned also proposed a form of regionalist monarchy as a means of regenerating the Spanish state—was for many years the Ten Commandments of Catalanist demands, but its importance lies fundamentally in the fact that it was presented directly to the king by a commission designated by the Centre Català, thus bypassing the parliament and government. This significant act was, to a certain extent, Catalanism's letter of presentation in the general politics of the Spanish state, but, above all, it marked the first time that important sectors of the Catalan bourgeoisie demonstrated their public commitment to an autonomous political action of their own, independently of the parties and official institution of the regime. What could be surprising about this in 1885, when the age of great fortunes of the *febre d'or* was coming to an end, and when the decline of Catalonia as an economic power led the Catalan bourgeoisie to demand some recompense for its unconditional support for the political machinery of the Restoration? As for Eusebi Güell, he was one of the authors of the document, responsible for drawing up the section dealing with economic policy, and, although this was not in fact the case, he was thought by his contemporaries to have been one of the members of the commission sent to King Alfonso XII, and that in itself is significant. On the other hand, he not only wrote the speech delivered to the Barcelona institutions at the banquet they gave in honor of the members of the commission, but read it, as well.[6]

The opposing positions of the groups assembled in the Centre Català regarding the Barcelona International Exhibition of 1888 resulted in their going sep-

arate ways.[7] While the more radical sectors, led by Almirall, launched an intense campaign against the holding of the Exhibition, those linked to the Renaixença emerged as one of its most important ideological and financial backers. Thus the official media would present Claudio López and, through him, his brother-in-law Eusebi Güell, to public opinion as generous financial backers of the works for the exhibition.[8] In 1887, when the most conservative group within the Centre Català split off to form another political club, the Lliga de Catalunya [League of Catalonia],[9] Güell—through a newspaper of which he was founder, pointedly titled *España Regional*—was with them. But the Lliga de Catalunya implied a shift, subtle but important, with respect to previous positions: indeed, while they continued to espouse apolitical patriotism as their most basic principle, they also manifested, now quite clearly, a readiness to serve as a bridge, as a platform for the actions of all those—even representatives of political parties, "whatever the party"—who were willing to act "in favor of Catalonia."[10] The change in degree that this willingness entailed was not long in revealing its consequences. Isidre Molas correctly described the main features of the Lliga—accidentalism, specifically Catalan organization, defence of a diffuse regionalism as a model of the state, platform for political action—as a foretaste and synthesis of what would prove to be the basic features of future political Catalanism. Not in vain did the Lliga play a key role in the creation of the Unió Catalanista and, through it, in the drawing up in 1892 of the *Bases de Manresa*,[11] a veritable constitutional declaration of conservative Catalanism and the most complete statement of its credo. Nor should we find it surprising that in the progression from the Lliga de Catalunya to the Unió Catalanista to the foundation in 1901 of the Lliga Regionalista[12] (this latter a true political party), those tenets, in spite of the false starts, remained present throughout, and that their variations manifest themselves as no more than changes in intensity.

But we have left Eusebi Güell in 1877, at the moment when, by way of *España Regional*, he was involved in the founding of the Lliga de Catalunya.

After that year we no longer find his name in direct connection with any of the actions that led to the embodiment of conservative Catalanism in a political party. Thus it would seem that his biographers are correct in insisting that his only political activity was that related to his posts during the early years of the Restoration, and that the nature of those posts was purely one of service. On the other hand, if we interpret literally the apoliticism of his speech in honor of the commissioners of the *Memorial de Grenges*, so much in keeping with the ideology of the most conservative wing of the Centre Català that we may consider it paradigmatic ("always turning a deaf ear to the tempting voice of the political sirens, we forsake any kind of political affiliation in order to follow with integrity the sacred standard of the motherland," and, further down: "above the turbulent waves of the ever stormy sea of politics there rises calm and steadfast the majestic figure of Royal power"),[13] we can see that this role of *service* is one that Güell was also playing when, while holding those posts, he acted from

within Catalanism. In adopting this attitude, then, Güell is declaring that he is not a politician but an industrialist who, given his social standing, nonetheless feels obliged to lend his legitimating presence, with unfailing generosity. In other words, it may be that the absence of Güell's name from the major political events following the International Exhibition reflects a more precise interpretation and thus a confirmation of this strategy. Indeed, although during the latter years of the century Güell's direct involvement in Catalan politics appears to diminish, the same cannot be said of his influence. It will suffice to point out a few events, extraordinarily significant ones, to get an idea of the meaning and the weight of that influence.

Firstly, the case of Ferran Alsina,[14] who held a high position—and in due course was to be a partner—in Eusebi Güell's industrial ventures, and into whose textile mills he had introduced new machinery and new working methods that considerably reduced the number of workers required: what was known at the time as the "English work sys-

*A. Gaudí, Palau Güell. Interiors*
*of the main floor photographed*
*at the end of the nineteenth century.*

*A. Gaudí, Palau Güell. Interiors of the main floor photographed at the end of the nineteenth century.*

tem." In fact, Ferran Alsina was also one of the most widely influential figures in *fin-de-siècle* Catalan society, not only for his economic treatises—with such suggestive titles as *Criteri econòmic general catalanista*—or his application of scientific research to industry (he founded the first experimental physics facility in Barcelona, which he subsequently turned into a museum and ceded to the city) but above all for his political activities. Alsina was one of the founding members of the Lliga de Catalunya, of which he became president, and, afterwards, as a member of the Unió Catalanista, one of the main authors of the *Bases de Manresa*, above all in its most directly economic aspects. Alsina was known as Eusebi Güell's "industrial right arm,"[15] and some of his books are prefaced with dedications to Güell. These facts would seem to constitute sufficient evidence that, in the eyes of his contemporaries, Güell stood side by side with Alsina in his political activities. Secondly there is the case of Ramón Picó i Campamar:[16] a somewhat mediocre poet and playwright whose presence in the cultural institutions of the Renaixença was always decisive, he was also closely linked to the institutions of Catalanism and to the Lliga Regionalista itself. In 1899, on the recommendation of Jacint Verdaguer, he became Eusebi Güell's personal secretary and representative, and thereafter dedicated to his patron almost his entire poetic output, which he conceived as a homage to Güell and his family. Finally, the third case, although less obviously striking, is without doubt the most telling: Enric Prat de la Riba,[17] the chief ideologue and head of the Lliga Regionalista, as well as being the unquestioned leader and most effective theorist of conservative political Catalanism (in 1914 he became the first president of the Mancomunitat de Catalunya, a limited attempt at autonomous Catalan government), dedicated to Eusebi Güell, in the crucial year of 1898, his fundamental book *Ley jurídica de la industria*,[18] dealing with what was euphemistically called the "social question." In that book Güell's industrial colony at Santa Coloma de Cervelló, founded seven years before, was implicitly put forward as a model and paradigm of industrial policy and, indeed, of political practice. In addition to all of the above, what else if not an indirect form of intervention in Catalan politics was the presence of Güell in institutions such as the Acadèmia de Sant Jordi or, above all, the Jocs Florals, of which he was president in 1900. For the latter he prepared the speech we have referred to above (a speech which beneath its fanciful philological theories betrayed a very clear political intention, despite being infused with the aloofness and generosity appropriate to a man whose counsels are above actual politics).[19] And then, in 1908, the government of Antonio Maura made Güell a count.[20] What was this if not part of Maura's strategy to win over the Lliga Regionalista, by flattering its most conservative sectors, to his own reformist policies? It was during 1908 and 1909 that, with the acceptance on the part of the Lliga of the government's proposal for a new draft of the Local Administration bill, this strategy of entente reached its apogee. The fact that in the wake of the events of the Semana Trágica [Tragic Week] the Lliga Regionalista gave its unconditional support to the indiscriminate repression unleashed by a Maura who was under pressure to resign speaks volumes about the extent of this entente.[21] Similarly, can we see the creation of Eusebi Güell's noble title in 1908 as anything other than an element of that strategy and, as such, an implicit confirmation of Güell's importance?

At the same time, in tracing Eusebi Güell's political activity and political presence, what have we done if not sketch, in step with the events of the time, the ideas and political strategies of a broad sector of the Catalan bourgeoisie of the period? Of a bourgeoisie initially committed to a Restoration that offered it the necessary stability for its business dealings, but which, with the *febre d'or* and the amassing of great fortunes a thing of the past, and now in the midst of crisis, strove to act against the Spanish government's free-trade strategy, on the one hand by creating its own pressure groups, and on the other by allying its economic demands with the historically-based cultural demands of the intellectuals of

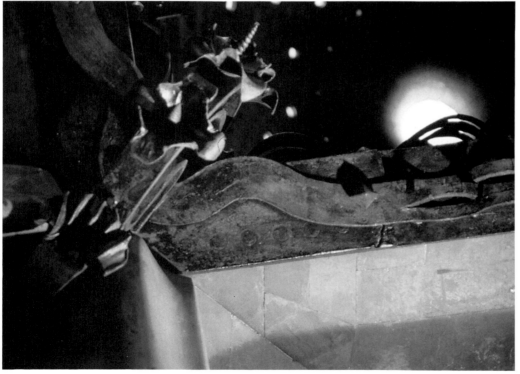

Catalanism in what would be its first overtly political actions. Of a bourgeoisie, finally, that on the threshold of a new century brought forth its first generation of professional politicians and supported, from behind the scenes, the creation of an organized modern political party, the purpose of which was to intervene in the policies of the Spanish state from the platform of Catalan self-government. In all of this Güell was always, as we have seen, at the privileged place, at the opportune moment: we could hardly find a better model for that bourgeoisie. On July 11, 1918, in the very lengthy obituary of Eusebi Güell published in the *La Veu de Catalunya*, mouthpiece of the Lliga, we read: "The body was draped, from the first moment, with the flag of the Lliga Regional, the same flag that had covered the coffins of Robert, Mossèn Cinto and Prat de la Riba."[22] Surely no comment is necessary.

But there are other aspects of Eusebi Güell's personality that also interest us, such as his education, for example. He studied law, political economy, mechanics and applied sciences, and in his youth spent long periods of time in France and England, dedicating himself above all to acquiring first-hand knowledge of how the textile industry worked in those countries. This varied and cosmopolitan education left a deep mark on him, and for our purposes this is of particular interest. Proverbial, above all, was his anglophile, or, more specifically, his idealized vision of something that we might call the "lifestyle" of the English aristocracy: that blend of reserve, refinement and ritual that is at the same time so apparent in every aspect of nineteenth-century European culture. The chroniclers of the period speak of how Güell liked to display with bland condescension certain aspects of his private life—those that demonstrated his exemplary character, or those to do with work and religion—while at the same time that frankness was accompanied by a deliberate, but too ostentatious to be sincere, reserve about other apparently more intimate features—those concerning his domestic life—which thus became secrets, but secrets that he always allowed to be intuited. On the other hand, a glance at

photographs from the period suffices to show the affected and somewhat pompous elegance of his personal appearance—the patriarchal long beard, for example—and to recall the ceremonial dimension of seemingly trivial decisions that were nevertheless decisive in determining the way his public persona was perceived, such as his obsession with traveling in a horse-drawn carriage rather than a motor car: all of them elements of a ritual invented by the British monarchy in the last quarter of the nineteenth century, passed off as authentic tradition by the English aristocracy and imitated in would-be aristocratic circles all over Europe.[23] We might think here of Baudelaire: remarking on how the clichés of that invention were making themselves felt on the continent, he wrote that "the English novelists, more than any others, have cultivated the *high-life* novel."[24] And it is Baudelaire again, just a few lines on, who says: "Dandyism appears especially in periods of transition when democracy has yet to become all-powerful, and when the aristocracy is only partially weakened and discredited. In the confusion of such times, a certain number of men, disenchanted leisured 'outsiders,' but all of them richly endowed with native energy, may conceive the idea of establishing a new kind of aristocracy."[25] These *manners* on which Eusebi Güell's appearance was founded had, when viewed from the perspective that Baudelaire offers us, a very definite impact. In 1931, for example, one of his sons, in a book of memoirs published in Paris, was to recall: "My father said … that everything the English do has a practical and simple purpose and that everything that is practical and simple, in this period of constant change in tastes, is what we call, in general, elegant."[26] We shall go on to see how direct a translation, in an age of unprecedented change, this appreciation of all that is enduring had in Güell's engagement with the arts. At the same time it is not difficult to find in the contemporary press, in accounts and reports from the period English words used in reference to Eusebi Güell: the term *dandy* applied to the man himself, or the word *home* in reference to his house. But above all Güell is consistently referred to in these

texts as a *gentleman*.[27] What might seem mere mannerism here is, I would insist, a studied concern with the effect of appearances. It is worth recalling that Joan Güell, Eusebi's father, was also referred to by his contemporaries in the English term as a "self-made man." A comparison of the two reveals a great deal about the distance that separates father from son; the distance between the shared ideology of immediate use of the generation of Joan Güell and Antonio López and the ideological veilings and sublimations of Eusebi, born into a very different culture and very different circumstances. If we have already dealt with this in passing in the last chapter, it is something to which we still have to devote a good deal of space.

Let us look first, however, at what is evidently the best-known facet of Eusebi Güell's personality, and one closely bound up with the above: his enthusiastic interest in the arts and sciences, his dilettantism. For example, he developed a singular theory of his own in the field of microbiology, which was published, signed with his initials, in Paris in 1889 and subsequently translated into English: *L'immunité par les leucomaïnes*.[28] And we have already referred to his picturesque philological studies of Catalan and the language of Rhaetia, which appeared in 1900. But his dilettantism finds its clearest expression in the arts: in addition to a sporadic practice as an amateur architect, draftsman and watercolorist, Güell was something of an expert, a connoisseur and, inevitably, a collector. A refuge of art: this was one of the qualities that his town house presented to the eyes of his contemporaries, and a glance at a few of the fairly numerous reports devoted to the building in the years following its inauguration will serve to show what this meant.[29] In 1894, for example, the Centre Excursionista de Catalunya published the first monograph devoted to what they significantly called the *casa palau i museu*—the "mansion and museum"—of Eusebi Güell:[30] the final section is a catalogue of the furniture, the paintings, the tapestries and the sculptures that adorned Güell's town house. It is no surprise to find a great quantity of medieval Catalan altarpieces and paintings in the inventory, just at a

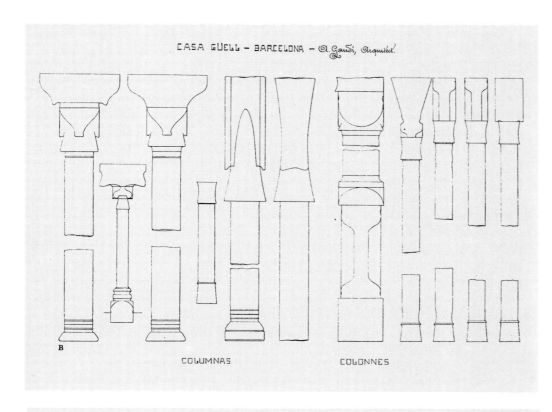

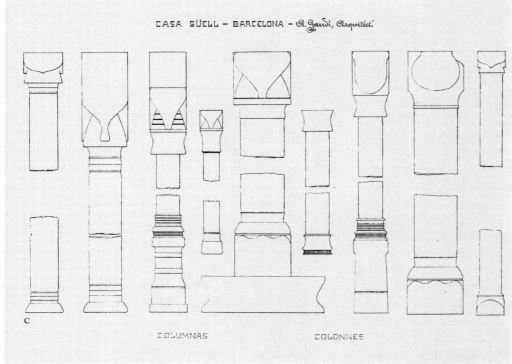

time when that legacy was being rediscovered; a discovery that was obviously historical and artistic, but also and above all political. In those same years its first historian, Raimon Casellas, spoke of it not only in terms of Catalan national art but a national style, thus infusing it with a sense of idealism and identifying it with a Catalan ethnic character that was the basis of the contemporary rebirth of a nation identified with its own art.[31] From this point of view, the preponderance of historic Catalan painting in the Güell collection is clear testimony to the simultaneously public and private nature of the artworks he acquired, and to the subtlety of that condition. Certainly, a collection is a means of ideally ordering and systematizing the world, but in Güell's case the order that is thus contemplated, an order that should have to correspond to the eye, to the particular vision of the collector, is informed by an exterior ideological condition. This is the double sense that comes from its being something more than art: Güell presents himself as custodian of the style, too, and as such at once watches over it and possesses it.

We shall have occasion to speak of that sort of doubling, present in so many aspects of the Güell mansion, in due course. Let us look now at the last link in the chain that articulates Eusebi Güell's public persona: his role as patron of the arts. There is no shortage of examples we might cite. Consider one extreme case. After a paragraph that makes very clear the profound ideological and political differences between the members of the editorial board and Güell, the Barcelona newspaper *El Radical* published the following lines on the occasion of his death in 1918: "For us it is enough that he helped the cream of our intellectuals to triumph (Gaudí, Canals, Picasso, García Robles, the great Isidre Nonell, Millet and so many other already consecrated figures) to say that Güell worked for the prosperity of Catalonia.[32] There are two surprising things in this excerpt: first, the medium in which it was published, a republican, anticlerical, anti-Catalanist newspaper that was noted for its violent demagoguery, and second, the heterogeneous list of artists mentioned, and especially the inclusion of

Timber paneling in various rooms
of the main floor. As in the ironwork
and the stained glass, the G of Güell
is a dominant motif.

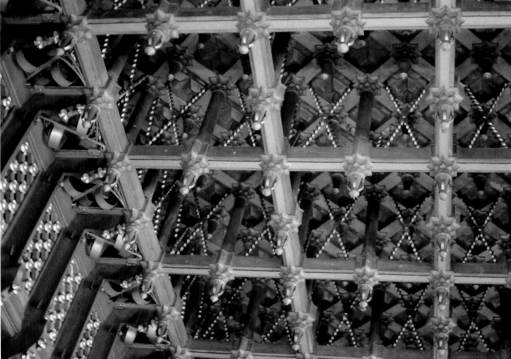

Picasso, who was already in 1918 a commonplace name in international modern art. But is it not precisely this, the commonplace, that the excerpt acknowledges? It had been conventional to refer to Güell as a patron of the arts for years.[33] Indeed, Güell's legacy rests on that identification, exemplified in his own family. The interest in the arts of all his children was proverbial: his daughter Isabel composed, and his son Eusebi was an amateur playwright and the author of curious treatises on geometry and fashion.[34] While it is not our business here to pass judgment on the artistic merits of the work produced by Güell's children, this seems at times (in the accounts of certain contemporaries) to have verged on the ridiculous. Adrià Gual, for example, recalls in his memoirs how Güell applied pressure on him by way of Àngel Guimerà to stage the play *Cassius i Helena*, written by the younger Eusebi, in his Teatre Intim in 1903. Gual describes how the performance finished to loud laughter prompted—he remarks with irony—by the envy of the "smart" companions of "that boy from a good family."[35] What is interesting is to see how here, too, there is a weaving together of the private and the public, drawing in the whole family, which thus takes on a transcendent significance. Art here is both example of and excuse for the greatest wealth, whose possession is inalienable, and of this, too, we shall speak at length in due course.

We have considered certain aspects of Güell's personality, those which most obviously reveal his political trajectory, and contemporary press reports and comment. The definitions, the words, the descriptions, the qualities perceived in and around him, some of which we have already noted, figure repeatedly over the years with surprising constancy and continuity right down to our own time. One thing, then, jumps to the sight: what we have here is a carefully measured construct, an effective mechanism. Eusebi Güell appears always as a model of political, social and cultural conduct, an example to be followed, above his peers, but the most important thing is the way the society in which he lived was willing to accept that example; that is, to embrace as part of its own ideological

system the image fashioned around the figure of Eusebi Güell. This is Darío Pérez, for example, writing in 1918: "No one would dare to deny that the noble gentleman of Calle Conde del Asalto should have been able deservedly to call himself the Count of Barcelona."[36] That title, pertaining to the Spanish royal family, was the first taken in Catalonia by the kings of the Catalan-Aragonese dynasty. The profound resonances that the author sought to give to his phrase have a significance that, in the light of what we have noted above, is hardly open to doubt.

But if we are to appreciate the *extent* to which the *image* of Eusebi Güell was perfectly defined, and which best explains the significance and the scope of his exemplary status, we must turn our attention to a book published in 1921, three years after his death, with the extraordinary title *The first Count Güell. Psychological notes and essay on the aristocratic sense in Catalunya*.[37] The author was Eusebi Güell's confessor, the Capuchin Miquel d'Esplugues, who exercised a great influence on the religious and cultural life of Catalonia through the journals of Christian philosophy he founded and edited, such as *Estudis Franciscans* or *Criterion*, and his presidency of the Fundació Bíblica Catalana. D'Esplugues also had an extraordinary personal ascendancy over some of the principal figures in the Lliga, such as Francesc Cambó. A few years earlier, in 1916, he had published an essay that excited considerable interest in Catalan intellectual circles, *Nostra Senyora de la Mercè. Estudi de psicologia ètnicoreligiosa de Catalunya* [*Our Lady of the Mercè. Study of the ethno-religious psychology of Catalonia*], in which he developed in the most irrational and antihistoricist terms a theory that he himself described as Christian nationalist.[38] Irrationalism, antihistoricism: these are also the principal characteristics of the personality of Eusebi Güell as reconstructed by Miquel d'Esplugues in his book. For Miquel d'Esplugues, Eusebi Güell was no less than the synthesis, the embodiment of the characteristics of a supposed Catalan *race* whose essential ethnic peculiarities are determined by its Roman origins. Thus, Catalonia would have

Stained glass on the main floor
and in the arches at the height
of the dome in the main salon,
and detail of the sofa in the main
salon.

been the *primaria sedes* of pacific Roman rule in Spain, not only the center of Roman government and culture but also, and above all, the place where the Christian elaboration of Rome's legacy penetrated the peninsula. Christianity had, for Miquel d'Esplugues, a very concrete meaning: Rome was as perfect from the civil point of view as it was imperfect from the religious, and the Christian religion carried out the historic mission of amending that fault. This was not a deviation from but precisely the sublimation of Roman culture. Miquel d'Esplugues is at pains to stress the Pauline origin of Catalan Christianity: the Roman and the Christian, with no trace of impurity or compromise, are inseparably fused in a kind of original perfection, with that perfection determining the unique identity of the Catalan people and its necessarily and transcendently religious spirit. Rome plus Christianity equals Civilization. That equation is, in effect, the basis for the various positions previously adopted by Miquel d'Esplugues; an equation that is imbued with the status of axiom: the origin of that Civilization (and the capital C always given it by Miquel d'Esplugues is evidently significant) is selective, aristocratic. Thus, citing Renan, he writes: "Civilization, from its origins, has been an aristocratic enterprise; the work of a small number (nobles and priests) who imposed it by those means that democrats call force and imposture."[39] It comes as no surprise that the irrationality of the positivism deployed by Renan, with his idea of the superior man dominating his environment, his anti-bourgeois positions (apparent in the anti-parliamentarianism implicit in the quotation), so prevalent among the Spanish intelligentsia of the late nineteenth century,[40] should provide the basis for the theories of Miquel d'Esplugues. The development of these, however, structured on rigid scholastic premises, leads to the most ineffable conclusions, literally to axioms. Thus, the Catalans are an essentially aristocratic people (Miquel d'Esplugues needs only a few lines to clarify the ethnic rather than class meaning he gives the word)[41] in the very fullest sense: that of being, from their very origins, the possessors of Civilization, and of being possessed by Civilization. For d'Esplugues this is an

evident historical condition that does not require demonstrating. On it is established the difference between Catalonia and the rest of the peoples of the peninsula ("They are two quite divergent religious sensibilities; ours absolutely Roman, that of the others Gothic and Mozarabic")[42] and its singularity before the world, above history: "First of all the *Senatus*, then the *populus*. The coincidence between the aristocratic sense of Catalonia and that of Rome is absolute."[43] The course pursued by Miquel d'Esplugues' history from this point on leaves little room for doubt. The disintegration of the Roman empire and the disappearance of Rome as *caput mundi* meant, literally, the end—albeit provisional—of Civilization. Catalonia, however, thanks to its Mediterranean loyalty—d'Esplugues always uses the Latin *mare nostrum*—has conserved in its count-kings something of that original sense, subsequently lost in the political union with Castile. With that union there began a long period of darkness and decadence, fundamentally characterized by the Castilianization of the Catalan aristocracy and its ultimate disappearance. In the nineteenth century, however, a new class emerged; not the bourgeoisie—egotistic, mediocre, interested only in their businesses and making money—but a class that was literally destined to be the guardian of the spirit of the nation (Renan's ideas continue to resound here in the theses of Miquel d'Esplugues), assuming naturally the mission of rekindling Catalonia's aristocratic sense and concentrating, as in the apex of a pyramid, the progress of industry, of trade, of the sciences and the arts that conventionally characterize the Catalan renaissance. And at the same time it would redeem the materiality of that progress in a spiritual, transcendent sense. In this class was to be seen the new superiority of Catalonia.

But in claiming all of this, Miquel d'Esplugues is simply redirecting—operatively, and towards perhaps insane ends—a series of elements that are present from the outset in the political and intellectual debate surrounding the nature of Catalanism. In Renan (so frequently invoked by d'Esplugues, and before him in Gibbon and subsequently in Ménard) there is a defence of

paganism against a Christianity that is always presented as the downfall of the Classical world; a Christianity with an evident Semitic component, on account of its origins in the East, and incompatible with the Classical reason with which the West identified itself. This idea had a very definite resonance in Catalonia. In Paris in 1880, Pompeu Gener published *La Mort et le Diable*, in which (very much in line with Renan and Ménard, whom he may well have known in person) he portrayed Christianity as the paradigm of negative and obscurantist doctrine. A few years later, in 1887, Gener, advancing ideas previously expounded by Valentí Almirall, put forward in *Heregías* the theory of the racial difference between Catalan and Castilian—the former of Aryan origin, the latter Semitic—and the superiority of the Catalan "race." Later still, an article by Gener in *L'Avenç* on the occasion of Renan's death in 1892 prompted a response from Josep Torras i Bages, who in the same conventional terms in which the Catholic orthodoxy had refuted his ideas disqualified the "lay cathedral" of Renan, a "docile and pampered nihilist."[44] It is not difficult to identify the heterogeneous strands that are pulled together in Renan's line of argument: exaltation of paganism over Christianity; equation of Semitism with decadence in the realms of both religion and race; racism. These find in Miquel d'Esplugues' formulation a new locus and a new direction. He upholds the racist thesis of the Aryan superiority of the Catalans and, sharpening his words with care, he replaces the pagan with the Roman; a Rome whose ideological identification with the Catholic Church, that eternal *Roma instaurata*, is part of a grand scheme constructed over many centuries. But there is more. The theses put forward by the Capuchin rests on another fundamental idea: that of the essential aristocratism of the Catalan people and, as a far from disinterested extension of this, the need for a new patrician class. Both Torras i Bages and Prat de la Riba had made that need a cornerstone

of their respective theories: Catalan society, they suggested, drew its model from the family itself and was in consequence an organically hierarchical, patriarchal society.[45] Prat, with much more clarity, spoke on more than one occasion of the need to reconstruct, in a Catalonia that was still a society in process of constitution, that governing minority that in traditional societies is represented historically by the aristocracy. In 1905, for example, he wrote: "Those peoples without an aristocracy are incomplete peoples"; and a little later in the same article: "Our society, undone by the secular domination of another race, is like a society in constitution. The new aristocracy must emerge from the land, always fecund, from its great economic enterprises, from the glorious crusade for freedom."[46] An aristocracy that springs from the land itself, in the charged words of Prat, which would in due course be harvested—and devoured—by Miquel d'Esplugues.

The figure of Eusebi Güell is, as we have said, the culmination of the reconstruction desired by Miquel d'Esplugues: that reconstruction, he tells us, is merely the pedestal on which the figure stands. The presentation of the personage in itself establishes all the conditions of his *necessary* personality, of his *presence*. Thus we read: "The first Count of Güell, great Catalan patrician, born in Barcelona; but Tarragonese by paternal ancestry and Genoese by his maternal lineage."[47] We have already spoken of the resonances of the title of Count, applied to Barcelona: there can be no doubt that in the first half of the sentence Miquel d'Esplugues wanted to make those resonances heard. The same purpose is served by the reference to Tarragona, which d'Esplugues had shown in his reconstruction to be the capital of Roman Spain, even going so far as to describe the Tarragona landscape in immanent terms: in its land and in its sky, in its Mediterranean condition, it already contained the essences of the original spirit that was to emerge from it.[48] Finally, the recollection of Eusebi Güell's Genoan ancestry takes us back to one of the tropes that was most insistently

81

*The corridor connecting the town house to J. Güell's old residence on the Rambla in its original condition, and a foreshortened view of the stable doors in the internal courtyard.*

woven around him: Güell the aristocrat would take the Renaissance Italian prince as its model.[49] Eusebi Güell's contemporaries frequently referred to him in this way, and there is even a famous phrase attributed to Gaudí in this vein: "Don Eusebi Güell is a great gentleman, of princely spirit, like the Medicis of Florence and the Dorias of Genoa, and the mother of Don Eusebi came of a noble and enterprising Genoan family."[50] Miquel d'Esplugues, in his book, repeats those same ideas again and again. A closer look at this in fact offers more of interest than the rhetoric of the commonplace might at first suggest. Surely it is from the stereotyped figure of the Italian prince—at least since Burckhardt, whose great study of the Renaissance in Italy is significantly far more concerned with the State than with art—that the patron derives his most meaningful tonalities. The prince possesses not only art, but the very will of the artists. But the context in which Miquel d'Esplugues situates his words lets us go even further. Commenting on Eusebi Güell's grandiose project for supplying Barcelona with water from the springs on his estates in Garraf, by way of miles of aqueducts, d'Esplugues writes: "The project, had it not proved unachievable, would have made ours a city better supplied with water than Rome itself."[51] The vast scale of Güell's endeavors is epitomized once and for all in the unachievable nature of this project. What is more, the allusion to a Rome that was spared from thirst thanks to the policy of its emperors or its popes, as princes of the first absolute State, leaves very little doubt as to the meaning of the comparison. The allusion evidently does not seem disproportionate to Miquel d'Esplugues, and nor did it seem so to Eusebi Güell himself, who also used it, albeit less explicitly, in his justification of the scheme. Thus Güell, citing his engineers, wrote: "these [waters] having a better claim to the title virgin than the celebrated *Acquae Vergine* [sic] of Rome."[52] He was well aware, *from experience*, of the double edge that such actions have: apparently conciliatory on the one hand; aggressively creating

dependence on the other. So it comes as no surprise to find the springs in Garraf taken up as the theme of a great lyric poem in five acts by Picó i Campamar, set to music by García Robles, and staged with great pomp at the expense of Güell himself, to whom it was dedicated; Güell put on three performances, two of them in honor of the Papal nuncio and the Spanish royal family, respectively.[53] But at that absolute pinnacle established by Providence itself at which Miquel d'Esplugues envisioned Güell, his clichéd image as patron of the arts was to shine forth with a new light. These were years in which the *Modernista* artists and intellectuals were urging on the bourgeoisie a greater consumption of artworks as a condition of their modernization—in other words, the creation of a market in which artists could directly introduce their work and live as true professionals,[54] *l'art pour l'art* being simply the ideology by which artists sought to justify the conversion of art into commodity—Güell sought to re-establish the figure of the patron in its most immediate sense, making the artist dependent both in his output and in the themes and subjects of his work. In opposition to the "art for art's sake" slogan of *Modernisme*, Güell's endeavors posited an integrated and thematic art, as we shall see. And above all, in contrast to an art market in which the bourgeoisie, as an anonymous public, simply purchase, Güell would recreate the uniquely identifiable figure of the patron who, above and beyond the alienation of the commodity, simply possesses. We shall return to these issues with specific examples, but by now one thing must be perfectly clear: when Güell's contemporaries referred to him as a prince, they were not only expressing themselves rhetorically.

*Ex unge leonem*:[55] for Miquel d'Esplugues the issue is not open to doubt. It is not so much in his business ventures, his political activities or his sporadic writings, but in his works—the town house, the park, the colony—that we recognize the greatness of Eusebi Güell. In those places where the role of the patron seems to be displayed most fully, where it is most all-encompassing, that the essence of the prince is apparent. It is,

*Entrance gates and dome.*
*The parabolic arch, leitmotif*
*of the town house for*
*the contemporary critics.*

in effect, through them that Güell can be distinguished as unique. There it is established, above all, Güell's Providential condition and place at the apex of the Capuchin's reconstruction: Güell is "monarch; that is to say: one who is above all others."[56]

Miquel d'Esplugues' theses will seem a good deal less preposterous if we take into account the specific social and political circumstances of Catalonia in 1921:[57] the identification with Christian Rome as the transcendent origin of the unique Catalan spirit; the racism not even draped in positivist trappings; the call for an aristocracy of its own as culmination of a vertically ordered (in the strict sense of normalized) society. All of this is closer than it might seem to the similarly normalizing ideology that the Lliga intellectuals—who by this stage were presiding over Catalonia's precarious attempt at autonomous government, as well as the principal Catalan institutions—had for a number of years been elaborating around the definition of Catalonia.[58] The difference is perhaps only of degree. The exaggerated irrationalism and anti-historicism of Miquel d'Esplugues seem, in fact, to mark the outer limit of the reasonable politics that the Lliga was pursuing through the government of the Mancomunitat: its mission was to sublimate as representation all of the things it was impossible even to dream of attaining. Barcelona once more the seat of counts, Roman Tarragona, princely Genoa: civilization itself condensed in pure images, immanent in time, was, quite simply, the chosen one.

But we should not imagine that Eusebi Güell was in any sense an instrument of Miquel d'Esplugues' book. On the contrary, the book could never have been written if it were not for the fact that Güell had dedicated his life to constructing the landscape within which his personality was to be described in a single, exclusive way, with no room for alternative interpretations. We saw in the previous chapter how in a period of crisis Güell sublimated the immediate ideology of his parents in a complex strategy of distinction, and now a couple of paragraphs more from Miquel d'Esplugues will serve to conclude this section: "The Barcelona of today has

*Other examples of the use
of the parabolic arch in the Palau
Güell.*

become bourgeois in excess, it is not sufficiently aristocratic and lives in ignorance of Catalonia's glorious past. Only those such as Güell who not only know that past, but possess it and are possessed by it, can be its guardians: his works are the example"; and he adds, a few lines below: "In modern Barcelona there are few palaces in the true sense. We have too many bourgeois villas and a shortage of lordly palaces."[59] Güell, as we have seen, was resolved to be not a bourgeois but a gentleman: to this end he built a palace, not a house. In it, his project began to take shape.

*Incarnation of Catalonia*
"The natural requirements of a comfortable home for a distinguished family consist primarily of abundant space, wide views and horizon, if possible in the open country, in order to provide the best possible conditions of health and hygiene, which are indispensable to existence and especially to a comfortable life. Of course we know that this is what everyone wishes for and that it is not always easy to obtain, even for the most affluent, especially if a site is chosen in the central part of a city such as our own, the main center of which is choked by a conglomeration of buildings with no open spaces and almost no clean air fit to breathe. Nor are we unaware that Mr. Güell was obliged by the abutment of another building with his property to make the best of favorable opportunities and circumstances in embarking upon the building in question, which has an averagely good situation but is located in a wretched and detestable part of the city."[60]
Amid his admiration for the richness and variety of spaces, solutions and materials, and the extraordinary quality of the furniture and works of art contained within it, Josep Puiggarí (in a monograph written in 1894 on the occasion of the visit by the Centre Excursionista de Catalunya to the town house that Eusebi Güell had built a short distance off the Rambla) allowed himself this one note of criticism concerning the location in the heart of the old town. Indeed this is the question that has been asked

most often and with greatest puzzlement in all subsequent writings on the town house:[61] why, when the open and airy Eixample was already under construction, did Eusebi Guëll choose to build it on a small site on a street in the dark old part of Barcelona? As we shall see, the question and the answer to it are more interesting than they might appear.

On June 30, 1886, Antoni Gaudí signed the official plans for his project, which were submitted for approval to Barcelona City Council, and in 1888 the town house—although not yet finished in all its details—was officially opened with a reception for the Spanish royal family. We need only recall the itineraries recommended in the guides to the International Exhibition of 1888 or, better still, Yxart's accounts of the same event, to realize that although there had been attempts at promoting a route around the old city (reduced to the small triangle bounded by the Gran Vía, the Passeig de Sant Joan and the Rondas—attempts that were to meet with no success until the early years of the next century) it was the old town that continued to be seen as the city proper, with the Ramblas, indisputably, as its main thoroughfare. From the principal hotels to the best and newest shops, from the new Academies to the most important theaters, all were to be found on the Ramblas. Above all, the Ramblas were—and still are—the site of the most prestigious mansions of eighteenth-century Barcelona: the Palau March de Reus, the Palau de la Virreina, the Palau Moja...[62] Is it really so strange, then, that Eusebi Guëll should decide to build on the Ramblas what was to be not a house but precisely a *palau*: a palace or mansion? *In concentrico loco*: there could be no more significant setting.

Puiggarí, it is true, calls this part of the city wretched and detestable, but it is equally true that he does so from a point of view, that of comfort, a quality which probably hardly entered into Eustebi Güell's expectations. On the one hand, when construction of the town house was beginning, the work of remodeling the

Torre Satalia had been completed, and all contemporary accounts agree that it was there that the Guëll family were most frequently in residence, while the town house just off the Ramblas was used for an essentially representational role. It seems clear that much of the family's private life was spent in the Torre Satalia.[63] In contrast, the town house is always associated, both in contemporary accounts and in memoirs, with social events, parties, concerts and receptions, such as that for the Spanish royal family mentioned above, or the famous receptions held for Grover Cleveland and Umberto I.[64] It is therefore quite natural that the building should have been officially opened precisely to coincide with the International Exhibition. On the other hand, however, is not *comfort* the neologism most frequently used, in all of *fin-de-siècle* literature, to define the ultimate aim of the bourgeois home? And is it not the idea of comfort that lies at the heart of Yxart's description of the house in which, according to him, Barcelona's new bourgeoisie wished to reside: "comfortable and luxurious?" "Gentleman" was the English word with which, as we have seen, his contemporaries sought to sum up the personality of Eusebi Guëll. It is obvious that just as "gentleman" evokes elitism, so "comfort" has bourgeois connotations. Not only that: the status to which the concept of comfort was elevated in the bourgeois philosophy of life gives us an idea of how it became an important subject for reflection by the aristocratizing sectors of the European intelligentsia in the second half of the nineteenth century. To them, this idea was without doubt the greatest expression of bourgeois mediocrity. An examination of some of the writings of Renan himself, whose importance in the formation of Eusebi Guëll's image we have already noted, is sufficient proof that we are not simply making generic suppositions. In 1859, in his *Essais de morale et de critique*, Renan wrote: "By no means does progress in art run parallel with those advances that lead a nation to acquire a taste for the "comfortable" (I find myself oblig-

ed to use this barbarism in order to define an idea which is scarcely French at all), and it could be said, without paradox of any kind, that the epochs and countries in which comfort became the principal desire of the people were those which were least endowed with artistic expression." Further on, he frankly affirms that "Comfort excludes style."[65] It seems clear that what the inhabitants of Barcelona saw in the town house, which was so hard to explain using the conventional models of judgment established in the city and was always described as eccentric or extravagant, was *style*. No doubt this is what Josep Puiggarí meant when he wrote that Güell "set out to, and succeeded in, creating a *sui generis* work, one without equal in Barcelona or, as far as we know, anywhere else."[66] And *Modernista* contributors to the newspaper *La Vanguardia* were also referring to it when, on the Spanish "Fool's Day" (December 28, the Feast of the Holy Innocents) in 1889, they published a hoax news item in which the Palau Güell is portrayed as an amusing archaeological discovery: "It seems unlikely that, in the *age of wrought iron*, space should have been squandered on columns of masonry, and of such thickness. The construction most probably dates from the time of Balthazar or ... the age of Nebuchadnezzar."[67] The authors of the hoax, without setting out to do so, accurately describe the building's rationale. Güell did not want to construct a building that was of his own century but, on the contrary, to create a place that was timeless, anachronistic. We have already seen how this was the case with the Torre Satalia in the last chapter, but in the Ramblas town house this objective takes on its most complex nuances. As the words of Puiggarí and the article in *La Vanguardia* suggest, the Palau Güell sought to set itself outside time. But outside of what time? Without a doubt, that time in which things have a verifiable, measurable value. Güell was building in a place in which not only space could be squandered, in all naturalness: in the extraordinary richness of the materials used in its construction, in the different

types of marble and wood and in the works of art it contains, the town house shows itself to be a place of exaggerated consumption, contrary to the rational logic of production. Not only that: concentrated in these same materials—in the highly complicated pieces of wrought iron that completely fill the house; in the obsessive variety of forms assumed by the 125 or more columns, each with a different capital of its own; in the applied arts of its drawing-room walls, its doors and fireplaces—there is an extraordinary quantity of human labor which, while it fills with absolute value all those places to which it has attached, in which it persists as a single thing, is in itself devalued. The Palau Güell is, in effect, the home of that which has no price. In it is displayed an inalienable kind of possession that is the possession not of the things themselves so much as the time spent in labor by the men engaged to make them. It is, in short, an anachronistic place in the sense that it is divorced from the time occupied by the market. Güell, in other words, set out to create a place of the most radical distinction, that distinction that comes from being outside the rules by which society is governed. The extravagances of the Palau Güell, all of them intended to display excess, have exactly the meaning suggested by some of Puiggarí's remarks: "That which distinguishes itself from the masses reveals itself to be in some way superior to them."[68] One of Güell's sons, in the volume of memoirs to which we have already referred, recalls the town house as "a moment of destruction." No doubt he was referring to a *social* destruction: to the distance that the town house established in relation to the contingent world of *change*, to that distance which he had identified between his father, who inhabited a *priceless* place, and his *peers*. In another part of the book, he writes: "One of the guiding ideas behind the conception and the distribution of my father's house was that it should be suitable for giving grand concerts."[69] Could there be any clearer expression of what constitutes *style* as opposed to *commodité*?

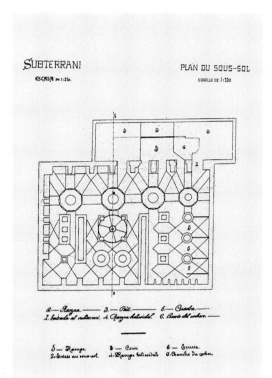

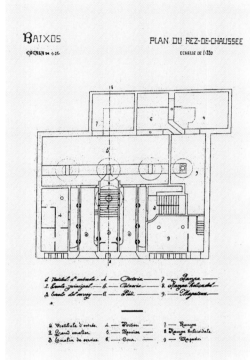

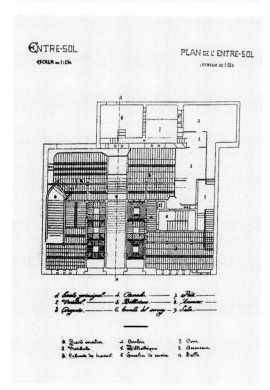

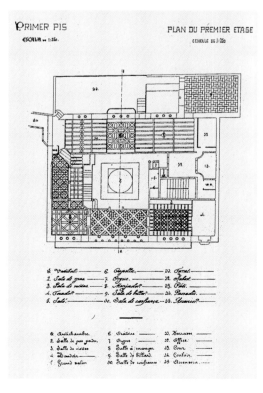

Another article that was also published in *La Vanguardia*, on August 3, 1890, and is certainly the first serious attempt at a public evaluation of the town house, may help us to understand this more clearly. The piece was written by Frederic Rahola, secretary of the Foment del Treball Nacional, (the most important employers' association in late-nineteenth century Catalonia) and founder of the Institut d'Estudis Americans (no mere coincidence), a prominent member of the Lliga and, lastly, a close associate of Güell's both in politics and in business.[70] Even in the first few lines there are words that make it clear what position the town house is intended to occupy within its environment. Rahola says of Gaudí that "his constructions battle against routine and fashion."[71] Against the flat, constant and mediocre time of the everyday and of habit, but also against the ever-changing, always "other" time of fashion: this is where the town house stands. We need only take note of the particular condition of the things it contains to see how the town house seeks to establish itself as itself, as its own absolute. Everything in it seems imbued with the notion of the *inmueble*, the building as immovable property. Everything seems to become one with the walls of the house themselves, to be fused with them. We have already mentioned the wrought iron and the marble in which the work is condensed: the ironwork weaves its way throughout the house like ivy, literally attaching itself to the walls and columns. These in turn, constantly varied in form, are so integrated as to display a condition that goes beyond functionality. And even the *muebles* or "movable" furniture which fills the house is characterized, paradoxically, by its immovability. Most of the furniture is antique, and when it is not, it consists of pieces that were specifically designed by Gaudí to occupy a particular place, such as the remarkable marble sofa with its alabaster back and brocade upholstery in the main salon, or Señor Güell's *chaise longue,* to be seen in period photographs next to a corner bookcase, or his wife's dressing table with its frozen dripping mirror. But this

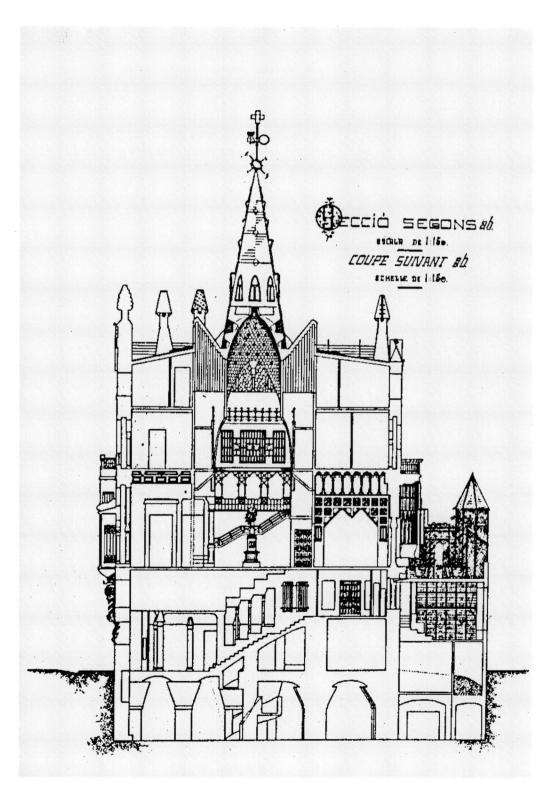

quality is perhaps most in evidence in the way in which the works of art occupy their place within the house. The many framed paintings both antique and modern were hung in their very own specially-designed gallery, a kind of corridor linking the *palau* with the old house of Joan Güell next door. The large rooms of the town house contain antique pieces such as reredos, triptychs and tapestries, and especially mosaics, stained glass and wall paintings. There is thus a clear distinction between movable works of art and the immovable art that is part of the walls of the town house, that *is* the town house—a distinction that at the same time places the boundary between the private and the public in an ambiguous compromise. The murals painted on the walls of the main salon by Aleix Clapés (who after a period as a fresco painter in Rome trained, significantly enough, under that most literary of painters Eugene Carrière) are particularly relevant here:[72] the nature of their integration into the architecture is evident even in the way they literally turn the corners of the walls rather than occupying the center. Everything that the house contains, therefore, is not only located in that absent time to which we have already referred but is also, and to an even greater extent, fixed to the immovable character of the house itself, to its inner and outer walls and to the ground on which the house is built; in other words, literally fixed to the property. This is yet another demonstration of the way the place has been taken out of circulation and out of the market, and imbued with an inalienable sense of property that is oblivious to the time of change. In another passage from his memoirs, Eusebi Güell's son speaks of the transcendent nature of this property, of the way that, within it, house, things and time become immovable: "It is interesting to note how this house, of ultramodern conception, creates an atmosphere that is in perfect harmony with the antique paintings and tapestries, so that some visitors have believed it to be several hundred years old, as though it were the fantasy of some Venetian artist of the

fifteenth century."[73] In sketching such a description, the viscount doubtless had in mind, anachronistically, not the studio of an artist of the *quattrocento* but the legendary Palazzo Fortuny in Venice. His words are nonetheless eloquent, however: what, in the last analysis, was Fortuny's Venetian studio but the continuation of the studio his father had on the Via Flaminia in Rome, which was so fashionable in the days when Güell was constructing his town house?[74] The ultramodern and the antique are condensed in an absolute instant, in an atmosphere from which every trace of temporality has been removed. This absence determines the most inalienable of possessions.

But the Rahola article, describing some of the town house's most singular elements, and commenting on the particularity of their constant presence in it, gives us other reasons to explain its unique character. Of the parabolic arc, for example—which as we have said was one of the signs of modernity most frequently used by the architects of Martorell's circle—he writes: "It is an elevated spiritual curve which tends to rise like a flame. Gaudí has adopted it as a constant motif in his design. Vaguely suggested in the basement, we find it complete in the two front doors, resting on the ground, then it emerges from the columns, springing forth everywhere. Thus in a grandiose *crescendo* it weaves in all directions in the great cupola of the main salon, where it achieves its greatest intensity, before disappearing into the chimneys of the upper reaches in swift spirals, in aerial fragments, dispersed like the single notes of a symphony's dominant motif that act as its final cadence."[75] It would not be too far-fetched to suppose that both Rahola and Güell were familiar with Toussenel's extraordinary book *L'Esprit des bêtes. Zoologie passionnelle. Mammifères de France* (which was first published in 1847 but came out in a second edition precisely in 1884),[76] in which—among a host of other things to which Gaudí's realism would not be alien, either—the author expounded a theory of the meaning of geometric curves,

and assigned to the parabola its familiar significance. But even if this were not the case, even if they did not know Toussenel's work, it would be hard to deny that the description quoted above belongs in a general sense to the same analogical-symbolic way of thinking. An architectural motif—one that no doubt appeared highly extravagant in the eyes of Güell's contemporaries—becomes in Rahola's description a spiritual flame that runs through the town house from top to bottom. In describing such a *continuum*, Rahola is clearly sublimating, in a nonphysical image, the bonding to the property in which all the things of the house engage. The parabolic arc draws together in a single ascending movement all of the parts of the building, and above all its meaning: in a sense, it gives the building a theme to interpret. It is also evident that such a sublimation must be and is, in fact, based on a clear concept: that of the total work of art so beloved of nineteenth century culture. This will undoubtedly help us to see in a new light the role adopted by Güell towards his work and his artists, and also the role he obliges them to adopt. The total work of art, an art that is necessarily thematic and integrated, is evidently brought forth—as we have already said—in opposition to the idea of *l'art pour l'art*, but at the same time as a condition of it. It is, in effect, none other than the ultimate, extreme product of the deepest of the tensions to be found in the art of the nineteenth century. This is an art that constructs an ideology to justify its conversion into merchandise—*l'art pour l'art*, in fact— while at the same time trying to oppose that inevitable condition by sublimating its destiny: no longer the anonymous public that buys on the market but society itself. The artist thus becomes, like the work itself, a total artist, the sole director of all the processes that lead to the ultimate and—because it is integrated—necessary determination of its form: there the much-vaunted freedom of the artist seems to become extreme. And yet the patron would also appear to be a necessary part of this process, as the per-

son who can guarantee the removal of the work from the market, and the one best placed to exorcize its modern condition as merchandise. It is not, however, a case of reverting to the old, feudal figure of the patron or of reconstructing pre-bourgeois modes of relation—that would be simply to undermine the position of freedom attained by art and so to reduce its value. On the contrary: only there can the extreme genius of the artist, liberated from his own time, find the protection that will comprehend his extravagance, an extravagance is capable of surprising the patron himself. The relationship is thus based on an ambiguous duality: the freer the artist's work appears to be, the more valuable it is to whoever possesses it—and the more it is reduced, in reality, to the small world of pure forms. We have already looked at the consciously anti-bourgeois stance on which the self-created cliché of Güell the patron was founded. In terms of all we have said here, Rahola's article could not be clearer. After criticizing the vulgarity of the modern city, which he blames for the "imposition that inhibits the artist's faculties, hindering the free movement of his fantasy," he writes: "Gaudí ... is a true eccentric."[77] But where could such eccentricity take on positive overtones other than in conjunction with the isolated singularity conferred by the patron? Only here can the eccentric move on beyond the merely capricious and shake off any pejorative sense to turn itself into *value*: a demonstration of original genius and a display of artistic freedom. It is worth recalling in relation to this how Baudelaire had juxtaposed precisely these two themes in his observations on Richard Wagner and *Tannhäuser*. He wrote, for example, using some of the same turns of phrase as we have seen in Josep Puiggarí's monograph: "An artist, a man truly worthy of that great name, must possess something essentially *sui generis*, thanks to which he is himself and no one else."[78] Rahola insists that "patronage has allowed the artist to act with complete freedom, with full confidence in his talent, without concerning himself about the excommunications of

*Colonnades and galleries
of the public rooms on the main
floor.*

the common herd."[79] Could any other possession confer such radical distinction? At the same time, the comment by Rahola quoted above, in which this possession was transcendently sublimated into the integrity of the work, contains a very significant musical simile. The parabolic arc is a dominant motif in the symphony form: the image is clearly Wagnerian. And if an architectural element can be described as a *leitmotif* without too much difficulty, this very obvious example is not the only instance of a Wagnerian idea presenting itself in Rahola's text. When he makes the at first sight surprising suggestion that the Palau Güell, in imitating natural forms, "signifies the triumph of realism in architecture,"[80] surely he is referring to the manner in which Wagner explained his concept of infinite melody,[81] comparing it, for example, with the effect of the murmuring of the forest, thus purposely confusing reality and idea? It would be unnecessary and beside the point to set out to describe here the extraordinary influence that Wagner's oeuvre had on the formation of the nineteenth century's concept of the total artwork. What does concern us, however, is the way in which this oeuvre was interpreted in Barcelona, a city that in the latter half of the 1880s—the same period in which Güell's town house was being built—was in the grip of its first great wave of Wagner fever, in which Eusebi Güell was an active participant.[82] In fact these were the years of the first complete performances of the German maestro's operas—very few of them, indeed, bearing in mind the great stir they caused among the public. What is more, events such as the first performance of *Parsifal* in Bayreuth and the death of Wagner himself led—in spite of the great distance and widespread ignorance—to heated debates in the city's newspapers, debates that were generally of greater sociological than musical interest. It was at this time, too, that much better informed writers such as Joaquim Marsillach and Josep de Letamendi wrote their first essays on Wagner.[83] Marsillach had been a personal friend of

Wagner and in 1878, at the age of nineteen, had published the first book in Spain on the composer's work; he was to die very young, only a few months after Wagner himself. Marsillach's work, which now seems excessively literal, is of less interest to us here than that of Letamendi, whose first essay on the subject (in fact it was an introduction to Marsillach's book) was so successful that Wagner had it translated into German and published it in his Bayreuth Blätter. Letamendi's work is far more purposeful and his comments of greater transcendence.[84] His aim was essentially to find the best way of applying Wagner's art to his own situation or, to put it another way, to show how the German master's art could be used—an operative approach to Wagner that would later be taken up by other Catalan intellectuals such as Maragall or Casellas.[85] On Wagner's death, Letamendi wrote that the composer's aim had been to achieve "the supreme social education by means of the perfection of the theatrical spectacle,"[86] and some years later he raised this idea to a higher level, giving it the circularity of an axiom: "He made Drama not only the school but also the measure of the culture of a people." This sentence is from a long article that Letamendi published in 1884 and entitled "The Music of the Future and the future of my country."[87] First and foremost, Letamendi is concerned to make very clear the applied nature of Wagner's total art. It is precisely this application that reveals its synthetic nature and its transcendence. "The glorious reputation of Richard Wagner consists in his having achieved, for the first time in history, the supreme synthesis of Art, not theoretically or abstrusely, and not Art for Art's sake, but—and this is the indisputable novelty—of Art applied to the higher education of peoples."[88] It is clear, therefore, that both Wagner and his work—what Letamendi calls the "Wagnerian fact"—are instruments of a necessary destiny that is prior to and also beyond those instruments. Letamendi is concerned with firmly establishing the necessary, ineffable character of Wagner's oeuvre: it is not, he tells us, "a thesis that is to any degree debatable," but rather "an overwhelmingly consummate fact."[89] In his text there is a clear intention to charge the words with this idea: Art, Culture and Drama always appear with an initial capital. How could it be otherwise in an essay that is concerned throughout not with persons but with peoples? In short, Wagner's merit—his "indisputable novelty"—is none other than to have given shape to that which is essential to a people, that with which it identifies most profoundly: its legends, its myths. He writes: "The Maestro adopted Myth and Legend as the sources of inspiration that were most cleansed of real ugliness, thanks to the constant, steady filter of the centuries."[90] The precision with which Letamendi chooses his words is significant: Wagner is not inspired by myth because he uses it, but because he adopts it. That is to say: myth is not only a model, a source for the artist's creation; it admits not only his interpretations, which are always contingent, but, above all, it exists—at one with itself, formed by the centuries and therefore in a time without temporality—waiting to be received once more. In the presence of myth, then, the artist must assent: Wagner does, and in so doing, adopts the myth. Myth is as much the stuff of peoples as it is of Wagner's art, and the artist is, after all, merely its custodian and transmitter. But what is it that so fires Letamendi's enthusiasm if not the very thing with which Nietzsche and others were so concerned? With Wagner, in fact, myth is no longer an artistic or literary resource, a medium for other allegorical or demonstrative purposes, but has come to be something that is brought forth and expands with the music itself. Myth and music have in common an absence of theses, of conceptualizations: they carry within them, and display, only images. Myth does not allow for demonstrations but only for its own imposition: that is why its manifestations are based on repetition and redundancy. What else is the leitmotif but the Wagnerian path of that imposition? Letamendi writes that Wagner "does not seek to humanize the divine but to sublimate the human":[91] a total and absolute re-mythologizing, then. In consequence, the course taken by his

works is vertical: through this work, the human becomes no longer human, precisely because all ugliness has been eliminated from it. Could there be any better expression of the total work of art as an attempt to impose myth on society? Letamendi's conclusions refer to the situation of his own country. Spain, he tells us, so backward compared to other European nations in material terms, has nonetheless a way forward for its restoration: "Wagnerism, considered as instrument and sign of national Culture."[92] He concludes by saying: "Precisely because we are the last to undergo a rebirth, we must be reborn according to the latest principle of progress which, from this day on, is no longer a battle for dominion but dominion by culture."[93] This is not only the most applied of the uses of myth—its most operative imposition—but literally a spell cast against the material world and, even more so, against the most immediate reality. Let us not forget that this was 1884: the great mercantile boom of the *febre d'or* was already over, and the economic crisis brought with it not only a period of great social instability but also a search for new political strategies on the part of the Barcelona bourgeoisie, which no longer felt itself to be represented by the machinery of the Restoration. When Letamendi concludes that "in this higher concept [that of culture], every advance made in the non-material order will be much more honorable and useful for Spain than the addition of a battalion to its army or a ship to its navy,"[94] he is simply consoling himself, by means of spells and incantations elevating the spiritual over the material, for his real powerlessness. But at the same time, what better ideology could there be for a time of crisis?

Dominion by culture: an exorcism. The Palau Güell is this, too. It is no surprise that these instructions for use *in society* that Letamendi sets out for Wagner's opera should be perfectly understood by a bourgeoisie that had been prevented by the crisis of 1882 from fully exercising its true powers. We have seen, in effect, how a sublimated power is represented in the Palau Güell, as a will to distinction and as an anachronism, and we shall see how myth was to be the conclusion of this sublimation. The Wagnerian simile with which Rahola describes the town house's continuous structure is thus something more than poetic license. The redundant and repetitive presence of the parabolic arch in the Palau Güell violently imposes, its image, an image that—far removed from any conceptualization—serves no other function than to show itself to itself and, in so doing, demonstrate its exclusive, self-sufficient superiority. There could certainly be no greater correspondence between this image that constantly manifests itself and the Wagnerian *leitmotif*. What other mechanism could turn the Palau Güell into a form of dominion by culture, in other words, of the imposition of myth? It is by no means surprising that the Wagnerian simile should have been so much in favor with commentators on Gaudí's architecture. Leaving aside the far-fetched parallels between Gaudí and Wagner drawn by Francesc Pujols in the 1920s (parallels of which Salvador Dalí was particularly fond), it is worth recalling a paragraph written by Vicente Gibert in 1928. Talking about the main salon of the Palau Güell, he says: "The author of *Parsifal*, a man of the theater, striving for the immediate staging of his work, contented himself—had to content himself, because he could not do the impossible—with stage illusion. His theory of the union of the fine arts, in so far as it touches on architecture, had a very deficient application on the surface of the painted canvas. It was Gaudí who constructed the cupola of Montsalvat."[95] We should not be misled by the apparent ingenuousness of this excerpt, which reveals so well the pertinacity of certain images: *Parsifal* had its first performance in Bayreuth precisely in 1882, and it had not been difficult for Catalan cultural circles to interpret the words in the libretto that situate the action—"Place of the action is the domain and hamlet of the Grail, called Montsalvat, in the characteristic landscape of the Gothic mountains of the north of Spain"—as an allusion to the mountain of Montserrat.[96] Would it be going too

One of the studies for the main
façade of the town house, drawn
by F. Berenguer; and the definitive
project presented to Barcelona City
Council, signed by Güell and Gaudí
in 1886.

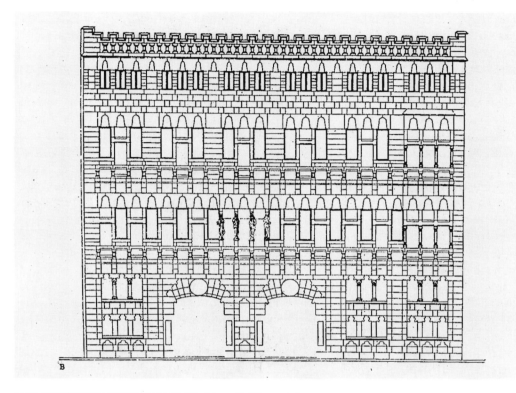

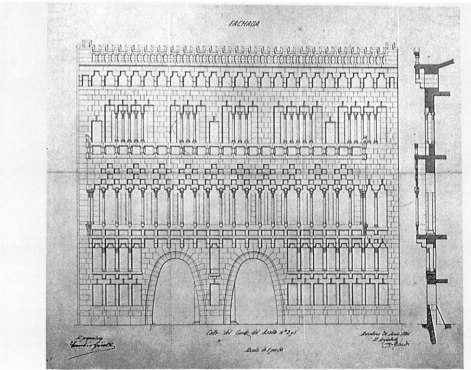

far to see in the Palau Güell reflections of the
fortress of Montsalvat, as contemporary accounts seem to suggest so insistently? It is not so
far-fetched, as we shall see in due course. What is
more, that absence of temporality that in the
Palau Güell is achieved, as a condition of inalienable possession, with the compression of time
and space into a single sensation, is perfectly described by Gurnemanz when he says: "You see,
my son? Here, space is born out of time"?[97] There
can be little doubt, then, that Letamendi's *theme*
is realized in the Palau Güell with absolute precision, with nothing wasted. There is no need to try
to establish here an explanation of the intellectual and cultural ties that linked Güell and Letamendi. Not only did Letamendi have the same
diversity of interests as Güell, ranging from the
scientific (he was a doctor and the author of exceptional theories in that field) to the artistic (he
was not only a music critic, as we have seen, but
also an occasional composer, as well as a philosopher, a poet and a painter); in addition, the two
were linked by their common membership of the
institutions of the Renaixença and in particular of
the Jocs Florals, of which both were president at
one time or another. The small circle in which
they moved makes a clear enough case for the
influence that Letamendi's operative theories—
which enjoyed considerable currency in different
Barcelona milieus, musical and otherwise—might
have had on Eusebi Güell's carefully meditated
artistic undertakings. The one crucial difference
is that Letamendi is the intellectual who proposes, Güell the patron who disposes. The idea of
dominion by culture is imbued, in Güell's works,
with immediate considerations. Who should understand better than he—son of Joan Güell and
son-in-law of Antonio López, he had already built
the Torre Satalia—the value of myth and the effect of its imposition? In the Palau Güell, this idea
is fully formulated: the myth here will be material disposed. Let us look at some of its facets.

On one of the side façades of the town house, the
one facing the Rambla, Aleix Clapés painted a
large mural, no longer extant, representing

*The main façade in a photograph
from the end of the nineteenth
century and caricature of E. Güell
leaning out of a window of his town
house (Picarol, L'Esquella de la
Torratxa, 1908).*

Hercules. The allusion to *L'Atlàntida* thus once again makes an appearance in one of Eusebi Güell's works. We can see what the painting by Clapés was like thanks to an old photograph: the Greek hero is walking with great strides, holding aloft a firebrand in his right hand and carrying a club in his left. Dramatically lit by the flame of his own torch, in a dark, vaguely defined landscape, it is obvious that this is not a representation of any specific landscape in Verdaguer's poem. Moreover, the firebrand and the club were the weapons used by Hercules in his struggle with the Hydra, not in his search for the Hesperides. We shall return to this apparent discrepancy in due course, but let us look now at the figure's strange appearance: out-of-proportion, with a small head and large limbs, he looks strong but not so much athletic as coarse. And if he has little in common with conventional idealized representations of the Greek hero, there is a clear link with the extraordinary *Hercules Hispanicus* in the cycle Zurbarán painted for the Salón de Reinos in Felipe IV's Buen Retiro palace, and which has been in the Prado Museum since that institution was established.[98] Like Zurbarán's Hercules, Clapés' is a crude, brutal figure, schematically represented with one overriding objective: that he should be evident. It is not strange that Clapés should take Zurbarán's canvases as models: hung at a height of more than three meters above the doors of the great Salón de Reinos, between paintings of battles that are much larger and of much greater thematic complexity, they exercise an exclusively symbolic function. This explains, as has been rightly pointed out,[99] their schematic clarity. Clapés' Hercules was also to be seen from a considerable distance and, moreover, was to present itself not as a narrative but as an emblem. We have already noted the symbolic role of the image of Hercules in the ideological discourse that was woven by the marquises of Comillas and Eusebi Güell. An emblem, then, was what the inhabitants of Barcelona were to see on the façade of the town house that Güell was building in the

center of the city: a sign of possession of the communal and collective, of radical distinction.

All of this takes us back to a question that can now be seen in a new light: the matter of the town house's location on a side street off the lower end of the Rambla. As we saw in the last chapter, in 1870 Antonio López had bought the Palau Moja, on the upper part of the Rambla, as a residence for his family. Two points should be noted about this highly prestigious building: firstly, it is entered not from the Rambla but from a side street, Portaferrissa; secondly, its spatial structure is truly exceptional within the tradition of eighteenth-century Barcelona town houses: it is unique in having its rooms laid out around a great double-height central salon.[100] Both of these unusual features were to be exactly duplicated in the Palau Güell, at the other end of the Rambla. We might see it as a coincidence, determined by circumstances, that the main entrance of each of the two houses should be on a side street.[101] However, the manner in which the Palau Güell is laid out around a main salon with a cupola that extends the full height of the building can no doubt be ascribed to a conscious desire to establish an analogy. The grand salon of the Palau Moja is decorated with frescos by Francesc Plà, "el Vigatà," depicting scenes from the history of the Cartellà family, the former owners; in the central salon of the Palau Güell the Clapés murals, too, with their scenes of Saint Isabel of Hungary giving her crown to the poor, or the image of Jaume Balmes, represent in their more indirect way not only the specific altruism of Isabel López, Güell's wife, but something more: the family's social policy. In addition, the salon was presided over by a bust of Joan Güell, set on a small pedestal that in its turn, in an obsessive play of redundancies, featured in bas-relief the monument erected in his honor on the Rambla de Catalunya, the significance of which we have already considered in sufficient detail. On the exterior, then, the great Hercules mural served to establish in emblematic form the identification between these two analogous town houses. At

*The organ in the main salon
and views from the gallery
on the bedroom floor.*

their opposite ends of the Rambla, they converted Barcelona's main thoroughfare into a virtual
circle, enclosing it within the inaccessible image
of power thus represented.

However, the symbols deployed in the Palau
Güell, as we have already seen in the Torre Satalia, are shot through with different interpretations. Hercules, in the myths of Barcelona's
origins, had always been the city's founder.[102]
Although there were already monuments to the
hero in Barcelona, and a number of its grand
houses were decorated with cycles depicting his
labors, the popular resurgence of the myth took
place, by no means accidentally, in the early
1880s thanks to the poetry of Verdaguer, as
would seem obvious—and not only through
*L'Atlàntida* but above all with the *Oda a
Barcelona*, which won a prize at the Jocs Florals
of 1883 and was published by the city council in
a special edition of 100,000 copies.[103] However,
the foundational significance to which the presence of Hercules alluded is further developed in
Eusebi Güell's town house by means of the other symbols that adorn its walls on every side.
Between the two main doors, bathed in the extraordinary tones of light created the remarkable mullion, a beautiful piece of wrought iron
depicts the four bars of the Catalan flag,
crowned by a helmet surmounted by a bird in
the act of unfolding its wings. On the one hand,
this is one of the most commonly-used symbols
of Renaixença imagery: the Phoenix rising again
over the Catalan flag, but the bird on top of the
helmet is also a clear allusion to the winged
dragon that, according to tradition, figured on
the crest of the helm of Jaume I, the king whose
conquest of Valencia and Mallorca in the thirteenth century marked the beginning of Catalonia's Mediterranean expansion. This bat (the *rat
penat* of popular lore), often mistakenly interpreted as a dragon, had since the sixteenth century at least crowned the coats of arms of Palma
de Mallorca, Valencia and Barcelona.[104] The bat
also finds a place at the highest point of the town
house, on the crest of the lantern where the

*Views of the double-height main salon and the dome.*

cupola cuts through the roof: on top of the globe of the world and beneath the cross, at the same height as the solar disk. Mythical Hercules and the conquering king: the the same story is invoked twice over. The Phoenix is born again atop this foundation that is both double and identical. There is little room for doubt about the meaning of the symbols that pervade the Palau Güell, nor is there about the fact that they are represented here, in a private town house, a *home*.

Is it possible that the highly cultured Eusebi Güell—and we have already seen the role of Verdaguer in determining his program of symbols—should be unaware of the significance of the figure of Hercules in association with a *palau* or town house? Since Antiquity, and especially since the sixteenth century, Hercules, as the image of Virtue and Strength, had been the most conventional symbol of the prince, and the labors of Hercules were an essential theme, a commonplace of the decorative cycles of the prince's palace. There is an almost endless list of palaces, throughout the four corners of Europe, with a salon dedicated to Hercules: from the Ducal Palace and the Palazzo Te in Mantua to the Palazzo Vecchio in Florence, the palace of Fontainebleau, the Villa d'Este in Tivoli, the Villa Farnese in Caprarola or the Farnese palace in Rome.[105] But if, as we have seen, this is a cliché, what reason could there be for choosing such an extraordinary model as the *Hercules Hispanicus* of Zurbarán? Precisely because this is the image of the Spanish monarchy, whose kings—like so many other European princes—claimed the Greek hero not only as a symbol but as an ancestor. And Hercules, again, is one of the main elements in the ideological discourse of *L'Atlàntida*: Hercules presented as king of Spain so that History is brought to a close at the moment in which Columbus, under Spanish reign, unites the continents once more. Conscious as we are of the ideological strategies of the Barcelona bourgeoisie, we should not be surprised at the apparent duality—Catalan and Spanish, with the latter specifically represented by the monarchy—with which the symbols of the Palau Güell can be read. But in this case we can establish a very specific equivalent. The opening ceremonies of the International Exhibition in 1888 had given rise to a major confrontation between the Centre Català and the recently founded Lliga de Catalunya. The latter had on the one hand argued for and obtained a postponement of the Jocs Florals so that, by coinciding with the Exhibition ceremonies, they might be presided over by the Queen Regent; and on the other, it had used the opportunity to present María Cristina herself with a document in which, in radical tones, it demanded wide-ranging autonomy for Catalonia.[106] Is it necessary to recall here, too, that the Palau Güell was inaugurated to coincide with the Exhibition celebrations, with a grand reception for the royal family?

This latter fact, however, is of such importance as to call for renewed emphasis: all of this took place in Eusebi Güell's *home*. The symbol of Hercules, then, as we see it here, admits of further consideration. As was pointed out earlier, his weapons are the firebrand and the club that he used to fight the Hydra, the seven-headed serpent. So it is Hercules the illuminator and the conqueror of discord—and not Hercules on his way to the Garden of the Hesperides—that we find represented in the Güell town house. Again, of course, this is a commonplace princely metaphor, but it is not only that. A few years later, in the Colonia Obrera built by Eusebi Güell in Santa Coloma de Cervelló, Güell would be represented as the conqueror of a very specific discord, "social discord," "discord between capital and labor." Ramón Picó i Campamar wrote a psalm, its music composed by Isabel Güell, Eusebi's daughter, that was to be sung by Güell's workers on the Corpus Christi processions: "Written in order for the inhabitants of the Colonia Güell to sing it in chorus on the said feast day."[107] Its words are as tendentious as the Hercules we have been referring to. "That there should be work, that discord and sloth should cease." This is a Hercules, then, who is perfectly

*Roof terrace with the spire
of the dome's lantern, detail
of the base and the interior
of the spire.*

in harmony with the "social philosophy" and the altruism represented in the Clapés murals in the salon. The themes of these, to which we have already referred, could hardly be more eloquent. Saint Isabel giving her crown to the poor, the dispossessed praying before a wayside cross, Jaume Balmes … In addition, have we not already noted that the bat shares its place at the apex of the town house with the solar disk, another conventional image of the prince associated, in this case, with Virtue, but, as always, by way of a Hercules whose twelve labors are equivalent to the twelve signs of the zodiac, in relation to which he is the sun?

The sense in which the town house became "immovable" property, then, the sense in which all of its elements were fixed to the property, immune from change, seems to attach itself with splendid circularity to the proprietor himself. The princely allusions are too numerous and too evident in the way they interweave with one another and tie in with the foundational symbols—also centered on two princes: Hercules and Jaume I—for us to doubt that their use is entirely conscious. What else did Miguel d'Esplugues have in mind when he referred to Eusebi Güell as unique or, even better, as monarch? Years later, Josep Yxart referred ironically to a particular type of cultural protectionism in Catalonia, exercised from above, shot through with paternalism, loaded with political connotations and allegiances: he was referring to the relationship of patronage that existed between the Infanta María Paz and Eusebi Güell, and he dubbed it *güellismo*."[108]

New light can also now be shed on the *power* that the total work of art contains and imposes, from this direction, from myth. Frederic Rahola concludes his article by drawing together again, with transcendent overtones, forms, work and symbols: "Everything seen and admired there is the work of Catalan artists, all of the materials have been taken from the bosom of our land, all of the products are the fruit of our industries. On the pinnacle of the cupola we find the vigilant bat

whose wings have protected the arms of Catalonia since the time of Jaume I the Conqueror; there it is, symbol of the powerful spirit of this land, animating that immense mass of stone, flesh of its flesh and bone of its bones." Having said that, however, who is it that watches over and protects but he who possesses the symbols? Rahola himself makes this quite clear: "The visitor, on leaving Señor Güell's abode, has an indefinable feeling of pride."[109] The town house seeks to present itself, in effect, as the *gift of foundation* of the land itself and its history. Rahola's image is striking, almost infectious: the Palau Güell is literally neither more nor less than the spirit of Catalonia made flesh and blood, *incarnate*. But at the same time—it could hardly be clearer, more stridently assertive—that flesh and blood are the *abode* of the gentleman, the *palau*.

### Axis Mundi

Flesh and blood of the spirit of the land, and at the same time abode of the unique. But what form was this incarnation to take? How should it be, in order to make the most of its symbolic identification?

The surface area that Gaudí had at his disposal for his project was certainly very small, if we bear in mind all that it was to contain: a plot of approximately 20 meters by 20, on a gap site between adjacent buildings.

The building's development is thus necessarily vertical: from basement to roof there are eight different levels. In 1910, on the occasion of the exhibition of Gaudí's works at the Palais de Beaux Arts in Paris, Eusebi Güell, his main patron, commissioned a set of meticulous and, as we shall see, highly purposeful drawings of the building, later published in an album: they shall serve us in our description.[110] On the ground floor is the main entrance hall. At the back of this hall there is access to the basement, which served as the stables. Two ramps lead down: one a straight, gentle slope, for the animals, the other a steep spiral, for the servants. Meanwhile, in the very center of the entrance hall is a

*Views of the chimneys on the roof
terrace with the cathedral
in the distance.*

single wide flight of stairs, set on the axis that runs between the two great arches of the entrance, leads up to the mezzanine, on which are the library and the offices from which Eusebi Güell directed his businesses. On the other side of the hall another stairway, in this case at the side, goes up to the main floor, whose spacious rooms—dining room, sitting rooms, visiting rooms—are laid out around a great domed central salon. This salon, decorated with the mural by Aleix Clapés to which we referred above, is the heart of the palace: here concerts, parties and receptions were held, as well as religious ceremonies. In an adjoining space, behind richly ornate doors of lignum vitae, bone and ivory, with panels painted by Clapés representing the Apostles, between the organ and the sacristy, was the chapel, no longer in existence. On the other side of the salon a transverse open stairway leads to a mezzanine in the form of a balcony overlooking the hall, in one corner of which a discreet door opens onto the stairway that gives access to family bedrooms on the floor above. Both on this floor and the one directly over it, housing the servants' quarters, the rooms are laid out around the void created by the great salon which, like an indoor courtyard, runs the entire height of the building as far as the roof terrace, with a conical dome surrounded by multi-colored chimneys encrusted with *trencadís* shards of glass and ceramic tile.

In this brief description of the distribution of the building one feature is immediately apparent: the spatial structure can basically be summarized as a sequence of volumes—basement, domed hall, roof terrace—in relation to which the rest of the spaces are absolutely contingent in character and function. And it is in these three singularly inventive volumes that the building's strong symbolic charge is concentrated.

First the basement. Despite its humble use as stables, it is clear that the form far surpasses the simple function. The space is quite extraordinary: it was the sight of these stables that led the writers from the daily newspaper *La Vanguardia* to compare the Palau Güell with Babylonian architecture. Lit through small high windows, the space here is

following pages:
*Examples of the ceramic* trencadís
*on the chimneys of the roof terrace.*

almost wholly occupied by overwhelming pillars of brick—some of them cylindrical, of colossal size—which widen out at the top to form immense round capitals, and whose placement, in some cases, does not even correspond to the structural load of the floors above. Nonetheless, it was absurd to accuse Gaudí, as did some critics from *La Vanguardia*, of having wasted the space with great pillars of exposed brick when he could have employed slender cast iron columns. It seems even more absurd that this should continue to provoke, right up to the present, ethical arguments about the sincerity or otherwise of the use Gaudí made of modern construction materials.[111]

In this basement, the space is indeed wasted, it is squandered in the most flagrant and explicit way, and not only in terms of quantity, but also and above all, in terms of quality. What is Gaudí playing with if not quality when he erects pillars eighty centimeters in diameter, less than three meters apart, that are not continuous with any structural element on the floor above? The suffocating presence of these pillars and, above all, their patent uselessness; the dramatic quality of the light that barely enters through the small skylights; the warm texture of the brick: all are there to manifest the brutality of a place whose inhabitants are, indeed, brute beasts. But this is not a mere exercise in decorative effect; as such it would be quite excessive. The place occupied by the beasts, by the irrational animals, is, like them, irrational; that is, subterranean, cave-like, and ultimately very much in keeping with a long symbolic tradition, hell. The basement of the Palau Güell is neither more nor less than hell.

Two levels radically separate the basement from the great salon on the main floor. This, as we have said, is a basically square space located at the center of the building. Nonetheless its location is far from evident as one moves about the floor. From the top of the stairs, in fact, access to the salon is either by way of two successive vestibules, leading into the main part of the salon, ritually positioned on the axis of the façade but set slightly off center with respect to the axis of the salon itself; or from the other side of the building, by way of the dining

106

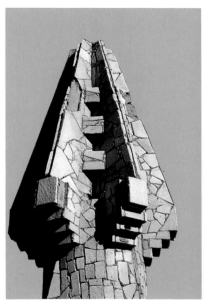

room and the more private sitting rooms, unexpectedly entering at one corner of the salon. Two itineraries, then, which by passing around the salon deliberately postpone the moment of its discovery, obliging the visitor to wait. But what do we find on each of these itineraries? In both cases, a succession of rooms in which the different realms of the fantastical nineteenth-century imaginary—those that had previously manifested themselves in the exterior decoration of the stables of the Torre Satalia—have been concentrated paradigmatically in the extraordinary richness and variety of marbles, mosaics and woods that the visitor comes across along the way. On the second of the itineraries described, the long private sitting room is divided diaphragmatically by wooden screens whose profile and placing are, as has so often been pointed out, an evocation of the Hall of the Kings in the Alhambra, as shown in the sections drawn by Owen Jones.[112] Greater complexity, however, is found on the first itinerary, where a series of four rooms aligned in *enfilade* along the length of the façade create a transition from evocations of a diffusely Oriental kind—Puiggarí, for example, can not decide whether the capitals of the columns remind him of "the Egyptian style of the colonnade of the temple of Luxor or of Ellora in India"[113]—to an equally diffuse rococo dressing room: "furnished in the tastes of the end of the last century or beginning of the present [nineteenth] century … clocks, cornucopias, candelabras…"[114] From the fantastic East to the coats and wraps: the tastes of that would-be aristocratic European and American bourgeoisie who bought its works of art from Goupil—and we should not forget that Fortuny had been perhaps the most paradigmatic of its artists—and considered, thanks to the Goncourts, the style of the eighteenth century to be the last great aristocratic art, finds here a very eloquent manifestation.[115] But that is not all. Puiggarí's meticulous description is impressive for other reasons: not only do the furnishings and works of art in each of these four consecutive rooms belong to different styles; so, too, the screens, the cornices, the floors, the coffered ceilings, the paneling in each of them is absolutely

diverse, always different. The taste to which we have referred is characterized in the Palau Güell by excess, by exaggeration. Yet is this not at the same time simply another example of the paratactic process of transposition and juxtaposition of images that we have seen Gaudí adopt in the stables of Torre Satalia? Here, however, it is not merely a question of fragments and details, but of complete enveloping ambiences whose images and appearance are superimposed and change as we pass through one door after the other. We looked in the last chapter at the origins of this summational form of composing in Gaudí's work, and at how this obsession with *varietas*, which is also manifested as a constant quest for novelty, coincides perfectly with a very specific demonstration of wealth: that display whose condition of exhibition is determined by excessive consumption. We have also seen how Gaudí's working process generated points of profound dematerialization in the stables and gatehouse pavilion. In the succession of interior ambiences we are describing here, this dematerialization is taken to extremes. Indeed, in three of these rooms, the wall of the façade is in the form of a system of filters, in the series of columns, arranged in parallel, with their different heights and their different syncopated rhythms. Thus, the inner series forms parabolic arcades while the outer series, which is lower to leave space for a skylight, supports an alternating sequence of lintels at two different heights. And there is a third filter formed by the wall of the gallery, also with an alternating sequence of windows of two different sizes. In each of the colonnades the elements—capitals, bases—are resolved according to different models, with the stepped clover-leaf plinths supporting columns of different series, syncopating further still the rhythmic sequences. We could hardly find a better example of disengagement engendered by the practice of an extreme *varietas*: the wall, of which the three rows of columns testify not only to its former existence, but as well to its virtual thickness, its mass, has literally disappeared, surviving only in a succession of syncopated rhythms and series described by the unexpected and arbitrary break

of the cadences they suggest, whose parallel arrangement evidences the contrasts even more clearly and underscores the absolute impossibility of their articulation. At the same time, this disengagement, this dematerialization, takes on an even more profound meaning when we consider the appearance of the façade: a wall of monotonously jointed grey stone, the small openings in which give it an opaque and impenetrable air that contemporaries were quick to interpret as the image of a fortress.[116] But without forgetting the relationship that the central salon establishes with the rest of the rooms, we should now take a look at another detail that is no less important for being less apparent. A look at the plan of the main floor of the town house suffices to show how the imaginary axes that cross one another perpendicularly in the center of the salon do not impose an order on the rooms around it: both the main door and the large window that communicates it with the family sitting room are slightly displaced with respect to one of these axes, and the same effect is repeated with even greater subtlety in relation to the other axis, between the door leading to the chapel and the stairwell opposite. Such displacements, although all but imperceptible at first sight, manifest themselves with stridency as a result of the construction solution employed by Gaudí to support the gallery running round the salon at the height of the first floor: large corbels whose regular arrangement contrasts with the irregularity of the lower openings, from which they are set far apart in some cases while, in others, they are almost superimposed on them, with ostentatious assertiveness. The question is, how are we to interpret these breaks, these deformations, this exaggerated representation of variety if not as a demonstration of the unity of a continuously surrounded center? In effect, from within the central salon itself, great openings, parabolic on one side, rectangular on the other, establish visual communication with all of the rooms and permit a continuous, transverse supervision of the whole of the building. So while the complexity of the itineraries, the displacements of the rooms and the extreme variety of ambiences and elements we

have described ensure that physical communication between the rooms is subject to the impossibility of perceiving the axes in their entirety, visual communication between the rooms is, in contrast, direct and immediate. Much more direct and immediate, indeed, than the visual communication between these peripheral rooms and the exterior, from which they are separated by filters of parallel colonnades, galleries and screens. If we look more closely at the floor plan we can see that the rooms immediately surrounding this great, obsessively interior salon configure, thanks to the sightlines created by Gaudí, a cross. A cross, nonetheless, that is purely virtual: the layout of the rooms, with their elements, as we have said, always set very slightly off the axes, alludes to a cross but does not actually form one. Nonetheless, the approximate order of the salon at the level of the main floor goes on thereafter to become a perfect order. From its four corners spring the regular parabolic arches on top of which the dome, also parabolic in section, rises rapidly, its vertical void running the entire height of the building. A glance at the form of this dome serves to reveal its meaning: perforated by small luminous apertures arranged in successive circular sections and crowned by a dazzling oculus, this dome *is* the sky. But it is also a condensed transcendent image of the world of variety we have just been looking at: the *oculus* is the *unicum* in which all the variety of the stars finds its significance, thanks to which it ceases to be mere arbitrariness to become firmament. At the same time the extreme *varietas*, crowned as it is by the inalterable rotundity of the dome, ceases to be disorder to become an image of the world: a transcendently vertical image—earth, heavens—in which the extreme formalization of its opposites as such brings these together in a mutual exaltation of their most profound qualities. What other goal, indeed, was Gaudí pursuing with his obsessive technique of contrasts? Higher still, on the roof, the dome projects up in a tall conical lantern. But this is not a smooth geometric solid devoid of properties. On the contrary, its surface, covered with small stones, seeks to evoke the natural ruggedness of a rock

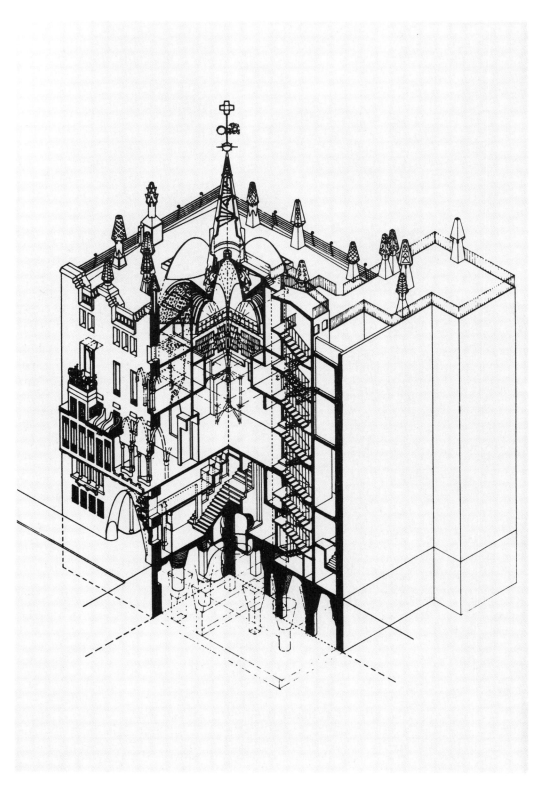

formation, a mountain: the allusions to the sacred mountain of Montserrat, charged with Wagnerian reminiscences and evocations, are obviously relevant in the symbolic context we described above, but not sufficient. This "mountain" is perforated in different ways in different sections: with a host of little grottos in the lower sections; with eight windows in the form of parabolic arches facing the cardinal points in the intermediate section; with alternatively ordered skylights in the upper parts. The cone, imminently vertical in its proportions, rapidly ascends to its vertex, topped with the symbols described above: the globe of the world, on top of which are the bat and the disk of the sun and, crowning it all, the cross—this is the first of Gaudí's buildings to culminate in a cross. From base to summit, this lantern has a height only slightly less than that of the interior salon from the floor to the *oculus*: it is not too difficult to deduce the inverted equivalence of the two structures. In effect, the vertical of the salon serves to unite the earth—the square room that was the hub of the family's social life, and like life itself ordered only virtually, given that it actually abounds in small but constantly repeated deviations—and the sky—the starry dome, absolutely symmetrical, rounded. This same cosmic order is represented in the lantern: pebbled, dotted with openings that are more intelligible in form and system the higher they are, with its crowning cross, as we have said, not only represents but *is* the sacred mountain, around which the variety of the chimneys with their shimmering colors and willful forms—a "dazzling and capricious multitude," writes Rahola[117]—ceases to be uncertainty, lightness, inconsequence, mere artistic caprice, and carries to the limit what occurred on the floors below to become a symphony. The unity of the world in its variety: this is taken to the limit in Gaudí's roof. But there is still more. The *trencadís* cladding on the chimneys, amid this ecstasy of forms, also takes on significant meaning. Rahola has given us a marvelous description of this roof: "Could there be anything more original than this cluster of fantastic chimneys fashioned from the waste of a building site? The shards of glass, useless bits of marble, fragments of broken tile, the remains of a lime kiln, combined at random in ingenious and fanciful forms compose a brilliant whole, rich in color, to show that a true artist can bring forth beauty from the very rubble itself."[118] Such a paragraph, closely contemporary with the opening of the building, could hardly be more telling. The leftovers, the waste, the remnants from the work—its rubbish, in other words—are no longer rubbish in the hands of the true artist, who puts everything to use. He makes use of it, evidently, but how? The lowliest material—the useless ends, the rubble from the wrecker's ball, the cast-offs, broken shards—is released from its contemptible insignificance at this highest point, the roof terrace: it is, in sum, redeemed of its condition, cleansed of its sin—the sin of being material abandoned to the vile state of uselessness—in a triumphant heaven. And what is this, if not the perfect summary of the meaning of the entire building, constructed as a conjuring away of the banal, as an exorcism enacted against reality, against the material? And we find this same representation arising at other, equally basic places around the town house. We might pause here to consider one of the most intimate of all, the master bedroom. A arcade of three arches, the highest in the middle, marks the access: the polished marble columns, with capitals in rounded forms whose turgidness is suggestive, are suddenly swathed in prickly bands of wrought iron that are literally nailed to them. The effect of this spiked iron is all the more unexpected and violent in its contrast with the smoothness of the almost liquescent marble. But what is this if not the image of sacrifice that overrides the temptation of the material? We shall have occasion in a later chapter to look further into this issue, which is fundamental to understanding the constant and painful contraction that the material suffers in Gaudí's work. Let us now return to the roof of the Palau Güell.

The sacred mountain, rising up out of rubble and variety, turns, as we have seen, disconcert into concert: it is evident that what is represented here is a world well founded at its center. The broken shards, Rahola tells us, are combined at random: for all that so many people have done so, it is absurd to think of Gaudí's work with bottle glass, bits of porcelain or ceramic an anticipation of collage or other techniques of contemporary art.[119] For Gaudí, the random had, as we shall see, a redemptive and therefore profoundly religious meaning: chance, then, is Providence, and the artist is no more than its vehicle. But if the lantern is the repetition of the great domed salon, at the same time, both encounter their finished image in the building as a whole. Together, the basement as hell, the salon as earth and sky and the terrace as triumphant heaven symbolically define the entire house as the image of cosmic order. Let us go back now to the plans of the building that Eusebi Güell had drawn up in 1910, to look at the cross-section. The design could not be more intentional: in it we see the exact coincidence of the three cosmic strata in a vertical succession that makes up the very center of the building. The spiral ramp leading down to the basement, literally embedded in the depths of the earth, is the starting point of an axis that continues without deviation through the lofty salon and culminates in the vertex with the cone crowned by the cross. Only the diagonal of the main stairway interrupts the sequence, and even then not essentially: it is simply a case of avoiding a direct connection between the inferior and the superior. Eusebi Güell's town house is thus an *axis mundi*: an axis of the world, a place of sacred communication, of the founding of order. In our description of the house we have looked at the labyrinthine nature of its itineraries, the absence of any direct, continual, communication between its floors and ambiences. We are now in a position to understand this lack of connection more fully: the unity of the building is only achieved transcendently, and is not demonstrable on the basis of use. One highly significant detail will help us to see this more clearly: there is only one element in the Palau Güell—the service stairs—that runs from top to bottom without interruption through all its floors, but Gaudí represented this stairway as a provisional structure: suspended from cables, it could be removed at any time.[120] In its contingency it could not compete with that other axis that also runs through the whole building (albeit invisibly, or at least not evidently) in a way that has nothing to do with function (or even, in the last

analysis, with architecture regarded as a mere medium), embedding it in the depths of the earth and the sky.

We now appreciate the extent to which the Palau Güell is immovable property. Gaudí has condensed myths and symbols in a material substance that, having been redeemed, effectively disappears. Air, pure spirit, carries with it the *axis mundi* that empties the palace. The foundation can only be total, foundation of the world: the prince, one and unique, lends it his credence.

[1] Despite his exceptional importance there is still no in-depth study, either global or partial, of his personality or his activities. What we have are hagiographies such as: M. d'Esplugues, *El primer Compte de Güell*, Barcelona, 1921, which we shall consider at some length in due course; P. Rodón, *Eusebi Güell, industrial*, Badalona, 1935; P. Gual Villalbi, *Eusebio Güell y Bacigalupi. Primer conde de Güell*, Barcelona, 1953. See, too, the disappointing: G.W. McDonogh, *Las buenas familias de Barcelona*, cit., pp. 112–20 and 280–90. It is well worth consulting Güell's own writings, especially those collected in: E. Güell y Bacigalupi, "Tres discursos," *Lectura popular. Biblioteca d'autors catalans*, vol. XVII, Barcelona, pp. 387–460.
[2] See: (various authors), "L'Ajuntament de Barcelona i el régim restauracionista. 1875–1901," *L'Avenç*, no. 116, June 1988. See, too: id., "La Restauració de 1875: una reacció conservadora," *L'Avenç*, no. 85, September 1985. In general: J. Varela, *Los amigos políticos. Partidos, elecciones y caciquismo en la Restauración. 1875–1900*, Madrid, 1977.
[3] There is a reference to Güell's supposed participation in the founding of the movement in: *Quaderns d'Estudi*, October 1918, p. 75, reprinted in: M. d'Esplugues, op. cit., p. 169. I have found no evidence to show that Güell was "officially" involved in the association. Here again, then, what is significant is the accumulation of "suppositions" that contemporary commentators produced in relation to the man as myth, something that happened, as we shall see, on a number of occasions. From here on, then, it will be unnecessary repeat that these are "exemplary suppositions," which is precisely what interests us here. On *La*

*Jove Catalunya:* M. Font, "La Jove Catalunya," *Revista de Catalunya*, III, vol. IV, no. 21, March 1926; L. Figueras, "La Jove Catalunya," *Lluís Domènech i Montaner i el director d'orquestra*, cit., pp. 45–47. After the present book was written an interesting study was published by M. Tomás, *La Jove Catalunya. Antologia*, Barcelona, 1992, in which there are no direct references to Eusebi Güell.
[4] Güell's supposed presidency is mentioned in almost all of the obituaries and notices published on his death. See, for example, those in *La Veu de Catalunya*, July 9, 1918 and July 11, 1918, in which the matter is raised on more than one occasion. Reprinted in: M. d'Esplugues, op. cit., pp. 139–50. See: J. Trías Vejarano, *Almirall y los orígenes del catalanismo*, Madrid, 1975; J. Galofre, *El primer congrés catalanista (1880)*, Barcelona, 1979, and above all the still indispensable: I. Molas, *Lliga Catalana. Un estudi d'estasiologia*, Barcelona, 1972, vol. I, pp. 16–21.
[5] See: J. Camps i Arboix, *El Memorial de Greuges presentat al rei Alfons XII*, Barcelona, 1968; J.A. González Casanova, *Federalismo y autonomía. Cataluña y el Estado español*, Barcelona, 1979, pp. 147–55; (various authors), *El Memorial de Greuges i el catalanisme politic*, Barcelona, 1986.
[6] E. Güell, "Discurs pronunciat en lo dinar donat en lo restaurant Martin a la Comissió que va anar a Madrid a fer entrega al Rey de la Memoria redactada per acord de la reunió de la Llotja," *Tres discursos*, cit., pp. 387–89. The ideas expressed by Güell are perfectly in line with the ideology of the Centre Catalá. For example, everything is due to "the fertile seed sown by our fathers, and cul-

tivated with faith and confidence by all of us"; or: "always turning a deaf ear to the tempting voice of the political sirens, we forsake any kind of political affiliation in order to follow with integrity the sacred standard of the motherland," and, a little later: "above the turbulent waves of the ever stormy sea of politics there rises calm and steadfast the majestic figure of Royal power."
[7] I. Molas, op. cit., vol. I, p. 24; J.A. González Casanova, op. cit., pp. 156–60. On the controversy surrounding the Exhibition: M. Jove, "Polèmiques, expectatives i valoracions a l'entorn del certamen," cit.
[8] See, for example: S. Lacal, *El Libro de Honor. Apuntes para la historia de la Exposición Universal de Barcelona*, Barcelona, 1889, p. 56.
[9] I. Molas, op. cit., vol. I, pp. 19–25.
[10] Ibid., p. 24.
[11] See: I. Molas, "Las bases de Manresa y la reforma del Estado español. Comentarios a la base primera," *Revista jurídica de Cataluña*, 1970, pp. 137–58; J.A. González Casanova, op. cit., pp. 161–66.
[12] See: I. Molas, op. cit., vol. I, pp. 37–46; B. de Riquer, *Lliga Regionalista: la burgesia catalana i el nacionalisme (1898–1904)*, Barcelona, 1977.
[13] See note 7.
[14] On Güell's relations with Alsina see, among others: P. Gual Villalbi, *Eusebio Güell y Bacigalupi...*, cit., pp. 21–22.
[15] M. d'Esplugues, *El primer compte de Güell*, cit., p. 98.
[16] On Picó i Campamar: M. Tomás, "Ramón Picó i Campamar (1848–1916)," *Randa*, vol. IX, 1979, pp. 159–70; the same author has published editions of Picó's writings: R. Picó i Campamar, *Obra poètica*, Montserrat, 1983; id., *Discursos*

*i parlaments*, Montserrat, 1985.

[17] On Prat de la Riba: R. Olivar Bertrand, *Prat de la Riba*, Barcelona, 1964; I. Molas, preface and edition of A. Rovira i Virgili, *Prat de la Riba*, Barcelona, 1968; J.M. Ainaud, E. Jardi, *Prat de la Riba, home de govern*, Barcelona, 1973; J. Solé-Tura, *Catalanismo y revolución burguesa*, Madrid, 1974.

[18] E. Prat de la Riba, *Ley jurídica de la industria. Estudio de filosofía jurídica seguido de bases para la formación de un Código Industrial*, Barcelona, 1898. This was an extended version of his doctoral thesis; we shall concern ourselves with its content in due course, in chapter 4.

[18] E. Güell, "Discurs presidencial dels Jocs Florals de Barcelona," *Tres discursos*, cit., pp. 393–406. We shall concern ourselves with this speech in detail in chapter 3.

[20] In almost all of the literature on Gaudí 1910 is given as the year in which Güell was made a count. In fact it was 1908: A. and A. García Carraffa, *Diccionario heráldico y genealógico de apellidos españoles y americanos*, vol. XXXIX, Salamanca, 1921, pp. 172–76; id., *El solar catalán, valenciano y balear*, vol. II, San Sebastian, 1968, pp. 318–19. It is worth noting that the motto used by Güell on his coat of arms (see the description in: J. Bergos Masso, *Antoni Gaudí i el Comte de Güell*, Barcelona, 1969, p. 7), "Ahir pastor, avuy senyor" ["Yesterday a shepherd, today a gentleman"], is from a poem by J. Verdaguer, "Amor y Ventura," *Jovenívoles* (J. Verdaguer, *Obres Completes*, Barcelona, 1943, pp. 947–49).

[21] On relations between the Maura government and the Lliga centered on the Semana Trágica, see the essential: J.C. Ullman, *La Semana Trágica. Estudio socioeconómico de las causas del anticlericalismo en España, 1898–1912*, Barcelona, 1972; see, too: A. Fabra Ribas, *La Semana Trágica. El caso Maura. El krausismo*, Madrid, 1975; and from a different point of view: J. Romero Maura, *"La Rosa de Fuego." El obrerismo barcelonés de 1899 a 1900*, Madrid, 1989 (reed.).

[22] Cit. in M. d'Esplugues, op. cit., p. 144.

[23] All of these data are repeated in the biographies or obituaries we have cited above. On the ceremonial of the British court as invented in the course of the nineteenth century and imitated by courts all over Europe: D. Cannadine, "Context, execució i significat del ritual: la monarquia britànica i l'invent de la tradició, periode 1820–1977," in E.J. Hobsbawm and T. Ranger, *The Invention of Tradition* (Catalan translation: *L'invent de la tradició*, Vic, 1988; pp. 101–60). On the image of

the British in Catalonia in the latter part of the nineteenth century it is interesting to consult an author who was, as we shall see in due course, close to Eusebi Güell: F. Rahola, *Los ingleses vistos por un latino. Impresiones de viaje*, Barcelona, 1908, but first published in instalments in *La Ilustración* during 1882.

[24] C. Baudelaire, "Le peintre de la vie moderne," *L'art romantique. Oeuvres Complètes III*, Paris, p. 91.

[25] C. Baudelaire, op. cit., p. 94. And a little later: "Dandyism is the last glimmer of heroism in its decadence."

[26] Vicomte De Güell, *D'Alphonse XII a Tut-Ank-Ammon. Perspectives*, Paris, 1931, p. 38.

[27] One or two examples may serve to draw attention to the subject. Thus, commenting on the difference between the severity of the façade and the richness of the interior of the Palau Güell, F. Rahola writes: "the cause of this disproportion we may perhaps find in the idea of the reconcentration of the *home*" ("Palacio Güell de Barcelona. Planeado y construido por Gaudí," *La Vanguardia*, August 3, 1890, pp. 45); or: "That slender, elegant and most proper silhouette of Eusebi Güell that displayed the wardrobe of a gentleman and the manners of a prince" (M. d'Esplugues, op. cit., p. 82); or, indeed, among many others, the obituary in *La Veu de Catalunya* (July 9, 1918) to which we have already referred, which begins: "The count of Güell, great nobleman, patrician, gentleman, is dead." There is also an uncorroborated legend, which no doubt springs from the association with Güell, that Gaudí himself was something of a dandy in his youth (this, it is worth noting, makes his subsequent religiousness all the more telling: it is the old story of Paul's conversion on the road to Damascus), first mentioned by his first biographer and repeated in all of the following histories: "(Gaudí) dressed with extraordinary elegance, his table was always set with the choicest foods, he did not fail to take his drive in the coach or in his regular attendance at the Teatro del Liceo during the opera season…," and, in due course, after having remarked on his relationship with Güell: "The dandyism of Antoni Gaudí ties in perfectly with Baudelaire's definition: to be rich and love to work" (J.F. Ràfols, op. cit., pp. 24–28).

[28] See: P. Gual Villalbi, op. cit., pp. 17–19.

[29] For example: "The count of Güell was a lover of books, of good sculpture, of fine fabrics, of beautiful architecture and lovely music. Those who have attended a party

in his town house on vía Nova will have appreciated this perfectly … from the harmonies that, in waves, have filled the marvelous perspectives of Gaudí's art, from the discovery on all sides, on a stretch of wall or in some out-of-the-way gallery, of extraordinary wonders of the sculpture or painting of times past and present" *(La Vanguardia*, July 9, 1918).

[30] J. Puiggarí, *Monografia de la casa palau i museu del Escm. Sr. D. Eusebi Güell y Bacigalupi*, Barcelona, 1894.

[31] See: R. Casellas, "La pintura gótico catalana en el siglo XV," *Centenario del descubrimiento de América. Conferencias leídas en el Ateneo Barcelonés sobre el estado de la cultura española y particularmente catalana en el siglo XV*, Barcelona, 1893, pp. 175–201. A fundamental work on the subject is: J. Castellanos, *Raimon Casellas i el modernisme*, cit., vol. II, above all pp. 75–91.

[32] "Nuestra réplica: D. Eusebio Güell," *El Radical*, July 12, 1918, reprinted in M. d'Esplugues, op. cit., p. 155. P. Gual Villalbi refers to the unanimity of newspapers of all shades of opinion to pay tribute to Güell (op. cit., pp. 12–13). This was obviously a necessary claim in relation to a man who, as we shall see, sought to make himself the "patriarch" of Catalonia: for example, in an account of a dinner for the press following a visit to the Colonia Güell in 1910, we read: "There we sat, the editors of all the newspapers, from the most advanced on the radical left to the most extreme right" (*Semana Social de España. Quinto Curso. 1910*, Barcelona, 1912, p. 170).

[33] A commonplace that culminates in his relationship with Gaudí. It is worth recalling here the comparison drawn by J.F. Ràfols in 1928, a comparison much in favor in hagiographies of the architect and his patron: "What Michelozzo Michelozzi was to Cosme el Magnificent [sic], Antoni Gaudí is in relation to Sr. Eusebi Güell" (op. cit., p. 25).

[34] Isabel Güell set to music the verses of Catalan poets such as Verdaguer and Picó i Campamar, and composed minor pieces of church music, including a *Stabat Mater* in 1917; the output of Eusebi Guell i López, viscount Güell, is more varied and surprising, and in many respects, interesting for its significance: *New Basis for the Foundation of Geometry*, Manchester, 1900; id., *Considérations sur le concepte de la Mode dans l'Art*, Barcelona, 1903; id., *Cassius i Helena. Poema dramàtic*, Barcelona, 1903; id., *D'Alphonse XII a Tut-Ank-Ammon*, cit.; id, *Espacio, relación y posición. Ensayo sobre los fundamentos de la geometría*, Madrid, 1924.

[35] A. Gual, *Mitja vida de teatre. Memòries*, Barcelona, 1960, pp. 154–69. The author himself recalls the play with some reserve: Vicomte de Güell, *D'Alphonse XII a Tut-Ank-Ammon*, cit., pp. 115–21. Nevertheless, it also attracted praise, such as Carner's appreciation in *La Renaixença*.

[36] D. Pérez, "Un catalán ilustre," *El Liberal*, July 24, 1918, reprinted in M. d'Esplugues, op. cit., p. 156.

[37] Op. cit. In addition to Miquel d'Esplugues' analysis it contains Güell's speech to the delegates of the Centre Català in the presence of Alfonso XII (pp. 131–34) and an important "obituary appendix," pp. (137–85), together with the many obituaries and death notices that appeared in Catalan, Spanish and foreign newspapers and magazines, and the telegrams and letters of condolence received by the family. On Miquel d'Esplugues: J. Massot i Muntaner, *Aproximació a la història religiosa de la Catalunya contemporània*, cit., pp. 59–83; id., *L'Església catalana al segle XX*, cit., pp. 79–81.

[38] On the aims and repercussions of this book, published in Barcelona, see the short but significant commentary by J. Massot i Muntaner, *L'Església catalana al segle XX*, cit., p. 79.

[39] M. d'Esplugues, op. cit., pp. 26–27. This was, as d'Esplugues acknowledges in a note, a quote from *La réforme intellectuelle et morale*, Paris, 1871, and it is not his only quotation from the latter book. See, too, p. 29: "No hi ha reialesa sense aristocràcia…" On the political significance of the book: J.F. Revel, "Les origins de la France contemporaine" foreword to E. Renan, *La réforme…*, Paris, 1967. The irrationalism of d'Esplugues may also stem indirectly from his tendentious reading of Renan. On the irrationalist strands in Renan's thought, see: H.W. Wardman, *Renan, historien philosophe*, Paris, 1979.

[40] On Renan and Spain, in addition to the references in H. Juretschke's classic study *España ante Francia*, Madrid, 1940, see: T. Pecchia, *Renan en España. Contribución al estudio de la expresión religiosa en la literatura española, 1870–1915*, Ann Arbor, Michigan, 1983; A. de Blas Guerrero, "Estudio preliminar" in E. Renan, *¿Qué es una nación? Cartas a Strauss*, Madrid, 1987; and above all: F. Pérez Gutiérrez, *Renan en España. Religión, ética y política*, Madrid, 1988, although the section on Catalonia is disappointing, pp. 252–59.

[41] M. d'Esplugues, op. cit., p. 27.

[42] Ibid., p. 33.

[43] Ibid., p. 66.

44 P. Gener, *La Mort et le Diable. Histoire et philosophie de ces deux negations suprèmes*, Paris, 1880, translated into Spanish in two vols., Barcelona, 1884; id., *Heregías. Estudios de crítica inductiva sobre asuntos españoles*, Barcelona and Madrid, 1887. On the article in *L'Avenç* and Torras i Bages' reply see: E. Valentí, *Els clàssics i la literatura catalana moderna*, Barcelona, 1973, pp. 152–87, as well as the references to Gener on pp. 15–54.

45 See for example: J. Torras i Bages, *La tradició catalana* (1892), Barcelona, 1981, especially pp. 66–70; E. Prat de la Riba, *Ley jurídica de la industria*, Barcelona, 1898, pp. 257–71; id., *La nacionalitat catalana* (1906), Barcelona, 1978, especially pp. 69–86.

46 E. Prat de la Riba, "L'Ignasi Girona," *La Veu de Catalunya*, September 2, 1905, cit. in J. Solé-Tura, *Catalanismo y revolución burguesa*, cit., p. 237.

47 M. d'Esplugues, op. cit., p. 74.

48 M. d'Esplugues, op. cit., above all pp. 28–30 and pp. 35–38. This idealization of the Tarragona landscape has also been used by a number of Gaudí's biographers as one of the origins of his architectural sensibility: Ràfols writes "the light of the Camp de Tarragona" with ineffable feeling in the opening lines of his book (J.F. Ràfols, op. cit., p. 9).

49 Eusebi Güell's Italian descent, which his biographers have used to great effect in constructing his image as prince and patron, was on his mother's side: in 1845 Joan Güell married Camila Bacigalupi Dulcet, Eusebi's mother, who came from a family of moderately successful Genoan merchants who had settled in Barcelona. After her untimely death he married her sister Francisca.

50 I. Puig-Boada, *El pensament de Gaudí*, Barcelona, 1981, p. 167.

51 M. d'Esplugues, op. cit., p. 111. The project, by the engineer S. Thos i Codina, proposed to carry the water across the River Llobregat by means of aqueducts, to a great cistern in Pedralbes. See: E. Güell, *Manantial de Garraf*, Barcelona, 1899, and also the alternative project by M. Durán y Gost, *Estudio financiero comparativo entre la aportada de las aguas de Garraf y la del canal de S. Pedro de Casseras*, Barcelona; id., *Abastecimiento de aguas a Barcelona Rectificación a (...) D. Eusebio Güell i Bacigalupi (...)*, Barcelona 1899.

52 E. Güell, *Manantial de Garraf*, cit., p. 12.

53 Picó and his poem are discussed at length in the first section of chapter 4.

54 See: J.Ll. Marfany, "La cultura de la burgesía barcelonesa en la fi del segle," *Serra d'Or*, cit.; id., "Estetes i menestrals," *L'Avenç*, cit.; id., "El modernisme," *Història de la literatura catalana*, cit., vol. VIII, pp. 87–93; J. Castellanos, *Raimon Casellas i el modernisme*, cit., vol. I, pp. 219–54.

55 M. d'Esplugues, op. cit., p. 111.

56 Ibid., p. 88, where he also treats Güell as a legendary figure, as he does elsewhere, for example, p. 5.

57 On the strength of the great business opportunities created by Spanish neutrality in the First World War, the Lliga (in the midst of dramatic social conflicts and a crisis of state power; and following the death of its leader Prat de la Riba) launched a campaign for Catalan autonomy, one of the consequences of which was the entry of one of its members, Cambó, into the Madrid government as a minister in 1918; the strategy failed, and on Cambó's return to Barcelona he pronounced his famous phrase: "Monarchy? Republic? Catalonia!." There was a continuing series of government crises, centered on colonial disasters in North Africa (the battle of Annual, 1921), worsening social conflict, and severe repression in Barcelona (between 1917 and 1922 there were more than eight hundred attacks, over half of them directed against workers; the province of Barcelona was under a state of emergency from 1919 until 1922, with constitutional privileges suspended), and the Lliga mounted a new campaign for autonomy that in 1921 put Cambó once again in charge of the Ministry of Finance; finally, the coup by Primo de Rivera in Barcelona (1923) imposed a provisional end to the situation. Very briefly, various aspects of the situation can be consulted in: A. Balcells, *El sindicalisme a Barcelona. 1916–1923*, Barcelona, 1965; J.A. Lacomba, *La crisis española de 1917*, Madrid, 1970; J.M. Poblet, *El moviment autonomista a Catalunya dels anys 1918–1919*, Barcelona, 1970.

58 There is an overview of various aspects of this normalization in (various authors), "La Mancomunitat de Catalunya" in *L'Avenç*, no. 3, June 1977. Nevertheless, the most acute interpretation of its significance is still to be found in Marfany's writings on the crisis of Modernism: J.Ll. Marfany, *Aspectes del modernisme*, Barcelona, 1975, pp. 13–96; id., "Modernisme i noucentisme, amb algunes consideracions sobre el concepte de moviment cultural," *Els Marges*, no. 26, 1982, pp. 31–42, and in Castellanos' study of certain specific aspects: J. Castellanos, "Josep Pijoan i els orígens del Noucentisme," *Els Marges*, no. 14, September 1978,

pp. 31–49; id., "Noucentisme i censura (a propòsit de les cartes d'Eugeni d'Ors a Raimon Casellas)," *Els Marges*, nos. 22–23, May–September 1981, pp. 73–95. And see, too: J. Cassasas i Ymbert "La configuració del sector intelectual-profesional a la Catalunya de la Restauració," *Recerques*, no. 8, 1978 pp. 103–31; id., *Intellectuals, professionals i polítics a la Catalunya contemporània (1850–1920)*, Barcelona, 1989.

59 M. d'Esplugues, op. cit., p. 104.

60 J. Puiggarí, *Monografía de la casa palau i museu...*, cit., p. 11.

61 The contrast between the "sumptuous palace" and the neighborhood in which it was built is a commonplace in histories of Gaudí. For example: Ll. Bonet-Garí, "Arquitectura en el palacio Güell," *San Jorge*, July 1954, p. 62; C. Martinell, *Gaudí. Su vida, su teoría, su obra*, cit., p. 250; S. Tarragó, *Gaudí*, Barcelona, 1974, p. 33, etc.

62 On the formation of the Rambla see: (various authors), *Inicis de la urbanística municipal de Barcelona*, cit., pp. 24–26; A. García Espuche and M. Guardia Bassols, *Espai i societat a la Barcelona pre-industrial*, cit., pp. 72–74. On the mansions mentioned here: A. Sáenz-Rico, *El virrey Amat*, Barcelona, 1967; M. Arranz and J. Fuguet, *El palau dels March de Reus*, Barcelona, 1987; S. Alcolea, *El palau Moja...*, cit.

63 This is borne out by Verdaguer's own personal reminiscences of the Torre Satalia in his letters and in the dedications and other writings to which we referred in the last chapter.

64 J. Bassegoda, *El gran Gaudí*, cit., p. 286.

65 E. Renan, *Essais de morale et de critique*, Paris, 1859, pp. 359–62. See, for example, Baudelaire's opinion: "L'idée d'utilité, la plus hostile du monde à l'idée du beauté" (C. Baudelaire, "Notes nouvelles sur Edgar Poe" [1857], in *Oeuvres Complètes*, Paris, 1975, vol. II, p. 327). On the aristocratism of Renan and others, see: P. Lidsky, *Les écrivains contre la Commune*, Paris, 1970.

66 J. Puiggarí, op. cit., p. 6.

67 "Notas locales," *La Vanguardia*, December 28, 1889, p. 8. For more on this, see: P. Voltes y Bou, "Cómo imaginaron Rusiñol y otros humoristas que sería la Barcelona de 1889," *La Vanguardia*, June 25, 1964, p. 27.

68 J. Puiggarí, op. cit., p. 6.

69 Vicomte de Güell, op. cit., p. 56.

70 F. Rahola, "Palacio de Güell en Barcelona. Planeado y construido por Gaudí," *La Vanguardia*, August 3, 1890, pp. 4–5, reprinted in *La Ilustración Hispano-Americana*, nos. 532, 533 and 535, January 11 and 18, and February 1, 1891.

71 F. Rahola, "Palacio de Güell en Barcelona. Planeado y construido por Gaudí," *La Vanguardia*, cit., p. 5.

72 Aleix Clapés—an interesting figure who has still to receive a satisfactory general or partial study—was, among other things, a furniture designer (see his pieces for the Ibarz family: *Guía de la Casa-Museu Gaudí*, Barcelona, 1989, p. 10), a photographer and the owner of the art magazine *Hispania* in its final period; but above all, like Carrière, he was a portrait painter. There is more on Clapés and his place in the Barcelona scene in J. Castellanos, *Raimon Casellas i el modernisme*, cit., vol. I: pp. 154–55 give Casellas' opinion of one of Clapés' paintings, *Els pobres*, of 1896, while pp. 265–68 have more information on his involvement with *Hispania* in its various phases. On responses to Carrière in late nineteenth-century Barcelona, see R. Casellas, "Paris Artístico, V:. Eugenio Carrière," *La Vanguardia*, May 26, 1893. Casellas saw Carrière as a representative of the new art and an example for modern Catalan artists to follow: J. Castellanos, op. cit., vol. I, pp. 134–39.

73 Vicomte de Güell, op. cit., pp. 50–51.

74 See: E. de Beaumont, B. Davillier and A. Dupont-Auberville, *Atelier de Fortuny. Oeuvre posthume. Objets d'art et de curiosité, etc.*, Paris, 1875. There are references to this in almost all of the published studies; for example: J. Ciervo, *El arte y el vivir de Fortuny*, Barcelona, 1921, pp. 9–17; see, too, the analysis by C. García, "Fortuny como coleccionista, restaurador y artesano," *Fragmentos*, no. 7, 1986, pp. 56–65. The relative wealth of published studies shows the extent to which Fortuny was in vogue in late nineteenth-century Barcelona; in addition to the numerous articles and albums, it is worth noting a couple of important studies contemporary with the Palau Güell, by J. Yxart (*Fortuny. Ensayo biográfico-crítico*, Barcelona, 1882) and F. Miquel i Badía (*Fortuny. Su vida y obras*, Barcelona, 1887). See: J. Ainaud de Lasarte, "La fortuna de Fortuny," in the catalogue *Fortuny, 1838–1874*, Barcelona, 1989, pp. 65–97.

75 F. Rahola, op. cit., p. 4.

76 A. Toussenel, *L'esprit des bêtes. Zoologie passionnelle. Mammifères de France*, Paris, 1884, pp. 89–92. For links with other contemporary phenomena and personalities, such as Grandville, see W. Benjamin, *Parigi capitale del XIX secolo. I "passages" di Parigi*, Turin, 1986, pp. 254–55, from which I quote here.

77 F. Rahola, op. cit., pp. 4–5.

[78] C. Baudelaire, *Oeuvres Complètes III. L'art romantique*, Paris, p. 249.

[79] F. Rahola, op. cit., p. 5.

[80] Ibid., p. 4.

[81] This is an idea Wagner developed in his *Music of the Future*. There is a Catalan translation from 1909 (R. Wagner, *Obres teóriques i critiques I. Musica del pervindre. L'art i la revolució*, Barcelona, 1909, pp. 66–67, in relation to the image of the forest and the infinite melody), but the text had already been warmly debated in Barcelona musical circles many years before that: see J. Marsillach, *Ricardo Wagner. Ensayo biográfico-crítico*, Barcelona, 1878, who expresses his disagreement with the idea on p. 95. This was a persistent source of controversy among Barcelona's Wagnerians. For example, Letamendi, in contrast to Marsillach, considered that Wagner "has resolved with judicious discernment the eternal and vexing question of realism in art" (J. de Letamendi, "La Música del Porvenir y el porvenir de mi patria," (1884), in *Obras Completas*, Madrid, 1907, vol. IV, p. 200, with which the quotation from Rahola is clearly related).

[82] On Wagner in Catalonia see, in the first instance: (various authors), *XXV Conferéncies donadas a l'Associació Wagneriana. 1902–1906*, Barcelona, 1908, and: A. Janes i Nadal, *L'obra de Richard Wagner a Barcelona*, Barcelona, 1983; id., *Wagner i Catalunya. Antologia de textos i gràfics*, Barcelona, 1983; and more generally: X. Aviñoa, *La música i el modernisme*, Barcelona, 1985. Güell, who was one of the sponsors of the Societat Filharmònica de Barcelona, is recollected by his son (Vicomte de Güell, op. cit., pp. 58–59) as attending the concerts at Bayreuth, and in 1899, for example, recommended the musician Antoni Ribera to Cosima Wagner (A. Janes i Nadal, op. cit., p. 210).

[83] J. Marsillach, *Ricardo Wagner. Ensayo biográfico-crítico*, cit., and also A. Fargas y Soler, *Observaciones al ensayo biográfico-crítico de R. Wagner por J Marsillach*, Barcelona, 1878, and J. Marsillach, *Contrarréplica a las observaciones...*, Barcelona, 1878. See: J. Pena, "En Joaquim Marsillach," *XXV Conferències...*, cit., pp. 29–46; A. Janes i Nadal, op. cit., pp. 43–56.

[84] J. de Letamendi, "La aparición de Ricardo Wagner deducida de la naturaleza del arte teatral" (1878), in *Obras Completas*, Madrid, 1907, vol. I. See: A. Janes i Nadal, op. cit., pp. 57–63; see, too: J. Pena, "El doctor Letamendi," *XXV Conferències...*, cit., pp. 207–22.

[85] See: J. Maragall, "Una mala inteligencia" and "Wagner fuera de Alemania" (1899), in *Obres Completes*, Barcelona, 1981, vol. II, pp. 112–14, pp. 114–16; R. Casellas, "Exposición general de Bellas Artes II. La pintura religiosa e histórica," *La Vanguardia*, May 1, 1894. On the former: J.Ll. Marfany, *Aspectes del modernisme*, cit., pp. 140–42; on the latter: J. Castellanos, *Raimon Casellas...*, cit., vol. I, pp. 152–53.

[86] J. de Letamendi, "Juicio postremo de Ricardo Wagner," (1883), in *Obras Completas*, cit., vol. I, p. 109.

[87] J. de Letamendi, "La Música del Porvenir y el porvenir de mi patria," (1884), in *Obras Completas*, cit., vol. IV, reprinted in gran parte, with commentary, in J. Pena, "El doctor Letamendi," *XXV Conferències...*, cit., from which I quote here, p. 217.

[88] Cit. in J. Pena, op. cit., p. 216.

[89] Ibid., p. 216.

[90] Ibid., p. 217.

[91] Ibid., p. 217.

[92] Ibid., p. 221.

[93] Ibid., p. 221.

[94] Ibid., p. 221.

[95] V. de Gibert, "Gaudí, músico potencial," *La Vanguardia*, June 17, 1928, p. 7. Francesc Pujols wrote a number of texts on Gaudí, but see above all: F. Pujols, *La visió artística i religiosa d'en Gaudí*, Barcelona, 1927, with its comparison with Wagner on pp. 19–21. See especially, in relation to the architecture of the Palau Güell, J. F[ranquesa], "Una vetllada memorable," *La Renaixenca*, Barcelona, November 4, 1894, pp. 6481–88.

[96] See: J. Pahissa, "La primera representación de Parsifal en Europa fuera de Bayreuth," first published in *Sendas y cumbres de la música española*, Buenos Aires, 1955, now in *Wagner i Catalunya*, cit., pp. 145–53.

[97] Gurnemanz says this as he enters the great nave of the church of the Grail and the set changes (act I). It is worth noting here the relationship between the domed central salon of the Palau Güell and the image of the Grail church in the sets for the 1882 performance by Paul von Joukowsky, later developed into paintings by Max Brückner: a central domed space, with galleries on the second floor, with a Byzantine structure and oriental decoration.

[98] On the Hercules paintings by Zurbarán see the catalogue *Zurbarán*, Madrid, 1988, pp. 234–45, and the analysis by J. Brown and J.H. Elliot, *Un palacio para el Rey. El Buen Retiro y la corte de Felipe IV*, Madrid, 1981, pp. 162–70.

[99] J. Brown and J.H. Elliot, op. cit., p. 170.

[100] S. Alcolea, *El palau Moja...*, cit., recalls another Barcelona town house of this period with a double-height salon: the Casa Bertrán, constructed by Elías Rogent in 1884. See: L. Monreal, *Casa Bertrán de San Gervasio*, Barcelona, 1885. Joan Martorell also constructed a double-height salon in the Antonio López mansion in Comillas.

[101] When the Palau Moja was built, the Rambla had not yet been urbanized, and it was difficult to arrive at it with the desired "dignity." In the case of the Palau Güell, although it was built on a side street it was connected to it by way of a house with a façade on the Rambla that had originally belonged to Joan Güell.

[102] See: Ll. Nicolau d'Olwer, *Mitología barcelonina*, Barcelona, 1934; A. Duràn Sampere "Mitología barcelonesa. Las representaciones de Hércules," *La Vanguardia*, July 14, 1935.

[103] A. Duràn i Sampere, "La Oda a Barcelona de Verdaguer," *Barcelona Divulgación Histórica*, Barcelona, 1947, vol. III, pp. 122–28; and more recently: R. Pinyol, "Notes sobre la génesi de l'oda a Barcelona," *Anuari Verdaguer 1987*, cit., pp. 35–45; M. Arimany, "Tendencia teatralitzant i movilitat expressiva en l'oda a Barcelona," id., pp. 47–56.

[104] A. Duràn i Sampere, "El escudo heráldico de Barcelona. Historia y significado de sus elementos," *Barcelona Divulgación Histórica*, cit., vol. III, pp. 225–29; M. Bassa Armengol, *El veratable escut de la ciutat de Barcelona. Origen, història i errors d'abans i d'ara*, Barcelona, 1964.

[105] For an overview of the question, see G.K. Galinsky, *The Herakles Theme. The Adaptations of the Hero in Literature from Homer to the Twentieth Century*, Oxford, 1972. On the palaces referred to, see the bibliography in J. Brown and J.H. Elliot, op. cit., pp. 292–93.

[106] J.A. González Casanova, *Federalismo y autonomía...*, cit., pp. 156–61. The association between the mural of Hercules in the Palau Güell and the Spanish monarchy was perfectly evident to contemporaries. On this point see the cartoons in the Barcelona satirical papers, such as the one published in *Cucut* in August 1905.

[107] See: *Colonia Güell y Fábrica de Panas y Veludillos de Güell y Cía. Breve reseña histórica...*, Barcelona, 1910, pp. 125ff. But we shall consider this at greater length in chapter 4 below.

[108] See: J. Castellanos, "Tres cartes: Josep Yxart, Santiago Rusiñol and Raimon Casellas," *Els Marges*, no. 10, May 1977, pp. 77–82.

[109] F. Rahola, op. cit., p. 5.

[110] Drawn by Joan Alsina Arús and published in a large-format limited edition with annotations in Catalan and French.

[111] This is the basis for much of the comments by J. Margarit and C. Buxade in "Otra visita al Palau Güell," *Arquitecturas Bis*, no. 45, December 1983, pp. 27–31.

[112] J.J. Swenney and J.Ll. Sert pointed out, in *Antoni Gaudí*, Buenos Aires, 1961, pp. 60–61, similarities between the section of the Palau Güell and the Mirador de la Reina in the Alhambra. For comparisons with the drawings by O. Jones, J. Goury and P. Gayancos in *Plans, Elevations, and Details of the Alhambra*, London, 2 vols., 1842–45, see: T. Torii, *El mundo enigmático de Gaudí*, cit., vol. II, pp. 40–41.

[113] J. Puiggarí, op. cit., p. 9.

[114] Ibid., pp. 10–11.

[115] The work of the brothers Goncourt on the eighteenth century first appeared in magazines from 1859 on, and in book form in 1875, with successive expanded and corrected editions (1874, 1881, 1882 ...). See J.P. Bouillon, "Les Goncourt: apparence et sensibilité," introduction to E. and J. de Goncourt, *L'Art du dix-huitième siècle*, Paris, 1967. More generally: S.O. Simches, *Le Romantisme et le Goût Esthétique du XVIII siècle*, Paris, 1964; P. Minguet, *Esthetique du Rococo*, Paris, 1966. On Goupil and his orientalist taste, see: H. Lavoix, "La Collection Albert Goupil II: L'Art Oriental," *Gazette des Beaux Arts*, no. 32, 1885, pp. 287–307. In general: G. Seligmon, *Merchants of Art: 1880–1960*, New York, 1961. However, we shall consider this at greater length in chapter 7..

[116] F. Rahola, op. cit., p. 4. As late as 1908, the town house was still represented as a prison in a caricature by the satirical cartoonist Picarol ("El verdadero conde...," *L'Esquella de la Torratxa*, July 1908, p. 491).

[117] Ibid., p. 5.

[118] Ibid., p. 5.

[119] An interpretation put forward in such studies as: J.E. Cirlot, *El arte de Gaudí*, Barcelona, 1950; C. Giedion-Welker, "Bildhafte Kachel-Kompositen von Antonio Gaudí," *Werk*, no. 42, April 1955, pp. 126–37; J.J. Swenney and J.Ll. Sert, *Antoni Gaudí*, cit., etc., that is still defended even today; indeed, the idea is supported by the authors of the supposedly critical texts in the catalogue devoted to Gaudí's collaborator Jujol: "Josep Maria Jujol, arquitecte. 1879–1949," *Quaderns*, nos. 179–80, in January–February and March 1989. See, too, chapter 4, note 110 below.

[120] In fact the stairs are embedded in the wall on one side and suspended from the rafters on the other. See: J. Margarit and C. Buxade, op. cit., p. 29.

## The Holm Oak and the Dolmen
Park Güell: Landscape, Theater
and Sanctuary of an Essential Catalonia

*Soil and Soul*

"Oh, beloved Catalonia! How your beautiful image follows me everywhere, how Europe's highest mountains remind me of yours and how the finest beauties of the creation fill me with nostalgia and love for your glorious beauties! Oh, Montserrat, Montjuich, Montseny and Canigó! I see you pass, one by one, before my eyes, which weep with nostalgia, and your sweet memory mingles with the mist to distract me from the dazzling view of the Jungfrau, robed in ice, and Mont Blanc, crowned with eternal snow, proud watcher over the neighboring ranges, like a shepherd watching over his white flock at first light in the mist."[1] Thus exclaimed Jacint Verdaguer in his account of the journey he made through various countries in Central and Northern Europe, in May and June, 1884, while writing his second epic poem, *Canigó*, so different in its meanings from his first.[2] At the sight of the magnificent Swiss peaks he is overtaken with a longing for Catalonia. Obviously, however, it is not the similarity or the memory that provokes this emotional disturbance, but the actual vision of the landscape itself, whose overwhelming power transports the poet, taking him inside himself, into his own deepest feelings, putting him directly in contact with his true native land, now more than ever at once mother and soul. The Romantic tradition of assigning symbolic values to each of the elements that make up a landscape, from rocks to trees, from rivers to mountains—one of the pillars, in the case of Catalonia, of the mythical and patriotic construction of the Renaixença, to which Verdaguer contributed so much with his own poetry—is suffused here with an unexpected sense of the whole. Mountains are an archetypal landscape: their height excites the desire of those who climb them and the imagination of those who seek the highest peaks. Faced with the sight of these mountains Catalonia becomes, for the poet, entirely mountainous: a land close to the sky. And it comes as no surprise that Verdaguer, when he again comes to compare this landscape to Catalonia, evokes Spring: "The apple, plum and other fruit trees are all in full blossom,

as they would have been a month ago in Catalonia."[3] Spring is the ripest image of rebirth, perfectly in tune with the feeling of ascent to the sky: meanwhile, in Catalonia (the reference is no mere casual trope) all is already in bloom. But there is more here: the earth itself is brought to life as a flock of sheep, watched over by the highest mountain. With this loving evangelical image of the shepherd and his flock Verdaguer colors the observed landscape to make it tie in even more completely with what he is evoking. Is it really necessary to point out, in attempting to understand in full the deeper meaning of this image, that the rest of Verdaguer's account consists of little more than the poet's constant, scandalized complaint about the crisis of Catholicism in Europe?[4] The Great Peaks are the essential landscape—the land that the Creator has presented for the eyes of mankind with the greatest majesty, in that they are nearer to Him in their height, watched over by the Lord Himself; the land, then, is that of the poet's own origins: Mont Blanc is only the chance evocation of Catalonia, which is the true land and sky.

As we have seen, Verdaguer went on this journey with Eusebi Güell as his traveling companion, and no doubt they would have exchanged impressions and thoughts on various occasions in the course of their trip. Their acquaintance with Switzerland, a federation of autonomous cantons, each with its own languages and legislation, would not only have affected the feelings of the Catalan travelers, sensitive as they were to these issues. The apparition of Catalonia summoned up by the Swiss landscape presents itself again, sixteen years later, in a speech written by Eusebi Güell: his presidential address at the Jocs Florals literary awards in Barcelona in 1900.[5] Certainly, in form and premises this text could hardly be more different from the lines by Verdaguer quoted above, but it can in fact be read as a functional, operative version of the poet's vision, which may well have affected Güell in the same place, at the same time and in the same way. And at a time when everything was in place for the founding of the Lliga

Regionalista within the year,[6] what was this but its concreted political expression?

Güell's discourse takes the form of a philological study of the language of Rhaetia, an ancient region of the Central Alps, but his thinking is, from the very start, eccentric. From the starting point that Latin was not a monolithic language but was in fact made up of a myriad of different dialects he puts forward the thesis that far from Rhaetian being a derivative of Latin, a surviving remnant of it, the opposite is true: that Rhaetian was one of the roots of Latin. Güell's interest in Rhaetian may have been sparked by the Romantic literary revival of its dialects and the efforts of institutions such as the *Retoromontscha* society (which, not by chance, was founded in 1885 and through its published *Annals* began the process of compiling a dictionary of the Rhaeto-Romanic languages). However, Güell does not back his arguments with the slightest scientific evidence: he does not even take into consideration the great dialectal fragmentation of the language and, in contrast to his interest in stressing Latin's diversity, he always presents the Rhaetian language, together with the region itself and its inhabitants ("The Rhaetian people are what remains of the ancient Etruscans"),[7] as single and monolithic. It can hardly come as a surprise, however, that Güell should seek the proof that Rhaetian is older than Latin not in the structure of the language itself but in the landscape where it is spoken. This is a landscape charged with symbolism in which the people are united around the voice of the poets, born to preserve their language: "The ancient Rhaetian language endures like one of those venerable holm oaks that shade the old dolmens, and lives and grows more beautiful day by day, cultivated with love and enthusiasm by the poets and prose writers of that land."[8] It would be hard to find a better image, not of the language but of the intentions that Güell is seeking to project onto it. The dolmen, druidical and ancestral, and a tree, the holm oak, dedicated to Jupiter by the ancients, symbol of strength and longevity, the material of

*A. Gaudí, Park Güell, ceramic*
*medallions on the walls of the park.*

Hercules' club: a dual image of the origin, of a world founded in the bowels of the earth and in time. For Güell the people are a tribe and the landscape atavistic. From this point onwards the discourse is conducted in almost strident tones into the operative sphere. Güell discovers, in the first instance, strong similarities between Rhaetian and Catalan. The conclusion could hardly be more logical: "Given the similarity and the kinship that are immediately apparent in comparing Rhaetian and Catalan ... is there no reason to believe, or at least to suspect, that these languages are older than classical Latin?"[9] The similarities, however, do not end there: "The Rhaetian people being ... of Etruscan origin ..., the Etruscan people having established themselves here, in Catalonia, and having left behind so many relics of their great civilization, it is natural that they should also have had a powerful influence on the formation of our language."[10] Finally, the conclusion adducing the antiquity of Catalonia, prior to Roman domination, and the origin of Catalan, as an influence on Latin rather than a derivative of it, comes to the fore: "These conclusions serve to corroborate certain opinions voiced by some of our modern historians who ... maintain that before the arrival of the Romans, Catalonia already had its own civilization and thus its own language, and that Roman influence was not as decisive as some might suppose."[11] We shall attempt in due course to establish the exact significance of these claims, but first let us go over the speech because, in fact, this conclusion is followed by a corollary whose immediate purpose no longer needs to be disguised. On the one hand, this corollary takes the form of a patriotic affirmation based on a defence of the language, an affirmation that is very little different in tone and wording from the many others that made the transition from the historicist ideology of the Renaixença to a conservative Catalan nationalism: "We too, like the Rhaetians, have been resisting foreign influence for centuries. Like them we have resisted, we resist and shall always resist changing our language, while there is still a breath of life in us. May we always

continue to do so, gentlemen; the only language we can have is the one we have now, which is ours because God gave it to us. Let us preserve it forever and we shall be a people with a personality of our own: let us never forget that as long as our language is alive, Catalonia will live as well."[12] On the other hand, however, it develops into a very specific political proposal: "The study of the causes of the manifest superiority of the peoples of the Swiss Confederation will convince even those least inclined to recognize it that this superiority is due to the federal constitution of the country."[13] In 1900, barely a year after Prat de la Riba had been busy giving its definitive form to the political ideology of conservative Catalan nationalism in the pages of *La Veu de Catalunya*, of which he was editor, and just months before the founding, also under the supervision of Prat, of a political party, the Lliga Regionalista, as the necessary instrument of that policy, Güell's speech—and above all its corollary—must be seen as charged with meaning.[14] Is it necessary to recall here that in the fateful year 1898, Prat had dedicated his fundamental *Ley jurídica de la industria* to Güell? Güell's text, then, is a perfect example of the way he engaged in politics from the outside. From a cultural and civic platform Güell gave his support to the thesis of federalism defended by Prat and the Lliga as one of the main pillars of its ideology,[15] giving it on the one hand a semblance of science endorsed by his reputation as a dilettante, and on the other, and above all, the immense weight of his authority and prestige in his role as patriarch, as father of his country, embodied in paradigm form in the vigilant presidency of the Jocs Florals. But this is no more than a confirmation of a strategy that we have already examined at length, in the last chapter. Let us now take this a little further. In the first place it is hardly surprising that Güell should focus on the Rhaetians and their language and seek to make of these a monolith that is evidently false. We hardly need to recall here that throughout the nineteenth century European Romantic nationalist movements, including the Catalan, had seen their own problems

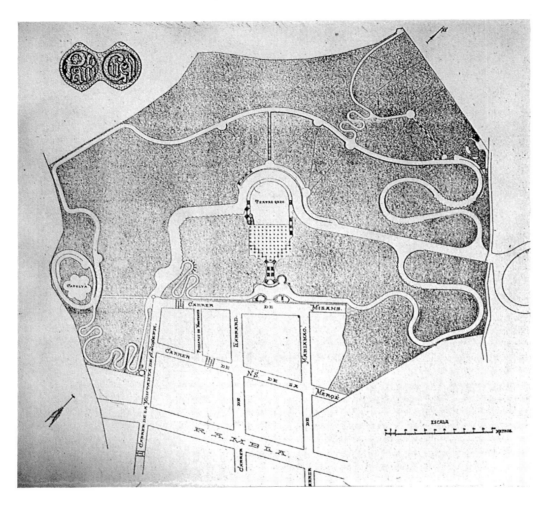

and aspirations reflected in those of other state-less peoples, all of them, from one end of the continent to the other, using the same mechanisms to mythologize their language, their geography and their history.[16] To this generic situation, however, Catalan Modernists had added some special characteristics, such as an admiration for the smaller States of Europe, such as Belgium or Norway, homelands of their beloved Maeterlinck and Ibsen, respectively: the emergence of such figures allowed them to see in the small State a dynamism and cultural vitality, and especially a capacity for creating new models, that were crushed by the very weight of the large States.[17] The small State, then, was identified with the sort of widely extended modernity they were aiming for. These issues were to become highly effective in the hands of the politicians. As early as 1897, in a series of articles and speeches that were to be summed up in 1906 in *La nacionalitat catalana*, Prat de la Riba had set out to demonstrate as one of his principal goals that Catalan nationalism was a movement absolutely in step with the times, absolutely modern: following "the latest and most scientific formula," he went on to declare that "nationality is a hydrographic catchment area."[18] In much more operative terms, between 1898 and 1899, above all through the agency of Francesc Cambó, *La Veu de Catalunya* was to launch a debate that took the Modernists' more or less explicit thesis as its starting point, with the aim of making a definitive identification between nationalism and modernity, not only presenting Catalan nationalist politics as the most up to date option but at the same time accusing its opponents of anachronism. This is the precise moment when, as aptly pointed out by Marfany, Modernism seems to fuse with Catalan nationalism.[19] In light of this, Eusebi Güell's drastic comparison in 1900 between Catalonia and ancient Rhaetia (which in its conclusion becomes a comparison between Catalonia and modern Switzerland) would not have been seen by anyone as a mere Romantic platitude or a scientific nonsense: on the contrary, it had a clear, identifiable political significance. It

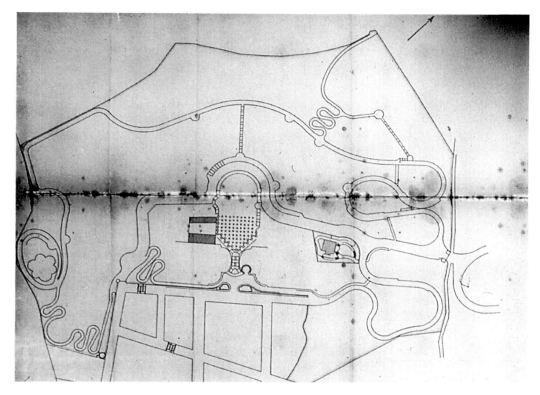

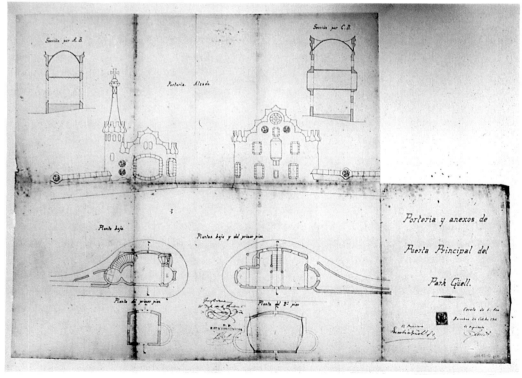

was a purposive gesture on Güell's part, but it was also more than that. In Eusebi Güell's discourse there are other less immediately apparent issues, situated in deeper ideological strata, that also tie in perfectly with Prat's theses. For one, the identification between language and nation, which sees the state of the former as a condition for the survival of the latter, is presented by both in almost identical terms. Prat de la Riba wrote with ineffable sublimity: "the people that has not managed to create its own language is a mutilated people, given that language is the most perfect manifestation of the national spirit and the most powerful instrument of nationalization and as such of the preservation and life of the nationality."[20] These words, published in 1906 in *La nacionalitat catalana*, had previously been pronounced in a lecture, delivered in 1897 at the Ateneo Barcelonés: the similarity with the resonant form in which Güell describes the survival of Rhaetians and Catalans, cleaving to their respective languages, is strikingly apparent. And there is more: in *La nacionalitat catalana* Prat de la Riba was also to establish, deriving his scientific support, as Güell had done, from the researches of "some of our modern historians," a historical origin for Catalonia, prior to Roman domination, which he calls *etnos ibérica* ("the first link that history reveals to us of the chain of generations that has forged the Catalan soul"),[21] already perfectly identifiable not only with the Catalan language but also with the future geographical boundaries of the country, with its borders and thus with its landscape. The elements that define a nation—which according to Prat are, in this order, "territory, race, language, law, art"—are informed by his own definition of nation: "The nation is, in consequence, a spiritual principle ..., a kind of moral state that takes hold of men, penetrating, molding and working them, from the cradle to the grave."[22] The resonance of these words—the foundational spirit of which is infused with the biblical account of the creation of the first man, fashioned from clay—is very much in keeping with the ancestral, atavistic terms in which

Güell had described the timeless, essential nature of Rhaetia and Catalonia a few years before. Güell's dolmen and holm oak, however, evocative of the ancient rites of a people that has sprung as they have from the earth itself, equally ancient, allow other and no less important strands of meaning to operate within the scientific and historical discourse that both adopt in presenting their theses. On the one hand, the pseudo-scientific work carried out during the 1890s by Pompeu Gener and Joaquim Casas Carbó in affirming the existence of a Catalan race whose being is consubstantial with the land itself, and on the other, the mythical poetry that Joan Maragall was producing in the same period, imbuing both these theses and Prat's definition of the national spirit with transcendental tones,[23] are no doubt responsible for Güell's poetic turn, however rudimentary it may be. "The soul of a people is the universal soul that springs up from a soil,"[24] Maragall had written.

In due course we shall come to consider all of this in greater depth: it is briefly introduced as a means to a clearer understanding of the coordinates and the ideological strata, perfectly apparent to his contemporaries, within which Eusebi Güell situated his discourse. This is the important thing: with his explicit references, identifiable without the slightest degree of ambiguity, Güell in his role as patriarch is endorsing an extremely concrete doctrinal construct that is no longer limited to mere generic manifestations of Catalan nationalism, but is now the ideological strategy of a political party.

But this public and very immediate declaration was to include other and even more spectacular constructs; more spectacular and at the same time subtler. The outcome of these would be to involve Güell himself in this construction of an ideology: his properties, his actions and, even more so, his very person. And it would involve him not merely as one of the many who supported the ideology of conservative Catalan nationalism but quite simply as a part of it, as one of its constituent elements.

What does Miquel d'Esplugues' book, on which we have commented at length, have to tell us if it is not the success of this strategy? In looking at the Palau Güell we have seen one aspect of that success, and we shall consider another, the Colonia Güell at Santa Coloma de Cervelló, in due course. It is time now to turn to the Park Güell.

*The Necessary Earth*
"The paths that cross the park have a total length of three kilometers, and in their course, given the necessity of making bridges, cuttings, embankments and so on, this has been covered in such a surprisingly delicate way that an operation that has been carried out since the origins of society has now taken on the character of a poetic innovation. The bridges here are viaducts with beautiful and seemingly daring spans, and the embankments are empty-bankments, if I may so call them, with apologies for the neologism. For, in effect, the space that would otherwise have been filled has been turned into porticoes, and so it is that on a day of rain, of wind, of fierce sun or some other inconvenience, people need not forego their walk, and can cover long stretches under these new arcades that are not at all discordant with the rustic aspect of the mountain as a whole. The inclined columns that bear the thrust of the earth, some of them fancifully worked, and all of them with a pleasing rusticity, some Solomonic, others cylindrical, with varying sections, some with exterior reinforcements in the form of natural stalagmites and stalactites, in which it seems that the caprice of nature has sculpted here a strange creature, there a head, over there a mummified caryatid of new design, in that it is made up of pieces agglomerated by the strength of the concrete, and all terminating in a capital in the shape of a rustic iris calyx, opening up to receive a tree, a buttress or a section of path. Each is joined to the next, they support each other mutually in their inclination, leaving openings for the roots, and finally, covered with earth, they are protected against sudden knocks that might damage them

*General views with the Doric
colonnade and the entrance
pavilions and details of these
during construction.*

and the pressure is shared out equally. Many of the hollow columns will feel the tickle of the roots of the palm trees as they search for liquids and substances to absorb, with which to augment the leafiness of their branches, and all of them provide not only shelter for the visitor but also natural decorations that are like the dreams of fervent imaginations."[25]

In spite of its length, it was necessary to quote this passage in full, since it is without a doubt one of the most profoundly meaningful descriptions of the Park Güell ever written, especially if we bear in mind that it is contemporary with its construction. When Salvador Sellés wrote these lines, to record the visit in 1903 by members of the Asociación de Arquitectos de Cataluña to the park then under construction on this large expanse of hillside looking out over Barcelona, consisting of the land acquired by Eusebi Güell between 1899 and 1902, only the famous bridges, viaducts and porticoed paths that he describes had been built or opened.[26] Several photographs of these structures, with tools and construction materials still scattered about on the ground, accompanied the text. In fact, although the Doric colonnade and the famous undulating ceramic bench were not built until some years later, the perimeter wall, the pavilions at the main entrance and the grand flight of steps would have been practically completed by this time. Sellés, however, makes only a passing reference to these, praising them politely but without enthusiasm:[27] there is nothing comparable to the ecstatic description of the more naturalistic part of the park, in which words and phrases seem to wind around the things described like the roots he refers to. It is precisely in these almost invisible aspects of union between nature and work, in these allusions to what is growing and tickling in the depths of the re-presented earth of Gaudí's park, that Sellés brings out its difference and the power of suggestion that it could exert, and was intended, to exert on its contemporaries.

Before going any further, however, one or two explanations are required. It is clear that parks in which nature is presented in those of its aspects that are most remote from human reasoning and human control, as a mysterious, constant, violently telluric force with a power only comparable to its ally, time, belong to a tradition that has existed since ancient times. It is also clear that ruins, grottoes and interior lakes had, in the course of the nineteenth century, become indispensable elements in the imaginary of the artificial landscape, whether constructed or described.[28] And this is so not only because of the very direct relation between these elements and with the emotions contained in the Romantic categories, that is to say as a specific cultural reflection: we have only to think of its constant presence in the great popular novels of the nineteenth century—beginning with those of Jules Verne, in which a grotto or a subterranean sea is a recurring feature[29]—or its indispensable and fantastic appearance in the more mundane settings of the Universal Exhibitions to see that this was a commonplace.[30] It was a commonplace, however, in that the nineteenth century utopia of progress has precise meanings: in effect, in the context of the *plein air* of science, technology, bourgeois art and the total secularization of the world these had provoked, the grotto or the interior sea represent the search, frustrated by the spectacular nature of the imaginary employed, for a space and a light that are once more enclosed, once more sacred. From the subterranean grottoes of the Jardin Reservé at the Paris Exhibition in 1867 to Ludwig II of Bavaria's Blue Grotto at Linderhof, a single path leads to the colored lights and the indoor fountain of Bruno Taut's Glass Pavilion at the Werkbund exhibition in Cologne.[31] And much closer to Gaudí and Güell, too, these aspirations had been manifested in concrete projects, ranging from the gardens of the Laberint de Horta to the reproductions of Montserrat in the Ciutadella park.[32] A single example, however, will serve: in Cambrils, on the coast of Tarragona, Josep Fontseré had begun in 1882 to lay out a fantastic park for Salvador Samà, Marques de Marianao, a wealthy "indiano," covering an area of more than twenty hectares around a magnificent mansion famous for its collections of paintings and its library.[33] Here were artificial lakes with oriental-style jetties; grottoes in the form of prehistoric caves, complete with living areas; other grottoes with stalactites and copies of Classical sculptures, such as a Farnese Hercules (clearly a meaningful reference); mountains whose peaks could be reached, like the volcano on Lincoln Island climbed by the colonists, by way of subterranean paths opened in its rocky entrails in the form of long galleries; medieval towers on rocky crags … But this example has not been chosen at random. It is not only one of the finest parks of this kind constructed in Catalonia during the nineteenth century, there are also important points of contact between its designer and its owner and Gaudí and Güell. In 1882, in fact, when the laying-out of the park began, Gaudí was still working as an assistant to Josep Fontseré on another park, this time in Barcelona: the Ciutadella.[34] As for the Marqués de Marianao, although he had a different political allegiance from Eusebi Güell—to the Liberal Party, a "Spanish" party, and the party in government—and a totally different focus—he was Mayor of Barcelona on several occasions, some of his terms in office clearly revealing the quality of his commitment, such as the period 1910–11, after the social and political repression following the Semana Tràgica—he shared with him important economic interests, centered primarily on the colonial trade with Cuba and the Philippines.[35] The following fact speaks for itself: the major part of the fifteen hectares of the Park Güell was purchased by Eusebi Güell in 1899 from the Marqués de Marianao, the former owner.[36] But while it is clear that the Park Güell is very much a part of that tradition so perfectly represented by Salvador Samà's park, the two are also different in many ways. One evident difference, above all, provides a starting point for any kind of interpretation: while the Marqués de Marianao's park was constructed in a small town on the coast, a long way from Barcelona, as a fantastic introspective refuge for its owner, Güell's is on an open slope,

like a great amphitheater, overlooking Barcelona. We should not be too ready to dismiss the idea that one of the hidden motives behind the project for the Park Güell was Eusebi's wish to emulate and surpass the achievement of a rival in business and politics—and what is more, to do so on his former property; as a matter of fact it is surprising that greater importance has not been given to the symbolic relation between the two parks. On more than one occasion it will be necessary to draw on elements of Samà's park in order to find explanations for features of Güell's: the important thing, however, is that we must always do so in terms of contrast. While it is true that the two parks have many similarities and belong to a common tradition—a nineteenth-century *topos*, as we have already noted—it is also true that Eusebi Güell's will to representation, condensed in another will (Gaudí's will to interpretation), goes far beyond the possible and probable coincidences between them, investing the Park Güell with highly particular meanings. A number of elements are already apparent, as we have suggested, in the Sellés description quoted above: let us return, then, to Sellés.

Let us look first of all at the actual structure of Sellés' long paragraph. As if carried along on a current, his words move smoothly and evenly from the description of the functional elements of the park—viaducts and porticoes—to a vision of these that merges with the roots inside them that search for moisture and nourishment. The naturalness with which the text passes from one to the other, and with which the two are ultimately conflated, is very characteristic: Sellés refuses to distinguish between porticoes, there to give shelter from the rain or hold up the earth, and their inner life, which is no longer that of a human construction with contingent aims but that of the earth itself and the plants that grow in it. What this paragraph does, then, is precisely to explain one of the main points in which the Park Güell quite intentionally differentiates itself from the tradition of the gardens we have been describing above. In that tradition nature is imitated in its strangest, most

singular aspects: hidden grottoes, subterranean lakes, extravagantly shaped mountains, as we have said. This capricious nature, however, which such parks seek to represent, transfers its caprice to the work itself. In effect, in these parks, the rock formations and the grottoes with their stalactites are designed to exhibit, with ambiguity, their human origin, to show that they have been constructed: in them, then, caprice is the central theme, and in line with this they are filled with equally arbitrary buildings: prehistoric huts, oriental pavilions, Gothic towers, classical ruins … nature has been stripped of its essence to become the guarantor of its opposite, artifice, and it is evident that the ambiguous frustration of the sacral character of its caves and interior lakes has a direct relation to an imitative form that has lost its grounding. Not only the relation to the supposed laws of a nature now regarded as merely arbitrary and capricious but all contact with the earth itself on which they stand are undercut by the extravagant forms bestowed on mountains, grottoes and lakes in these parks. To the consciously purposeful Gaudí and Güell, with their gestures, as we have seen, always oriented towards a program, this could only have been regarded as a loss: the loss, precisely, of nature's original essence, negatively represented there. Given their public intentions, how else could they have seen such a persistent pursuit of surprise in Salvador Samà's private park? What the Park Güell sets out to show is, in fact, something very different. All of the human work in the Gaudí park is presented as telluric necessity, as something configured, not as an imitation of nature, and far less of its stranger aspects, but with nature itself, following nature's own laws, its own rules. Sellés' initial reference to what he calls "empty-bankments" is highly significant: where it has been necessary to remove some earth to construct a path, the resulting void has been occupied by a gallery. In this way, Gaudí eliminates the traditional retaining walls and subsequent earth fills, or at least—and this is even more significant—he explicitly represents their elimination and non-existence. In other words, he

wipes away the wounds that man's works produce in the earth. It is the expression of the violence that such constructions and such movements do to the natural configuration of the land—the expression, therefore, of its artificiality—that Gaudí is trying to do away with in the natural spaces of the galleries. The forms these take are presented as logical, as determined by the laws that structure the earth and at the same time give it weight and form. It will come as no surprise, then, that the image of these "empty-bankments," represented in section with a diagram of compression and tension forces should be one of the principal illustrations of an important article published several years later by Joan Rubió i Bellver, one of Gaudí's collaborators, entitled "Dificultats per arribar a la síntessis arquitectònica."[37] The importance of this piece rests above all on the way Rubió seeks to give a transcendent interpretation of some of the construction practices of his master: in short, he sets out to theorize these practices. For Rubió, the principal problem of architecture down through the centuries has been to achieve an absolute continuity between load-bearing elements and those being supported; an integral continuity manifested both in the forms of these elements and in their laws of equilibrium. In this endeavor, he tells us, is to be found the ultimate definition of styles, and from such premises it is no surprise that he should see in Roman or Byzantine architecture only a system for the summing of forms determined geometrically and not statically, while the continuity of Gothic moldings is, for him, a manifestation of this endeavor, undoubtedly the closest to the ultimate solution, synthetic but nonetheless frustrated by its exclusively formal condition; by the need, in short, of Gothic structures for external elements to balance and hold them up. It is only when a single form coincides with a single law of equilibrium that architectural synthesis is achieved: this, according to Rubió, has been the main aim of Gaudí's architecture and its most important achievement. From the parabolic sections of the Palau Güell to the complex *funiculus* of the studies for the church of the Colonia at Santa

Coloma de Cervelló, the coincidence of form and tension, that eternally sought-after synthesis, is achieved in full. In due course we shall come back to this very evident reduction to which Rubió subjects the highly complex work of his master, but for the present let us focus on just one of its aspects.

Rubió recognizes that structures designed according to the laws of their own equilibrium—bridges, for example—are now relatively abundant. They are always, however, the work of engineers and "this case of scientific rigor that dispenses with all the laws of harmony is not architectural." Clinging to the old *querelles* or controversies with strident conventionality, Rubió attributes to architecture, as opposed to civil engineering, an added value that derives ineffably from "the beauty of its results."[38] In the ensuing explanation of Gaudí's pragmatic methods, however, this distinction between architecture and engineering takes on a concrete meaning: what Rubió is opposed to are the rational methods of calculation used by engineers; in other words, the abstract nature of their geometrical and mathematical procedures, which, he objects, are always carried out away from the site itself, on a drawing board. Gaudí's method, on the other hand, is immediate, carried out on the object of calculation itself; a method in which the process and the result are now, like form and law of equilibrium, one and the same thing and in which, in short, the reason is not speculative but resides in action and in the hands. What Gaudí has done is to "escape from abstraction and approach the framing of the problem with real, positive means, with no shadow or reflection of scientific rigidity."[39] And what is the form of this single element—in whose interior there flows the continuous tension of a law of equilibrium that is born and dies in it, without interruptions, in its foundations or rather in the earth itself—if not the most perfect image of Gaudí's experimentation? The conclusion is obvious: remote from all speculation, Gaudí's work is supremely logical because its logic is that of the things themselves; the most rational because its reason is the reason of the very

*J. Rubió i Bellver, diagrams
of the systems for retaining earth
used in the Park Güell, published
in 1913.*

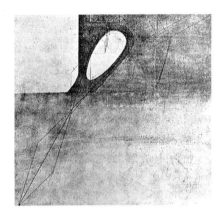

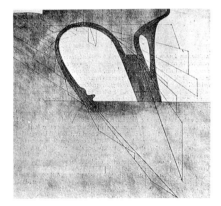

equilibrium of these things and, in the last analysis, the most real because it is arrived at not through abstract calculation but on the basis of experience and practice. It comes as no surprise, then, that the integrity with which Rubió is so concerned, his architectural synthesis, should find its most finished form in the porticoes of the Park Güell, and not only because in them (as the illustrations accompanying the article make clear) the diagram of tensions is in perfect correspondence with the form of the section itself, but because the path followed by the lines of this diagram not only comes to rest in the ground but comes out of it. The earth thrusts and receives its own weight, then, through the most logical, the most rational form: the last trace of caprice has thus disappeared from that form; and not only caprice, but every trace of speculation. What more sublime example could we hope to find than the porticoes of the Park Güell, in which this integrity is produced by the very force of the laws of the earth? Because when all is said and done, where does the particular nature of Gaudí's experience come from if not from an earth that is slowly but surely traversed by transcendent reasons? In the final paragraphs of Rubió's article, in fact, the words are charged with extreme resonances: on the one hand, in the way Rubió chooses these with care in extolling the patronage of Eusebi Güell, thanks to whose generosity Gaudí was able to carry out his experiments: "The first instances conceived with this integral criterion, making a place in the architectural synthesis for a greater delicacy in the application of the laws of mechanics, have been carried out for the private constructions of D. Eusebi Güell y Bacigalupi, to whom, as for so many other things, our land owes its gratitude."[40] Not only, then, is this universal synthesis produced by the will of a private individual, on private property, but it is the land itself that should be grateful. It would be naïve to imagine that the use of the word "land"—whose atavistic strength in comparison with other, more abstract terms such as country or even society is beyond doubt—is unintentional. At the same time, however, Rubió's closing sentences set out to forge a synthesis around the description of the Park Güell that goes considerably further than the merely architectural. In the last paragraph of the article we read: "Up until now the most synthetic architectural constructions to have been carried out are those of the Park Güell, a glorious moment for architecture in general, the first manifestation of a complete architectural circle, whose growth and extension concern us all, perhaps the most transcendental of the fruits produced by our renaissance, sculptural form, stony creation, visible and palpable manifestation of our innovative and practical, idealistic and scientific spirit, fond of soaring to distant horizons and enamored of simple and practical means for obtaining grand effects."[41] The Park Güell has ceased to be merely the coincidence of the section and the diagram in a drawing. Rubió moves perfectly naturally from the definition of an architectural achievement to a description of the character of a people. This depiction of the Catalans as a practical people who although they engage in great endeavors do so without losing contact with what is real and immediate—the same characteristics, indeed, that Rubió alleged in vindicating Gaudí's experimentation over the speculation of abstract calculation—was a standard stereotype at the time this was written, but this should blind us to the fact that it had been one of the essential aspects by which the Catalans sought to differentiate themselves from the rest of Spain. For example, both Almirall and Torras i Bages—with different aims but, in spite of this, drawing on broadly the same support—had put forward this practical character in opposition to a supposedly dreamy and mystical Castilian spirit.[42] It was easy enough to dress up these idealistic concepts in supposedly scientific arguments drawn from the positivist theories of the time so as to give a racial interpretation to this difference, and Casas Carbó and Pompeu Gener, among others, did just that. For example, the latter wrote that "the soil ... constitutes the MOLD that gives form and cohesion to the race."[43] The earth, then, as clay—like the clay in the story in Genesis that

is molded to create the first man—thus makes its appearance here. We are close here to some of the basic definitions that Prat de la Riba put forward in *La nacionalitat catalana*, as we saw above. All that was needed to arrive at these was for the people to receive, like the man of clay, the divine breath: a collective spirit. Joan Maragall, in his poetry and in his articles in the press, was to construct the myths necessary for the definition of that spirit.[44] In 1904, as we noted in the last section, he wrote in *Alma catalana* that the soul of a people springs from the soil itself and, indeed, the whole article takes the presence of the earth as a referent. So if, in keeping with a character little given to dreaming, Maragall says, the Catalans are "accustomed to triumph through work," this is because "the Catalan earth is hard, but grateful," and what is more, "if resting they look at the sky" this is simply because "they see in the sky a beautiful rest extended above the work of the earth."[45] But it is in his poetry, of course, that this character takes on its more transcendent aspects and becomes definitively symbolic. The personae of his *Visions*—a series of poems of fundamental importance, to which we will turn our attention in due course[46]—feel the earth beneath their feet and carry it in their eyes. Count Arnau, for example, expresses his deepest meaning in lines such as this: "I find the sky pleasing only when, from the earth, I see it extended over me."[47]

Slowly but surely, then, the earth enters into the character and the spirit, which come to identify with it to such an extent that Catalonia's heroes smell of the earth itself or cry out as King Jaume does, in words that go beyond the terms of the article just quoted: "What a gift is the earth! / How well the sky above it becomes it!"[48] This intense identification seems to cast a good deal of new light on Rubió's article and on the meaning of the park. Gaudí's method is more than just a quintessential expression of the Catalan spirit; it goes further, and Rubió has no hesitation in declaring that the Park Güell is the finest fruit of the renaissance of this spirit. He clearly states that a sculptural form has there become a visible, palpa-

*Helicoidal ramp at the end
of the Washerwoman portico
in period photographs.*

ble manifestation of the Catalan spirit. So it is hardly surprising, then, having said all this, that Rubió should emphasize above all the rocky, telluric quality of that form, for does the spirit not also have a telluric origin? The way that Rubió draws together Gaudí's architectural experience, the plastic form of its results in the park, the spirit of the earth and finally Güell himself is highly revealing. When work commenced on the Park Güell in 1900, Eusebi Güell was envisioning the origin of peoples in terms of ancestral continuity and the atavism of the dolmen and the holm oak: there could scarcely be more earth, or an earth more terribly remote, in such images. It is perhaps not so far-fetched, then, to suggest that in his project he set out to express the profound essence of a land, or that Gaudí's synthesis was the best path—continuous, unique, like the plastic form it produced—for such an expression. We should not forget that the construction of the park commenced with the most naturalistic part, the part described by Sellés. Let us go back to his article.

In spite of appearances, then, Gaudí's work is not capricious but as rational as the laws of the earth itself: this idea, which Rubió's article reaffirms, is already present in Sellés' resonant description, and we have already spoken in this context of telluric necessity. That the description finds its corollary in the moving image of the root that, tickling its way among Gaudí's stones, searches for its food, is thus obvious. But there is more for us here. Sellés commences his article with some lengthy paragraphs devoted to a geological analysis of the terrain where the park was being laid out. The geological studies, encouraged from the outset by Eusebi Güell, in which leading geologists such as Jaume Almera and Artur Bofill i Poch were involved, were conducted with a thoroughness that clearly went far beyond the basic requirements of the laying out of the park, but in so far as they bear witness to the antiquity of the land and its most profound forces and movements, prior to the history of its human inhabitants, this thoroughness contributes to its symbolic image.

Sedimentations, stratifications, faults: everything here speaks of an earth that is gigantic in the scope of its movements, a living thing in its own right, as it was long before man first walked it. In the rocky forms of galleries and viaducts the antiquity of the earth, as demonstrated in the scientists' evocative descriptions, becomes evidence of a landscape with a will to the archetypal. A series of happy accidents, which Eusebi Güell was not slow to exploit, helped to reinforce the image of the park as essential earth. There was, for instance, an underground spring whose water was rich in magnesium, the temperature and qualities of which were widely remarked on at the time: springs have always been associated with the symbolism of birth, and the origin of life, but in this case the water was also seen as possessing the very properties of the earth through which it flowed. Güell had it channeled so as to put forth from a spout in a semi-cave (although it is also true that years later, and rather more prosaically, it was bottled and sold commercially).[49] But other and far more important discoveries were to be made on the site. Thus, in December 1900, laborers working on the south side of the park found a cave containing a considerable quantity of fossils. A study of these immediately got under way, at the instigation of Güell himself, and in 1901 Norbert Font i Sagué published no fewer than six articles on the subject in various scientific journals, in both Catalan and Spanish.[50] There seems to be little doubt, then, of Güell's interest in making this discovery known, especially if we bear in mind that in Font's articles, interspersed with the scientific data, which are in themselves evocative, in the context created by the discovery, there are continual observations of all kinds concerning Güell himself and his property and the work of constructing the park. But this is not all: in 1902, the Centre Excursionista de Catalunya, of which Ramón Picó i Campamar was president, organized a visit to the cave, and in 1903 Font i Sagué, together with the aforementioned Jaume Almera and Artur Bofill i Poch, presented a long report to the Real Academia de Ciencias; a report whose

*General view of the three bridges
on a postcard published
by A. Toldrà in the early years
of the twentieth century,
and the Pont de Baix in 1904
and as it is today.*

tone, in referring to Güell, differs little from that of the earlier articles.[51] Without a doubt the discovery was consequential from the point of view of the geological and palaeontological history of Barcelona, but in terms of the symbolic aims of the Park Güell it was simply providential. In comparison with the artificial grottoes of other parks—ambiguous, if not impotent images of the sacred profundity of the earth—the cave in the Park Güell could demonstrate, with incontestable authority, its ancestral reality. Among its ancient strata it was thus the bones of animals that had populated the earth before man rather than the roots of plants that spoke with atavistic evidence of this sacral dimension, as images of a time preceding history that were not merely symbolic but tangible. What can compare with this cave, emerging as it does from the depths of the material earth, in revealing the maternal myth of the tectonic inherent in the soil and the plastic forms of the Park Güell. Everything here is grist for the owner's mill. Consider, for example, the following lines from Sellés' description: "And now let us say something about what lies between these paths. We have seen between the viaducts … dark openings made in the terrain like burrows dug there by some living being from troglodytic times; and in the light of the flickering torches we have followed with cautious steps the rough and labyrinthine tracks of the cave… In the blackness of these spaces, a pleasing sensation of coolness has caressed our bodies and now and then, on rounding a bend, we can hardly contain an exclamation of surprise when we see appear, like some inimitable diorama, the landscape outside, a patch of sky or the distant huddle of the buildings of our city, spread out there in the distance on the sands of the Mediterranean and climbing the plethoric dark green slopes of Tibidabo."[52] What appears at first to be a description of the natural grottoes has within a few lines become a description of a tour of what seem to be carefully orchestrated surprises. It is not easy to determine here whether Sellés is writing about the natural structure of the terrain or its remodeling by Gaudí's

hand,[53] and it is precisely this confusion that is significant: it is what serves to endorse the telluric necessity of Gaudí's forms, the archetypal profundity of an earth that is the more sacred the more plastic and more explicitly material it is, with its sacral dimension extending through the interior space of the grottoes and galleries, and it is there that the problem of whether its origin is natural or artificial finally disappears. Equally significant is the way that Sellés, mirroring what we have just seen in those verses of Maragall's, is only aware of the sky when he sees it from the depths of the earth, and the landscape itself only reveals its grandeur when seen from the grotto: the sky, the sea, the sands of the beach and Barcelona are all captured in Sellés' flash of vision. What else did the profound Park Güell aspire to be, if not the mechanism of an essential contraction of landscape, history and time?

The three viaducts that Gaudí constructed on different levels of the terrain—the Pont de Baix, the Pont del Mig and the Pont de Dalt[54]—offer us a further image of this contraction, or at least of the desire to represent it. This is due not so much to the way these structures are formally resolved that is of interest to us here: the heavy, rough-dressed ashlar blocks, set at times (as in the vaults of the Pont del Mig) in a seemingly unstable equilibrium, or evoking clusters of stalactites, are little more than a commonplace rustic image; nor is it the virtues of their equilibrium or their constructional values, which have so attracted Gaudí's hagiographers from Rubió to the present time;[55] rather it is the way in which Gaudí combines and articulates their elements. The lowest viaduct is composed of two rows of inclined columns. Their shafts, of different-sized stones, open into truncated conical capitals that merge smoothly into the curve of the vault, the whole section finally taking on a parabolic profile. Column, capital and vault, then, present no sign of discontinuity, revealing the absolute homogeneity of the resulting structure. Minor details, carefully established, contribute to this effect. The columns, for example, rise directly out of the lev-

el ground, with no socle or plinth, like the trunks of trees, and as if to confirm this evocation the laying of the stone in the capitals is subtly different from the rest of the shaft and the vaults: the stones, spindle-shaped rather than rectangular, form up in files that open out like the branches of a palm tree. It is important to emphasize, however, that these transformations take place within this essential continuity: these are not immediate images that might interrupt that continuity but diffuse variations that effectively reinforce it. What, then, do we find in this portico but the single element, constructed according to the laws of its own equilibrium, in which form and tension become indistinguishable, with which Rubió was concerned: the structure of his "architectural synthesis"? At the same time, the way its arboreal image emerges from the earth and merges with it surely suffices to justify the transcendent tone of Rubió's theorization. But what is achieved here can only be understood in full by comparing it with the other viaducts. In these there are three rows of columns, those in the two outer rows inclined and those in the center vertical. In both cases the bonding of the ashlars, although rustic, is quite regular, inviting a different interpretation of that naturalistic spirit pursued in the Pont de Baix. The fact that in the highest portico, the Pont de Dalt, some of the stones in the shaft project outwards like lopped-off branches affords a key to the line of interpretation invoked here. In its contrast with the regularity of the masonry elsewhere and in revealing both the utopian image of the column and its constructional reality, the stonework is clearly operating on a literary plane, or to put it another way, it alludes to a tradition of the rustic—that of the Vitruvian legend of the tree as the origin of the column and, by extension, of the natural origin of architecture is anecdotically explained—that is absent from the absolute immediacy of the pillars of the Pont de Baix. But it is not only in these details that we find anecdotic references: the vaults that these columns support are ribbed, and very visibly so. In fact, between the rough-dressed stones of these vaults (in

Stone trees on the upper part
of the Pont de Dalt on two postcards
from the early years of the twentieth
century and as they are today.

the Pont del Mig, as we have seen, the stones are reminiscent of stalactites) the tensed ribs inlaid with small stones manifest, like the ashlar blocks of the shaft, a constructional order that the contrast intensifies. The absolute correspondence between the form and the laws of equilibrium in the Pont de Baix, the perfect homogeneity of its structure, is not present in the other two viaducts: indeed it is this very absence that they seem to declare. The columns rise from high socles and terraces or, like buttresses, form part of the retaining walls; on top of them the capital—the trunk of a pyramid in one case, a ring in the other—interposes between the shaft and the ribs of the vault and these, as we have said, clearly divide the rustic intrados. But it would seem that even this evident separation of the elements is not sufficient: the tendency towards a parabolic section that the outer columns of these viaducts suggest is violently interrupted by the verticality of the central row. The small span of these porticoes—about six meters between the bases of the outer columns, and appreciably reduced between the capitals—manifestly demonstrates the redundancy of the robust central colonnade. This can only be understood as one of those external supports to the formal and structural continuity necessary to achieve the architectural synthesis that Rubió spoke of. In this way these viaducts visibly take on, in their rhetorical over-complication, tonalities of the imperfect, and this would seem to be the effect intended. The most essential aspects of that history of styles to which Rubió refers are already present here in these three viaducts. In effect, the apparently conventional allusion to the myth of the natural origin of architecture has been loaded with ulterior meanings. Thus, while the architecture of the upper bridges, broken down into its elements, reveals the analytical process of the steps of its construction and in so doing "demonstrates" its speculative, artificial origin, exhibiting its rusticity as literary *topos*, that of the lowest bridge makes visible a homogeneity that, rooted in the earth itself, extends beyond architecture. In other words, what the architecture sets out to do, on the

basis of that homogeneity, is not to explain that it derives from nature but to show beyond all doubt that it is returning to it. Rubió was right in seeing the structures of the Park Güell as an ineffable paradigm: the whole of his theorization was already contained in this series of viaducts. The Pont de Baix is, in effect, the definitive correction of the imperfections of the other two: Gaudí's technique, then, reflecting any kind of narrative discourse, immediately redeems the corrupt naturalness of architecture. Here, nature is not a mere evocative image but the sacred beginning and end of all technique.

But we have already seen the resonant significance with which, in the environment in which Gaudí and Güell built, nature was identified with a transcendent land of origins. Rubió described the stony character of the structures of Park Güell, and there is no doubt that one of its most eloquent effects is petrification: in the upper viaducts, petrification as the image of the cul-de-sac of the "history of styles," of an imperfect architecture, corrupted by abstract speculation, evidence of which is found in its analytical decomposition, or, in contrast, in the lower viaduct, petrification as a symbol of a return, of a new merging of the work of man and nature, and Gaudí would be Gorgon to the former and Deucalion to the latter. In any case, however, petrification as the image of a time without temporality, of that most ancient time of a land that contains history, forms and technique. It is hardly surprising that the vegetation of the park is made up of pine, carob and palm trees, springing forth sporadically from amid the woody shrubs (broom, rosemary, thyme), figures of this essential land in which water scarcely exists, nor that on the uppermost viaduct, the Pont de Dalt, Gaudí should have erected two rows of stone trees crowned by large pots in which pitas were planted. Emerging implausibly from the stone trunks, their disturbing points pointing, for all their scrawniness, defiantly up at the sky, these are the most terrible metaphor of the aridness of a land within whose bowels there are only remote underground

streams of warm water and fossils resting in silence. Surely all of this can only be seen as constituting a symbol, like the dolmen and the holm oak, of the atavism of a land. Indeed, all the signs, even the most apparently random, point to the same thing. Sellés, in the description with which we commenced this section, said that in the stone galleries of Park Güell nature seemed to have sculpted recognizable forms—a strange animal, a head, a mummified caryatid.[56] This can also be referred, initially, to a *topos* of the artificial landscape. In the Samà park, for example, the caves with their stalactites contain, as we have noted, reproductions of classical sculpture, that sculpture in which European culture has seen deposited, with greater intensity and exemplary perfection, *idea* and *tekhne*. The work of man is even more perfect in view of the formlessness of a nature that manifests itself in the cave in its most rustic form. *Ratio* as opposed to *natura*: in the last analysis this is the cliché represented in such a contrast. In Gaudí, it is all very different. On one of the arcades there is a buttress in the form of a woman balancing a basket on her head with one hand, while the other hand, which rests on her abdomen, once held a wooden stick: the mummified caryatid of which Sellés speaks. The adjective could hardly be more sinister, but what, in effect, is evoked in that image—fashioned from the stone itself, frozen in stone forever with the small pebbles in the cracks that afford a glimpse of an ancient age—if not the victim of some terrible punishment? She is shut up with her conscience, like Lot's wife or the sisters of Belle, who were turned into statues at the door of their palace, and like them she is the daughter of a myth that reveals itself here in its most remote facet. The petrified image is a terrible echo of the fossils discovered in the caves of the Park Güell, and its intrinsic ridiculousness, its crude, grotesque resolution, which might suggest naïvety on the part of the craftsman, only serves to underscore the absence here of *opera*. Not *ratio*; on the contrary, what we have here is a totemic dependence on *natura* that its sudden and extraordinary appearance reveals.

But there is another place where this dependence seems to be even denser or, strictly speaking, more inevitable. Among the columns of the Pont del Mig Gaudí left a carob tree, its gnarled branches and thick leaning trunk emerging from among the petrified succession of pillars to create an echo of primordial images from which every trace of naïvety has utterly vanished.[57]
There is little room for doubt that in the Park Güell an archetypal landscape seeks to manifest itself: every part of it emanates a totemic spirit. Other values, however, have marked it through history. Sellés in fact explains that Gaudí himself recognized an ancient Roman *iter* in one of the tracks that crossed the land: the route that connected Barcino with the Castrum Octaviani.[58] The identification is not in the least trivial: this was the road that, according to tradition, the martyrs of Barcelona trod in search of refuge during Diocletian's persecution of the Christians in the early years of the fourth century AD. The footsteps of the martyrs thus reinforce the originatory significance of this land on which they left their mark, setting up new resonances in the ideal landscape of the Park Güell. It is history, one part of that history, that is now condensed in its stones. Sellés' conclusion is highly meaningful: "How interesting it is ... to contemplate the amicable proximity of this vigorous modern work with the venerable work of twenty centuries ago, if it were even contemporary of Augustus' castle in the Vallès, which you all know has presided over these green plains since before the age of Christianity and has suffered the vicissitudes of serving as a prison, a convent of the nuns of San Antonio, a Benedictine monastery founded by Charlemagne, the prize of the Arabs in their victory over count Borrell, and fuel for the voracious flames of the insanity of 1835!"[59] Rome, the martyrs of Christianity, and a Middle Ages of mythical convents and legendary counts: a history of Catalonia marked by glorious disasters seems to be concentrated here. The last reference to the destruction of the convents, unleashed by the alienating laws of the Liberal State, is an eloquent inclusion here.

*Buttress of the Solomonic column
with Ionic capital
and the Washerwoman.*

The fact is that criticism of the parliamentary State, image of the centralized Spanish state, was one of the ideological foundations of conservative Catalanism. From Torras i Bages to the *Bases de Manresa* to Prat de la Riba,[60] the State is always presented as something artificial, cut off from society: something in opposition to which Catalanism advocates the regional and corporate State, in which tradition and nature are united once again, and where the presence of the land is, as we noted above, so resonantly significant. In 1905, for example, Durán i Ventosa could write: "The regionalist movement is primarily founded on a reaction of reality against fiction, of natural life against the artificial organizations that oppress it."[61] This is precisely what the Sellés paragraph above, littered with recollections of destruction, evoke: the naturalness of a history whose ills have an external origin, which is precisely the case with what is defined as oppression. For Sellés the meaning of Park Güell is, in this respect, pivotal: a visit to it allows us to engage with "the memory of such ill-fated traditions" and "compensate ourselves for the grief suffered."[62] Indeed, what else is exhibited in this atavistic land—concealing in its bowels fossilized remains, traversed by the *iter* of the martyrs, watched over by the foundations of Augustus and Charlemagne, dotted with totemic appearances and restored, in short, to its natural state, corrupted by history, by the hand of Gaudí—if not the confirmation of its own configuring sacredness?

But the reference to a land marked by the imprint of a Christian Rome invites us to admit other interpretations. In 1899, Jacint Verdaguer published a brief poem dedicated to Santa Eulàlia, patron saint of Barcelona and one of the martyrs of those persecutions to which Sellés referred.[63] In it we find a description of Barcino: temples, baths, gymnasiums, amphitheaters and aqueducts lend a monumental quality to the setting of the martyrdom of the saint, who is already Catalan: "most sweet crucified compatriot,"[64] Verdaguer calls her in his bitter prologue. At the same time, this architectural setting of classical marble is given very specific nuances in Verdaguer's poem. Here, for example, he describes the basilica in which the praetor awaits the saint: "Thirty-four gigantic columns, / tattered scions of the neighboring / hills, serving her as a harmonious peristyle: / each one seeming a mountain height / that to the attic beauty / unites something of the Catalan profile."[65]

The Roman columns, then, are not Roman at all, but fragments of the mountains of Catalonia, and still these fragments of the earth blend in, ultimately, with the country's women, who are formed, in effect, from the land itself, whose tectonic and maternal symbolism echoes most loudly in this succession of figures. So implicit in these lines is the image of an essential land, sacred and configuring, as to render any explanation superfluous: in much the same way, Gaudí fused earth and technique in Park Güell. Still, in the prologue, the primordial figure of Eulàlia seems to mark every corner of the Catalan lands and their history with equal intensity. Towns, streets, tracks and springs, counts, kings and bishops, are signalled by her name, in a continuity that goes beyond places and events: "Judith of our race,"[66] Verdaguer calls Eulàlia, with primordial emotion. At a certain point, however, the discourse seems to take on quite a different tone. Verdaguer writes: "Her own Cross, which shines over the stripes on certain old Barcelona coins, might perhaps be a fine solution for the paralyzed Plaça de Catalunya, crossing it with two intersecting boulevards... Where better could her four provinces be symbolized than between the four arms of the cross of our Heroine?"[67] There is something disturbingly vulgar in this proposal for a town planning improvement, dashed off among so many essential signs. At the same time it tells us a good deal about Verdaguer's faith, naïve and, for that very reason, so powerfully immediate in the power of symbols. We need only recall the way that Güell, too, moved from symbols to proposals in the speech with which we opened this chapter, to see that we are dealing with a specific mentality: that which sublimates the world in its signs. So this consideration of Verdaguer's poem is not a generic

recourse, a mere comparison, and the coincidence noted here is not the only reason. This Catalonia in which the Roman forms and the primordial figures of Christianity are molded from the earth itself, and ultimately reflected in immediate symbols, is quite simply one of the means by which Eusebi Güell himself becomes part of an ideological imaginary—the most profound of all. It was necessary, then, that this *iter* that embraces the Roman and the Christian should cross the ideal landscape of Park Güell, a necessity to which other signs also bear witness. Is there any need to recall here the precision with which, years later, when Miquel d'Esplugues was constructing the patrician personality of Eusebi Güell, he would establish his origins in the Christian sublimation of the Roman legacy, recalling the Pauline origin of Catalan Christianity?[68] It is not surprising that in referring to Park Güell, Miquel d'Esplugues should write: "He preferred it to any of the other works and it was his last love, which is often the most serene, firm and ideal." A very specific atmosphere, then, is concentrated in this blending of land and history that takes place in Güell's works. We get a good idea of the necessity—and the pertinence—with which the signs are superimposed on and impregnate those works from the unpublished memoirs of Joan Matamala, a sculptor who, like his father before him, had worked with Gaudí on the Sagrada Familia. The description of the Palau Güell in Matamala's recollections is characteristic, and it is to this, rather than to the description of the park, that we shall refer in particular. An angel guides a hypothetical visitor, not through the rooms of the palace, but through its symbols. Finally, "from the vestibule, she accompanies him outside to admire the portals of the entrance, showing him the 'milestone' in the center of the façade of the building on the verge of the ancient Via Paulus, bidding him to note its orientation towards Montserrat, spiritual beacon of the Catalan lands."[69] All of the signs that permeate the Park are concentrated, then, in the description of another of Eusebi Güell's works: a Roman road significantly dedicated to

St. Paul, and an immanent land condensed in its sacred mountain. Are we still to believe in chance or coincidence?

A lost project by Gaudí, which Ràfols, his first biographer, saw and classified among his papers, reveals another and, if possible, even more radical feature of this symbolic link between Eusebi Güell and the land that is represented by Park Güell. Thus, among Ràfols' notes we find this laconic comment: "1895. Funeral chapel for the counts of Güell on Montserrat. To be carved out of the rock of the mountain with a vestibule for use as a chapel."[70] Laconic, indeed, but rich in meaning. Güell's body was not to rest in a mausoleum erected over insignificant foundations in the ground, or in a cemetery alongside his peers, but in a cavern dug out of the sacred mountain of Catalonia. Neither a haphazard architecture nor the decorous symbols that always accompany it, but the mountain itself was to have represented Güell's triumph over death, and constituted his last and definitive monument. And this is very far from being some delirious fantasy; it is that same ideology that we have seen constantly reflected in the Palau Güell and in the park taken to its logical conclusion. The ideology of the monarch whose gesture is always double-edged: apparently conciliatory on the one hand, and in fact aggressively dominating on the other. What is it if not the figure of Güell himself that this domination imposes by way of all the signs? The project was never carried out, and apart from the description quoted above, we have no further information regarding it, but Ràfols' words could not be more significant: "carved out of the rock." The evocation of the tomb *par excellence*, the Holy Sepulchre, is obvious. However, this leads us without a break to another project by Gaudí on Montserrat. The fact is that between the end of 1900 and the middle of 1907—at the same time, then, as he was working on Park Güell—Gaudí devoted himself, with varying intensity, to the construction of the First Mystery of Glory of the Monumental Rosary that was built on the mountain between 1896 and 1916.[71] A cave drilled out of the rock was to contain the

*A. Gaudí, First Mystery of Glory
on Montserrat. The Christ
by Llimona originally placed
by Gaudí in the void of the cave,
the model by Llimona with his
proposal and the definitive solution.*

empty sarcophagus, while above it would rise Josep Llimona's cast bronze figure of the resurrected Jesus. A number of financial problems, as well as probable differences between Gaudí and Llimona,[72] ended up deforming the architect's initial idea, of which all that survives today is a faint reflection. A photograph taken in 1911 shows the state of the work at that moment in time: while in the definitive solution—executed by Jeroni Martorell and Josep Llimona in 1916—the image of Christ is suspended from the rocks with banal obviousness. In Gaudí's proposal, of which the period photograph affords a glimpse, the profound darkness of the cave is a dense void that envelops the figure of Jesus, which literally floats in the emptiness. It is Christ's tense body, seemingly suspended with no support other than the air, that gives the void such density: the opening in the rock becomes the material echo of this unexpected density. Finally, the stripes of Catalonia are cut into the stone above the Saviour's body: the resurrection of Christ, then, is the image of that land in which His body resonates. A bronze plaque bears Maragall's eloquent words: "The Spiritual League of Our Lady of Montserrat, on behalf of the devotion of Catalonia, offers this mystery, sign of all resurrection."[73] It seems likely that the tomb of Eusebi Güell would not have been very different: in the depths of the earth lie the sacred origins of his ideology. In these two frustrated projects the "representation" of Park Güell without doubt attains its supreme plane: in it, in effect, everything presents itself, time and again.

*Doric Temple, Greek Theater and Omphalos*
However, the Park Güell is not just an archetypal Catalan landscape, its most hallowed ground. At its center, in the middle of this landscape, stand the eighty-six Doric columns of the famous hypostyle hall that supports the great esplanade above, the park's open plaza. The plan that accompanied the much-cited Sellés article of 1903 shows the group of columns, although in an evidently schematic fashion: there are ninety-three columns, regularly laid out on a grid marked by

the diagonals of the front part of the hall. The number of columns and their distribution is thus very different from the finished result. The plan submitted by Gaudí for approval by Barcelona City Council, meanwhile, dated October 26, 1904 —by which time the viaducts and pathways discussed in the previous section had already been constructed—does no more than indicate the triangular perimeter of the space, with no sign of any columns.[74] It seems clear, then, that although the intention had always been to support the great terrace on classical columns (Sellés refers, as if he could already see it, to the "complete order" that produces in the observer "a profound impression of classicism"),[75] the definitive solution was not decided on until construction started, probably around the middle of 1906. A photograph taken in October of that year shows the column shafts built up to a height of almost two meters. Another photograph, taken in November of the following year, shows that the columns have been completed, but not the entablature, which to judge by other photographs taken at the end of 1908—showing scaffolding at the front of the hall—must have been completed early in the following year. Finally, construction of the ceramic-tiled bench that runs around the upper terrace continued until at least the beginning of 1914.
Firstly, let us try to describe the Gaudían order. Its intention is obvious: the evocation of archaism. While it is pointless—and over-generic—to look for models for this Doric order among the temples of ancient Greece, Sicily and southern Italy, Gaudí did nevertheless use a series of specific methods to establish the proportions and decide upon the most eloquent details of his order. If we take as our module the radius of the column at the base of the shaft, as recommended in the treatises, the ratios could hardly be more heterodox. The fourteen modules that, for example, Vitruvius allocates to the column with its capital also include, in Gaudí's Doric order, the entablature.[76] But we can try a different approach, dispensing with the Gaudían diameter and in determining the vertical proportions alone use the module given by the

height of the architrave, including fascia and guttae, which—again according to Vitruvius' description of the Doric order—corresponds to the radius of the column, and hence to the module. In this case, the result is quite different: the column, with its capital, has exactly fourteen modules and the entablature, excluding the final repeated cymatium, three and a half—a perfectly orthodox result in terms of our accepted source. At the same time, the individual elements, as a result of distortions produced by their interpretation, coincide more approximately with this set of dimensions, although without major variations. The capital, for example, despite irregularities in the echinus, is the same height as the architrave, while the frieze (with no appreciable difference, taking into account the inclination of the pseudo-modillions and the absence of a capital in the triglyphs) corresponds to one and a half times that height. Gaudí therefore adheres—very precisely in the modulation of the whole and more approximately in the case of individual elements—to the proportions Vitruvius established for the Doric order in Chapter III of Book IV of *De architectura*. And still other of Gaudí's Doric variants can be related to the recommendations and stories of the Augustan architect: Gaudí's inclined pseudo-modillions are, for example, an echo of their constructional origins, a memory of the stoneworkings to which Vitruvius refers in Chapter II of Book IV, and even the naturalistic interpretation of the guttae could be indirectly derived from Vitruvian legends about the origin of architecture, taking the word in the least rigorously philological sense. But we must not get carried away in our search for references.[77] What is important is that Gaudí turned to an ancient source for the essential proportions of his Doric order, rather than to some fundamentally academic text book such as Vignola.[78] However, once he had obtained this sequence of ratios, Gaudí amended the Vitruvian Doric and went beyond its classicism to evoke an archaic time that is thus closer to the origins of architecture. First, then, without altering these relations in height, he increases the diameter by almost one whole module and reduces the number of flutes, from the twenty prescribed by Vitruvius, to twelve, making the column less slender. This is not the only way in which Gaudí creates a greater sense of weight: in the cornice, he doubles the cymatium by more than a module and in the capital, the chunky echinus sitting very low, looks as if it were about to be pierced by the sharp-arrissed shaft. Innumerable details help to give this impression of mass: the chiaroscuro of the undulating entablature and the way it is continuously broken up into different shapes, the visible continuity of the octagonal abacuses, the naturalistic interpretation of the mutules, triglyphs and guttae to which we have already referred, and so on.

Gaudí thus employed the means he needed to create a new vision, which in many ways is not so different from those totemic presences that punctuate the porticoes and viaducts. In fact, in the essential landscape of the Park Güell, the evocation of archaism achieved with this Doric order is not restricted to an allusion to the original meaning of architecture. All archaic art diffusely evokes that which is very ancient, and this endows it with a profoundly sacred significance. Even in the Augustan era it was common for classical authors such as Vitruvius himself to attribute to archaic forms—which Augustus had so astutely reintroduced—an essentially sacred, religious aura, indissolubly linked to the prestige possessed by everything ancient.[79] In an atavistic and ancestral land such as that represented by Park Güell, in which history and myth inhabit the same realm, the Doric columns imbue their surroundings with a climate of sacred solemnity, an atmosphere of old, essential religiosity and, like the other elements here, a sense of the arcane, of mystery. It is hardly surprising that the hall should have been referred to from the very first as a temple. The effect of the flattened necking, the naturalistic correspondence of the guttae and the thickness of the doubled cymatiums is heightened when seen from below, from the ritual access by way of the double staircase that ends not in an opening but in a column, set on the central axis of the hall. A power-

ful but suspended sculptural plasticity pervades the darkness of the interior, barely glimpsed from below, while the column comes forward on the axis above the nymphaeum, in front of which the staircase branches in two for the last time, and is illuminated, suspended in its heavy antiquity, its original *auctoritas*. But we shall try to interpret this arcanum using a more specific approach.

We have already said that when Sellés visited the Park Güell, the hypostyle hall had been conceived but not yet built and probably not even planned in the strict sense of the word. Indeed, in his article, Sellés relates the columns to the esplanade they partly support, which he compares to a Greek theater and which is in fact marked as "Theater Grec" on the plan he published. This is no mere allusive comparison, however. Sellés explains that not only dramatic performances but sports events will be held there, and that there are plans for temporary tiered seating, to be made of steel and wood. He describes, with some emotion, the monumental backdrop of the theater, formed by the view over the plain of Barcelona down to the sea.[80] The way in which Sellés relates the Greek theater with the "very intense classical feeling" created by the yet-to-be-built columns,[81] which evoke "the venerated creations of Greek Doric," and ultimately links the whole thing to sport—"races, football, lawn tennis and other appropriate games"[82]—might seem merely picturesque, but it takes on a very specific significance if we bear in mind that only a short time before, in 1896, the first Olympic Games of the modern era had been held in Athens. Even more significant is the way in which the Games were interpreted by the sports reporter Charles Maurras, in a series of articles that made a great public impact and were subsequently published in 1901 in book form under the title *Anthinéa*.[83] In these articles Maurras not only sets out what he calls a "philosophy of classical art" but also frames an ideology in which the words classicism and Mediterraneanism are endowed with precise meanings. Two other books that Maurras published at this time, reflecting the same ideas, clearly expand on these specific meanings: in 1898, after visiting the Greek Rooms at the British Museum, Maurras wrote *La Naissance de la Raison* and in 1902 he published the first sections of *Avenir de l'Intelligence*.[84] In the meantime he had also founded Action Française and given a specifically political slant to these ideas about the classical cast of mind: his "integral nationalism."[85] There can be no doubt that Maurras and his work had more influence on the ideological development of Catalanism than they have been credited with in the past.[86] The archaic solemnity of the Park Güell's Doric temple, supporting a Greek theater whose backdrop is a panoramic view of a Barcelona reflected in the *mare nostrum*, is by no means alien to all of this, although the relationship between them, as we shall see, is not direct but problematic, and takes the form of a complex crisis. Many other factors, on many different levels, go to make up the jigsaw of that cast of mind. Let us try to put the scattered pieces in order.

The Park Güell's open-air theater had at least one antecedent in Barcelona, and one that was similarly laden with classical allusions. On October 16, 1898, the Laberint gardens—a Romantic park complete with a pond and dotted with classical pavilions and rotundas, which belonged to the Marquès de Alfarràs—hosted the first performance of Joan Maragall's Catalan translation of Goethe's *Iphigenia*.[87] It was by no means unusual at the turn of the century for Barcelona's high society to make the ritual journey, in carriages specially laid on for the occasion, to private gardens on the outskirts of the city, to listen to, amid columns, classical statues and cypresses, the strophes of a Greek tragedy. From Beziers to Reading, open-air theaters had been built in which that same high society assembled to watch classical drama. It was a period when all of European high society—and Barcelona was no exception, as we have seen—seems to have been seized by a vogue for all things Greek. Eloquent examples are found in the pseudo-Greek tunics worn by Isadora Duncan, not so much on international stages as in the Paris salons of the Countess Greffuhle and the

BARCELONA. 59 - Parque Güell - Columnas del Teatro Griego.

A. T. V. - 47 - BARCELONA, Parque Güell, Vista parcial

Princess de Polignac (who were less interested in Duncan's artistic revival than they were under the spell of the Eriphyles and the Aphrodites of Moréas, Pierre Louys and Maurras himself); in Fortuny's pleated satin Delphi gowns, worn by Duncan herself (as well as Eleanora Duse and Ruth St. Denis) and the ladies at whose parties she danced—and by Princess Murat and Lady Diana Cooper, among others; and of course in painting, with Leighton and Moore, and in the pictures of Alma Tadema assuming an almost ridiculous degree of cliché. In addition to its more mundane and evidently superficial aspects—Madame Lemaire gave a famous party in 1903 with the theme "Athens in the time of Pericles," at which guests were asked to wear "classical Greek costume": Proust attended in evening dress—this fashion for things Greek did, however, have a more significant side. Scandals such as that occasioned, to take one example, by Nijinsky's appearance, half-naked and surrounded by classical nymphs, in the Paris première of Debussy's *L'Après-Midi d'un Faune* in 1901, were no longer symptoms of a fashion but of a profound change in customs and in mentalities. Lastly, the fact that, to a great extent, this atmosphere was created by writers such as the aforementioned Moréas and Louys, and others such as Hérold or the young Claudel, and above all by Maurras, is a clear sign that the fashion for things Greek, having been converted into a Mediterranean—that is to say, racial—reasoning and intelligence, attained new levels of significance, and as we have said, these levels were ideologically and politically very profound.[88]

But let us look at how something so diffuse manifested itself in the specific Barcelona example we are considering here and examine its specific features. In the first place, one thing seems to stand out: *Iphigenia* was indeed staged, but in the Goethe version. It was not unusual, of course, to look at the classics through more modern eyes, and Isadora Duncan herself continually borrows lines from Byron to describe her journey to Greece.[89] But Goethe is not Byron, and the choice—quite apart from the personal taste of the translator, Maragall, which is in any case symptomatic in itself[90]—has a precise significance. Adrià Gual, creator of the Theater Intim and responsible, along with Miquel Utrillo, for putting on the performance of *Iphigenia* in the Laberint gardens, recalls the circumstances in his memoirs. Above all, the "noble" setting was the most suitable scenario:[91] "the Laberint, free from artifice, imbued with imported Italianism and with the same neo-classicism represented by the literary Hellenism of the *Iphigenia* by the author of *Faust*."[92] The classicism of these gardens exudes is not in fact ancient but Italian—that is to say, Renaissance—and neo-classical. This is, then, a classicism informed by the different overtones of its interpretations, like the play itself, whose power to evoke Antiquity is in any case established by a specific order, the Goethean order. In Gual's memoirs, then, one idea is clearly reflected: that of the strictly representative significance of the performance. He insists on this elsewhere in the book: "The Laberint gardens absolutely fused as one vision of the nineteenth-century poet with that of the famous poet of the Periclean age…, like those statues and pavilions, with the blue sea in the distance, those cypresses and those steps screened by Spanish cedars and the symmetrical, architectural topiary of the box hedges."[93] The ancient author and his modern interpreter thus meet in a *hortus conclusus* that includes all the elements to be found in a contemporary version of the classical *otium*: the exquisite pervaded by a banal ideality. The following excerpt is even more eloquent: "As on one occasion, when in the gardens of the park at Weimar, Goethe's *Iphigenia* was performed before the court, with Goethe himself in the role of Pylades, his short cloak covering his breeches but concealing neither his silk stockings nor his silver-buckled shoes."[94] In the memoirs of its main promoter, the representation was a two-fold evocation, the evocation of an evocation. This seems to invite us to interpret its elements in different ways. The pleasure of imagining Goethe himself, in his paradoxical costume—the most

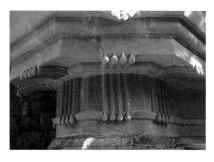

*Detail of the Doric entablature as it is today.*

brilliant image of this *institutio* of the ancient contained in the neo-classical category—is simply a picturesque but nonetheless significant way of recognizing the authority of a Greece which does not retain that authority within itself, but acquires it in being reinstated in the words of none other than Goethe, Privy Councilor to that most ideal of states, the intellectual who determines both policy and customs. The name of Weimar, linked to the memory of Greek Antiquity, figures as a symbol of that order that imposes itself, if necessary, on justice and indeed on life itself. Not for nothing does the passage above remind us that Goethe himself performed before a very specific audience, a courtly audience. And finally, those silver buckles reflect another very specific aspect: the pleasure with which Gual describes the buckles glittering beneath the tunic, reveals the Versaillesque, *ancien régime,* origins of his classicism, more influenced by the Goncourt brothers and by Goupil than by the Greece of its contemporary interpreters.[95] The principal significance of the performance of *Iphigenia* was, it seems clear, the order that emanated from all this. The interpretation not of the classical but of a specific neo-classicism that took place in the aristocratic *hortus conclusus* of the Laberint was the rite of a precise social sublimation, and its significance can be found precisely in its imperfections and contaminations.

While the première of *Iphigenia* in the Laberint gardens is a telling symptom of the way the vogue for things Greek was received in Barcelona society, and of the meanings with which it was invested, there was another manifestation of this, perhaps less spectacular but more lasting and more influential. In two stages, between February 1898 and March 1900, the magazine *Catalonia*—whose contributors included the organizers of the Laberint *Iphigenia*—came to be the principal platform for a particular, subtly mediatized recovery of the classical.[96] It should first be noted, however, that *Catalonia* presented itself as the successor to *L'Avenç,* the *modernista* review *par excellence,* which had ceased publication in 1892;

its successor or, even better, a new version of it.[97] *Catalonia* was the center of efforts to rebuild a *modernista* front with the same premises and assumptions as those that had motivated the editors of *L'Avenç* and their contributors, most of whom were in any case involved with the new magazine. Like *L'Avenç* before it, the main aim of *Catalonia* was to promote all things modern. It was guided by the same eclecticism as *L'Avenç*, which accepted everything that was new simply because it was new. In principle, then, all of Europe's innovative figures and movements, from the symbolists and the decadents to the most radical and vitalist tendencies, were to find a place in its pages, either in their own right or by way of their Catalan representatives. This, as we have said, was in principle the magazine's premise. In reality, however, *Catalonia* was characterized by two highly definitive traits, as Marfany has so acutely noted. First, it clearly sought to be something that *L'Avenç* never was: a platform for *modernisme*, with all the sense of being a movement and the unifying and organizing role that this implies. Second, and as a consequence of the above, while it proclaimed the same eclecticism towards the new as the *modernistes* of previous years, its actual content reveals an opposition, at times implicit and at others very explicit, to the symbolist and decadent tendencies, in favor of a new vitalism. The paradigm for *Catalonia*'s literary reviews was Paris, and the choice of model immediately suggests that the decadent Nordic mists have been dispelled by the Mediterranean luminosity of the Ecole Romane, which as its very latest manifestation, constitutes a higher expression of modernity.[98] But this is not the only reason why *Catalonia* was in favor of the classicism and Mediterraneanism of the latest movements in Paris, or of the classical Greeks. The fact that it championed such things; that its writers contributed texts and verses that were classical in mood or meter; that it published translations of works such as Aeschylus' *The Persians* by traditional writers such as Artur Masriera, for whom the vogue for classicism represented a means of gaining entry to modern

149

magazines; and lastly, the fact that Maragall's translation of Goethe's *Iphigenia*, as performed in the Laberint gardens, should appear in its pages: it is also necessary to consider all of these things in a different light. To begin with, the name of the magazine is itself charged with meaning. The title of *L'Avenç*, like those of other publications of its kind all over Europe, resonates with ideas of action and progress. No such associations are evoked by *Catalonia*, and not only for reasons of chronology, because combative names for magazines had gone out of fashion. In 1900, another new publication aiming to draw together the different strands of modernism called itself *Joventut*,[99] and even in 1907, the title chosen for the new magazine, whose leading light was Gabriel Alomar, was *Futurisme*. In contrast, *Catalonia* is the name of the country invested with the *auctoritas* of its most erudite and ancient, Latin form. Clearly, the name was intended to communicate a sense of solemn order and institution, of an eternal culture rather than of progress. And while the masthead of *L'Avenç* proclaimed it to be a "literary, artistic, scientific" journal, *Catalonia* announced its contents, in contrast, as "political, literary and art criticism." The replacing of "artistic" with "art criticism" is a significant change of emphasis, but changing the "scientific" that gave the masthead of *L'Avenç* a strong sense of bourgeois optimism to "political," in pride of place, is even more significant. The first issue of *Catalonia* included an article by Alexandre Cortada, one of the magazine's guiding lights, who had been one of the most radical contributors to *L'Avenç*. The title of Cortada's piece purposely confuses the name of the magazine with that of the country: *Ideals nous per a la Catalonia*, or "New Ideals for Catalonia."[100] Although, formally, this was nothing more than a renewed profession of that faith in the new that had motivated the editors of *L'Avenç* in their campaigns to modernize Catalan society, there is an underlying difference of tone in Cortada's article that is merely the outward sign of other, deeper differences. In place of sweeping rejections and condemnations there is a will to seek

integration and agreement, and instead of the old radicalism there is a desire for operative effectiveness. It could not have been otherwise: between 1898 and 1900—the same years in which the magazine was published—the first Catalanist political party was formed, and the modern, independent Catalonia dreamt of by the modernists of *L'Avenç* thus became a concrete political objective, integrated into a timely ideological program. As Marfany has so rightly observed,[101] these were the years when modernism was absorbed into Catalanism: *Catalonia* was one of the first steps in this process of absorption. In this context a taste for the classics —and for writing imitations of them—is more than a mere reflection of the latest fashion from Paris. The very name *Catalonia* is an evocation of *auctoritas* outside of time, of integral perfection: of the order, in short, that comes from an *aurea aetas*. The dream was of something very much like that. The institutional and academic components of classicism, as well as the racial components of the Mediterraneanism associated to it, were felt in all their force by those whose aim was no longer merely the revival of a country but the creation of a State by very concrete political means. While classicism and Mediterraneanism were the key watchwords of the "normalizing" ideology of cultural affirmation of the Lliga intellectuals, the specific perception of the Greek vogue in Catalonia at the turn of the century was its first sign, its beginning. There is no need to insist any further on the aims and the name of *Catalonia*, but it does allow us to understand certain other things more clearly: for example, the fact that a Greek tragedy should be performed in Barcelona in the form of a translation (and the word is charged with meaning) by Goethe. The passion for all things Greek was also a passion for the *ancien régime*, and its meaning is the institution, the perfect State.

This completion needs to be looked into. When Adrià Gual remarks in his memoirs that the performance in the Laberint gardens was part of his project for a new kind of theater, and lists his European models—Castelnaux, Lugné-Poe and

most of all, Eleanora Duse—for this,[102] they all lead implicitly to D'Annunzio. There is nothing strange about that. D'Annuzio's work had been extremely popular in France since 1894 at least, and it was almost always by way of France that new developments reached Barcelona's artistic and literary circles. In *Catalonia*, in fact, D'Annunzio was, together with the writers of the Ecole Romane, the most important point of reference for the new modernity, because the magazine's editors saw in him a reflection of their own eclecticism, a new kind of synthesis between the decadent and the classical.[103] In Gual's case there was an even more important factor: since 1898 D'Annunzio had been planning, with a great deal of publicity and propaganda, to construct an open-air theater on the shores of Lake Albano.[104] The new Italian theater, in which the drama was to be reborn, was thus to have been a classical theater, and it is no accident that Gual's references should coincide with D'Annunzio's contact with a similar initiative being carried out in the Roman am-

phitheater at Orange. The project for that theater was offered to the "architetti latini" and, no less importantly, its backers included the ladies who held the most fashionable society salons of the day: from Countess Pratolini to the Countess de Bearn and the Princesses Wagram and de Potenziani. The opening ceremony was set for the first day of spring in 1899, and it was planned to stage *Persefone* by D'Annunzio himself. The other plays to have been performed leave no doubt as to the theater's orientation: an Aeschylus (*Agamemnon*), a Sophocles (*Antigone*) and D'Annunzio's *La città morta*. Alessandro Guiccioli described how those grand ladies dreamed of dressing up, in the woods beside Lake Albano, with their "intellectual acolytes" like "old nymphs with old fauns."[105] This ironic treatment of the degeneration into snob appeal of D'Annunzio's supposed revival of the theater, with its evocation of a classical landscape inhabited by happy deities, is simply the reflection of a social sublimation of exactly the same kind, if more modest in degree, as that

which took place in Barcelona's Laberint. However, in D'Annunzio's planned restoration, the theater is only one facet of a many-sided prism. It is worth recalling that, at the same time as he launched his campaigns to promote the Albano theater, he was portraying the parliamentary state as the source of all social evils and the mirror of a decadent society, in such widely acclaimed works as *Le vergini delle rocce*. The redeeming vision of art embodied in his project for a classical theater is not, of course, alien to this élitist and aggressively anti-democratic ideology; on the contrary, it is inseparable from it. The Catalan intellectuals who took such an interest in D'Annunzio in the final years of the nineteenth century were by no means unaware of this aspect. Joan Pérez-Jorba, a literary critic who wrote for *Catalonia* and was one of the contributors with the closest links to the French classicist groups (in fact he settled in Paris in 1901), published a series of articles in *La Publicidad* in 1896 exploring various aspects of D'Annunzio's work (the first of these dealt with *Le vergini delle rocce*), and it was not unusual to find interviews with D'Annunzio or reviews and translations of his work in the Barcelona press at that time.[106] It was precisely that élitist ideology that gave specific importance to the forms that D'Annunzio's theater took when it had the opportunity to manifest itself. In 1900 he published a novel, *Il fuoco*, which included an account of his stormy relationship with Eleanora Duse, and was an immediate success. In this novel D'Annunzio clearly spells out the significance of his project for the theater at Albano, as voiced by the central character, Stelio Effrena. The relevant dialogue is as follows: "The drama must be nothing other than a rite or a message," declared Daniele Glauro. "It is necessary that the performance be once again as solemn as a ceremony, including the two elements that constitute every cult: the living person who embodies on the stage, as if before an altar, the word of a Revealer; the presence of the silent multitude, as in the temple..." "Bayreuth!" interrupted Prince Hoditz. "No, the Janiculum," cried Stelio Effrena, suddenly emerging from his vertiginous silence, "a Roman hill. Not wood or bricks from Upper Franconia; we will have a marble theater on the Roman hill."[107] D'Annunzio obviously felt compelled to acknowledge his debt to the Wagnerian conception: the enacting of the drama is a sacred ritual of social communion in which the artist becomes the celebrant and the work manifests itself as the sublime synthesis of all the arts. But D'Annunzio immediately marks a difference. This society governed by priests is not to be identified, as it is in the Wagnerian project, with its myths—in other words, with its soul—but is suspended before the liturgy of an arcane religion, silent before the fear of the gods. In D'Annunzio's vision, society does not recognize itself, as in the re-mythologizing undertaken by Wagner, in its own primordial spirit; instead, with priest and temple interposed between society and its origins, it discovers in the altar its order and its hierarchy. In the marble theater described by D'Annunzio, the static form of the sacrifice is itself the message. That qualifying "marble" is not used for nothing: together with the allusion to the Roman hill and the intended name of the theater, Teatro d'Apollo, it invokes a very specific neo-classicism, the time of an *institutio* as precise as the Augustan. With its marble temples and ancient rites, that first imperial age had also replaced the Hellenistic and republican *pathos* with the solemnity of the classical and the archaic. The commonplace that sets Apollo and Dionysus in opposition to one another is precisely manifested in a number of pertinent D'Annunzian phrases and, on more than one occasion, in *Il fuoco* non-Latins are referred to as "barbari." But that is not all. In 1898, Sarah Bernhardt starred in the Paris première of D'Annunzio's first play, *La ville morte*. It is pervaded with images of Antiquity in the form of the dazzling treasures of Mycenae: the air of sacred mystery that always surrounds the archaic is made to resonate even more when concentrated in the secret mysticism of the treasure. At the Italian première of the play, with Eleanora Duse in the leading role, the set featured genuine archaeological relics loaned

by the Brera Museum, and copies were made of the Mycenae treasure:[108] the cult was thus made real on a stage imbued with *sanctiona auro*.

It is time to shuffle our cards once again. Evidently the use we have made of the example of the performance of *Iphigenia* in the Laberint had a symptomatic purpose in establishing not only a diffuse atmosphere, but also a series of specific references. It is true that although *Iphigenia* coincided with the sources, and to a great extent with the purposes of D'Annunzio's project, a comparison of the two clearly reveals its modest scope and taint of the mundane, the causes of which we have already noted. But perhaps this is largely a matter of historiographical prejudice. We need only recall Guiccioli's ironic remarks to see that the mythical ground of D'Annunzio's grand venture also had its mundane and even ridiculous elements. We do not easily find such failings, however, in the impressive distance that the order of the Park Güell establishes in relation to its society. In the presence of its Doric hall and its Greek theater, constructed in the heart of an essential land, those prejudices disappear, and not only because almost eight years had elapsed between the Laberint *Iphigenia* and the start of work on the Park Güell. The archaism of the grove of columns spreads around it the same sacral mystery that D'Annunzio sought for his Teatro d'Apollo, but planted as it is in the heart of a primordial landscape (we should not forget that it supports the plaza above, and has been perceptively referred to as a Doric womb)[109] its solemnity is all the more resonant and its discovery is invested with more intense atavistic tonalities. It stands, then, at the heart of this land and, as we have noted, it was known from the outset as "the temple." But we must also bear in mind its geographical location: of the range that overlooks Barcelona. The hill on which the Park Güell is laid out is the one that penetrates furthest into the plain.[110] The way the Greek theater dominates the city from that hill is highly significant, as we have already suggested: making the city its backdrop, a panoramic scene that terminates with the sea on the horizon. Tem-

ple and theater, then, on the hill above the city and the sea: in them the gold of the *tesorí di Micene* shines with a special lustre.

At this point it is time to mention an especially interesting fact. The Vicomte de Güell, in the volume of memoirs from which we have already quoted a number of times, recalls that under the "elliptical vault of oriental alabaster" of the great salon of the Palau Güell, a great concert was held on a certain occasion: "I recall that my father could give a concert in which a hundred voices took part, while an orchestra of a hundred instruments played and the chords of the organ were heard."[111] Despite the probable exaggeration on the part of Eusebi Güell's son, this must have been an event of great magnificence. But what is most important is the music that was being performed: the hymns to Apollo, two fragments of music from the second century BC that were found at Delphi in 1893, among the very few surviving examples of Greek music. The Vicomte de Güell tells the story with a wealth of detail that reveals his great satisfaction: "It was the first and only rendition in Spain of the Hymn of Apollo, found at Delphi. This hymn, discovered in May 1893 among the ruins of an Athenian treasury at Delphi, was attributed to an Athenian composer who lived around 138 BC. The Hymn was inscribed on a marble slab, kept in the museum in Delphi, and according to H. Weil and T. Reinach the music was published in its definitive version by Reinach in the book *Fouilles de Delphes*, 1912."[112] In view of the scholarly caution and rigor with which any performance of such music would be undertaken nowadays, it is difficult to imagine how the notation on the ancient marble was followed by Eusebi Güell's musicians and singers, or how modern instruments were substituted for their ancient counterparts—the organ in place of the *hydraules*, for example. But such things are of little importance: clearly this was not an archaeologically correct interpretation, a scientific reconstruction, but a ceremony with precise meanings. In the first place, Eusebi Güell himself was the principal protagonist: his role was not

Á LA FESTA DEL PARCH GÜELL

—¿Ahónt va ab parayguas, Caimitu?
—El duch per quan plogui. ¿No sab que la sardana, ballada aquí, es un crida-pluja infalible?

that of the occasional concert promoter but of the patron of the arts whose action stands outside of the contingent time of fashion. The chosen venue, moreover, was not a public place but Güell's house, that salon whose sacred solemnity we have already considered at length. Secondly, the music was not some recognizable composition readily assimilated by public taste, as a classical tragedy translated into a modern language by a contemporary author might be, but a strange hymn to an ancient god, a piece as authentic as the marble tablet on which it was found. Thirdly, the carefully selected audience, there by personal invitation, was not the public. The rudimentary music of those hymns, with their melody moving in short intervals and constant returns to a keynote, with their disjointed rhythmic sequences, must necessarily have had a ritual fascination for those present, no doubt intensified by their well-primed sense of its religious character; music that, in all its strange originality, breathed an air of the most arcane Antiquity, of the most sacral mystery. But, above all, the sensation of hearing sounds that had come to them from a distance of two thousand years, sounds that must have reverberated in some temple of far-off Delphi, long since in ruins, would have exercised a special power over their imaginations. With this concert Güell demonstrated a similar interest in things Greek to that which was sweeping the salons of Europe, but in choosing to perform that sacred hymn, that archaic music, he purged the event of every trace of the mundane. This was, without a doubt, a profoundly ritual ceremony, charged with sacred connotations, not only on account of the music performed, but also by virtue of the place. In his evidently ingenuous but nonetheless reliable memoir the Vicomte de Güell bears witness to this in the lines with which he concludes his description of that concert: "In this house only concerts have been held; my parents never liked dancing."[113] Only at a concert—and especially at that concert—does the audience observe the solemn silence of the temple. As on so many other occasions Eusebi Güell is intensely involved in a potentially banal situation

that is sublimated in his hands. The double-edged figure of the *princeps*, making patronage the subtlest and at the same time the most effective demonstration of power, reveals itself once again. Güell's distinction is affirmed here by bringing not only the most secret and sacred, but also the scarcest of the treasures of ancient Greece to a most select audience that, yet again, is only so thanks to the condescension of the lord who admits them to his house, in which the fire of the temple is kept. But that temple in which hymns are sung in praise of Apollo, with the authentic sound of Antiquity, is not only the domed salon of the Palau Güell: it has another site. In due course we shall consider the relationships between this concert and the hypostyle hall in the Park Güell in greater detail, but who among the people who attended the concert could have failed to be aware of them? That hypostyle hall is the Teatro d'Apollo, but it is also, in its way, the temple of the god himself.

In its way; but first of all we must insist on one point: the hypostyle hall in the Park Güell, the Doric temple, is the womb of a primordial, atavistic, animate land, the archetypal landscape of Catalonia. As such it is also a dolmen. But on the emotional level, how were that Doric temple and that Greek theater interpreted?

A late testimony will help us here. In 1928 the musician Vicent M. Gibert published an article in *La Vanguardia* about Antoni Gaudí, in which he referred to the Park Güell in the following terms: "The Greek theater in the Park Güell was to be the established seat of a new and essentially Mediterranean Catalan lyric theater. We may recall in passing that the performance of *El comte Arnau* by Pedrell was proposed for there, but did not take place; it was not the most appropriate work for that site, but there is no doubt that Gaudí must have liked it, especially for the theological implications of its conclusion, with which the composer felt obliged to give a dramatic termination to the previously unfinished poem by Maragall."[114]

Gibert thus clearly connects the Greek theater in

the Park Güell with the project of creating a Catalan lyric theater: a project that had, since the success of the 1897 prèmiere at the fourth Festa Modernista in Sitges of *La Fada*—an opera by Jaume Massó i Torrents and Enric Morera in which the mythologizing of Catalonia's history and landscape in the libretto and the continuity of the music drew on the Wagnerian paradigm[115]—mobilized artists, intellectuals and patrons, and a project in which the dramatization of *El comte Arnau*, the poem by Maragall in which the "voices of the land" were to be heard most clearly, was one of the most cherished objectives. Maragall was never to write the libretto, but the poem, although composed independently of the musical project, was influenced by that atmosphere, and Pedrell took Maragall's poem—by then a mythical work of Catalan culture—as the basis for his opera, prèmiered in 1904. If that project for a lyric theater ultimately met with little success, the part that an opera of Wagnerian inspiration centered on the legends and the geography of Catalonia was to play in the formation of the myths of the Catalanism is obvious. It is not so surprising, then, that Gibert, so many years later, could still relate that failed project with the archetypal scenario and the primordial land of the Park Güell. At the same time it is worth noting the last attribute that Gibert ascribes to a Catalan lyric theater: Mediterranean. Is not this very adjective that reveals to Gibert the unsatisfactory nature of both the project and the setting? Why was *El comte Arnau* not the most appropriate work for that place? To attempt to answer those questions is to introduce further complexities into the interpretation of the Park Güell. On the one hand, Gibert had not only witnessed the failure of a Catalan lyric theater, he had also seen how a Greek-inspired D'Annunzio had gradually usurped, in the eyes of certain sectors of the Catalan intelligentsia, the place of an increasingly Nordic Wagner; and on the other he knew, in 1928, when the processes of *Noucentista* cultural affirmation had already completed their cycle, that classicism, if it was to underpin a universal "civil-

ity," had to be less emotive than the Doric order of the Park Güell, suspended in its rapt fascination with the sacred and as such opposed to the academy, although certainly not on libertarian grounds. But perhaps Joan Maragall himself can help us to clarify the evidently unsatisfactory nature of the Doric temple and the Greek theater. We have already encountered Maragall, as the author not only of *El comte Arnau* but of the translation of *Iphigenia* staged in the Laberint. If there, for quite specific reasons, Goethe interposed himself between Maragall and the classical drama, Maragall's interest in the Greek classics gradually liberated itself from such cultural interferences, although only to set others in their place. In a series of letters from the early years of the twentieth century Maragall tells Pijoan of his growing interest in reading the Greeks; but, as has been so rightly noted, his interest is loaded with sentiment, closely related to his intense emotional response to the Catalan landscape,[116] almost always sublimated in a mythical Mediterranean land-

scape—the vegetation, the light, the sea—that evokes in his mind idealized scenes of ancient Greece. But it is not only those associations of the landscape that inspire Maragall, but the landscape itself, nature pure and simple, unadorned. In his *Elogio de una tarde de agosto* we find a perfect example of this. Maragall recalls a performance of *Oedipus Rex* in the open air, at a resort in the French Pyrenees.[117] At the start of the poem, the size of the mountain meadow, the trees on the slopes overlooking the scene, so rich in concrete sensations—"strongly fragrant of the new-mown hay and full of the murmur of running water"[118]—makes the presence of the actors seem exotic and ridiculous: dressed in their white robes, their almost inaudible voices scattered by the breeze, their declamation is "poor and pitiful artifice, alien to that ambit where oft vibrate only the rumors of the waters and the wind, the rustic flute of the shepherd and the sonorous lowing of the herds."[119] Maragall hears only the voices of nature, charged with an Arcadian beatitude. But the

*The tripod and the dragon
on the central stairway
in their original state.*

afternoon is overcast, and when it starts to drizzle the "immobile coryphaei tremble in their languid flesh under the rice powder and the subtle cloaks of white linen stirred by the chill breeze."[120] Yet in spite of all this, "Oedipus is a great actor," and from time to time there flashes forth "with terrible momentary sheen in his eyes, the classical mask."[121] This lasts only an instant before the performance once again reveals its impotence before the imbalance between the works of man and nature. The actors go back to being "marionettes on the over-large stage of the green hill, of the august mountains…, of the towering sky."[122] Finally, as the play is coming to an end and Oedipus and Jocasta leave the stage, the storm breaks: "Terrified, the people whirl and scatter and flee in all directions. The fences are first leaped, then broken; chairs and benches and boards fall, and in the few moments the meadow is left deserted and sown with ruin, amid … the din of the tempest that fills all the valley."[123] Maragall's evocation of the spectacle eloquently expresses the role he assigns to each of his components: "Beautiful crown for a tragedy in the open air of the mountains!";[124] then, taking refuge in the hotel, he asks the "frivolous group of ladies about the inconvenience they have suffered,"[125] and still contemplating the lightning through the windows they answer: "What does it matter?"—a response that Maragall was to set down with care.

What, then, constitutes the grandeur of this spectacle? On the one hand there is the personal power of an old actor, the only one capable of revealing—in flashes—the tension of the ancient tragedy; in flashes, just like the phenomena of nature themselves: in the whole of the text Maragall offers no opinion on the play by Sophocles, but only on the specific quality of its transmission through the voice and the *pathos* of an actor. On the other hand there is a nature idealized by contemplation, which finally reveals itself, however, in its most indominable aspect, in the total violence of the storm. Here, then, the tragedy is recalled explicitly through an actor and the place and circumstances of its performance, of that thrilling day.

Maragall expressly avoids everything that makes Greek tragedy, or classical Antiquity, an object of devotion in itself, an object of static and solemn devotion. It is hardly surprising, then, that Maragall should focus on the actor and on untamed nature when D'Annunzio's project for the Teatro d'Apollo, with its call for a temple-like silence, was directed specifically (and paradoxically, in view of the presence of Eleanora Duse) against the *teatro d'attore*. All of this is reinforced in the last lines of Maragall's poem. Returning to those mountain meadows on a sunny day, the poet tells us, he no longer finds in them "the pure peace of the fields, but it seemed to me there remained there, hovering, the sacred terror of the ancient tragedy."[126] A fiercely individualistic sacral quality that is thus very different from that of D'Annunzio's temple is opposed to all collective sublimation. It is in the individual and not in society that Greek tragedy and nature, imbued with the same emotion, resonate. In effect, Maragall concludes: "Where is all that? It is in me."[127] Private sentiment thus warms the marble of the ancients.

Only by appreciating the resonance of the individual response in Maragall's *Elogio*—that sense of a higher emotion that corresponds, in its ideology, to the poet alone—can we begin to understand why Gibert saw the Greek theater in the Park Güell as unsatisfactory. Where does it come from, indeed, if not from the manipulation of that same sentiment? What is the purpose of that Doric order, so willfully archaic, in the womb of the Catalan land but to be the medium of a higher emotion that in Güell's hands is immediately transformed, as had happened already in the Torre Satalia and still more in his *palau*, into an ideological statement? To quote Maragall: "What does time matter? When the remote Oedipus groaned under his tragic fate, where was Sophocles? And what did Sophocles know of the Pyrenean August afternoon, or of our emotion before his work? … And, nonetheless, for this heart to be moved in a certain way, it required the patricide and the incest and the atonement of an obscure king of Thebes, the genius of a Sophocles revived and an after-

*Details of the tripod and the dragon as they are today.*

*Medallion with the sheild
of Catalonia in the central part
of the stairway.*

noon of passionate feeling in the Pyrenees with thousands of years between these things that co-existed together and were merged in an instant of fortuitous emotion."[128] Time, then, in the form of things great and small, is abolished as temporality, and contracts into the instant emotion of the individual, engraving itself forever in his memory, or rather, in his experience. That same abolished time, contracted in an essential land that is the object and objective of a construction, is represented in the Park Güell: to it the archaic temple is dedicated.

But is this not the culmination of its ideological significance? Eusebi Güell was to make the Doric column, the Greek theater, the most evidently public spaces of the park the site where his identification with the restoration of Catalonia, now a political objective, is most indissolubly manifest. Can there be any doubt that in the Park Güell the very feeling that Maragall expressed in his *Elogio* was being manipulated, made operative? Once again, then, it is Güell who determines: in him, individualism becomes the public projection of power. The classicism of his temple represents the same private sentiment that Sophocles' tragedy aroused in Maragall, because only in it can a will to individual rivalry crystallize. The classicism of the Park Güell, so autobiographically loaded, was not conceived as an emblem of social virtue. For those who attended the many Catalanist rallies and festive events held in the park throughout the early years of the twentieth century, of note among which was the Garden Party marking the First Congress of the Catalan Language in October 1906,[129] what did that setting represent but the overwhelming presence of the *princeps*? His temple, his land, his house, his name, alternating with the word "Park," repeated so many times in the ceramic medallions that Gaudí set all along the wall that symbolically separates the enclosed precinct from the city, placed there as a reminder of him. Miquel d'Esplugues wrote that "Don Eusebi … never refused the use of the Park if it was requested of him for the succour of the Catalan soul, radiant in the glory of triumph," granting

the request "with a patriarchal spirit."[130] At such mass events, then, the ideological significance and the symbolic value of the place attained its most intense expression. In the archetypal land there represented and of the architecture with its sacred aura of the archaic that the land contains and which at the same time crowns its grandest scenario, Güell is made one with the Catalan soul: he is in it. The power that is expressed in the ambiguity of the public and the private thus takes on extreme tonalities. Like the princes of the past, *spectari monumenta sua voluit*: in this way a whole program is defined. The autobiographical resonance of that setting, however, was not lost on Güell's more critical contemporaries. To take one example, a cartoon by Picarol, published in the republican satirical weekly *L'Esquella de la Torratxa*: a man and a woman meet in the park, under a blazing sun, during one of those Catalanist rallies. Seeing the man with an umbrella, the woman shows some surprise, and he says: "I brought it in case it should rain. Don't you know that the sardana, danced here, is an infallible rainmaker?"[131] There may well be contingent motives in the joke, but it is hard to escape the sensation of primordial sacral essence thus proposed: in the land, in the tribe, in the totem and in the enchanter.

As we have seen, Miquel d'Esplugues describes Güell's relationship with his park. He presents that relationship as the result of the "melancholy evocation of the first impressions of life," thus making its autobiographical character a radically exclusive value to which every image is literally attached. But this is also an aspect of princely virtue: "Possibly for this reason, in the Park Güell there is made patent—in spite of Gaudí's highly original luxuries—the influence of those youthful impressions … complemented by a thousand more of the same kind, the fruit of studies, travel and creation, and especially, in its innate elegance, polarized by the laudable obsession with accomplishing great things."[132] The classical stereotype of the secluded life in the perfect refinement of the villa seems to resonate here. However, the con-

Stone "rosary beads" on the paths
of Park Güell and general view
of the park in 1905. In the distance,
on top of the hill, the Calvary
in the location originally proposed
for the chapel.

stant ambiguity between the public and the private returns here to inform the meaning of this evocation: of the possible paradigms, not the privacy enshrined in Pliny the Younger's Laurentine letters, that radically sequestered *otium*, but the paradoxical privacy of Hadrian's villa, product of his travels and his culture, but the product, too, of the subtler power expressed in the idea of an inverted *publica magnificentia*." There is no exaggeration in referring to such models. We have already seen Miquel d'Esplugues merging and confounding, with precise intentions, the image of Ancient Rome and that of the sixteenth-century popes, and he is doing the same thing here. In the grounds of the Park Güell there was an existing eighteenth-century mansion, which Güell fitted out as his residence: he began to live there, intermittently at first, in 1906, and died there in July 1918. D'Esplugues describes it thus: "A princely mansion, a sketch of a palace such as those that characterize the Rome of the sixteenth and seventeenth centuries, for example, and are sadly lacking in Barcelona."[133] The project for re-aristocratizing Catalan society led by Güell and sublimated in his works informs what d'Esplugues, ingenuousness aside, interprets here in the Park: the private imposes its forms on the public. The infectious ambiguity of the result, its double edge, underwrites the power of the *princeps*, his constant and unavoidable presence. D'Esplugues' implicit criticism of Gaudí's exaggerated originality can hardly surprise us.

Eusebi Güell's house, that "esbós de Palau," is next to the Doric hall, on the left when seen from the foot of the steps. And this flight of steps, the only monumental element in the park, has a particularly eloquent form, dividing into symmetrical sections in each stretch, terminated by a small nymphaeum—in fact a covered bench—and crowned by the Doric columns. This can only be a re-creation—on a very small scale, of course, but with a precision that leaves no room for doubt—of a classical *topos*, always constructed as a perspective of power, such as we find in the system of terraces that crowns the Fortuna Primigenia in

A. Gaudí, sketch for the
monumental cross for the Calvary.
Never executed.

Praeneste, replaced in the fifteenth century by the palace of the Colonnas, and repeated in the succession of large spaces of Bramante's Belvedere, culminating in the exedra in which Julius II kept his collection of antiquities. And it is, of course, the *topos* passed down by Michelangelo's Capitol—now as "identifying model"—to arrive by way of many other works at our own time.[134] A very concrete *topos*, an image of memory, whose ritual requirement of a unique point of view invests the neighboring house with its princely significance and definitely establishes the hypostyle hall as a temple. But that is not all: superposed on this rhetorical *topos* is an endlessly redundant succession of veiled associations, of emblems, in which the autobiographical origin once again determines, as it did so many years before in the gate of the Torre Satalia, a mechanism of radical exclusion and distinction. It has been suggested that the dragon of colored ceramics that serves as a fountain on the flight of stairs, framed by the two palms on the top terrace, may be an allusion to the coat of arms of Nîmes, a city in which Güell spent some time in his youth and whose Parc de La Fontaine Miquel d'Esplugues cites as an analogous model for the Park in Barcelona.[135] No doubt, many other elements of that ritual ascent contain veiled autobiographical references, but of these there is one and one alone that coherently embraces all the others, and in it the symbolic program we are considering here is asserted with absolute precision.

Let us begin by describing the stairway from bottom to top. Between the twin flights of steps at either end of this, Gaudí introduced a sequence of containers or basins filled with water, wet vegetation and fantastic animals, as if the earth had opened up to expose its entrails. In the first of these, the lowest, there is a tiny landscape of grottoes and rock formations, a kind of *koniwa* or Japanese miniature garden,[136] which project up from the pool with its little waterfalls, fed by the series of fountains on the stairway. The second, with a stylized rockscape that is simpler than the first, supports a ceramic medallion bearing the

flag of Catalonia. From the center of that medallion, framed by a white ring, emerges a strange head that has traditionally been thought of as a serpent—contrary to the visual evidence, since its ears are clearly apparent, making it look something like a mouse. Above this is the landing giving access to the house in which Eusebi Güell lived, and above that the third element: the famous dragon with its sinuous bands of variegated colors, from the mouth of which flows the water that feeds the whole system, with its four feet resting on the parapets behind which, under its belly, we see the same kind of arrangement of rocks and water as in the other two containers. After the dragon, above the white ceramic lip of a well, we come to the base of a ceramic tripod, originally topped by three arms that branched out from one another and joined again a little higher up. This piece, though it can be seen in period photographs, has long since disappeared: all that remains today is the base of the tripod. After this structure—whose size in relation to the other pieces was considerable; indeed, it was clearly the culminating point—is the nymphaeum and the Doric columns that support the Greek theater. There is only one thing to be added to this description: something that is out of sight. In fact, under the Doric temple there is a large hypostyle cistern, made to look like a grotto, which stores the rain-water channeled down through the pipes inside the Doric columns, the overflow for which is the dragon on the flight of steps: by way of the land seen in the succession of containers of the stairway, the depth of that cavern is symbolically revealed on the exterior. There could have been little doubt in the minds of the select group of guests who had attended that great concert in the Palau Güell at which the Delphic hymns to Apollo were performed as to what all of this meant. The cavern under the columns of the Doric temple, pouring out the waters of its interior lake through the mouth of the dragon; the land, emerging in its most fantastic forms from the depths of the discontinuous fissure that separates the white order of the two sections of the stairway, from which

163

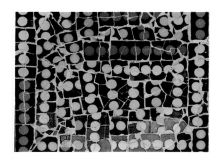

*Fragments of ceramic* trencadís *by J.M. Pujol on the undulating bench and the stairway of the Park Güell.*

the moisture-laden air of the cavern emerges; the ring on which the tripod rose above the well: what are these but images of the sanctuary of Delphi, of its myths and its ritual artefacts? There, in effect, in the *opisthodomos* of the Doric temple of Apollo, in the center of the sacred walled enclosure at the end of the Via Sacra, the cleft between two rocks from which flowed the fountain Castalia was believed to be the mouth of Gaea, the earth mother. Of her was born the serpent Python, from which Apollo stole the oracle. Set atop the cleft was an iron tripod, which ancient Greek vase paintings show supporting a cauldron over which the pythoness pronounced the oracles. In the *cella* of the temple was a conical stone of marble, which the Greeks held to be *omphalos*, the *umbiculum terrae*, the tomb of the hero embodied in the serpent.[137]

The extent to which all of this coincides with the succession of elements in the flight of steps of the Park Güell is too precise to be seen as mere coincidence. A man like Eusebi Güell, who felt such an interest in the sanctuary of Delphi as to overcome all of the difficulties involved in putting on that concert in his town house, could hardly have been ignorant of these aspects of the Delphic rites, the myths contained in them, the elements and instruments of the cult. All of these motives were already present in the hymns sung in the salon of the Palau Güell. "You, son of the great Zeus ... reveal to us mortals your imperishable oracles and ... take possession of the prophetic tripod guarded by the enemy dragon, many-colored monster of tortuous folds." What is more, Güell had at his disposal not only works that ranged from Gótte's *Das delphisch Orakel*, first published in 1839, by way of the *Mémoires* of Delphi by Foucart and Mommsen's *Delphika* (1865 and 1878, respectively) to the then recent *Beiträge zur Topographie von Delphi* by Pontow, published in 1889, but above all the reports that the French archaeological expedition that had discovered the hymns had been publishing in the *Bulletin de correspondance hellénique* since 1893, subsequently collected in the monumental *Fouilles de Delphes* from

1902 on. Indeed that French expedition, which had begun its excavations in 1892 by destroying the village of Castri, had made Delphi fashionable with a succession of sensational discoveries. The famous pleated satin Delphi dresses by Fortuny—inspired, as we know, by the *Auriga* discovered there—is one example of this, but there are many others.[138] A more trivial example may give some idea of the extent of the Delphi vogue in Catalonia: a popular series of statuettes in black clay by Fidel Aguilar (the sculptor, who died in 1917 at the age of twenty-one, created ceramics for architects such as Rafael Masó, influenced by the subtlest strands of classicism) represented women in hieratic archaic poses, dressed in "Delphi" tunics.[139] Of course, what Eusebi Güell set out to achieve with his park, while related to that vogue, went far beyond mere fashion, but Delphi serves to explain many things. The sacred precinct of Delphi, enclosed in a more or less rectangular wall, was situated on the side of a hill. At its center stood the temple of Apollo and above this, at the highest point, was the theater. The Doric columns of the Park Güell, supporting the Greek theater like a plaza in the middle of the hillside, are manifestly a contraction of that image. And again, the Via Sacra that zigzags across the enclosure at Delphi to reach the temple was flanked by countless gifts and ex-voto offerings to the oracle. We have already mentioned the totemic figures that punctuate the walk beneath the porticoes, but of course the principal path through the Park Güell is bounded by large stone balls that represent the beads of the Holy Rosary, another characteristic of a Via Sacra. And this Via Sacra was to have led finally to a chapel on the highest part of the terrain, the form of which on the general plan of the park is precisely, that of a rose.[140] The same symbolic overlapping that we saw in the gate of the Torre Satalia is thus repeated here, and the symbols and the Marian invocations inscribed on the undulating bench are secret, almost hidden, lost among the fragments of broken ceramics that once again embody a redemption of the most contemptible material, of

waste matter can be seen as the conclusion of that superimposing.[141] Just as in the sacred enclosure of Delphi each stone, each tree, each topographical feature was imbued with a sacred value, in the Park Güell it also has an autobiographical value. Miquel d'Esplugues wrote that the Park Güell "monopolized the preferences of Don Eusebi in his last years. He preferred it to any of the other works."[142] It might seem, then, as if Güell were repeating here Maragall's question and answer: "Where is all that? It is in me." But, as we have already suggested, it only seems to be so. In fact it is Güell himself who is there, embodied in all those forms, rather than the other way around. Who, I repeat, among the people who attended the concert in praise of Apollo could have failed to see the Park as a gigantic emblem of Eusebi Güell?[143] Veiled emblems, once again: autobiography, then, as the ubiquitous presence of the *princeps*. But not only that: in a society that saw itself as pyramidal, what was the figure of the *princeps* but the pinnacle to which all eyes are directed, the supreme model? The public and the private are mixed here again: by no means casually, but with a very clear intention. And the highly cultivated Güell could not have been unaware of the extraordinary importance, not only symbolic but religious and political, of the Delphic oracle in Greek society. It prophesied, it issued warnings and established rules of conduct; but above all, its power was directly related to the processes of Mediterranean expansion and colonization that configured the pan-Hellenic world. No Greek colony or city could be founded without first consulting the oracle of Delphi, and from this point of view the moral guidance it exercised was decisive in forging a sense of identity and solidarity among the Hellenic peoples.[144] "Forward, illustrious Attica, nation of the great city, who occupy an inviolable soil," declaimed the hymns that Güell had had performed in his house. The archetypal landscape of the Park Güell, which is the essential land of Catalonia opening out like a fan above the city stretching down to the sea, is thus invested with complementary meanings: it contains the *omphalos*, the

center of the world, and from it, too, that world is guided, led. But if this reinforces the primordial character of that land, from whose depths, as in the Delphic oracle, its voices emerge (Maragall's "voices of the land"), the classicism of the temple of Apollo represents another aspect of its soul. What is represented on the first landing of the flight of steps is the head not of a serpent, but of the oracular mouse: another of the attributes of Apollo worshipped at Delphi, the mouse was associated with the protection of people, livestock and crops. What other meaning could it have, emerging as it does from the coat of arms of Catalonia, but that of the protection of the country's enterprises and their expansion, "radiant in the glory of triumph"?[145]

This facet, complementing the telluric, ancestral character of the land, its myths and its soul, is clearly present in the political formation of Catalan nationalism: in fact, it is those myths that legitimate an expansionary ideology, and Güell, repeating in a different way the same gesture he made with his inauguration speech at the Jocs Florals, with which we commenced this chapter, could hardly have been indifferent to this. "Imperialisme" was the title that Prat de la Riba had given, in 1906, to chapter XI of *La nacionalitat catalana*, the political credo of conservative Catalanism, precisely articulating in its ideological construction an issue that had been present from its first beginnings, in the *Compendi de doctrina catalanista* of 1894.[146] Prat is perfectly consistent with the thinking of his models—Emerson, Roosevelt—in seeing imperialism as simply a higher form of nationalism: "Imperialism is the triumphal period of nationalism: of the nationalism of a great people. This is the true substance of imperialism. For this reason the masters of imperialism are fervent nationalists."[147] In the book's conclusions Prat applies this idea to Catalonia in a section entitled "Començament de l'etapa imperialista." There he writes: "The nationalist process continues: it has not taken control of the State, the Law or the language; we have not attained full interior expansion, but Catalan nationalism has

already initiated the second function of any nationalism: influence over the exterior, the imperialistic function.[148] He then goes on to enumerate those areas in which Catalonia has already begun to exercise an influence abroad. Among a series of legal, economic and political aspects, it is worth noting the following phrase: "Catalan art is beginning, like Catalan literature, to irradiate the whole of Spain."[149]

A new version of the old regenerationism, then, but also something more. It is evident that in Prat's formulation there is a great deal of ideological sublimation of the real weaknesses of the bourgeoisie he is addressing here, but his discourse is no less effective on that account. We need only read the articles devoted specifically to this subject, such as "De lluny," in 1904, or the eloquently entitled "Greater Catalonia," of 1907, to see that the significance of the concept in the political ideology of his party is far from generic.[150] For our present purposes, however, certain aspects of Prat's expression of all of this are of particular interest. In the first place there is his historical identification of what must be the initial focus of this new Catalan imperialism: the lands of the former Corona de Aragón, in whose Mediterranean expansion Catalonia had been the driving force: "Meanwhile, let us do the same as the English with their *Greater Britannia*, that imperial flower on the verge of crumbling: let us speak of the Great Catalonia, that is confined not only to the Principality, Mallorca, the Rousillon or Valencia; but Valencia and Mallorca, the Principality and the Rousillon, and all of this together."[151] The new imperialism, legitimated in a glorious past, thus ceases to be new and becomes the latest, climactic stage in the restoration of Catalonia, inseparable from its historical tradition—and not only of Catalonia. Prat invokes an image to give resonance to his project, to transform it into a vision: the contemplation of the landscape: "From the vantage point of Durtol in those past hours contemplating the plains of the Auvergne and the snow-covered ranges of the Cévennes, how many

times had I dreamt that immense nation, that group of peoples that could understand one another and extended from Valencia along the Mediterranean to the Rhône and the foothills of the Alps; stretching along the Pyrenees to meet the Basque lands and touch the Atlantic and border it to the mouth of the Loire."[152] There is only a difference of degree, the degree of the operative, between this vision and that of the Swiss mountains that had so moved Verdaguer. The nation in expansion is conflated, then, with the landscape, with the very form of the land contemplated, as befits the visionary on his vantage point. But this is also the "nation of the great city." The center of that land informed by one soul is a Barcelona discovered anew, with the power that gives the bird sight: "From there … it seemed to me I discerned our present problem … in this Barcelona, head of Catalonia, that has formed and enamored our souls, that is the center of our strengths, forge of Catalanization, heart of our race, that receives in torrents the turbid floods of foreign multitudes to transform them into the body and blood of Catalonia."[153] Body and blood of Catalonia: this was also, of course, the matter of which the Palau Güell had been made. What, then, was the primordial, archetypal land of the park? With good reason the *omphalos* of that expansion had been installed there.

But there is a second strand, inseparable from the first: "Imperialism is the aspiration to constitute the Empire-State, to gather a flock of nations under the power of a single shepherd."[154] The shepherd connotes the ruling people as a chosen people, but above all gives implicit justification to the patriarchal organization of that people. In due course we shall develop this point that we merely note here more fully, in terms of our central concerns, but it is worth recalling that, as we know, Prat also declared that "peoples without an aristocracy are incomplete peoples."

Finally, it is hardly surprising that that same chapter XI of *La nacionalitat catalana* should begin with a philological reflection on the word "empire": "The Roman people conceded to their

magistrates, whatever the degree they held, the *Imperium*, that is, the faculty of imposing their decrees by force. The idea of force was as essential to the notion of *Imperium* as military power was to the *Imperium* itself; and the one magistrate that, by assembly of the ancient magistratures, concentrated all the power, all the force of the public authority, Rome designated 'emperor,' *imperator*."[156] The Roman essence contained in the very origin of the word further legitimates Prat's idea: imperialism is thus both the highest state of civilization and its origin.

The nation as essential landscape; the people uplifted by the vision of the patriarch; the archaic essence of the classical—of the initial symbol, in effect, of civilization—as the womb of that land, erected over the *omphalos* of the colonizers' oracle under a Greek theater whose backdrop is Barcelona, the great city of the inviolable nation, converted into a panorama that stretches to the *mare nostrum*: all of the emotive aspects of Prat's ideology were condensed by Eusebi Güell in his great emblem. When Rubió i Bellver wrote that the Park Güell was "perhaps the most transcendental of the fruits produced by our renaissance," and that because of this "our land owes its gratitude" to Eusebi Güell,[157] he was not only expressing himself rhetorically.

It is worth insisting on this issue: it is the emotive aspects of Prat's vision that certify Güell's emblem and justify the gratitude that the land owes to the shepherd. There is not much difference here, as we have already said, between these images and the ones suggested to Verdaguer by the Swiss mountains, and Gaudí's Doric temple is not very different from that Augustan temple whose columns, in the presence of Eulàlia, forcibly united Attic beauty and the Catalan profile. Out of the land itself there emerges the soul that not only liquefies the guttae of the temple's metopes, but transforms it into a cathedral: Gaudí's Doric columns, in effect, support not a system of architraves but vaults in whose cells Jujol created the famous ceramic incrustations in which old coffee cups and scent bottles would find, as in a gently

concave sky, their redemption. This is what Rahola, commenting on certain aspects of the Palau Güell, referred to in Wagnerian terms as Gaudí's realism. The vision of Güell and Gaudí is steeped in all those atavistic feelings, their landscape is concentrated around the dolmen and the holm oak in the time of the tribe and the priest, their endeavor has an oracular justification: to the oracle is devoted the primal expression of the *ratio* that the Doric, subterranean and profound, symbolizes. This temple gives civilization a sacred rather than a social origin. Güell's patriarchal status obliges him to stop one step before that emotion becomes, with Prat, explicitly political. How can we forget that what really crowns the Park Güell, that world of earth and myth configured by the monarch, is a Calvary?

This brings us back to the discomfort evident in Gibert's comments on the Greek theater in the park. We have already touched on one reason for this, but there are more. In effect, the imperialist theme expounded by Prat, and the classicism implicit in this, were to receive a rather different interpretation in Catalonia (at least after 1904, although with little subsequent continuity). An example will help us here. In 1906 the Liceo theater in Barcelona premiered an opera entitled *Emporium*, composed by two one-time *modernistes*, Morera and Marquina.[159] The reference to the town of Empúries, in the Empordà, on the Catalan coast, has an immediate relevance: Empúries had been the first Greek settlement on the Iberian peninsula. The fact is that systematical archaeological excavations had commenced there at the very start of the century, financed by the Diputación (Barcelona County Council) and directed by Josep Puig i Cadafalch, an architect with a direct commitment to the program of the Lliga who in due course succeeded Prat de la Riba as president of the autonomous government of the Mancomunitat. These excavations had a strongly symbolic value: the name of Empúries, in effect, was used by *noucentista* intellectuals to substantiate the Greek (that is to say, classical and Mediterranean) origin of Catalonia, and be-

fore long the clear lines of its columns, mosaics and statues were to take their place in the mythology of Catalonia, supplanting the medieval mists of the Pyrenees, in all their particularism. Eugeni D'Ors, for example, commenting on the ancient sculptures unearthed in the excavations, wrote: "An Aesculapius, a Venus! ... How they resonate in one's heart ... these sounds, that are the strains of humanity, and that universally signify, whether in Athens, Paris, Rome, Oxford, Boston or Heidelberg, the salt of culture! This find gives us nobility, makes us new men in making us ancient men."[160] But let us return now to *Emporium*. D'Ors himself wrote a commentary on the opera, which begins: "*Emporium* ...—Ampurias ...—The breadth of an immense horizon is opened within us under the spell of the word. A blue horizon on which father Mediterranean extends his murmurs."[161] Nothing of land, of physical contact with the soil, of souls or primordial voices, but a bright vision of the sea transformed into a category, a universal concept: father Mediterranean. After the evocative resonance of the Greek city, the concept is clarified: "I often think that the ideal sense of the act of redeeming Catalonia might now be reduced to discovering the Mediterranean. To discover what there is in us of the Mediterranean and to affirm it to all the world, propagating it as an imperial endeavor among men."[162] While it is clear that Eugeni D'Ors' imperialism, expressed in such terms, has more than a touch of political propaganda, of support for Prat's nationalist corollary, it is also fundamentally different.[163] D'Ors, in effect, dispenses entirely with the historicist justification of the new Catalan Mediterranean imperialism—that justification for which imperialism has ceased to be new—and abandons the contemplation of the Catalan land and its immediate neighbors—the former realms of the Corona de Aragón—as a condensed vision of Catalan expansion. If Prat's imperialism was the result and culmination of a nationalist restoration that has its origin in a specific history, a specific language, a specific land, for D'Ors imperialism is inseparable from other concepts directly apprehended as values in their own right: the imperial endeavor is for D'Ors simply a condition of the Mediterranean, in Catalonia or anywhere else, from Athens to Heidelberg. Antoni Ras, in 1907, with the schematism typical of the publicist, made it clear what the means and objective of D'Ors' interpretation were: "The form of civilization is imperialism; that is to say, what in Ancient Greece was called democracy: the active and effective aspiration through intervention (the strong and temporary paternal guidance of the superior) that every one of our contemporaries may arrive at the supreme archetype of a higher humanity ... Order, Norm and Method must be incorporated into our action, to make these powerful means to our end ... All together, for D'Ors this orientation is *Noucentisme.* "[164] For those intellectuals who saw an opportunity in a commitment to the State policy advocated by Prat de la Riba, epochally dubbed *noucentistes* by D'Ors himself, the situation was perfectly clear. If the consolidation of the Lliga as a hegemonic party in Catalonia brought in its wake a wide-ranging process of normalization in every sector of the life of the country, rigidly directed from above, the situation created by all this led in the field of art and culture could not be more specific, and in becoming a project—a political rather than an artistic project—it effectively inverted the old system of relationships. In other words, if Catalonia had until then been a receiver of influences of all kinds—as had been the case with *Modernisme*—it was to be from that moment on the active center of a new culture, essentially unitary and universal in character. It would no longer be the same privileged few with their private rivalries who would represent and reconstruct the collective myths of the people in their work, like latter-day seers, priests or princes; instead, the community itself would be reflected in a precise, controlled social ritual, ideally directed to the masses and invested with urbanity in which the ancestral land would be replaced by the city. In 1906, Pijoan wrote: "City you will not be until you have a theater for the art of the multitude, an agora for the policy of the estates, a gymnasium for collective education. You ought to possess these things, I might add, and not only in appearance, but also in spirit, so that there may be that typically urban sensation of civil life."[165] Pijoan is thoroughly modern in his conception of the multitude: a conception that sees them as—and wishes them to be—a spectacle to themselves, idealized, the threat of conflict neutralized; a society, precisely, of the spectacle. Could any theater be further removed from this, intended to educate to such a multitude, than the Greek theater of the Park Güell?

But it is time to return to D'Ors' commentary on *Emporium*: "Father Mediterranean, our sea! If in these instants the spirit were to reveal itself as music! What a moment! I dare not expect it of the present work."[166] D'Ors, then, did not believe those artists would prove capable of carrying out their work, and in the event his misgivings were justified. Although in the opera, Ròdia, "the classical soul," overcomes her enemies, this only takes place "on the exterior, in the anecdote, in the plot; but in the interior, in the music of the poet and most certainly in the music of the composer, Ròdia is constantly defeated."[167] Where, then, does D'Ors see the failure of *Emporium*? Is it in the interpretation of the artist who in his prejudice-ridden individuality loses the essence of things, their authentic universality? Yes, but not only there: that, too, is the exterior. For D'Ors, as we have seen, the world has above all a form: imperialism, classicism, Mediterraneanism—they are all exactly the same thing, the natural expression of the community, its normality, and not something that can be interpreted. On the one hand, D'Ors can write: "We, in turning aside from classicism, disobey the essential law of our Race,"[168] and on the other, for example: "The Mediterraneanizing of music has been undertaken. Others will undertake the Mediterraneanizing of poetry. And in the future everything will be interwoven: music with sculpture; metaphysics with the elections."[169] Art and politics: everything is explained in visual, plastic terms. In D'Ors' sublimation everything is formal: "We make beautiful sculpture and, the time has come of say it, beautiful elections. Nobody will ever persuade me that the recent parliamentary election held in the German Empire can be of as much aesthetic interest as those that we are preparing. These, too, will be sculptures in their way: we model them."[170]

Imperialism, Mediterraneanism, classicism: everything, then, is condensed in a racial necessity, an obligation of destiny. In the collective consciousness of this obligation, this destiny, the "act of redeeming Catalonia" will be accomplished. But was not Catalonia itself (if by Catalonia we understand what we have been talking about up until now, explained in the profundity of its myths, its landscapes, its history and of its language) starting to become indifferent to so much absolute, so much universal law? What was left of that Pratian nationalism, so firmly rooted in the land and in the traditions of the land? Absolutely nothing. D'Ors' imperialism was not the logical conclusion of the nationalism, as Prat had sought to see it, but an autonomous concept that went beyond it: ultranationalism. It is evident that if D'Ors supported Prat politically, he did so from an ideological position that was not his own: the Maurras of classical order, of the racial intelligence, of the Mediterranean reasoning to which we referred in a previous section finds here its place and closes, with no break in continuity, but introducing the sinister radicalism of the abstract, the ineffable *novitas* of the absolute, the classicism that from *Catalonia* to the Laberint, from Maragall to the Park Güell, had been investing itself with particular tonalities. From the philosophy of classical art to integral nationalism: this, and not Catalanism—Prat's as much as Güell's: conservative, traditionalist, integrative, politically realist and contemporizing—is the origin of D'Ors' thinking, and the sustained interpretation he was to make of the form as a process of political purification places this beyond question, if his subsequent and deeply committed engagement with fascism could leave any possibility of doubt.[171] D'Ors reiterated his ideas with absolute clarity many years later, recalling the visits he received from José Antonio and commenting on his personality: "Not nationalist:

imperialist, yes … he was coming to be, on the point of concluding his combat with the Angel, our Jacob, that is to say, José Antonio. A believer in the absolute of Culture (that this means being classical) and not in the relativity of the Nation."[172] What has changed in D'Ors' ideas since the years in which he acted as cultural pontiff of Catalonia? Nothing: only the means, the circumstances. Now then: although his ideological origins were so different from Prat's, D'Ors effectively set himself up as the cultural conductor of the first stages of the normalization and institutionalization of Catalonia undertaken by the State policy of the Lliga, and his ideas were a formative influence on those intellectual and professional élites who, by their commitment to that policy, designed and shaped Catalan culture for decades. In the event, Prat could hardly have found a more directly and spectacularly effective strategy for his purposes. In that *nova cultura* would be sublimated—and sometimes rather more than sublimated—the limitations of his policy of commitments: in it an impossible State was to find its most perfect image.

But if D'Ors regarded *Emporium* as a model of imperfections and deficiencies, what was the classicism of the Park Güell? In due course we will consider D'Ors' disdain for Gaudí and his architecture; Güell's name, on the other hand, ever present as a political paradigm and a model of behavior in Prat's writings, does not appear once in D'Ors' *Glossari*: what place could there be in the *nova civilitat*, social and cosmopolitan, a blend of civil virtues, urbanity and aesthetics, for someone such as Güell, who had sought not only to support but to be himself part and parcel and symbol of the ideological construction of political Catalanism? The construction of his personality elaborated by Miquel d'Esplugues was a definitive demonstration of the significance and the reality of that strategy of power, but also, in its delirium, of its limits—which are, precisely, its lack of limits. The nostalgic tones of d'Esplugues' description of the signs of autobiography in the Park Güell are highly significant, as are his criticisms of Gaudí's exaggerations. It is clear that there was no place in D'Ors' *civilitat* for medieval patriarchs, only for modern caudillos. What we have here is the difference between the conception of the multitude as a people who are one with the land and that of the multitude as a spectacle to themselves: the two strategies may come to complement one another, but they nonetheless clearly need different times in which to develop. Much has been said of the failure of the Park Güell, and certainly, the garden city Güell planned to build there came to nothing: only one plot was sold.[173] But we must not forget that Güell, in addition to imposing draconian conditions on the purchase of land acquisition and the construction of houses in the park, did not provide any special form of transport with which to reach a place that was then a long way out of the city,[174] and not through any lack of examples: in those same years the urbanization of the Avinguda Tibidabo, also destined to become home to the upper classes, had been structured as a continuation of one of the principal arteries of the city, served by a tram line and connected by funicular railway to the summit of Tibidabo.[175] But these were evidently not decisive factors: who, in practice, could live in a place impregnated with symbols, in which the presence of the *princeps* was immanent in every stone, every tree, every image? Güell's *ou-topos*, symbolically separated from the city by a wall set with some ceramic medallions rhythmically repeating his name, would be inhabited by almost no one but Güell himself and his architect: nothing could be more eloquent.[176]

The great emblem that remained was simply condemned by the times: in silence, *civilitat* converted it into a symbol of the caprice of a bygone era. Güell died in his house in the park in July 1918, a few months after the death of Prat de la Riba. Then, only a Gaudí devoted exclusively to his work on the Sagrada Família, increasingly enveloped in his own legend, lived there, until eight months before his death in 1926, by which time both Gaudí and the Sagrada Família—the two together, not the work, as we shall see—had already for many years been established as fundamental myths of *noucentista* Catalonia: myths of a very different good nature from those contained in the Park Güell. It had also been a number of years since the heirs of Eusebi Güell had severed their links with the park and ceded it to the city. The campaign that was mounted against that cession, rousing him like a ghost from another time—a time at once so close and so remote, silent without its owner, who had aspired to signify so much—was simply the final consequence of Eusebi Güell's strategy of distinction: the revolt of his peers.

[1] J. Verdaguer, "A vol d'aucell. Apuntacions d'un viatge al centre y nort d'Europa," *Excursions y viatges (Obres Completes VII. Edició Popular)*, Barcelona, p. 91.

[2] J. Verdaguer's *Canigó. Llegenda pirenayca del temps de la Reconquista*, Barcelona, 1886 (in fact, late 1885) is an epic poem about the mythical origins of Catalonia. The dedication eloquently expresses a very precise patriotic sense: "*Als catalans de França.*" For an overview of the poem, see: J. Molas, "Jacint Verdaguer," *Història de la literatura catalana*, cit., vol. VII, pp. 270–79. For specific aspects, see: J. Guillamón, "El cavaller i la fada. Geografia fantàstica al Canigó de Verdaguer," in *Serra d'Or*, nos. 322–23, July–August 1986, pp. 23–27; R. Torrens, "Els corrents ideològics en el Canigó de Verdaguer," *Revista de Girona*, no. 119, November–December 1986, pp. 63–70; R. Torrens, "Contribució al estudi de la gènesi de Canigó de Verdaguer," *Anuari Verdaguer 1987*, cit., pp. 71–98; P. Tio, "Aportació d'una lectura romántica de Canigó," id., pp. 133–47; J. Pare, "La recepció immediata de Canigó a la premsa (1885–1890)," id., pp. 175–186. As we noted in chapter 1, *Canigó* was partly written in Eusebi Güell's Torre Satalia, and seems to have been sponsored by him (see the relevant data in: J. Bassegoda, "Verdaguer, els Güell i Gaudí," *Anuari Verdaguer 1986*, cit.).

[3] J. Verdaguer, "A vol d'aucell. Apuntacions d'un viatge al centre y nort d'Europa," cit., p. 92.

[4] See chapter 1, note 90. Also useful on this point is: J.M. Fradera, "Entre la Muntanya i Babilónia: nota sobre el sustrat ideològic del primer Verdaguer," *Anuari Verdaguer 1986*, cit., pp. 131–38.

[5] E. Güell y Bacigalupi, "Discurs presidencial dels Jocs Florals de Barcelona, 1900," *Tres discursos*, cit.

[6] See: I. Molas, *Lliga Catalana...*, cit., especially vol. I, pp. 42–46, and B. de Riquer, *Lliga Regionalista. La burguesía catalana i el nacionalisme. 1898–1904*, cit.

[7] E. Güell y Bacigalupi, op. cit., p. 399.

[8] Ibid., p. 398.

[9] Ibid., p. 398.

[10] Ibid., p. 399.

[11] Ibid., pp. 399–400. Undoubtedly Güell is referring to J. Balari i Jovany (1844–1904), a philologist and historian who had specialized in Rhaeto-Romance dialects, and

whose speech on taking his seat in the Academia de Ciencias y Artes in 1888 dealt with Roman influence on Catalonia in terms of orthography. His great unfinished work was *Orígenes históricos de Cataluña*, published in Barcelona in 1899, based on a study of Catalan etymology. On the relationship between Güell and Balari see P. Gual Villalbi, *Eusebio Güell...*, cit., p. 12, although Gual implausibly argues for the influence of the former on the latter.

[12] E. Güell y Bacigalupi, op. cit., p. 401.

[13] Ibid., p. 404.

[14] See note 6.

[15] For the debate on federalism in the context of Catalanist movements on the basis of the texts, see the fundamental: J.A. González Casanovas, *Federalisme i autonomia a Catalunya. 1868–1938*, Barcelona, 1974, especially interesting for the section covering the years 1880 to 1904.

[16] See for example, the cases discussed in E.J. Hobsbawm and T. Ranger, *The Invention of Tradition* (Catalan translation: *L'invent de la tradició*, Vic, 1988), especially those relating to Scotland and Wales. There is an excellent study of various aspects of the Catalan case: Ll. Prats, *El mite de la tradició popular. Els orígens de l'interés per la cultura tradicional a la Catalunya del segle XIX*, Barcelona, 1988.

[17] See: J.Ll. Marfany, "El modernisme," *Història de la literatura catalana*, cit., vol. VIII, pp. 113–16, for an analysis of the convergence between the ideas of the modernists and political Catalanism.

[18] Quoting Odisse-Barot: E. Prat de la Riba, *La nacionalitat catalana*, cit., p. 71.

[19] J.Ll. Marfany, "El modernisme" in *Història de la literatura catalana*, cit., vol. VIII, pp. 113–16 and 132–42. On p. 115 he discusses Cambó's campaigns and quotes from the articles he published in 1898 in *La Veu de Catalunya*: "Pirineu amunt i Ebre avall" and "Les noves corrents a França."

[20] E. Prat de la Riba, op. cit., p. 84.

[21] Ibid., p. 87.

[22] Ibid., pp. 84–85.

[23] On the ideology of race among the modernists see: E. Valentí, *El primer modernismo literario catalán y sus fundamentos ideológicos*, Barcelona, 1973, pp. 167–69; and above all: J.Ll. Marfany, *Aspectes del modernisme*, cit., pp. 113–15 and 136–40. Casas-Carbó, brother of the painter Ramón Casas, contributor to *L'Avenç*, director of its popular library and already in 1892 the author of *Estudis d'etnogènia catalana*, collected his political articles in J. Casas-Carbo, *Catalònia (Assaigs nacionalistes)*, Barcelona, 1908,

when *noucentisme* had already begun to lose ground; our subject is touched on by Pompeu Gener, one of the most active members of *L'Avenç* and subsequently of *Joventut*, in his: *Herejías. Estudios de crítica inductiva sobre asuntos españoles*, Barcelona-Madrid, 1887, and in *Cosas de España*, Barcelona, 1903. See chapter 2, note 44.

[24] J. Maragall, "Alma catalana" (Januaary 24, 1904), in *Obres Completes*, Barcelona, 1981, vol. II, pp. 681–82. On this subject see: J.Ll. Marfany, *Aspectes del modernisme*, cit., pp. 97–185; id., "Pròleg" in J. Maragall, *Articles polítics*, Barcelona, 1988. See, too: M. Vilanova, *España en Maragall*, Barcelona, 1968.

[25] S. Sellés, "Park Güell," *Anuario de la Asociación de Arquitectos de Cataluña*, Barcelona, 1903, pp. 57–59. Another important contemporary text is: B. Bassegoda, "Cuestiones artísticas: el Parque Güell," *Diario de Barcelona*, January 14, 1903, pp. 567–69.

[26] On the chronology of the Park Güell it is worth consulting: I. Paricio, "El Park Güell de Barcelona: una lección de construcción," *CAU*, no. 70, March 1981, pp. 45–62; T. Torii, *El mundo enigmático de Gaudí*, cit., vol. I, pp. 247–53, 278–86 and vol. II, pp. 300–19; E. Rojo, *Antoni Gaudí aquest desconegut: el Park Güell*, Barcelona, 1986, and J. Bassegoda, *El gran Gaudí*, cit., pp. 387–424, all of which offer slightly different versions.

[27] S. Sellés, op. cit., p. 65.

[28] On the "picturesque" garden and its elements see: N. Pevsner (ed.), *The Picturesque Garden and its Influence Outside the British Isles*, Dumbarton Oaks, 1976; D. Wiebenson, *The Picturesque Garden in France*, Princeton, New Jersey, 1978; *Jardins en France. 1760–1820*, Paris, 1978. On other aspects: J. Baltrusaitis, "Jardins et pays d'illusions," *Traverses*, nos. 5–6, October 1976, pp. 94–112. The theme of the cave in Gaudí's architecture is the subject of the second part of the study by T. Torii, op. cit., vol. I, pp. 187ff, but the most stimulating comment is still the article by J.M. Sostres, "Sentimiento y simbolismo del espacio," *Proyectos y materiales*, September–October 1949; now reprinted in id., *Opiniones sobre arquitectura*, Murcia, 1983, pp. 15–21, together with other notes and writings on Gaudí. Sostres is in part the basis for the also very interesting opinions expressed by J.E. Cirlot in *El arte de Gaudí*, Barcelona, 1954, pp. 45–47, in a chapter entitled "Africa" that is itself the basis for the study by Torii cited above. Cirlot's book is also of

interest for its surrealist vision of Gaudí.

[29] See: B. Giblin, "Jules Verne, la géographie et *l'île mystérieuse*," *Hérodote*, no. 10, 1978, pp. 76–85, and also J.J. Lahuerta, *1927. La abstracción necesaria*, Barcelona, 1989, chapter 2, devoted to Verne.

[30] There is a great deal of graphic material on the imaginary of the International Exhibitions in relation to Gaudí in: T. Torii, op. cit., vol. II, pp. 61–77. For a traditional perspective on the International Exhibitions, see: E. Schild, *Zwischen Glaspalast und Palais des Illusions*, Frankfurt-Berlin, 1967. More interesting is the introduction to H. Sedlmayr, *Der Tod des Lichtes*, Salzburg, 1964.

[31] I have tackled the subject in: J.J. Lahuerta, "Cathédrale de Metz à louer," *Arquitectura*, nos. 275–76, November–February 1988–89, pp. 110–17.

[32] For graphic material see, above all: T. Torii, op. cit., vol. II, pp. 80–119.

[33] See: J. Solà Altes, *El parc Samà*, Barcelona, 1981 (unpublished, Cátedra Gaudí); T. Torii, op. cit., vol. I, pp. 232–33.

[34] On Fontseré: (various authors), *Miscellania Fontseré*, Barcelona, 1961; R. Grau and M. López, "La gènesi del Parc de la Ciutadella: projectes, concurs municipal, i obra de Josep Fontseré i Mestres," *Actes del I Congrés d'Història del Plà de Barcelona*, Barcelona, 1984, pp. 441–67. See, too: J. Fontseré, "De la caracterisació de la arquitectura," *La Renaixença*, X, 1873, p. 8. And on his connections with Gaudí and the latter's involvement in the Ciutadella park in the wider context of his early work: A. Pabón-Charneco, *The Architectural Collaborators of Antoni Gaudí*, cit., pp. 1–13.

[35] The background of figures such as Salvador Samà is ably situated in general context in: J.M. Fradera, "Catalunya i Cuba en el segle XIX: el comerç d'esclaus," *L'Avenç*, cit.

[36] J. Bassegoda, op. cit., pp. 387–434 sets out all of the data with reproductions of the documents relating to purchase, development, etc.

[37] J. Rubió i Bellver, "Dificultats per arribar a la síntesis arquitectònica," *Anuario de la Asociación de Arquitectos de Cataluña*, Barcelona, 1913, pp. 63–79. On Rubió: I. Solà-Morales, *Joan Rubió i Bellver y la fortuna del gaudinismo*, Barcelona, 1975. The article cited is reproduced on pp. 120–36.

[38] J. Rubió i Bellver, op. cit., p. 76.

[39] Ibid., p. 77.

[40] Ibid., p. 79.

[41] Ibid., p. 79.

[42] This is the Almirall of *L'Espagne telle*

*qu'elle est*, Montpellier, 1886, and *Lo Catalanisme. Motius qu'el llegitiman, fonaments científichs i solucions pràcticas*, Barcelona, 1886, but also the Torras i Bages who sought to oppose a Catholic vision to Almirall in *La tradició catalana* (1892), cit., especially the "Disertació preliminar" in the second part, where the meaning is well explained in the way in which he reproaches Almirall for having invented a Catalan character as generic as the Castilian character he criticized: "in criticizing the Castilian people as idealist, generalizing and fond of abstractions, he offers us as a symbol of Catalanism, perhaps without being aware of the connection, the Hegelian Idea ... seeking in vain to model our practical and realist race with the abstruse and false idea..." (p. 127). See: J. Solé-Tura, *Ideari de Valentí Almirall*, Barcelona, 1974; J.J. Trías Vejarano, *Almirall y los orígenes del catalanismo*, cit.; A. Jutglar, "Estudio preliminar" in V. Almirall, *España tal como es*, Barcelona, 1983; and the forewords by J.M. Figueres in V. Almirall, *Articles polítics. Diari Català (1879–1881)*, Barcelona, 1984, and id., *Cultura i societat*, Barcelona, 1985. On Almirall's role in the origins of modernism, one of the essential references is still: E. Valentí, *El primer modernismo literario catalán y sus fundamentos ideológicos*, cit., pp. 111–45.

[43] P. Gener, *Cosas de España*, cit., p. 35. See note 23.

[44] On the evolution of Maragall's political writings, see the indispensable foreword by J.Ll. Marfany to J. Maragall, *Articles polítics*, cit.

[45] J. Maragall, "Alma catalana," cit., pp. 681–82.

[46] J. Maragall, *Visions & Cants*, Barcelona, 1900 (I cite from the *Obres Completes*, cit., vol. I, pp. 131–87, which includes the later parts of the "comte Arnau" published after the 1900 edition). Essential here are the studies by J.Ll. Marfany, *Aspectes del modernisme*, cit., pp. 97–185; id., "Introducció" in J. Maragall, *Visions & Cants*, Barcelona, 1984.

[47] J. Maragall, "El Comte Arnau," III, in *Visions & Cants*, cit., p. 140.

[48] J. Maragall, "L'estimada de Don Jaume," IV, in *Visions & Cants*, cit., p. 135. On these verses in particular, and those in the previous note, see: J.Ll. Marfany, "Joan Maragall," *Història de la literatura catalana*, cit., vol. VIII, p. 212.

[49] Referred to S. Sellés, op. cit., p. 54, who also mentions the geological studies Güell commissioned from J. Almera and N.

Font. See: E. Rojo, op. cit., p. 161.

[50] In the *Butlletí de l'Institució Catalana d'Història Natural*, no. 2, February 1901, pp. 9–10; *Butlletí del Centre Excursionista de Catalunya*, no. 75, April 1901, pp. 124–25; id., no. 84, January 1902, p. 4; *Revista de la Cámara Mutua de la Propiedad*, no. 14, September 21, 1904, pp. 99–100; *La Veu de Catalunya*, June 27, 1908. I have taken the data here from J. Bassegoda, *El gran Gaudí*, cit., pp. 388–90 and 422.

[51] J. Almera and A. Bofill, "Consideraciones sobre los restos fósiles cuaternarios de la caverna de Gracia," *Memorias de la Real Academia de Ciencias y Artes*, vol. IV, no. 33, 1903, pp. 447–59.

[52] S. Sellés, op. cit., p. 60.

[53] In Park Güell there is a whole series of artificial caves, now closed off (see e.g., T. Torii, op. cit., vol. II, p. 309), in addition to the fossil cave (J. Bassegoda, op. cit., p. 390).

[54] So named on contemporary postalcards such as those produced by Jorge Venini or Angel Toldrà Viazo.

[55] Among the latter see: I. Paricio, "El Park Güell de Barcelona: una lección de construcción," cit.

[56] S. Sellés, op. cit., p. 58.

[57] The trunk twisting between the columns was photographed by Man Ray and used to illustrate the article by Salvador Dalí, "De la beauté térrifiante et comestible de l'architecture modern style," *Minotaure*, nos. 3–4, June–October 1933, pp. 69–76, which we shall consider in chapter 7.

[58] S. Sellés, op. cit., p. 49.

[59] Ibid., p. 52.

[60] See: I. Molas, *Lliga Catalana...*, cit., vol. I, pp. 187–90.

[61] Ll. Durán y Ventosa, *Regionalisme i federalisme* (1905), Barcelona, 1922, p. 43.

[62] S. Sellés, op. cit., p. 52.

[63] J. Verdaguer, *Santa Eulàlia. Poemet (Obres Completes XVIII. Edició Popular)*, Barcelona,

[64] Ibid., p. 8.

[65] Ibid., pp. 34–35.

[66] Ibid., p. 18.

[67] Ibid., p. 15.

[68] M. d'Espluges, *El primer comte de Güell...*, cit., pp. 39–42, among other references.

[69] J. Matamala, *Mi itinerario con el Arquitecto*, Barcelona, 1965 (unpublished, Cátedra Gaudí), p. 46.

[70] Cit. in J. Bassegoda, op. cit., p. 341.

[71] See: J. Elías, "Gaudí en Montserrat," *Templo*, XCI, February 1956, pp. 8–11; E. Casanelles, "Gaudí ante Montserrat," *Destino*, May 26, 1962, pp. 54–55. For data and

bibliography: J. Bassegoda, op. cit., pp. 429–33, which also reproduces a number of documents.

[72] It will suffice to note that when Gaudí abandoned the project, Llimona moved the figure of Christ from where Gaudí had left it in 1911, "restoring it" to the place he himself had decided on in his first plaster maquette. There are no satisfactory studies of Gaudí's relationships with the artists who worked in his works or collaborated with him, but for the present case see: R. Rucabado, "José Llimona y Antonio Gaudí," *Templo*, June 1965, pp. 6–7.

[73] The project was an initiative of the Lliga Espiritual de la Mare de Dèu de Montserrat, to which Gaudí belonged (a circumstance we shall explore more fully in chapter 6). The purpose was "to request of God, through the mediation of Our Lady of Montserrat, the complete spiritual and temporal reconstitution of the Catalan People"; it brought together a range of Catholic Catalanist sectors, and was, in fact, an extension of political groupings such as the Unió Catalanista and, a little later, the Lliga Regionalista itself. See: J. Massot i Muntaner *L'Església catalana al segle XX*, cit., pp. 137–43. But it also enabled Catalonia's modern Catholic artists to develop contacts with a specific likeminded clientele. See: J. Castellanos "Un arte al servicio de la edificación social," *La Vanguardia. Cultura y arte*, October 17, 1989, p. 4; id., "Torras i Bages i Gaudí," *Gaudí i el seu temps*, cit., pp. 143ff.

[74] On the differences between the alternative versions see: E. Rojo, op. cit., p. 79.

[75] S. Sellés, op. cit., pp. 62–63.

[76] The proportions of this Doric order have been studied in different ways by: J. Bergos, *Autoni Gaudí. L'home, l'obra*, Barcelona, 1954, pp. 104–05; T. Torii, op. cit., vol. I, pp. 282–83. However, the deformation of the elements introduces a series of "deviations" that invite other interpretations, although there are no grounds for seeing these as exercises in irony on Gaudí's part, a widely held view first posited by J.M. Sostres, "Interpretació actual de Gaudí," (1953), and since reprinted in *Opiniones sobre arquitectura*, Barcelona, 1983, p. 122: ("the classical architecture satirized so cruelly in the hypostyle hall in Park Güell") and taken up by O. Bohigas, *Reseña y catálogo de la arquitectura modernista*, Barcelona, 1973, p. 160, among many others.

[77] Nor gratuitously multiply vague references to some "neo-classicism" such as we find, for example, in the generic: G. Barbe Coquelin de Lisle, "El teatro mer-

cado del Park Güell de Gaudí y el mito del Mediterráneo en el arte catalán de 1900," *Fragmentos*, nos. 15–16, 1989, pp. 123–29. It is worth adding that there is only a very diffuse relation between Gaudí's Doric and the by then remote discussions about Greek art that had occupied architects, artists and thinkers between c. 1750 and 1850. See: D. Wiebenson, *Sources of Greek Revival Architecture*, London, 1969. There was, however, as we shall see, a specifically Catalan awakening of interest in Ancient Greece, in everything from politics to fashion, around the turn of the century. For a schematic overview, see: L. Litvak, *El sendero del tigre*, cit., pp. 218–20.

[78] Despite a well-known anecdote that has Elías Rogent publicly burning a copy of Vignola during his first year as a student at the Escuela de Arquitectura in Barcelona (O. Bohigas, *Reseña y catálogo de la arquitectura modernista*, cit., p. 116), it continued to be the "classic" treatise. For more information, see: F. Calvo Serraller, "El tratado de arquitectura de Vignola y su difusión en España," introduction to *Regla de los cinco órdenes de arquitectura de Giacomo Barozzio de Vignola*, Murcia, 1981; J. Berchez, "La difusión de Vitruvio en el marco del neoclasicismo español," introduction to *Compendio de los diez libros de arquitectura de Claude Perrault*, Murcia, 1981.

[79] For more on this, see: P. Zanker, *Augusto e il potere delle immagini*, Turin, 1989, pp. 259–61.

[80] S. Sellés, op. cit., p. 62.

[81] Ibid., pp. 62–63.

[82] Ibid., p. 62.

[83] C. Maurras, *Anthinèa. D'Athènes à Florence*, Paris, 1901. See: L.S. Roudiez, *Maurras avant l'Action Française*, Paris, 1957, and, in general: M. Mourre, *Charles Maurras*, Paris, 1958.

[84] C. Maurras, *L'Avenir de l'Intelligence*, Paris, 1905, but also before; id., *Le Chemin de Paradis*, Paris, 1895, and after; id., *Athènes antique*, Paris, 1913.

[85] In 1900, in conjunction with legitimist monarchist exiles, from the *Gazette de France* he launched a series of polls on the restoration of an antiparliamentary monarchy, which led to the creation of the Action Française group. See his: *Enquête sur la Monarchie*, Paris, 1901.

[86] But there are references to his influence on Eugeni D'Ors; see, for example: E. Valentí, *Els clàssics i la literatura catalana moderna*, cit.; C. Garriga, *La restauració clàssica d'Eugeni D'Ors*, Barcelona, 1981; J. Tusquets, *L'imperialisme cultural d'Eugeni D'Ors*, Barcelona, 1989.

[87] *Ifigènia a Tàurida*, in *Obres Completes*, cit., vol. I, pp. 301–63. The laying-out of the gardens was begun in 1791 by Jaume Valls and Domenico Bagutti.

[88] For first-hand accounts of this extraordinarily diffuse "ambience" see the memoirs of some of those involved, from Isadora Duncan (*My Life*, New York, 1927) to Lady Diana Cooper (*The Rainbow Comes and Goes;* London, 1958), for example.

[89] I. Duncan, op. cit., (Spanish translation, Madrid, 1931, p. 117).

[90] See: E. Valentí, "Maragall i els clàssics," *Els clàssics i la literatura...*, cit., pp. 55–69.

[91] A. Gual, *Mitja vida de theatre*, Barcelona, 1960, pp. 57–93. On Gual: A. Artis, *Adrià Gual i la seva obra*, Mexico, 1946; M.A. Surroca, *Els pre-rafaelites a Catalunya*, Barcelona, 1981, pp. 340–52; E. Gallen, "El teatre," *Història de la literatura catalana*, cit., vol. VIII, pp. 433–39.

[92] A. Gual, op. cit., p. 84.

[93] Ibid., p. 85.

[94] Ibid., p. 86.

[95] See chapter 2, note 115.

[96] On *Catalònia* and its origins: R. Pla i Arxe, "L'Avenç (1891-1915): la modernització de la Renaixença," *Els Marges*, no. 4, May 1975, pp. 23–38; J.Ll. Marfany, "Modernisme i noucentisme, amb algunes consideracions sobre el concepte de moviment cultural," *Els Marges*, no. 26, 1982, pp. 31–42; id., "El modernisme," *Història de la literatura catalana*, cit., pp. 106–11.

[97] J.Ll. Marfany, "El modernisme," cit., p. 106.

[98] J.Ll. Marfany, "El modernisme," cit., p. 110. He also writes: "In 1893, when modernism was the *dernier mot* in Paris, modernism was, for that very reason, symbolist. In 1898, and for exactly the same reasons, it began to be classicist" ("Modernisme i noucentisme...," cit., p. 41).

[99] See: J.Ll. Marfany, "*Joventut*, revista modernista," *Serra d'Or*, XII, 1970, pp. 885–88.

[100] A. Cortada, "Ideals nous per a la Catalonia," *Catalonia*, no. 1, February 25, 1898, pp. 8–12.

[101] J.Ll. Marfany, "El modernisme," *Història de la literatura catalana*, cit., vol. VIII, pp. 113–16.

[102] A. Gual, *Mitja vida de theatre...*, cit. See, for example, his references to E. Duse on pp. 59–60 or his explicit declaration of the model of Lugné-Poe's *L'Oeuvre* on p. 61. See also: Lugné-Poe, "Rencontres avec D'Annunzio," *Scenario*, April 1938, pp. 176–77.

[103] See: E. Gallen, "El teatre," *Història de*

*la literatura catalana*, cit., vol. VIII, pp. 444–45.

[104] See: C. Pascarella, "Il sono del Teatro d'Albano," *D'Annunzio romano e altri saggi*, Rome, 1963, pp. 149–70; A. Sironi, "Caratteri e ruolo della scenografia dannunziana nel rinnovamento del teatro all'inizio del secolo," *D'Annunzio e la promozione delle Arti*, Milan-Rome, 1988, pp. 65–69; P. Chiara, *Vita di Gabriele D'Annunzio*, Milan, 1988, pp. 106–15.

[105] Quoted by P. Chiara, op. cit., p. 111.

[106] They appeared in *La Publicidad* on January 1, 1896, October 16, 1897, January 19, 1898, January 31, 1898. And also in *Catalonia*: March 25, 1898, April 30, 1898, September 15, 1898 and September 30, 1898, and elsewhere. E. Gallen ("El teatre," cit., p. 444) also refers to the early attempts to translate his work.

[107] Quoted in: A. Sironi, "Caratteri e ruolo della scenografia dannunziana…," cit., p. 65.

[108] See: M. Corsi, *Le prime rappresentazioni dannunziane*, Milan, 1928; A. Camilleri, *I teatri stabili in Italia (1898–1918)*, Bologna, 1959. See, too: G. Tosi, "Les relations de D'Annunzio dans le monde du théâtre en France," *Quaderni dannunziani*, VI–VII, 1957, pp. 30–60; G. Gullace, *Gabriele D'Annunzio en France*, Syracuse, 1966.

[109] M. Tafuri and F. Dal Co, *Architettura contemporanea*, Milan, 1976, p. 92.

[110] S. Sellés, op. cit., p. 54.

[111] Vicomte de Güell, *D'Alphonse XII a Tut-Ank-Ammon*, cit., p. 56.

[112] Ibid., pp. 56–57. See also: J.F[ranquesa], "Una vetllada memorable," *La Renaixença*, Barcelona, November 4, 1894.

[113] Ibid., p. 57.

[114] V.M. Gibert, "Gaudí, músico potencial," *La Vanguardia*, June 17, 1926, p. 7.

[115] For the whole background to *La Fada* and the *Teatre Líric* see: X. Aviñoa, *La música i el modernisme*, op. cit., pp. 260–328.

[116] See: E. Valentí, "Maragall i els clàssics," *Els clàssics i la literatura catalana moderna*, cit., pp. 55–69. Maragall's letters to Pijoan of April 1, 1904 and June 18, 1906 in *Obres Completes*, cit., vol. I, pp. 1035–36 and 1045–46.

[117] J. Maragall, "Elogio de una tarde de agosto" in *Obres Completes*, cit., vol. II, pp. 74–76.

[118] Ibid., p. 74.

[119] Ibid., p. 74.

[120] Ibid., p. 74.

[121] Ibid., p. 74.

[122] Ibid., pp. 74–75

[123] Ibid., p. 75.

[124] Ibid., p. 75.

[125] Ibid., p. 75.

[126] Ibid., p. 75.

[127] Ibid., p. 76.

[128] Ibid., p. 76.

[129] "La Garden Party al Parch Güell ab motiu del Congrés internacional de la lengua catalana," *La Ilustració Catalana*, no. 177, October 21, 1906, pp. 664–65. See, too, for example: "Festes catalanes de Beneficència," *La Ilustració Catalana*, no. 232, November 10, 1907, pp. 725–27: the events were organized in Park Güell by pro-autonomy groups.

[130] M. d'Esplugues, op. cit., p. 107.

[131] *L'Esquella de la Torratxa*, May 1908, p. 292.

[132] M. d'Esplugues, op. cit., p. 107.

[133] Ibid., p. 107.

[134] See: M. Manieri Elia, *Architettura e mentalità dal Classico al Neoclassico*, Rome-Bari, 1989, pp. XX–XXIII.

[135] M. d'Esplugues, op. cit., pp. 106–07. This datum is the basis for much of the thesis of E. Rojo, *Antoni Gaudí, aquest desconegut. El Park Güell*, cit. But see the perceptive foreword by M. Izard: "La Bonanova o Icària," pp. 9–13.

[136] So called by T. Torii, op. cit., vol. I, p. 250.

[137] On various aspects of the foregoing see: R. Paribeni, *I grandi santuari dell'antica Grecia*, Milan, 1947, pp. 12–28; P. de la Coste-Messeleiere *Au Musée de Delphes*, Paris, 1936; id., *Delphes*, Paris, 1943; G. Roux, *Delphi*, Munich, 1972; A. Doxiadis, *Architectural Space in Ancient Greece*, (1937), Cambridge, Mass., 1972, pp. 39–47.

[138] See: F. Muller, "Mariano Fortuny y la moda," *Mariano Fortuny y Madrazo. Pinturas, grabados, fotografías, trajes, telas y objetos*, Madrid, 1988, pp. 28–30; and above all: G. de Osma, "Fortuny, Proust y los Ballets Rusos"; id., pp. 31–40. On the "Auriga": F. Chamaux, *L'Aurige de Delphes*, Paris, 1955.

[139] On Fidel Aguilar see: E. Ribalta, "A la recerca de Fidel Aguilar," *Presència*, no. 299, Girona, 1971; J. Fàbrega, *Fidel Aguilar*, Girona, 1972.

[140] See chapter 1, note 101.

[141] Regarding the inscriptions on the bench, see: J. Matamala, *Álbum de las inscripciones*, 1967 (original in the Cátedra Gaudí); J. Bassegoda, "The inscriptions on the bench at Park Güell as transcribed by J. Matamala i Flotats in 1967," *Sites*, no. 15, 1986, pp. 12–14. The idea of *trencadís* as redemption of the material is discussed in chapter 2 above.

[142] M. d'Esplugues, op. cit., p. 106.

[143] J. Bassegoda has related a number of the elements of the stair, especially the dragon, to various aspects of Delphos and its myths, among other less plausible associations, but only in very general terms, without attempting to interpret any specific intentions that might underlie such a relationship (*El gran Gaudí*, op. cit., pp. 409 and 413).

[144] For more on this, see: R. Martín, *L'urbanisme dans la Grèce antique*, Paris, 1956, pp. 32–34.

[145] M. d'Esplugues, op. cit., p. 107.

[146] On this subject see: J. Solé-Tura, *Catalanismo y revolución burguesa*, cit., pp. 195–206.

[147] E. Prat de la Riba, *La nacionalitat catalana*, op. cit., p. 108.

[148] Ibid., p. 117.

[149] Ibid., p. 117.

[150] E. Prat de la Riba, "De lluny," *La Veu de Catalunya*, January 1, 1904; id., "Greater Catalonia," *La Senyera*, January 12, 1907, since reprinted in *La nacionalitat catalana*, cit., pp. 144–48.

[151] E. Prat de la Riba, "Greater Catalonia," cit., p. 147.

[152] Quoted in J. Solé-Tura, op. cit., p. 197.

[153] Ibid. A little later in the same text he famously refers to Barcelona as "the Paris of the south," although the image had already been coined by J. Verdaguer in his "*Oda a Barcelona*" parting from the same vision of the landscape: "… the neighboring Pyrenees / will ask, smoothing their snowy mane, / if that Paris of the Seine has moved to here." There has been no serious study of the extent to which Prat's political slogans drew their images from poets such as Verdaguer and Maragall.

[154] E. Prat de la Riba, *La nacionalitat catalana*, cit., p. 108.

[155] In "L'Ignasi Girona," *La Veu de Catalunya*, September 2, 1905.

[156] E. Prat de la Riba, *La nacionalitat catalana*, cit., p. 107.

[157] J. Rubió i Bellver, "Dificultats per a arribar a la sintesis arquitectònica," cit., p. 79.

[158] In fact by 1909 a Calvary had probably already taken the place of the rose-shaped chapel in the scheme of the Park. On this hill, now known as the Turó de les Tres Creus, see: E. Rojo, op. cit., pp. 124–27.

[159] On *Emporium* see: X. Aviñoa, *La música i el modernisme*, cit., pp. 319ff.

[160] E. D'Ors, *Conferència inaugural. Cicle d'educació civil. CADCI*, Barcelona, 1911. Cit. in: J. Cassasas Ymber, *Intel.lectuals, professionals i polítics a la Catalunya contemporània*, cit., p. 148.

[161] E. D'Ors, *Obra catalana completa. Glossari 1906–1910*, Barcelona, 1950, p. 53.

[162] E. D'Ors, op. cit., p. 54.

[163] On all of this see: C. Garriga, *La restauraciò clàssica d'Eugeni D'Ors*, cit.; J. Cassasas Ymbert, *Intel.lectuals, professionals i polítics a la Catalunya contemporània*, cit., pp. 136–155.

[164] A. Ras, "Ors y su Glosario," *La Cataluña*, no. 7, November 16, 1907, p. 7.

[165] J. Pijoan, "Les académies catalanes" (1906), since reprinted in *La Iluita per la cultura*, Barcelona, 1968, p. 100.

[166] E. D'Ors, op. cit., p. 53.

[167] Ibid., p. 54.

[168] Ibid., p. 1325, in a 1910 annotation.

[169] Ibid., p. 394, in a 1907 annotation.

[170] Ibid., p. 393.

[171] See: J. Tusquets, *L'imperialisme cultural d'Eugeni D'Ors*, cit., pp. 100–11.

[172] E. D'Ors, *Nuevo Glosario*, III, Madrid, 1949, p. 657.

[173] See data and transcripts of documents in: J. Bassegoda, *El gran Gaudí*, cit., pp. 394–99.

[174] Although he did give thought to other matters, such as security; he had a Guardia Civil barracks constructed next to the Park. See: J. Bassegoda, op. cit., p. 404.

[175] The developer was Salvador Andreu, by way of the Sociedad Anónima del Tibidabo, founded in 1889, and the urbanization was supervised by the engineer Marià Rubió i Bellver. It was a kind of linear residential estate for the wealthy bourgeoisie (who came to live in the large private houses designed by Rubió i Bellver, Puig i Cadafalch, E. Sagnier and others) served by an electric tram inaugurated in 1901. See: J. Mínguez, *Salvador Andreu*, Barcelona, 1926; S. Rubió i Tuduri, *El funicular del Tibidabo*, Barcelona, 1971 (unpublished; in the Historical Archive of the Collegio d'Arquitectos de Cataluña).

[176] Gaudí lived from 1906 until a few months before his death in the house that Francesc Berenguer had built the previous year in one of the plots in the Park as a show house. See: J. Bassegoda, op. cit., pp. 400–04.

## Redemptive Labor
Eusebi Güell and the "Spirit of Work":
The Opera *Garraf*, the Industrial Colony
and the Crypt

*Garraf*

August 4, 1892, saw the première, before an invited audience of artists, musicians and poets assembled under the starry dome of the great salon of the Palau Güell, of the lyric poem *Garraf*, written by Ramón Picó i Campamar and set to music by Josep García Robles. Excerpts from the opera were subsequently performed on two further occasions: the first, in 1894, before Monsignor Cretoni, the nuncio of Pope Leo XIII; the second, much later, in 1910, before the infantas María Paz and María Pilar, princesses of Bavaria.[1] Finally, in 1911, the work was published in a handsome edition. This series of incarnations, over a period of almost twenty years, bears witness to the importance that Eusebi Güell attached to the work, for all its mediocrity.

The Quadra de Garraf was an estate that Güell owned on the coast to the south of Barcelona, near Sitges, remarkable for its dramatic cliffs.[2] Three of its best-known geographical features, the crags of Vallbona, Ginesta and Falconera, are personified in Picó's opera as the three daughters of Garraf, the ancestral lord of those lands. Below the Falconera is a system of caves with underground springs and deposits of fresh water, which Eusebi Güell had begun to exploit in the late 1890s: these are the Garraf springs of which we spoke in the last chapter, whose waters Güell proposed to bring to Barcelona by way of miles of aqueducts in a controversial project of 1896.[3] In Picó's drama, the spring is Dona d'Aygua, Garraf's fairy wife who is held captive in the depths of the earth. Labor is the name of the angel God sends to Garraf and his family to urge them to fulfill their mission of giving life to those lands by means of work. The enfeebled condition of Garraf's wife is the cause of her punishment: what were once fertile lands are now, with the spring held captive, arid rocks. The sea god Poseidon appears amid a retinue of mermaids, ancient deities and sea monsters to tempt Dona d'Aygua to come with him, but Garraf blocks his way and defeats him, at the same time overcoming Fatigue and his own fears. Finally, with the aid of a redeeming Labor, Dona

d'Aygua is rescued from her captivity. Their reuniting ensures that not only the land but also human intelligence and knowledge will be reborn: "As soon as Dona d'Aygua, springing from the earth, runs to embrace her daughters, the region returns, as if by magic, from death to life; along the coast bloom the rock rose, myrtle and rosemary; the pines bring forth new verdure, the birds trill, and what was sandbank is a meadow of fragrant flowers on which appear in long procession all the Arts and Sciences that ... slept in the intellectual power of that man whom ... we have called Garraf."[4]

Two things about Picó's opera are of fundamental interest for us here. In the first place, its significance as such within the wider context of the project for the creation of a Catalan lyric theater to which we have already referred in the last chapter—a project that was to find in those middle years of the 1890s its moment of greatest optimism, which would culminate in the première of *La Fada* in Sitges, in 1897, five years after the first performance of *Garraf*, which was, as we have already seen, a strictly private affair: two significant questions to which we shall refer in due course. Secondly, we have the content of the work, its message, what it seeks to transmit as part of a more general symbolic production: that of the enterprises set in motion by Eusebi Güell himself. Güell, to whom the opera was dedicated, thus personified in one of his properties, and under whose roof and for whose guests it was performed, unites these two questions in his own person.

Let us begin, then, with the first question. A very useful basis for this is an article by Joan Sardà published in *La Vanguardia* in 1894 and subsequently reprinted as the foreword to the 1911 edition of the book. The title of Sardà's text tells us a good deal about the position and the role that the author assigns to Picó's work: "A Catalan lyric drama."[5] First of all, according to Sardà, *Garraf* derives from what he calls the spirit of popular legend. It is the "overwhelming need to personify the forces and accidents of nature and to translate into rudimentary dramatic action their clashes

*Pamphlet for the opera* Garraf
*and project by Gaudí for a hunting
chalet in Garraf for E. Güell,
around 1882. Never constructed.*

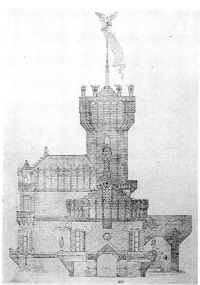

and relations"[6] that gives rise to the ideas and the methods of Picó's drama. Sardà here is in fact simply describing one of the most conventional aspects of the Romantic mentality: the obsession with sacralizing the landscape, attributing a meaning to each tree, each stone, each geographical formation. The primordial spirituality that underlies the urge to mythologize the necessary setting of the legend is also described by Sardà, with the specific tonalities this assumes in *Garraf*: the "geological catastrophe" that shaped the rocks, the caves and the underground lakes of those coasts, he tells us, was transformed into "poetic myth that sought to find something like a germ of inspiration in the biblical tradition of the fall of the man."[7] In Picó's drama, however, that initial posture—like the transparent orthodoxy and the exaggerated and clumsily didactic obviousness of the religious allusions (consider Sardà's veiled criticism, perhaps the only one to be found in this impeccably polite essay, of the recital of the Lord's Prayer which at the end of the work the personae who embody the land offer up to the Creator)—is finally transcended by the symbol in which all the characters, and especially Garraf himself, are sublimated: this is, in Sardà's view, "an artistic concretion of the great mystery of the destiny of the human race."[8] Legend, myth, symbol: the successive elements of Sardà's description continually evoke, although up until now without citing it by name, the Wagnerian model. As in Wagner, "this conception ... assumes in the lyric drama *Garraf* a religious aspect."[9] In Picó's opera, however, the "ideal matter" from which the drama is constructed and the "terrain" in which it is set attain a higher concretion. Sardà immediately sets out to clarify the specific, non-metaphysical nature of this spirituality: its "aspect" is "not so much religious as theological, of the purest medieval Christian theology."[10] There is no lack in Sardà's commentary of very concrete references that serve to emphasize the essential Christianity of the opera on other levels, too, such as the more strictly formal: for example, the prose in which some of the scenes are written has been musically adapted, "recalling and applying the decisive example of ecclesiastical plainsong."[11] But there is, for Sardà, yet another decisive feature of medieval Christianity that permeates *Garraf* even more deeply, and is apparent above all in what he sees as constituting the essence of its "rare novelty and singularity": its classicism. A classicism that is present in the first instance in the "pagan cycle" introduced by Poseidon and his retinue of mermaids and divinities, and even more so in the presence of the Chorus: "the Chorus of ancient tragedy ... a persona forgotten in the machinery of the modern theater, which is and wishes to be a more or less elevated diversion rather than the genuinely civic and religious ceremony or solemnity it was in the golden age of Greece."[12] Thanks to the Chorus, then, *Garraf* is definitely set apart from the mundane superficiality to which the present age has condemned the theater, and restores its former sacral solemnity. In fact, in the Prologue to the work, after the sounding of trumpets, a Herald addresses the audience to this effect: "you are not now in the Circus, but in the interior of the sacred precinct of a Temple that demands silence and concentration."[13] The stage thus becomes "sacred precinct": it is not difficult to imagine the impact of that admonition in a work that was only ever performed in private, under the dome of the salon of the Palau Güell, that *axis mundi*.

The recourse to classical tragedy consists, then, not in the appearance in the third act of what Sardà calls "the picturesque world of mythology," but in the deliberate invocation of its sacred dimension: it is the Christian essence of the opera that is to be sublimated by this resource. After a long succession of what might seem to be cautious hints to this effect, in commenting on the Prologue of *Garraf* Sardà finally clarifies what for him constitutes its ultimate significance: "In this prologue are the substance and the sum of the work; the revelation of the poet's purpose; the artistic formula of his way of conceiving the lyric drama. The Wagnerian formula, spiritualized and Christianized."[14]

*F. Berenguer, Güell wine cellars in Garraf, begun in 1895.*

The interpretation that underpins this statement of the obvious (reserved by Sardà, in a significant rhetorical exercise, for the last line of his article) finds an interesting continuity in certain circles of the Catalonia of the last decade of the nineteenth century. In 1897 (by no mere coincidence a year of the renewed upsurge of modernist and Wagnerian euphoria sparked off by the première of *La Fada* in Sitges), Torras i Bages gave a speech to the Cercle Artístic de Sant Lluc (an association of Catholic artists at which we shall look more closely in the next chapter), including extensive references to Richard Wagner.[15] His analysis, if such it can be called, is based on the simplifications and didactic schematism of the apologist: thus Wagner's art derives directly from "Hegelian subjectivism," which can only be interpreted as a manifestation of human egoism. The whole of "Germanic metaphysics" is nothing other than "a volcanic elevation" of this egoism, the ultimate origin of which is "the echo of the preaching of Luther." The conclusion is obvious: "The art of those whom this [preaching] informs—specifically, that of Wagner—must possess those same qualities."[16] Such considerations are complemented here and there in Torras i Bages' speech with others of a more formal nature, voiced in a more insinuating, less evident manner. Thus, for example, Germanic metaphysics is "as misty as the sky of those lands":[17] we can hardly fail to relate this to the "great ambiguity" of the music of Wagner, whose art, furthermore, is "mysterious, overwhelming, silent, apt for the dark."[18] We looked in the last chapter at the racism that was inherent in a certain classicist restoration: it is not irrelevant to indicate here the Catholic overtones that are already in evidence at this early date. In private notes probably drafted for the Sant Lluc lecture, Torras i Bages is even more explicit about this. Wagner here is simply a representative of the "semi-oriental Germanic spirit, more Asian than European."[19] The racism that serves Torras in his disqualification of the Wagnerian aesthetic, which he uses in his lecture as a kind of "ground bass," has an obvious and immediate purpose: the implied comparison with classical clarity, a clarity that is based above all on concretion. "The language of art requires a concretion or definition,"[20] writes Torras, amid references to Greece and Rome, but what is that concretion, in fact, but the absence of art as such? It is hardly surprising that in his critique of the *art pour l'art* of which Wagner is so extreme an exponent, Torras should choose the classical example: "Hence the identification between people and Art that existed among the Hellenes; they did not make Art such as it is made today, but sought to express religious belief, love and patriotism."[21] It is the absence of the liturgical that, for Torras, causes the Wagnerian project to fail. Of that grand attempt at constructing a mythology, Torras says in his notes that "myths *per se* are of no interest,"[22] and adds that "the Wagnerian fables are a kind of sphinx."[23] To that sphinx Torras' discourse opposes "the spectacle of the eternal and traditional Art, born in Greece and purified and fertilized by Christianity,"[24] and declares that, for him, the greatest beauty resides in the ceremonies of the Catholic liturgy, and especially in the Gregorian chant (which, as he takes the trouble to remind us, is "the pagan vocal music of Rome and Greece adopted by the Church"[25]), so that the silent mystery of the Wagnerian myth must be replaced by a different mystery, far richer in its resonances. "We love the mystery, we are interested in the figure; that is to say, that the visible should be the manifestation and face of the invisible; but we wish this figure, this form, to be real, because here in the natural order is included that which in the supernatural order we find in Holy Scriptures. And even in the historical events of the Old Testament, which although being more than real and true, are at the same time figure, symbol, manifestation, enigma and prophecy of something higher."[26] These schematic opinions were to become a persistent presence in certain Catalan Catholic circles, shaping their conception of the mission of art. Many years later, Josep Tarré gave an important lecture on art and liturgy (to which we shall turn our attention in due course), in which

he declared that the "supreme reunion of all the arts ... has only been assumed in full by the Catholic religion," adding that this is something the Protestant peoples "have felt the want of, and has been pursued without rest by the genius of Bayreuth."[27]

The sacral dimension of the arts in Antiquity, allusions to the New Testament as inspirational mystery, the specific beauty of the Catholic liturgy and especially of its music: quite clearly the critique that Torras directs against Wagner draws on the same elements as Sardà's commentary on the lyric drama of Picó i Campamar. Both set out from the same vision: that of an egotistically godless, despiritualized Wagner, who fails in his mythologizing venture because, seeking inside himself for inspiration rather than waiting for God to grant it, he is unable to transcend the human plane. A shared vision, then, and the same elements: the difference, obviously, is that while in Torras' text this stance determines a negative critique, in Sardà it is the basis for his positive appraisal of *Garraf*, presented as a transcendent contrast to the "Wagnerian formula." It is perhaps not going too far, then, to see the opera dedicated to Eusebi Güell and composed to exalt and celebrate him, and performed on one occasion before the Papal nuncio, as forming part of a bid, albeit unsuccessful and with no apparent continuity, to create a Catholic Catalan lyric theater directly opposed to the modernist appropriation of Wagner—that is to say, to the danger of a despiritualized Catalan lyric theater—and, indeed, a very early part of that project: the five years between the premières of *Garraf* and *La Fada* is, in a period of rapid change, a long time. The aim, then, was to construct on the basis of Wagner a traditional, conservative system, an opera at once modern and at the same time, in the most radical sense of the term, antimodernist: that and nothing else is the intention of Sardà's last point. The time we have devoted to Torras' views on Wagner (significantly, as his notes make clear, based on Wagner's writings and not on his music, which Torras may not even have heard)[28] has been well spent. It has served to show how Güell and Picó's undertaking, described by Sardà, did not vary in the slightest with regard to the orthodox Catholic assessment of those operas: it was simply made operative. But that was not enough. In reality, that "medieval Catholic" Wagner was also subtly bound up with a certain indisputably modern vision of his work, which could not be ignored by a Güell who, observing a late nineteenth-century bourgeois rite, regularly attended the concerts in Bayreuth.[29] In light of this, it is worth referring to Baudelaire's articles on various aspects of Wagner's work, precisely those aspects in which, as Benjamin was to remark in his observations on the poet, the concept of modernity enters into conjunction with Catholicism.[30] But where Benjamin sees the idea of the demonic, our Catalans undoubtedly saw objectifiable and directly usable words and ideas. And not so much in the effects of sacral magic that the music produces in Baudelaire "I had experienced ... a spiritual operation, a revelation"—as in its causes—"frequent repetitions of the same melodic phrases ... implying mysterious intentions and a method I knew nothing of."[31] It is evident that one of the principal intentions of Picó's opera, in exactly the direction marked by Torras' words, was to counteract those "mysterious intentions," that sphinx, in order to make the work more resonant. In this respect (that of method or, as Sardà says, that of the "Wagnerian formula") the assumption of some parts of Baudelaire's critique could not be, to the personages' eyes as ours, more telling evidence: "With not the least surprise I have found in some of those works that have been translated, especially in Tannhäuser, Lohengrin and the Ghost Ship, an excellent method of construction, a spirit of order and classification, that recalls the structure of the Greek tragedies."[32] This vision of Baudelaire's of what was part of a declaration of intentions, in Wagner's theoretical writings more than in his operas, becomes the actual material from which *Garraf* is constructed. In Baudelaire, however, the vision does not stem from an apparent prejudice, but leads on to a new complication.

**179**

*Procession in the Colonia Güell,
1910.*

Thus he writes: "Aphrodite, the radiant Venus of Antiquity, born of the white foam, has not passed through the horrible shadows of the Middle Ages with impunity... On descending below ground, Venus approaches the Inferno and, without a doubt, certain abominable solemnities, paying regular homage to the Archfiend, prince of the flesh and lord of sin." And he concludes: "Similarly, the poems of Wagner, although they manifest a sincere taste and a perfect comprehension of classical beauty, nevertheless partake, in great measure, of the Romantic spirit. The majesty of Sophocles and Aeschylus is evoked, and yet they oblige the spirit to recall the Mysteries of the most visually Catholic age. They are like those grand visions that the Middle Ages represented on the walls of the churches or wove in magnificent tapestries."[33] From that descent to the underworld of the pagan divinities to that artistic vision of Catholicism and its mysteries, a literal reading will suffice to exorcize the demon that Benjamin saw—and that certainly accompanied

Baudelaire in the depths of his thought—and assimilate it to the formula, to the method: in short, it was simply a question of objectifying what in Wagnerian opera emerges dramatically from its own contradictions. What is more, the visual forms of the Catholic faith—in its liturgy, in its rites, in its solemn processions, always ambiguously but necessarily associated with the mysterious and the demonic—constituted some of the favored sites on which the authors of the reactionary modernity of nineteenth-century European decadence liked to gaze, from the remote Barbey to the immediate Huysmans, by way of so many others?[34] In light of all this, what difficulty should there be for our personages in interpreting, as they did, the Wagnerian formula? If the negative criticism of the Church and the Catholic orthodoxy, as represented by Torras i Bages, was one end of the scale on which their construction had to be made operative, that Catholic visual aesthetic was without a doubt the other, that which determined its claim to modernity. Indeed,

*A. de Riquer, Saint Isabel spinning,
fireplace on the bedroom level
of the Palau Güell.*

we have already seen Eusebi Güell put a similar interpretation into practice in his town house. Letamendi's watchword, that "dominion by culture" that so perfectly translated the forms of social imposition represented by myth, assumes in *Garraf* quite different tonalities: but only tonalities, tonalities that make necessary other means and other immediate objectives (determined, however, by the same ends).

As "the Wagnerian formula Christianized," *Garraf* was, as we have said, a failed project, with no continuity—although it seems clear that the attempt to turn Maragall's poem *Comte Arnau* into an opera, and above all the final form given to that attempt by Pedrell, was a pale reflection of that project.[35] Nevertheless, the importance of that never explicitly revealed project, reduced forever to the intentions and the example of *Garraf*, can be inferred from the enduring presence of the ideas that had fueled it in certain *fin-de-siècle* Catalan intellectual circles.

The case of Doménech Español is symptomatic of that enduring presence and its subsequent fate. A music critic and composer, and one of the leading lights of the Associació Wagneriana de Barcelona, in 1902 Doménech published the extraordinary *Apothéose musicale de la Religion Catholique. Parsifal de Wagner*.[36] In this book he gives a symbolic explanation of the Wagnerian drama, focusing in detail on each step, each scene, each character, each element. Thus, the knights of the Grail are Catholic society, the chalice is the doctrine of Christ, the spear is the will of God; similarly, Kundry is the concupiscence of the flesh, Klingsor is the Antichrist and Parsifal the image of man illuminated by the Holy Spirit. Meanwhile, the first theme is the voice of Christ and the dominant theme is the God glory, the first act is constructed like a Gloria Mass and the third like a Requiem, the finale is the Last Judgment, and so on. Every note, Doménech assures us, has a divine origin and meaning: nothing in *Parsifal* escapes his explanation, and all of these explanations lead to the same end, which the title of the book clearly announces. In other words, *Parsifal* is the musical

apotheosis of the Catholic faith, and at the same time a prophecy in which Parsifal is the third man, the third Adam. For Doménech, then, Wagner has become an instrument of God: "It is by the inspiration of the Holy Spirit that Wagner wrote *Parsifal*."[37] The cautious hints of the authors of *Garraf*; Sardà's cares and the simplistic criticisms of Torras i Bages are radically overstepped by Doménech's claims. Thus, for example, the fact that Wagner was an atheist, to which Doménech specifically refers, was immaterial to the divine purpose of which he was to be the servant. Similarly, his work, directly inspired by the Holy Spirit, is sacred in a sense that goes beyond the normal use of the term, comparable to the sacred status of the proportions of the Temple dictated by God to Ezekiel, and, in short, given all of this, there is nothing strange in the fact that the Wagnerian technique—the elementary and repetitive leitmotiv that is at the same time rich in symbolic depths—should be the same as that found in Holy Scriptures. Doménech's manifestly far-fetched thesis, which he continued to put forward in a long series of no less curious articles and lectures, provoked a debate in the Barcelona press that was often fiercely critical, contemptuous and sneering.[38] But what is this if not the extreme expression of that project for a Catholic lyric drama initiated with (and at the same time frustrated by) *Garraf*? When even the very impossibility of implementing that project must have been long forgotten, Doménech looked for the Catholic essence in Wagner's work itself, specifically in its source, sublimating the inspiration and the consciousness of the artist, presenting him as literally alienated, a medium whose hidden motives only the inspired critic can perceive.[39] But for all that Doménech's venture seems slightly ridiculous and pathetic, it is worth bearing in mind that almost twenty years on, *Garraf* was performed again in 1910, for the Spanish royal family, and was not published until 1911. And many years later, in 1927, the eccentric and interesting Francesc Pujols was to add a further chapter to the story, bringing together Richard Wagner and Gaudí in a similarly controversial work

that was roundly condemned by the architect's most loyal supporters. True to his paradoxical nature, Pujols saw the exaggeratedly Catholic Catalonia that could construct a church such as the Sagrada Familia as precisely the country in which Catholicism would meet its end: the grand visions of Wagner and Gaudí were drawn together and equated in the perplexity of that fate. The title of Pujols' pamphlet was *La visió artística i religiosa d'en Gaudí*,[40] and with it, a circle was closed.

But let us return to *Garraf*. Between the two extremes of Torras i Bages' negative criticism and Doménech Español's enthusiasm, Picó's opera—prior to both, of course, and as such already present in them—represents a moderate middle ground. But it is precisely the seriousness of its public purpose that gives significance to a number of other essentially related aspects. One thing above all we must not forget: the opera was dedicated to Eusebi Güell, and set out to celebrate the man and his properties. The new spring that with the victory of Labor and the freeing of the underground stream, Dona d'Aygua, covers the dry cliffs of *Garraf* with verdure is an unmistakably direct allusion to the owner of the estate. Sardà, in his article, writes that the land "is today reborn in the hands of its proprietor, Don Eusebio Güell..., and the Catalan manorhouse stands once again within the rustic walls a home to honorable lifegiving work";[41] and a little later, recalling the surveys commissioned by Güell with a view to exploiting the underground springs of the Falconera, culminating in the project to supply water to Barcelona by aqueduct, Sardà is perfectly explicit: "from the spectacle of the work in search of the spring there emerged in the author's mind ... the first idea for his lyric drama."[42] It is hardly surprising, then, that in Picó's imagination the geographical features of the land become the characters of the drama, and pagan deities mix with the angels of God: the lyric drama composed in honor of Eusebi Güell is thus a clumsy imitation of the grandeur of *L'Atlàntida*, the extraordinary poem that Verdaguer had dedicated to Güell's father-in-law, Antonio López. What is even less

surprising, familiar as we are with the strategies of Güell's symbolic production, is that *Garraf*, so laden with public intentions in terms of the project for a Wagnerian opera (that is to say, a modern and at the same time Catalan and Catholic opera), was always performed in private; and performed, indeed, in the salon of the Palau Güell, the perfect setting for the *princeps*. The significance of this is eloquently expressed by the Herald, who, as we have seen, reminds the audience that they are in a sacred precinct. Güell is thus the protagonist of *Garraf* twice over: protagonist as the sponsor of an artistic project with far-reaching ideological connotations (in other words, as patron) and protagonist of the poem itself, as lord of Garraf.

This brings us to the second of the factors that make *Garraf*, for all its meagre artistic quality, a work of fundamental importance: its message, inextricably bound up with the persona of its protagonist, in which we shall find much to interest us. It is obvious that *Garraf* is an exaltation of work. In the Prologue itself the Chorus proclaims: "Let us intone a hymn to Labor!,"[43] and, as the conscience of the defeated Garraf, it never ceases to remonstrate with him: "...if you wish to recover the lost good, bestir yourself...,"[44] or, to take a few lines almost at random: "Garraf, Garraf, never abandon Labor!.../ Follow him always!... Only with him will you attain / the highest summit / where desires flourish... / Follow him always and you shall be strong and free!..."[45]

This, then, is work illuminated by God, and at the same time a symbol of redemption and resurrection: everything flourishes once again thanks to work; not only the land, but the Arts and the Sciences.[46] But it is not joyful work: the recollection of work as the punishment for man's original sin is there, but transformed into Law, into a reason loaded with connotations of the absolute, of the necessary. It is significant that it should be the personification of fatigue and not, as would seem logical, of sloth, that tests Garraf. Labor reviles Fatigue: "Impious one... / I am the Law, you the punishment!..."[47] Work as redemption from sin

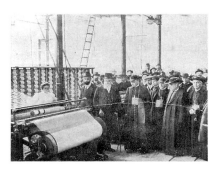

and work as the only path to prosperity are indissolubly united in the great Catholic-bourgeois convention that informs Picó's drama. A convention, obviously, but a convention with concrete applications. In the last verses of the Prologue, the chorus sings: "Oh, Mother Catalonia! Oh, Our Homeland! / Labor raises you from the ruins of your past greatness!... / Labor will weave you a mantle richer than that once torn from you!... / Labor will circle your brow with a crown more prized than that you lost as Queen!"[48]

It is evident that these verses generically reflect another great convention: that of the hard-working Catalan character that, in contrast to the lordly disdain for work of the Castilians or the oriental apathy of the Andalusians, had produced the Romanticism of the Renaixença as well as the Spanish popular genres of *costumbrismo* and the picturesque. But this, as we have said, is a stereotype. What is much more specific is the identification that this stereotype permits here: Catalonia will flourish as Garraf does thanks to the work of the ancestral lord of those lands, who is their personification. Eusebi Güell and his property, then, are not only an example, but work itself and Catalonia itself. This is not a story from which we are to draw an obvious moral, but an identification, pure and simple: the identification that takes place at the pinnacle of society between that society, conceived as the land, and its lord. Here again, then, Güell—his person, his deeds, his properties—is Catalonia. So there is nothing strange in the fact that many of the elements of *Garraf*—the deep caves and the voices that issue from inside them, the underground springs and lakes and the great geological movements they evoke, the very personification of the land and its accidents—should subsequently come to form part of the necessarily essential landscape of Park Güell.

At the same time the leading role assigned to work has, in the wider context of the symbolic production of Eusebi Güell, yet another meaning. Again, in the Prologue of *Garraf*, the chorus exclaims: "Hungry Poverty, turbulent Discord and

destructive War flee from Labor as soon as they see him come, singing joyfully, surrounded by the daughters of Peace, the sweet Joys that, linking their hands, skip smiling around him."[49] But, what are these lines from the "Hymn to Labor" but a further commentary on the program embodied in the murals Aleix Clapés painted in the great salon of the Palau Güell? Of these four paintings, let us look first at three in particular: the poor praying before a wayside cross, Saint Isabel giving her crown to the poor, and a ring of girls dancing among flowers. The exaltation of charity and prayer is their theme, but a theme that, in the image of the queen who gives her riches to the poor, has very specific implications: not only in terms of the paternalism of Eusebi Güell's ideology in relation to the "social question," to the specifics of which we shall refer in a moment, but, once again, the total involvement of the family in that ideology. We should not forget that Isabel was the name of Eusebi Güell's wife, and that the picture in the salon is not the only representation of the saint in the Palau Güell: a delicate mosaic by Alexandre de Riquer on the main chimney breast on the bedroom level depicts Saint Isabel spinning, and thus alludes not only to charity, but also to the condition of the wife who waits at home.[50] Still less should we forget that the performances of *Garraf* took place amid the murals of the salon, in which the words of the chorus found a precise echo: here Labor was united with Charity, and gaily dancing around them, both in the opera and in the murals, were the daughters of Peace and Joy, the girls decked out as spring. It is surely not surprising that one of the performances of the opera, the one for the Bavarian princesses, was given on November 17, Saint Isabel's Day.[51]

But the "Hymn to Labor" in *Garraf* has, in the setting of the salon of the Palau Güell, still other associations. The fourth of the Clapés murals is a portrait of Jaume Balmes, the first Catalan—or Spanish—thinker to look clearly at the new problems being created by the processes of industrialization; Balmes went on to elaborate, between 1844 and 1848, the year of his early death, a

*F. Berenguer, general plan*
*of the Colonia Güell, published*
*in 1910.*

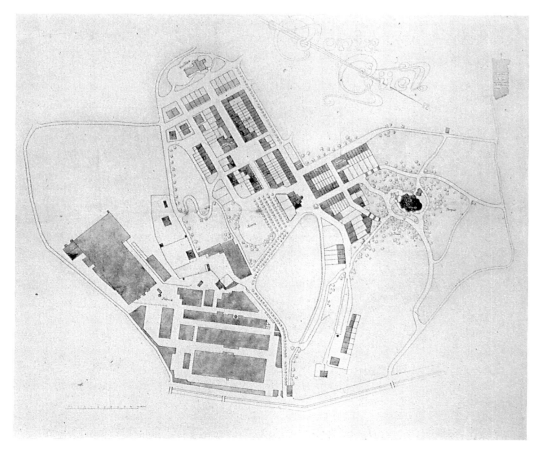

coherent, all-embracing social philosophy on this basis.[52] He set out from an immediate fact: in Catalonia, industrialization was irreversible and therefore, so, too, was the radical change in social relationships that industrialization had brought about. A new class, the industrial bourgeoisie, the new aristocracy of wealth, was taking over from the old aristocracy of noble blood. The hegemonic aspirations of this new class were, for Balmes, intrinsic to its capacity to create new wealth. Therefore, this bourgeoisie had to impose itself definitively on the old aristocracy, or, to put it another way, conquer State power. The strategy that can be deduced from Balmes' writings is highly significant: the Catalan bourgeoisie was to extend its interests to the rest of Spain, and ensure that the whole of Spain—the nation—identified with those interests. At the same time that bourgeoisie should impose not only its political hegemony, but also its social hegemony. Another social class, as new as the industrial bourgeoisie, had been born alongside it: the working class. For Balmes it was apparent that this was where the real danger for the new order lay, and here too his strategy was clear: the progress of science, technology and industry had to generate not only wealth, but a new morality. In other words, the bourgeoisie had to envisage, right from the outset, the integration of the working class in the system of relationships it had created.

Once again, Balmes' recommendations are precise and detailed, from the encouragement of saving and the ownership of property among the workers to the creation of mixed social, political and economic institutions in which employers and workers would be united by shared interests.[53] For Balmes there was obviously a Christian imperative in this way of proceeding—namely, charity—but he was also motivated by the need to prevent the working class from organizing independently. The new social ideologies that the far-sighted Balmes had discovered on his trips to Paris and London in 1842 (those of Robert Owen in particular), which still contained strands of the French apologetic school from Lacordaire to

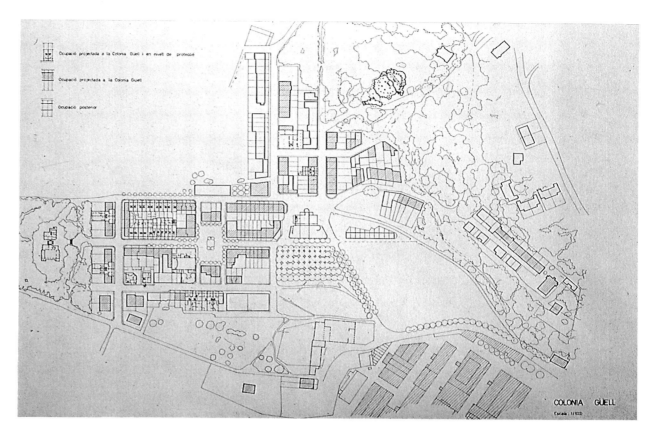

Montalembert and a Romanticism rooted in Chateaubriand, are condensed in his formulation, which put forward an authentic program for a bourgeoisie that in due course was to make him, rhetorically speaking, the philosopher of Catalonia.[54]

In fact, however long it was to take—Balmes died in July 1848, ostracized by the very classes he had sought to convince with his social and political thinking, and passionately devouring the latest news to reach him from revolutionary Paris— very few of his ideas were to fall on barren ground. Prat de la Riba subsequently drew those ideas together in his own political synthesis, while Eusebi Güell, as we have seen, simply turned them into an emblem of his ideology of work. It has rightly been said that Balmes' ultimate aim was to arrive at a mutual ethical and social commitment between the classes: depicted alongside Balmes, Isabel of Hungary takes on a clear social

significance that the Hymn to a redeeming Labor reinforces.[55]

But the elaboration of the program we have traced from the salon of the Palau Güell to *Garraf* involves yet another specific identification. As we know, on the side façade of the house there was a large mural by Clapés depicting Hercules, vanquisher of the Hydra, and of course that monster with seven heads was traditionally interpreted as an image of discord. In the Prologue to *Garraf* the Chorus specifically refers to "turbulent Discord" and "destructive War" as evils routed by Labor:[56] can there be any doubt that these are the discord and violent conflict that may arise within the social fabric itself? How else could it be Labor who vanquishes them? In other words, this is "social discord": class struggle. We might recall here a source that fully confirms this, in the verses of the Corpus Christi Psalm written by Ramón Picó i Campamar, with music by Eusebi Güell's daugh-

ter Isabel, "in order for the inhabitants of the Colonia Güell to sing it in chorus on the said feast day": "That there should be work / that discord and sloth should cease."[57]

The inhabitants of the Colonia Güell were to sing in chorus, then, a hymn to work very much like the one announced by the Herald in *Garraf*; not only in the murals of Eusebi Güell's mansion, but in the united voices of his workers, too, that hymn would resound. Güell's aim, in effect, was to construct a city of work from which all the discord would be utterly banished. His colony was to be the material embodiment of a whole program that in the aspects we have considered so far—Labor and Hercules, Isabel of Hungary and Balmes—had done no more than find its symbolic expression.

## "Capital and Work, Brothers"

We have already had occasion to note how the critique—in origin, regenerationist—of the Spanish State was one of the essential bases of the Catalanist ideology that would culminate in Prat de la Riba's synthesis and the founding of the Lliga Regionalista. But what were the grounds of this critique of the State? First and foremost, its artificiality; that is to say, its remoteness from civil society: a thesis of Romantic origin that, as Catalanism became consolidated politically, was gradually to lead to the identification of that society with the interests of the industrial bourgeoisie. As an alternative to the centralist State and the parliamentary regime, Prat and the intellectuals of the formative stage of the Lliga proposed a regionalist State and a corporate regime: only there

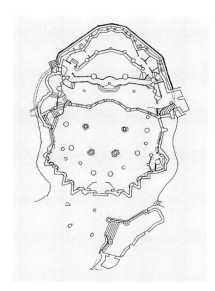

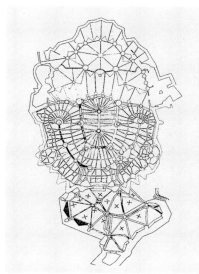

was it possible to find a naturalness with direct links to the land, to tradition and history.[58] But we have already looked at all of this: what interests us now is one very concrete aspect of the expression of that ideology. In 1898, the year in which Spain lost its last overseas colonies after a disastrous colonial war and when, in the light of the increasingly evident failure of that State, the regenerationist thesis of Catalanism begin to receive the support of key sectors among the Catalan upper classes, Prat de la Riba published an important book, *Ley jurídica de la Industria*, in which the critique of the existing State becomes a theory of the privatization of its functions. Chapter six of Prat's book is particularly important for our purposes, because that theory is there given concrete expression in a very specific case: that of the industrial colonies. Let us consider this case more closely.[59]

The starting point of Prat's analysis is the following quotation from Joan Permanyer: "I would go so far as to cite, among the factors that are perhaps to provide the basis for reform, these great industrial colonies that have been organized and are now operating in different parts of Catalonia and principally in our river basins. The facts are plain. Private enterprise, in places once all but deserted, encloses for days, weeks and even months under a single key, in the material sense of the word, thousands of persons of both sexes and all ages, whole families; in a word, a population of workers with their managers, supervisors and foremen, their groceries, shops, medical care and even the cure of their souls, all under a single direction and under the imperative of a sovereign will."[60] Three ideas are contained in embryo in Permanyer's words, which Prat hails as literally a revelation: the reforming potential of the colony, its radically private nature and its condition as a "little world." To each of those ideas Prat attaches a precise meaning, which we shall attempt to analyze in that order.

For Prat, Permanyer's ideas describe, above all, one of the solutions that "the genius of the Catalan people would give to the profound contemporary social crisis, if it were free to implement the inspirations of its legal criterion."[61] Here, then, the reforming function that Permanyer attributes to the workers' colony is immediately interpreted by Prat as a "regenerating virtue," and from the outset this is linked in his thesis to the Catalan character, thus giving a transcendent dimension to the critique of State policy in relation to the so-called "social question." At the same time, the force for social regeneration that Prat discerns in the colony has certain concrete aspects. The first words of the chapter are very clear in this sense: "The social question is not a merely economic question; it is not enough, then, to extend material well-being, it is not enough to guarantee the worker his daily bread: it is necessary to transform his soul, when it has been corrupted."[62] The great urban concentrations generated by industry are the cause of that degeneracy: "a medium in which swarm all the germs of evil."[63] Prat uses the metaphor of contagious disease, of the microbe that must be fought with vaccines and isolation (images that were in due course to take on, as we shall see, a literal significance), to give his words a crusading resonance. Prat knew how to exploit the discursive mechanisms of the French social Catholic writers, and understood the value of their effects. In his metaphor of the "infected medium," the physical images in his vivid descriptions of the birth of the working population intuitively provoke in the reader a sense of repugnance at the disease that is transmitted; however, this disease is not biological but moral and social. Moral and social, in effect: "the greed of the worker, stimulated by all over attractions of the populous cities, slowly engenders in his soul terrible hatreds, hatreds and class resentments." A radically antiurban ideology thus underlies proposal: "The industrial colony combats the accumulation of the population in the cities, moves it to the countryside, disperses the population … in small isolated nuclei, helping in this way to re-establish the equilibrium of the social body."[64] It is perfectly evident, then, that if there is one factor that is glaringly absent from the Pratian thesis it is the

Gaudí's original drawing relating
to a photograph of the model
of the east façade, published in 1910.

189

economic: it is not even mentioned. Prat can see only one benefit in adopting the model of industrial dispersion offered by the workers' colonies: the social benefit. That, and none other, is the added value that can be expected of it: mitigation of the threat posed by large concentrations of workers in the cities.[65]

In this way, antiurban reaction is converted directly into a proposal for restructuring society. The gist of this, as we shall see, is very clear: there where the remote State is incapable of establishing order, private enterprise can do so, by means of the colony. And this idea derives from the second question that Prat perceives in Permanyer's words: that of the colony as site of the "imperative of a sovereign will." On the one hand, Prat defines the State as "a colossus bristling with cannons and bayonets, condemned to look on impassively as around it there germinate errors of all kinds…, efflorescence of ideas and doctrines that make it systematically impotent."[66] On the other, however, in contrast to the colossus that, encompassing all things, is unable to touch any, there is a very different power. "A power less extensive and, as such, closer, more difficult to evade, more specialized and therefore more fitted to its object and more cognizant of the needs of the particular case: the power of the employer, head of the industrial family."[67] And there is one reason above all that makes such a power effective, that is to say, real: its direct relationship with things and people, its physical concretion. This is Prat: "In the present social breakdown the only civil power that, in spite of the attacks it has suffered, remains robust and vigorous is the *potestas in re*, the dominion over things."[68] That concretion, the kind of dominance that seems to make itself effective in the very hands that a man lays on the things and the people around him, derives its strength from the right that, literally as a gesture, he creates: the right of property. From this, in effect, there stem the powers that the employer needs to create the desired "medium" in his colony: "the faculty of permitting within his house only certain practices or customs, of expelling those who stray from these practices, of imposing on those who wish to live in his house observance of its rules…"[69] What better way of explaining one of the qualities that determine the effect of the colony, that condition it and define it: its isolation? At the same time, in opposition to the abstraction of a State reduced to an "efflorescence of doctrines," the right of property is invested in Prat's text with all the attributes of the real: it is not a juridical concept but a self-evident fact that demonstrates its naturalness in the very act of its exercise. A naturalness that Prat upholds in two ways. On the one hand, with a historical analogy, presenting the restructuring of society to be achieved by the adoption of the industrial colony system as a return to the Christian Roman mode of colonization. "The great transformation of ancient society," Prat writes, "was effected within the *dominium* or villa." In effect, "in the rural *dominium* there lived … under the orders of the prefect or *villicus* a numerous population of servants … without organization, without structure … And, nevertheless, from that formless chaos … there emerged the most robust and most stable family the centuries have seen, that patriarchal family that in the rugged mountains of our land still survives as an example to our own people and outsiders." A little later, "with the conversion to Christianity of the lord of the villa, immediately there was constructed by the side of the *praetorium* the temple of Jesus Christ; each *dominium* had its church and its pastor; baptism dignified the slaves; indissoluble marriage put an end to promiscuity…; one day the needs of agriculture caused these families to be dispersed throughout the *dominium* … and then the family of servants was complete."[70] After this vision, Prat's conclusion is ineffable: "Something very similar must be effected today. The situation is similar." Similar, in short, because Prat sees that "population of servants without organization, without structure" reproduced in the "immense working population without traditions and without a home, confused, uprooted, easy prey to all the corruptions":[71] the corruptions that urban industrialization has gen-

190

erated. And similar, too, because the solution is to be found, as in the past, in that same act of will: by "placing a vigorous, unshakeable personal power in the service of a moral and religious doctrine."[72] Prat's proposal, then, could not be clearer: in place of the inoperative State, the privatization of power. And as we have seen, this is no new invention; on the contrary, it is a return to tradition and established customs. The allusion to the patriarchal family that survives as a lasting example in the mountains, where the moral and social crisis of the big cities has not arrived, is eloquent. That patriarchal family is uncontaminated social organization, guardian of the values that need to be re-established: from this perspective, the vision of the colonies extending across the territory is thus literally the image of a project for the refounding of society. And in this respect, too, Prat's words are transparently clear: "Society as it is must be re-created, it must be created anew."[73]

This brings us to the third question to be inferred from Permanyer's words, that of insisting on the need for the colony to be isolated, presenting it as a "little world," a cell in which the whole of society is already contained in miniature. We have already seen that it was the right of property—and, consequently, the will of the employer—on which the possibility of constructing that microcosm was based: Prat tellingly refers to the colony as the employer's house. The naturalness that Prat claimed for the origins of the patriarchal family, the truth that is enshrined in its immutability through the ages, is sufficient justification for the equivalence of the two terms, "colony" and "house," and legitimates the will of the owner, who directly assumes the role of father. In Prat's proposal, in effect, paternalism is something more that ideological myth-making: "The formation of that medium adapted to the regeneration of the workers, entails the active exercise of an ener-

**191**

getic will, which shall hold sway within that medium just as the father does within the family."[74] At the same time, the description of the medium itself could hardly be more thorough: the industrial colony is "a nucleus of population that is to be formed under the eye of the director or owner; it is he who chooses the site, who constructs the building, who provides dwellings for the workers; it is he who appoints the workers and foremen; in his precinct there is a place only for those who live by the work of the house. Idleness is not permitted there. The incentives to vice can also be thoroughly rooted out. The dwellings of the workers should be separate, so that each family has its own home and this should be sufficient for its needs. Amusements may be ordered in such a way and disposed in such a form as to educate and instruct instead of corrupting. The education of the children may be in hands of those who shall truly shape their souls for good, instead of being left to those who would brutalize their intellect … Finally the meetings of the club may be replaced by religious solemnities, and its furious ranting by the simple and serene sermons of the priest."[75]

But it is worth stressing the fact that no economic argument figures in Prat's vindication of the colony system: only moral and social advantages will follow from its application. In other words, the colony is to be the "medium" in which the Catalan industrial bourgeoisie—a minority, and endemically weak—will find the labor-relations and consequently the political stability necessary to consolidate its hegemony. But given the genuine complexity of the new industrial processes, given the obvious fact of irreversible urbanization, could such a proposal go beyond the merely symbolic? Prat himself wrote, advisedly: "we shall refer always to the kind of perfection that must constitute the ideal of the colony."[76] And in his important study of Catalonia's industrial colonies, Ignasi Terradas remarked in this regard: "the colony system, as it is presented ideologically, has never existed, not even in its most minimally perfect form."[77] And yet perhaps that is not entirely true. The little world in which, mimicking the cho-

rus of a Greek tragedy, the workers intone a hymn to redeeming Labor—the vanquisher, like Hercules, of discord—comes close to that perfection, and does so in precisely the terms of Prat de la Riba's enunciation of the theory: by manifesting itself as example, as symbol and as emblem. From the minute details of the project itself to the legends and the miracles that were woven around it, everything to do with the industrial colony established by Eusebi Güell is a demonstration of the re-created society that Prat had called for. Why else did he commence his book with a dedication to Eusebi Güell?

In 1890 Eusebi Güell had begun to construct a new factory for his corduroy company on an extensive property acquired many years before by his father some twenty kilometers outside of Barcelona, in Santa Coloma de Cervelló. In 1891, when the machines perfected by Ferrán Alsina were set in motion, there had been built around them a whole new community that at its height, around 1917, was to number more than a thousand families: this township was called (officially so from 1892 on) the Colonia Güell.[78] There is good reason, then, to linger for a moment in the early 1890s, some years prior to Prat de la Riba's theorization of the industrial colony. In advance of the theory, then, the Colonia Güell had already been constructed as a genuine heterotopia of social and production relations. Prat's dedication of his book to Eusebi Güell was simply a due and necessary recognition of an existing fact. Although other late-nineteenth century Catalan industrial colonies had institutions, services and "internal laws" similar to those in the one founded by Eusebi Güell, none of these, as we shall see, was to make such a public paradigm of its constitution as the Colonia Güell.[79] While it certainly seems that no public statements of intention were made by Güell or his collaborators at the time of the colony's foundation (there are a number of sufficiently eloquent subsequent declarations, as we shall see), this is perhaps because its founding itself said so much more than words could have done. Right from the start, the workers of the

Colonia Güell, installed in new single-family houses that were described in a contemporary account as "authentic chalets surrounded by garden,"[80] saw the colony's own organizations and institutions growing up around them, from the savings bank to the friendly society and the co-operative shop; from the "atheneum" cultural association to the dramatic society and the two choirs that the colony at one time boasted, and from the confraternities to the school and the chapel (which as early as 1892 had become a parochial tenure).[81] Underlying all of these institutions there was an evidently functional rationale, always conceived in terms of one of the essential conditions of Prat's thesis: the need to isolate the population of the colony; an isolation that should not be seen, then, as simply spatial, but as something directly physical, applied to every member of the community.[82] The atheneum, the theater and the choir were evidently designed to make it unnecessary for the residents to leave the colony in search of amusement, just as the confraternity and the parish church made it unnecessary for them to go elsewhere for their religious observances. But this explicit demonstration of ideological control that we find inside the colony, ultimately deriving from the inseparability of private life and public life that its institutions suppose, is relativized by the purely economic control that is implicit in its running. The function of the co-operative, the friendly society and the savings bank in ploughing the workers' wages back into the economic continuum of the colony, where production and consumption are bound up with one another, is incontrovertible.

This circularity of every aspect of the life of the colony, essential to ensuring its isolation and the dependence of its inhabitants—essential, in effect, to making it the microcosm it was intended to be—is well documented. In 1910, a visit to the Colonia Güell was, significantly, one of the central acts of the Semana Social de España, or "Social Week," in a Barcelona still shaken by the revolutionary events of the Semana Trágica. One of the journalists who made the visit, after describing

the colony as a "social venture that ... in this sense outshines ... the excellent industrial achievement" of the factory, went on to describe life there, focusing above all on one thing: the houses of the workers. Of these houses he writes that they are "authentic chalets surrounded by garden," and continues, "so that he may be well looked after and cared for, he ceases his work in the factory at noon on the Saturday, in spite of which he is paid the full day's wage. In this way, on the Saturday afternoon, the worker becomes a small farmer, and can devote his Sunday completely to genuine rest, to the observance of the religious practices that the Church requires of him."[83]

All of the elements we have been describing seem to be summed up in these words. The very basis of the colony as such—property, the property—here becomes fiction. The fiction of property—the house and the garden: this it was that a number of years later enabled Miquel d'Esplugues to observe that, in the Colonia Güell, the "simple worker finds himself set up as a petty bourgeois,"[84] is constituted in the ultimate goal of all the mechanisms that were to make the colony a society apart.[85] The inhabitants of the colony are definitively tied to it and the closed hierarchical order it represents by way of that house that makes them small property-owners. Nevertheless the work on their little plots of land creates the fiction not only of property, but also of self-sufficiency, effectively converting the isolation of the workers into a virtue. And that ties in with a last fiction: that of the rural, also a virtue. What is more, the work done on the individual patch of land, in which contact with the soil and the sweat of the effort of digging it are not a mystification (in contrast to the work done in the factory, which is necessarily alienating and in which it is therefore so hard to discover the qualities assigned to it), serves to reaffirm the values of work and above all—with symbolic eloquence and biblical resonances—its redemptive value. From this point of view the observation made by the journalist we quoted above is clearly significant:

on Saturday, the worker tends his small plot, "in spite of which he is paid the full day's wage." What better example of the circularity of public life and private life, of work and consumption, described here? Indeed, other statements make those bonds perfectly explicit. Thus, in 1917—another symbolic date for the "social question" in Catalonia—the Colonia Güell produced its own propaganda exercise, a pamphlet giving a summary of its history and an explanation of its functioning.[86] The exemplary purpose is manifest, here, from the very outset: the colony and its inhabitants are merely the objects of that exemplarity. Commenting on the "dramatic society," the pamphlet says: "The purpose of this group is to entertain the people on the major holidays with evening performances, in order to avoid, as far as possible, that families should go out of the colony."[87] And this, on the savings bank: "The youngsters, in just a year or two, have acquired stamps to the value of five thousand pesetas, a sum entered in this savings bank instead of being spent on sweets or toys or—even worse—in one of the new cinemas in the neighboring towns."[88] Prat's theorization, the whole vision of the colony as heterotopia, is stripped down here to its bare bones. But it is this stripping down, which lays bare a panorama, an actuation and a set of aims by no means exceptional in the numerous industrial colonies created in Catalonia around the turn of the century, criticism of which had begun to appear with the colonies themselves—for example, Morote's *El feudalismo en las fábricas* [*Feudalism in the Factories*] was published in 1891, predating Prat by several years[89]—that by contrast enables us to identify the distinctive aspects of the Colonia Güell. The overtly purposive symbolic sublimation that was practiced there derives directly from that "ideal colony" of which Prat spoke, whose ideal status was specifically defined as a rationalization of the feudal excesses of the employers. It is this sense of public exemplarity that makes the Colonia Güell not only a solution, but a project.

But there was more. In the same 1917 pamphlet we read: "In the Colonia Güell, capital and work

are always twinned."[90] This is quite clearly the ultimate aim of the whole symbolic process that the colony embodies. We have already seen that "social peace" was, in Prat's theorization, the only return that the employer received from founding a colony. But we have also seen how to achieve that peace required the re-creation of a naturalness that fused necessity and tradition, whose ultimate image was the land itself. The pamphlet also gives an account of the significance of all this: "Let it be known to all the beings of Catalonia, of Spain and of the entire world, and to the coming generations, that in spite of the satanic efforts currently being put into practice by the false redeemers of the working class … the faith of our forefathers still holds firm, and in the Catalan breast there still springs hope, and charity continues to be the most prized inheritance of Catalonia."[91] Social peace, then, is the peace of the family, the most traditional and most uncontaminated, the closest to the origin, in which the natural truths are conserved. And also the most widely extended: that which transmits faith and virtue from bosom to bosom and finds comfort in a hierarchy that halts the time of the generations, and in a crowning point at which patriarch and country become one.

In the Colonia Güell this process of symbolic concentration can culminate nowhere else than in the person of the master: Eusebi Güell. That sacred inheritance, charity, but also that other inheritance to which the workers intone their hymns, redeeming work, are condensed in his founding action. One concrete fact points to the premeditation with which that contraction is produced: the land on which the Colonia Güell was built, as we have seen, was an old rural estate, in the middle of which there was an eighteenth-century *masía* or farmhouse. This farmhouse was the only one of the existing constructions to be conserved, and it was there that Eusebi Güell and his family stayed when they visited the colony. The presence of the old *masía* in the middle of the new township could hardly be more eloquent. In effect, the literature of the Renaixença had made the *masía*, that characteristic form of occupation of the Catalan countryside, one of the basic elements of the symbolic sys-

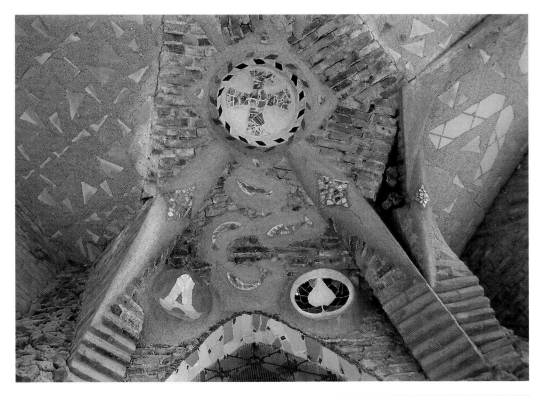

tem of tradition, a constant presence at the center of the idealization of the rural world as the world of natural values—which in this case are also intrinsic to the spirit of Catalonia—determining it hierarchically. In the farmhouse, in the ancestral home, all is sacralized around the household in which the patriarch, halting time, conserves and passes on old customs; here are the generations in whom the soul of the land itself subsists. In its characteristic architectural form, whose origins can be discerned in the profile of the classical temple, patriarchal family and tradition, the soil and work, nation and religion, are simultaneously identified.[92] Like an ancient seed: between the factory and the township, at the heart of that re-created society, such is the house of the lord, the family home.

Once again it is Miquel d'Esplugues who provides a synthesis of the personification that is effected in the Colonia Güell. Between quotes from Jaume Balmes, he writes: "in the Colony the first factor is the spirit." Certain key words make this more concrete: "religion, culture, liberty, even a certain refinement of, let us say, proletarian civilization are discernable realities that emerge of the central industrial reality, but are so much alive as in some way to surpass it."[93] To surpass the industrial fact: could there be a better explanation of the kind of added value obtained in the colony? Only one thing is still lacking for that sublimation to coincide, point for point, with Prat's analysis: the concretion of this in the order of the family. "This is not a Colony," writes d'Esplugues, "it is a real family, under the loving action of a most intelligent patriarch."[94] But there is still a further transcendentalization waiting to take place. A little further on we read: "Under his paternal yoke he desires nothing but sons and daughters, free beings dignified by work and love, that raise their hands to bless the bread earned in his factory, blessing at the same time he who has given them it: that is to say, the great father of all, as collaborators in his industrial thought, bold fighters for the glory of the race, of Catalonia, mother of the employers, of the workers, of the Catalans."[95] It would be difficult to find a better expression of the

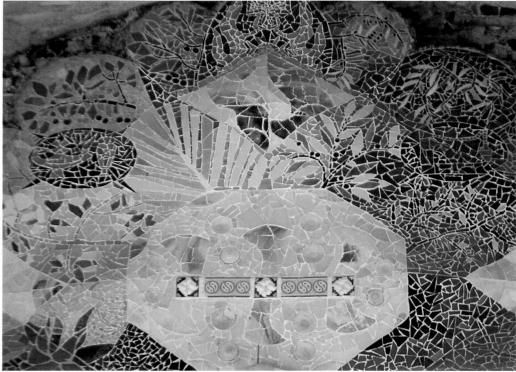

ideology we have been describing here, the ideology that causes the colony as a "society apart" to function, and constitutes its heterotopia. Each of these concepts finds in Miquel d'Esplugues' words its precise place in this order. Here, then, the symbolization that culminates in the person of the patriarch himself is made transcendent in the simultaneous, superposed vision of Catalonia as mother of all. The use of the image of the family as form of the necessary natural order could hardly be more persistent, but d'Esplugues goes even further: if Catalonia is the mother, Eusebi Güell is the father. Indeed, was this not the ultimate significance of the union of the lord of Garraf—Güell himself—and Dona d'Aygua—the secret resources of the land? And did the seed of that union, duly blessed by Labor, not bear fruit in the rebirth of a formerly barren land? In the identification of nation and patriarch that takes place at the symbolic apex of the Colonia Güell, the characters of Picó's drama resound with force. Could it be otherwise?

But this sublimation, however important, is relatively unexpected. There was also another, more radical sublimation, in that it was determined by an action. In 1905, a young factory worker accidentally fell into a vat of corrosive liquid, badly burning his legs. The doctors came to the conclusion that only a major graft of skin from human donors could save him. Eusebi Güell's own children came forward as volunteers, together with forty-three workers from the colony, and the operation was carried out successfully.[96] The story immediately caused a great sensation, and the titles of the articles that were written about it clearly reflect the precise sense in which it was interpreted: "Heroic sacrifice," "Heroes who love their neighbor," etc.[97] What is more, right from the start it was invested with the significance of a prodigy, a miracle. The boy was literally resurrected, and this miracle was to lead to others: an appendix to the propaganda pamphlet of 1917, for example, speaks of several cases of sick people being miraculously healed thanks to prayer, of extraordinary cures right there in the Colonia

Güell.[98] Miquel d'Esplugues, in his synthesis, says: "It has been written that a happy people has no history. Of the inhabitants of the Colonia Güell it could be said that they are not even aware of it."[99] The Colonia Güell is a "society" without history: what does this statement amount to but an affirmation that this is a place cut off from the everyday world? Instead of history, then, we have prodigies: the miraculous has installed itself there, making of its order a static and transcendent truth from which the defects of the temporal have disappeared completely.

So there is only one possible interpretation of the prodigy: that outside of the world, everything is possible. Juan José Laguarda, bishop of Barcelona, was to ask Eusebi Güell in 1910 to erect around the colony "a very thick and very high wall so that the doctrines of socialism may never penetrate,"[100] and that same year, Torras i Bages wrote that the cured boy revived "thanks to the love of his brothers and lives through the skin of the priest, the worker and capitalism."[101] The pregnancy of these words, in which the allusion to human skin is no mere mystification, definitely establishes the symbolic significance of the colony: if there is a re-created society it is that in which prodigies are a mark of God's favor. However, when Torras pronounced those words their meaning was already becoming brutally visible in the church that Antoni Gaudí was building there.

### *"Idealism through the Material"*

Ràfols, Gaudí's first biographer, tells us that the makeshift chapel in the *masía*, which was Eusebi Güell's residence, having grown too small for the needs of the colony, Güell commissioned the architect to design a new church as early as 1898.[102] The fact remains that the first stone was not laid until October 4, 1908, and that from 1914, with the crypt completed and some projects of the church above it under way (the great portico with its monolithic lintel still stands at the top of the stairs) the work began to tail off; it was definitely halted in March 1916, two years before the death of Eusebi Güell, who, perhaps having abandoned

*Longitudinal and cross sections
of the crypt by R.M. Bolet
and G. Goday.*

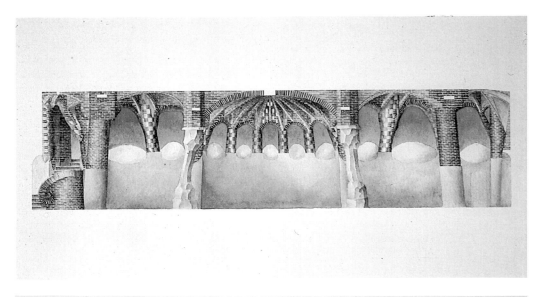

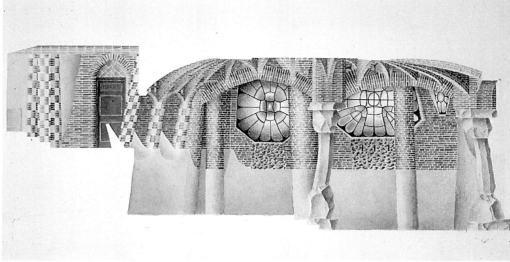

other projects, had considered being buried there. In any case, on November 3, 1915 the crypt was solemnly consecrated, and was used as the parish church.[103]

The plan of the Colonia Güell makes it quite clear that the siting of the church was carefully chosen.[104] Set a little distance away from the grid of houses laid out around the sides of a rectangular square, at the opposite end of the colony from the industrial bays and the factory, the future church was to stand on the crest of a small hill covered with pine trees. The road leading up to it was also thought out with care. After crossing a little parabolic-arched bridge, the path winding through the pine grove would have offered constantly changing perspectives of the church.[105] Every aspect of this layout, then, is charged with symbolism, and the symbolism of the church's position within the colony as a whole is directly apparent. The church is raised up on a hill, set apart from the township, effectively crowning it: its vaults constitute a synthetic vision, crowning the life of the colony. But not like the Romantic Gothic church, proud emblem of the city that sublimates its identity in the towering height of its spires; this is quite simply like the temple of Jesus Christ, built next to the *praetorium*, of which Prat de la Riba writes. In effect, this church on top of its hill is the temple built on its little acropolis:[106] the integrating image of the city, but first and foremost the image by analogy of its hierarchy. The church in the Colonia Güell is not inside the fabric of the township; as the temple raised by the patriarch, it stands alongside him, on another level, to confirm and preserve his order and to reveal, above all, the prodigious (that is, exemplary) character of the colony he founded. The propaganda pamphlet of 1917, in effect, spoke of the "prodigies and marvels that can take place in the shadow of the factory chimney, when this is not in opposition to the belfry."[107] The watchful temple, then, must be erected, like the factory, in a place governed by a different time: both order, with their shadows like the hands of a clock, the time of the town. Gaudí's surviving drawings of the pro-

ject give an idea of the size of the planned church. Looking at them, it is hard to believe that this is only a church intended to meet the needs of the colony. Its fusiform vaults, clustering about a central cupola, rise up from the hill above the tops of the trees to compete with the tall chimneys on the other side of the township, as can be seen in a drawing on the celebratory parchment presented to Pius X in 1913.[108]

But if that symbolism, so immediately official, could be reflected without distortion in an emblematic drawing, there is another and more secret symbolism, associated with other values: a symbolism that is perhaps reinforced by the very fact that only the crypt was actually constructed. In contrast to the disarticulated, merely juxtaposed relation between township and factory (a disarticulation that very forcefully expresses the alienated time that travels that road), the path to the chapel follows, as we have said, a route that is invested with precise tonalities of ritual. In fact the only thing that can be glimpsed of the church is the top of its central cupola rising blue above the clustered tops of the pines. The road to the church, zigzagging up the slope of the hill, can thus be seen as a path of ascension, but also as a path leading into the heart of the wood. That perennial wood, in the center of which the church was to stand (and where it was forbidden to cut down a tree), clearly assumes a sacred value. It is not difficult to guess the resonance of its meaning for a man such as Eusebi Güell, he of the dolmen and the holm oak, for whom, as we have seen, a sacral ancestral spirit rooted in the soil was a palpable reality. The church competes in size and height with the chimneys of the factory—under the shadow of both the prodigy of "social peace" is achieved—but enveloped in the penumbra of the pines (an essential tree) it recovers—in the conventional vision of the forest as a place where life grows in profusion untamed by man, in which the earth itself reveals its abundance—its own superiority, its uniqueness in comparison to what is repeated, which is all that remains beyond the edge of the trees. The forest, with the mysteries of its

depth, was the primeval sacred place, the branches of its trees hung with the offerings and the trophies of men, and this is precisely the significance, in contrast to the everyday time of the factory and the township, of that little wood that guards the church in its heart, and was expressly preserved to do just that. The one is sublimated in the other. But at the end of the road that leads into the pine wood, there stands not the grand church of the drawings but the crypt, half hidden, confounded with the land itself, with the inclined pillars of its portico that have so often been described in the now trite image of their confusion with the pines. The solitary large-linteled doors of the future upper church rise above the crypt, and scattered in the long grass lie the great unworked blocks of granite that were to have been used in its nave and aisles. A few years ago, when the place was still very much as it was when Gaudí knew it, with the pine wood still intact amid a now vanished solitude, the unfinished crypt and church and their constituent elements scattered between the trees like the remains of a ruin that had never even been construction, only intention, could create a very strong sensation of sacral mystery. But let us not be misled. In Gaudí and Eusebi Güell's project the little wood enclosed not a half-concealed crypt but a church with tall vaulting domes clad in colored glazed ceramics, green, purple and blue, grouped about a central cupola that in some drawings bears a great clock, and on the path leading to it there would have been not the litter of an abandoned construction, but changing views of the great church, seen always from different perspectives among the trees, as the evidently formalized goal of the ascension. The imposing colored domes of the church, with their symbols and written invocations, visible from afar, manifest the emblematic significance of the project and do away with any sense of intimate in that ascension, in that venturing inside the wood. We have already considered the significance the church accrues to itself in competing with the factory, determining by its analogous presence the hierarchical integration of the life of the colony,

*Views of the interior of the crypt.*

over which it watches. It is only as public ritual, then, that this ascension in which the church itself characterizes its setting can be understood. The solemnity of the procession, for example, makes explicit the kind of sacral dimension that exists in this place and takes shape in this ascension, and the limits of its expansion, without any of the evocations of the sacred that we have noted losing their resonance. On the contrary, the procession converts the road itself in spectacle. And it may well be that the doubling and the need for eloquence that this representation of the sacred entails imply are the very mechanisms that determine the built object.

Each of the eleven pillars of the portico of the crypt as built has a different form and a different material treatment. The outer pillars, inclined like flying buttresses that spring directly from the ground following the line of tension, unashamedly expose their shafts with their apparently arbitrary mix of bricks of different tones and textures, with their masonry of varied types and jointing, with parts of their surfaces rendered with an almost untreated mortar that retains all the roughness of the elemental paste. The outermost of these pillars has a stellate section, with warping surfaces and sharp edges; condensed into the small space of the column, these create the impression of a petrified tensed musculature. The other pillars, circular in section, spring directly from the ground or from the parapets of the ramp that would have led up to the church above. Opening out in capitals with truncated conical forms, these are continued in other, smaller buttresses to other points on the roof, or splay out in a palmate system of brickwork ribs that are rendered in places, so that these fragments of continuous surface, unexpectedly standing out from the other materials, are perceived as points and arrises. Between the ribs are vaults rendered with mortar and decorated with triangular ceramic inserts, forming an obsessive pattern of St. Andrew's crosses whose virtual homogeneity is suddenly concentrated in a great red cross. These vaults look as if they had

been inverted, hanging down like sail canvas: the curve of their section seems to be not concave but convex, suspended.[109]

Those inclined shafts with no base, delighting in their very roughness, with an absence of refinement that they themselves thus interpret as an absence of artifice, declare with an almost strident obviousness their resemblance to tree-trunks, while in the buttresses and the ribs, spreading out and crossing under the belly of that vault whose ceramic triangles shimmer like trembling leaves, it is easy to see the dense foliage of the forest. But we have already remarked on the staleness of such comparisons. Indeed the analysis of the porticoes and viaducts of the Park Güell has shown us how mistaken it is to interpret such aspects of Gaudí's work in a naturalistic vein, that is to say, as the imitation of nature, and even more so in this particular case as integration into the natural landscape.[110] It is certainly not these pines in this little wood that Gaudí sought to extend here with his arboreal portico; his aim, without a doubt, was to embody a vision in which the things of nature, of the material world, are transcended, literally disappearing behind the intentionally powerful presence of the symbols that possess them. Gaudí was not attempting to imitate nature, but engaged in a project of re-naturalization, a restitution of the natural. That word is loaded in Gaudí's project with resonances in which there is no place for nature as such: it is simply an image in which society manifests itself. The re-naturalization that Gaudí's architecture aspires to and is explained by is, in effect, social.

In the Park Güell the columns did not come from the trees, but went towards them, returning to their own myth in order to make evident the sacral dimension of a piece of land and a technique whose rationale is its own experience. They were, then, the complete, circular image of a land that was being shaped, through the technique displayed in its construction, into precisely the character, the soul of the people that inhabited it. And the same is true of the petrified forest that is the portico of the Colonia Güell crypt. The columns

and pillars do not follow the random distribution and the form of the trunks of the pine trees; on the contrary, it is the trees that imitate the columns. In fact, the portico has been built as the last stage in a return to the center. If the little wood is sacred it is because it has that heart fashioned from essential stone and earth, in which the work of building forcefully exposes its original roughness. The inclined columns, at times twisted on their axes, the discontinuous and abrupt movement of buttresses and ribs, the unexpected suspension of the vaults, whose directrices exhibit with pleasure the chaotic variety of their directions and, above all, the brutality of materials that mix, collide with or superpose themselves without bonding in any way, exhibiting in their infinite encounters an awkwardness—amounting in some cases to violence and rupture—that seems to be the only guiding will obeyed in every detail: what are all of these but demonstrations of the effort, the difficulty, the pain of building? And what are effort, difficulty and pain but demonstrations of the effort, the difficulty, the pain of building? And what are effort, difficulty and pain but the attributes of the work to which man was condemned? The opponent of the ancestral man of *Garraf*, remember, was not Sloth, but Fatigue: it is by mastering that enemy that man masters himself and embraces the redeeming power of Labor.

Re-naturalization, redemption: they are certainly very close to one another. In the arduous toil that the brutality of the crypt represents, the two literally coincide, and do so above all in one image that, among so many resonances, seems unique. In the inner part of the portico, in effect, a column gathers together all of the tensions in the unexpected repose of its verticality, thus establishing itself as the virtual center of the system. This column is different from the others not only in its position, but also in its execution: the shaft is a monolithic block of basalt, with two truncated conical blocks of the same material for its base and its capital. The three elements are simply set one on top of the other. The irregularly leaded joints serve only to stress their juxtaposition and

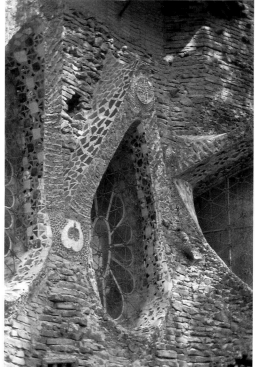

the elemental weight, the weight of each stone that is its immediate rationale, the immediate rationale of its order, its height. This interior, central pillar does not, as the others do, rise out of the ground to be displayed then, without solution of continuity, in the branching system of ribs; instead, divided into the three canonical parts of the column, it holds up the roof and rests on the floor, on a foundation that Gaudí chose to make mildly visible. This shaft, this base and this capital are, at the same time, as we have said, three simple blocks of stone. The schematic cuts that have given them a more or less prismatic or truncated conical form reveal the marks of the tool that made them, and thus attest to the arm of the man that with his strength wielded it. It is not so much the basalt block itself that impresses us—in comparison to those in the interior, it is modest in size—as that schematic and elemental yet also skilled and strong work that separated it from the quarry or, better yet, from the defile in which it had rested in darkness since the beginning of time. But Gaudí has halted the process here. There is no further step, no elaboration through which the first work is made to disappear by the hand of man again: a hand, then, that instead of striking hard molds gently, working to erase its own trace in an opaque perfection. On the contrary, this block has been set in its place to become a column, without more ado. It is hardly surprising that such a column should occupy this central position, or that, here too, there should be a change in the direction of the tensions in the portico, or at least of the representation of those tensions. All of the minor details in which the expression of the work, of its traces, is dispersed in a deliberate awkwardness are suddenly compressed in the single totemic presence of the most essential of the columns, still revealing the original blow that cleaved the block from its age-old bed of stone to set it upright. That blow, then, re-naturalizes and refounds the only possible nature, the nature that man by his labor rouses from its slumber and dominates: the nature that extends, in short, this side of paradise. But at the same

time, in permitting the contemplation of the primordial meaning of work in the essentiality of its trace-laden result, whose simple presence humbles the artful presumption of all perfection, it also cleanses of guilt; it redeems. The sharply projecting outer pillars resonate in the vertical weight of the single column that occupies the center and seems more than any other to bear the weight of the structure. The hands that have clumsily distributed the materials and resolved encounters without bonds discover their meaning in those earlier hands that cut and raised the stone with precise blows, leaving it thus so that all the effort and the pain of toil, so strong a presence elsewhere, comes here to its culmination and is halted. So this re-naturalization of Gaudí's is a return not to nature but to the first work, that work in which the tool is the direct and perfect extension of the hand, and the construction is the immediate result of the shock of the tool against the sleeping material, without further transformation or elaboration. As such it is also redemption.

The pain, the effort, the difficulty of the arm that beats are literally apparent in the imperfections of the faces and edges of the basalt blocks, just as a hand laden with earth can be seen in the crude bonding of brick and stone in the pillars and walls. This exhibition of manual work in the concrete form of the material also has more literary expressions that enable us to take our interpretation a little further. In the interior of the crypt everything seems to suggest a repetition of what occurs outside in the portico, and yet some things have changed. It is true that in walls and pillars, brick, stone and rendering are deployed with the same brutality as outside, while the arches and parapets that support the roof are crossed and superposed, turn or meet, with the same explicit awkwardness, but in contrast to the portico, Gaudí is seeking here to make visible in certain details a working process, something like a very elemental method. In some of the pillars, for example, perfectly squared blocks of Garraf stone alternate with bricks, laid on top to form a chequered pattern that, however strange as a bond,

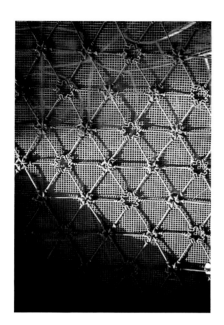

effectively creates the simplest of compositions: that based on the alternation of two colors or two textures. On other pillars, the rendering of the lower part of the shaft stops at the parabolic line determined by the catenary curve of a chain suspended from the top of the pillar. The immediacy of work represented as force, as pain, in the intentionally crude and brutal jointing of the materials in pillars and walls seems, in details such as the ones we have just described (and especially in the latter), to amount to a process that, nevertheless, in its striking elementalism, once again humbles presumptuous perfection, definitively denying all subsequent elaboration. Thus, at a few chosen points (it is hardly surprising that the very slight decorative nuancing of the gestures of construction should occur precisely in the pillars around the altar) there is exhibited, literally, the limit of all refinement, manifesting at the same time the ingenuous—that is to say, pure—wisdom of the constructor: these little compositions of materials next to the altar are his elemental, simple homage. And what else is that ingenuous wisdom but an image of the ultimate goal of redemption? But there is one other place where such an image is invested with complementary meanings. The windows in the exterior wall, set around with brilliant *trencadís* ceramic fragments, are protected with hexagonal metal grilles made of needles from the weaving machines in the factory. What could be more natural than to find the *trencadís* next to those pieces from the looms? We have already spoken at some length of *trencadís* as the redeeming of worthless matter, the waste of the work, and the same holds for the needles from the factory, although in this case, as we have said, the meanings can be extended further. In other words, those pieces from the machines effect the redemption not only of a waste material, but also of the machine itself, of the machine that still represents (as we saw in the ambiguities of Prat de la Riba's text) the source of all the evils of the century: the corruption of customs and traditions, the dissolution of the family. However, Prat proposed to re-create society through an act of will directed

not only at its members but at the factories and the machines that are the image of property and of the concrete: this was the whole purpose of the colony. Could there be a better metaphor of that purpose than the grilles of the crypt? In them, tools that had been a medium of alienated labor are redeemed of their sin by the hands of the artisan who has converted them, by his real work, into window grilles, and these transmit a new value that transcends them. It was by a similar act of will that the man in *Garraf* who listened to Labor triumphed over himself: that, and no other, is the ultimate meaning of the work that is made present here.

These grilles, then, like the artisanate simplicity of the interior details we described above—in one of which the weight of the chain itself, determining the curve, gives expression to the most concrete of presences—are a humbling of the will to perfection, which, in light of the primordial nature of the work exhibited there, the value of that immediate work, brutal and essentially grievous, can only be interpreted as presumption, as vanity. It is caprice, sophistication, any sort of virtuoso display, that must be humbled, whether it be through the brutality of the first work with which man wrests the material from nature or through the naïve simplicity of the first elementary decoration with which he qualifies his work as offering. Those ever-present hands that grasp the tools and touch and beat the material humble the presumptuous desire for rootless novelty and wealth. In each trace, in each wound, in the difficult encounter of each of the materials in the crypt, what Gaudí is trying to show us are hands—hands that continuous contact with the material teaches to be humble towards it and for which the very experience of work, rendered arduous by awkwardness, is the road of elemental wisdom, opposed to all sophistication and therefore purer. It seems clear that in the tormented condition of his work Gaudí offers us a pacification laden with paradoxes: that of man not with the material but with the violence that he must enact on it in order to build; that is to say, with the work. The will to re-naturalization

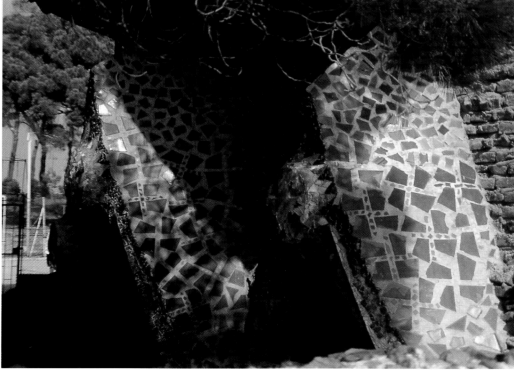

thus seems to take on a more precise form, but also new tonalities. Everything in the crypt, beginning with those carefully selected materials, is opposed to the absence of a past, to a novelty without roots.[111] The ironwork is wrought from what were once weaving needles, the cutting of the basalt blocks recalls the defile in which they had lain since the beginning of time, and even the bricks Gaudí uses are special: he personally chose the overfired, burnt bricks, which in manifesting those stigmata that made them imperfect and dispensable, at the same time escape the standardized uniformity of correctly fired bricks. Everything, then, has to bear some trace, some mark of a past time that in this way continually manifests itself in it. What is more, that past distinguishes things, avoids the ordinary and commonplace: there is no place for routine in the long, deep time that the materials and the traces of their working reflect in every element, in every detail of the crypt.

But all of this can also be seen as a very specific declaration of traditionalism. Opposition to a rootless novelty for its own sake, and to the alienated repetition of the same that robs things of their authenticity and desacralizes gestures: this is the way in which tradition defines itself as a place of safety in times of major change, and these were the terms in which the late European Romanticisms of the turn of the century set about inventing the tradition of their peoples.[112] But in the case of Gaudí the references are not merely generic. In effect, Josep Torras i Bages, in *La tradició catalana* (the most influential expression of Catalan neo-traditionalism, first published in 1892 and re-issued, significantly, in 1906, at the same time as Prat de la Riba's great political synthesis, *La nacionalitat catalana*) devoted an entire paragraph, which concludes the first part of the book, to the theme of *Tradició i renovació*—"Tradition and renovation." There, among references to Vico and scholasticism, he writes: "Tradition and stagnation are antithetical even in their grammatical meaning: because the word tradition, and consequently the concept it expresses, includes the idea of movement, of journey, of transmission, in oppo-

sition, as we can see, to the sense of quietude of the second term, so that all generations, all men, even, work in the heritage of tradition, that is constantly changing while remaining always the same."[113] This vision of generations of men down through the ages that have worked to create, always anew, values that are always nonetheless the same seems to find an extraordinary translation in the exhibition of primordial toil that is produced in Gaudí's crypt, in the way that the hand always finds there, with pain, its limit, but also its redemption, in the material. The ideological and political thrust of Torras i Bages' vision, which finds its fulfillment in the conclusion that everything changes precisely because and in order that nothing changes, is transmuted in Gaudí's work into pure construction and, in effect, into pure work: it transcends itself in taking shape.

We can also consider these issues from a different point of view that will help us to follow them from the outside. During the Catholic Social Week in 1910 to which we have already referred, in which the visit to the Colonia Güell was one of the most important moments of the program, Torras i Bages himself delivered the inaugural speech, whose title was "The spirit in the problem of work."[114] Pronounced so close to the colony, so closely in line with the objectives the colony had set itself (the latter part of the speech was devoted specifically to its exemplary character), its content could not be more significant. And not so much for its championing of the patriarchal family as the model of "unity of spirit" for "a social body that is dislocated,"[115] which is essentially a repetition of the ideas developed by Prat and an extension of the self-same aims that underpinned the exemplary status of the Colonia Güell, as in the form in which it sublimates the very essence of this staging. In effect, if Prat set out to rationalize the excesses of the employers, to impose order on exploitation, Torras i Bages declares that the purpose of his words is "to try to bring wealth to book";[116] that is to say, to regulate the product of that exploitation and its most strident manifestation. And do we not see in that insidious

mirroring of objectives the sublimation, as I have said, of Prat's pragmatism in what Torras calls "the spiritual"? Torras speaks not of actions, but of something subsequent to actions: consciences. "Wealth," Torras says, "without being evil in itself—on the contrary, being a gift of God—in view of the conditions of our nature, produces in man, if it is not mastered and enslaved, deplorable effects, and is a focus of corruption in society. Therefore it is important to humble it, to bring to light its miseries, to proclaim its inferiority, and to set at the pinnacle of the hierarchy of human things the spirit."[117] Prat's "sovereign will," without ceasing to be sovereign, thus also becomes virtue attained through the mortification of what has been justly earned, so that in this way the discipline imposed on what is private is converted, by being exemplary, into the most public of representations.

It is hardly surprising that in a speech that ends up citing the Colonia Güell as an example of all that it wishes to say we should once again find an ambiguity about the public and the private: the strategies of Eusebi Güell are clearly apparent here. In his biography of the patrician, Miquel d'Esplugues wrote that the industrial colony beyond the outskirts of Barcelona nevertheless reverberated in the very heart of the city, in the townhouse. "A great industrial colony on the outskirts or in the suburbs tends to have a double repercussion in the city: that of an office or spacious warehouse, in which the manufactures are deposited, ready to set out from there to try their fate in the world; and that of the lordly mansion that is the home of the great manufacturer, as head of the family, businessman and citizen."[118] This vivid image that locates the bustle of the factory and the noise of the machines on the periphery, and the peace of the great man's home in the heart of the city, making of the two extremes a single resonance, is highly effective: it reconstructs, before our eyes, the actions of Eusebi Güell in the overall context of his project. But in doing so it casts a new light on mansion and colony, and enables us to understand more fully, in both, the meaning of Torras i Bages' words. We have seen, in effect, how the Palau Güell represented an incredible exhibition of wealth. Not only in the exotic exuberance of the materials used—materials that, always fixed, immovable, made the town house the place of property *par excellence*—but above all in the human work that was condensed in the material, in its eccentricity, in its obsessive *varietas*. That lavishly squandered human work served in the last analysis only to devalue the material, however precious it might be on the market. But was not its detachment from the market precisely what the house demonstrated? The impressive wealth that is embodied in the most radical, mostly immovable property, that extends from the depths of the earth to the sky by way of a transparent *axis mundi*; that wealth, expressed in the heart of the city, in the peace of the great man's home, is obviously just: "a gift of God." The mansion resounds in the industrial colony, and its wealth and its peculiar work resound there also, since in both places they constitute the culmination of what is represented. If in the Palau Güell a prodigal work triumphed over the materials to the extent that it despised them, in the crypt the essential work of the first gesture, of the primary tool, of the hands, triumphs over the materials in marking them brutally; that is to say, in uniting itself in them by injuring them it is reunited with its own origin. We have already commented at length on the way the immanence of the work thus represented was at the same time a humbling of vanity and the selfish desire for perfection: we can now see that to do this, turning away from temptations, is to humble wealth. What better resonance could the "gifts" of the palace have in the colony?

We have already noted that in the crypt, the material—from the unbonded overfired bricks to the great monolithic blocks of basalt—seeks not to display itself, but to reveal the work of the hands that roused it from its inert sleep. And it is precisely with a panegyric to manual work that the speech by Torras i Bages which we have been referring to commences. Its virtues, Torras de-

*The crypt during construction
in 1911 photographs.*

*Funicular model of the church
in the architect's workshop
on the site.*

clares, are the virtues of the Catalan people and their particular path towards the highest idealism.[119] This is a new version of the realism and practicality traditionally attributed to the Catalans, a popular stereotype to which we referred in the previous section. Voiced here, however, Torras' expression also aims at a very specific sublimation: we should not forget that, although he is talking about "manual work," he is doing so in a speech that deals with what was euphemistically called the "work problem." And that sublimation seems to condense much of what Gaudí sought to interpret in the primordial condition of his crypt. Torras says: "Our people ... saw idealism through the material."[120] There could hardly be a better description of the "sovereign will" of Eusebi Güell.

That "collective intuition" of the value of manual work is not represented in the crypt alone. Even a superficial examination of the rest of the constructions in the colony, for the most part by Joan Rubió i Bellver, makes it clear that this is the principal theme of all the architecture.[121] The so-called manager's house is the most striking example. The stone and the brick of the walls of this average-sized house are combined, on this occasion, in orderly bonds. In the case of the brickwork, however, there are a number of places where this comes into its own in a virtuoso display of craft skill: the corbels on the corner that, in an equivocal interpretation of Gaudí's dematerializations, support the little rotunda; the cornices and balustrades that crown the walls; the tall windows with their schematized Gothic tracery; the chimneys and skylights, and the open-work: on the rotunda-like turret, around the cistern and, above all, in the very beautiful gallery, folded like a screen and the most permeable of all. The dignity of this house for the factory manager comes not from the materials, which are the same as those used in the industrial bays, for example, but from the great skill and experience demonstrated in their working.

In principle, then, there is no difference between the intention manifested in this house and that

manifested in the crypt, although it is clearly not same thing to interpret that intention by means of craft skill that as a naked invocation of the primary gestures of construction. And not only for the most obvious reason, because Rubió is not Gaudí. There are other and more weighty reasons that explain the immeasurable difference of degree between the crypt and the rest of the constructions in the colony: the foremost of these is the fact of its being a church.

At the beginning of this section we looked at the way the church figures as the emblem of the colony, in symbolic balance with the factory. The shadows of the chimney and the belfry are cast across it in parallel from the first moment of its definition as a project: there is no need to insist further on something so immediately evident. We also saw, in the previous section, how Rubió i Bellver brought together in his "Dificultats per a arribar a la sintessis arquitectònica" what was for him the eternal problem of architecture and the specific resolution of the form and structure of the temple. This identification came, obviously, from Gaudí himself, and we shall have occasion to consider it more closely in relation to his interventions in cathedral of Mallorca and the evolution of the Sagrada Familia in Barcelona. Let us focus now on another issue, one with a more direct bearing on the crypt, and more decisive than it might seem: the way that the temple seeks to humble not only wealth or vanity in general but the specific vanity of its creator.

A reading of some of the addresses delivered to the Congrés d'Art Cristià a Catalunya held in Barcelona in 1913 provides a key to the way that idea was effectively presented by the Church itself.[122] Thus, among references to the school of Beuron and quotations from Guyau, Kurth or of Callewaert—and, of course, from Chateaubriand, Ruskin, Taine and Huysmans: commonplaces of a general nostalgia for the cathedral—all of the addresses to the Congrés revolved around an issue that we will examine in greater depth in the next chapter: the claim that the Catholic liturgy is, in itself, the most sublime expression of art. How-

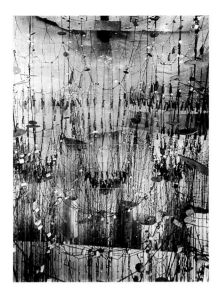

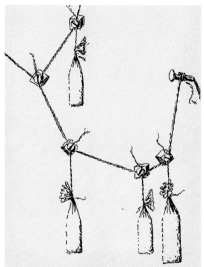

ever, one aspect of this is worth stressing now: the vehemence and manifest intentionality with which all of this was presented. Thus, Josep Tarré, in a discourse entitled "L'Art i la Litúrgia," spoke of "the processions, the devout gestures of the multitudes, the imposing and meaningful ceremonies of the ministers of the Sanctuary, who, vestured with magnificent ornaments, move about the altar, where nature has offered her finest flowers and the sculptors and goldsmiths the fruits of their ingenuity, both in the liturgical furniture and in the images, sacred vessels and candelabras": of everything, in fact, that constitutes "this supreme union of all the arts, brought together to co-operate for a single end; that is to say: to make intelligible to a congregated people the highest and deepest ends of humanity, an aspiration that has only been assumed in full by the Catholic religion, and that the Protestant peoples have felt the want of, and has been pursued without rest by the genius of Bayreuth."[123] We have already referred to the last words of this quotation, which are particularly relevant here. What is Tarré's purpose in suddenly concluding his speech in these terms but to issue an indirect warning to artists to devote their efforts to a cause in which—and only in which—they will find true satisfaction? The Wagner alluded to here is a Wagner frustrated by his inability to infuse his works with the divine inspiration that would have made them not a representation of the sacred but the sacred itself; that which is consubstantially present in the ceremonies, the gestures and the instruments of the Catholic faith. In effect, as Tarré tells us elsewhere: "The first law constitutive of the Liturgy is the consecration of all that is used, setting it apart from profane use, consecrating it to God, transforming and spiritualizing it through His supernatural efficacy."[124] The liturgical elements, then, imbued with divinity, are the elements of the one true and inalienable total work of art, the only one that brings together, without mystifications, the celestial and the earthly, God with the people transmuted in it. Could there be a more desirable content than that sketched by such

ideas for the mission of art, and hence of the artist? Quite simply, a priesthood. But a priesthood, of course, with all of its consequences, as consecration, as vow: this, too, is present in Tarré's words. It is hardly surprising, then, that his speech should contain phrases such as this: "In no other genre as much as in the sacred is that theory of art for art's sake so deficient and so disturbing."[125] The two modes with which nineteenth-century art had set out to justify itself, *art pour l'art* and its paradoxical culmination, the total artwork—and, indeed, the phantasms of the artists—are placed, then, under a new order: that of the priesthood. Genius itself will thus be subtly led: in its ineluctable feeling will be found the sin of pride and the need for gratitude: in other words, sin, confession and repentance.

Another of the speakers, the Jesuit Ignasi Casanovas, of whose great influence on Gaudí there is telling evidence,[126] is even clearer in this respect. In a long section of his discourse on "L'Art en el Temple" he declares: "I have no desire to dissimulate here a fear that besets me and constantly returns, which is that, precisely by way of the paths of regeneration I preach, religious art may falsify religion, and aesthetics dilute piety. If the liturgy, in an access of artistic fever, were to appear to us as a pure feast of beauty, it would be a mere counterfeit of the supernatural life, we ourselves would be hypocrites, and the artists would have arrived at the most refined idolatrious and simoniac cult of themselves, which until quite recently they renounced. The artist will always feel the temptation to linger over the facile aesthetic elements of religion, instead of coming by greater effort to the essential sources of the religious life, such as the dogmatic and doctrinal content of the sacred literature, the supernatural efficacy of grace, lived in daily practice, individual training in the solid and perfect virtues. The Christian religion is a way of life, and as such it is either lived in its entirety or it is a pure phantasmagoria."[127] Ignasi Casanovas' tone could not be more vehement. This is a warning to artists about the dangers of art itself, an admonition against its

*Gouaches by Gaudí, painted over
photographs of the funicular model,
showing two versions of the project.*

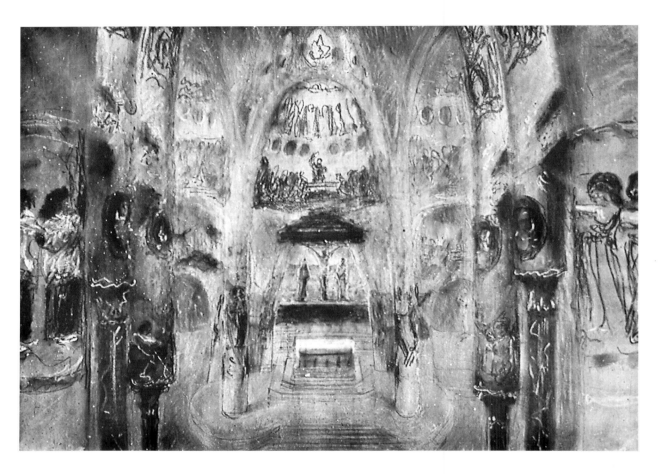

temptations. Who could propose so radical a vision of a total art, of an art that embraces in its compelling destiny not only this life but also, under the threat of sin and the warning of eternal damnation, the next? "The worm of a useless and misleading aestheticism": this, the text tells us, is what must be defeated if the artist wishes to avoid the lamentable situation of Hermann Ronge, who "was an artist, yet without being a Christian; he thought himself religious, but possessed only an aesthetic sentimentalism."[128] Not for nothing had Casanovas affirmed, a little earlier: "The Holy Church, with its liturgy, has vanquished all the artists."[129]

The dire tone of these treatises might lead us into the error of believing that these admonitory sermons were marginal to Barcelona's artistic circles. Far from it. There is well-documented evidence, as we have said, of the profound admiration that Gaudí felt for Father Casanovas, and we know that he regularly attended the Jesuit's courses. But this is merely an anecdotal detail: we shall refer in due course to the Cercle Artístic de Sant Lluc, an association of modern Catholic artists, and to religious associations such as the Lliga Espiritual de la Mare de Deu de Montserrat, in which many of the Cercle artists rubbed shoulders with a pool of potential clients who shared the same religious, political and social aims.[130] Like so many other influential Barcelona artists, Gaudí was a member of both associations: his devout public image, so meticulously constructed on the paradoxical humility of the genius, makes it hard to doubt that he sublimated his own invincible phantasms in the conventional sermons of Tarré, Torras i Bages and Casanovas.

We should have no difficulty here in going back to the process of re-naturalization pursued in the construction of the crypt from this new point of view; a point of view that, far from excluding, actually complements the crypt's representation of a "collective intuition," exemplified in the person of an artist-priest. We have already seen how the humbling of wealth is made concrete at the point at which the crypt becomes the resonance of the town house, but surely this could have been achieved, as in the house for the manager, simply by using "poor materials" that were nevertheless handled with a great degree of craft skill, in a display of pure virtuosity? In the crypt, however, the materials are not merely poor but discarded—burnt bricks, old weaving-loom needles, broken ceramics. At the same time they endure a deliberate renunciation of any kind of artistic elaboration, manifesting a brutality, an awkwardness, a decorative naïvety in which the humbling of vanity is made concrete for the second time, endured on this occasion by Gaudí himself. By Gaudí himself: what is that pregnant materiality that traverses every element, that painful limit that brick and stone mark for the hand, but the world of an artist in flight from the temptation of giving form to things? What is the shock between a brutal material and an equally brutal work that the whole crypt exhibits but a renunciation of the superficial show of all phantasmagoria?

But perhaps even more than the result itself, the procedure Gaudí adopted in designing the crypt bears witness to what we are talking about here. As we know, in order to work out the structure of the church Gaudí built what he called a stereo-static model, a system of strings from which he suspended little canvas bags filled with lead pellets whose weight was proportional to the real loads at each point.[131] Under these stresses, the strings automatically assumed the inverted form of the real structure of the church, at the same time indicating the direction of the terminal thrusts. In this way they determined almost instantly not only the exact profiles of the arches, but the inclination of the pillars and the walls on which these would be supported. The result of all this was an absolutely homogeneous hyperconnected structure, each one of whose points was necessarily determined by the whole, and vice versa. Gaudí built this model in a workshop on the site where the church was to be constructed. On the ceiling of the workshop was a wooden board with the plan of the church marked out on it. Fixed to the points that represented pillars or angles of wall were the strings from which the little bags of pellets were suspended. Period photographs preserve the image of this impressive model, four meters in height, but its homogeneity is attested to, above all, by the accounts that various authors managed to collect concerning the process of its construction—a process that, if we are to believe Ràfols, it took Gaudí more than ten years to perfect: for example, it was necessary to readjust the whole model every time Gaudí introduced some variation in the project, however minor; or the way that the vast assembly trembled from top to bottom at the mere touch of a finger at any point. We have here, then, a structure that, in its pursuit of "architectural synthesis," has definitely eliminated the distinction between supporting and supported elements, evolving on itself in an organic sequence that can only be compared to the processes of natural growth, and a procedure in which Gaudí has ostentatiously renounced a purely mental speculation, replacing mathematical calculation—that is to say, abstract thought— by a stridently empirical "making with the hands": but we have already considered the significance of such questions in sufficient detail in relation to the porticoes and viaducts of the Park Güell. But the emotive reminiscences of the astonishing homogeneity of the model and the vivid period photographs we mentioned above also show a model that declared itself to be not an instrument of the work but a liberation of it. The model, in effect, is a hyperconnected world, but one in which everything has been reduced to almost nothing, a world in which the material has in fact all but disappeared. Strings, pellets, little canvas bags in the quantity necessary to enclose

nothing but air. And yet contained in that incredibly precarious system is the most absolute synthetic perfection, the ultimate secret of all construction. The model of the Colonia Güell church is thus a paradigm of Gaudí's work: not only because all of that work, from the radicalism of its dematerialization to its incomparable hand-crafted perfection, is simultaneously present in it, but also because it is the only image of the consciousness of the work that, once built, will inevitably be reduced to banality or—no paradox—destroyed. Indeed the covering of the model with a skin of very fine paper, which in order to reveal the plastic form of the future church had to conceal the pure vision of the tensions of a development that was utopian in the most technical sense of the word; and, still more, the upside-down photographs of the model on which Gaudí painted the symbolic colors and forms of that concrete temple in gouache and pastels: what are these but the banal steps that Gaudí had to follow in order to complete a project? And in the moment of execution, what is the brutal materialization of the crypt that we have described but a demonstration of the abyss that separates matter from spirit—that spirit Gaudí nonetheless believed he had captured, in the model, with his hands? That model, like a pathetic metaphor of the inescapable necessity of taking one or other of those paths— banality or destruction—was an inverted structure whose perfection did not support itself but, for all that it was made of almost nothing, was manifested only by its weight. The air it enclosed was a dream of the spirit, and this was to install itself like a terrible void in Gaudí's work. In the crypt, that void made a place for itself from the first moment. The plan, in effect, is nothing but a system of rings surrounding a center determined by the structure itself, and the four monolithic columns that lean in towards that center seem to seek to sacralize with their totemic presence a point that does not, however, coincide with the altar.

It has been suggested that financial reasons were responsible for construction of the church being abandoned in 1916,[132] but by then it was already more than a year since Gaudí had given up supervising the work on site, and even longer since he had stopped accepting private commissions in order to devote himself exclusively to the work of the Sagrada Familia, an undertaking that was, as we shall see, increasingly integrated into the operative political project of conservative Catalanism. Quite clearly the "re-created society" of the colony, based on the "sovereign will" of the patriarch, had come to seem anachronistic in comparison to that project of State, of the masses, urban; a project that, as we saw at the end of the last chapter, was also to render the emblematic landscape of the Park Güell anachronistic at the same time. But there is no need to insist on this now: there will be time for that when we come to consider the role that other temple, the Sagrada Familia,

was to fulfill in this political project as a sublimation of pacts and commitments.

But perhaps there is something more here: how could a man such as Gaudí, having seen the perfect spirit of the temple in the precariousness of that model that a breath could set trembling, carry on with the work? If "death comes of the flesh,"[133] neither the one nor the other could be far from the man whose presumption was humbled by imperfection. And Gaudí would also have seen, between the four imposing columns at the center of the crypt, that the void, when it ceases to be a spectacle of the perfect, has no name: in the face of that void his work had no choice but to stop. Gaudí's own convictions made it impossible for him to continue the crypt and complete it.

[1] Garraf. Poema lírich en cinch actes y un prólech, written in Catalan by D. Ramón Picó y Campamar, music by Joseph García Robles, Barcelona, 1911. The data mentioned on p. 123. On Picó i Campamar see chapter 2, note 16.

[2] On Güell's properties in Garraf see data and bibliography in: J. Bassegoda, El gran Gaudí, cit., pp. 343–55. It seems that in 1882 Gaudí had already designed a hunting pavilion for Güell in Garraf, the elevation of which, the only known document, was published by J.F. Ràfols, Gaudí, cit., p. 26. Subsequently, between 1895 and 1898, Gaudí's collaborator Francesc Berenguer—the only one to whom Ràfols gives special attention in his biography of his master ("Breu homenatge a Francesc Berenguer," Gaudí, cit., pp. 66–72)—designed and built the famous wine cellars. Gaudí's contribution to the latter—he was probably responsible for the initial conception, but not the project and certainly not the construction—and the personality of Berenguer have been the subject of long and ultimately sterile polemics that have involved authors from Joan Sacs to Toshiaki Tange, by way of David Mackay. For a basic bibliography see: J. Bassegoda, op. cit., pp. 348–49. There is a careful analysis in: A. Pabón Charneco, The Architectural Collaborators of Antoni Gaudí, cit., pp. 38–59.

[3] See chapter 2, note 51.

[4] Garraf, cit., p. 102.

[5] J. Sardà, "Un drama lírico catalán.

Apunte expositivo," Garraf, cit., pp. 3-8.

[6] Ibid., p. 4.

[7] Ibid., p. 5.

[8] Ibid., p. 6.

[9] Ibid., p. 6.

[10] Ibid., p. 6.

[11] Ibid., p. 7. On the subject of Gregorian chant see chapter 5, note 31.

[12] Ibid., p. 7.

[13] Garraf, cit., p. 13.

[14] J. Sardà, op. cit., p. 8.

[15] We considered La Fada in the last chapter. For everything referring to this opera see: X. Aviñada, La música i el modernisme, cit., pp. 265–86. We shall look in greater details at Torras i Bages and the Cercle de Sant Lluc in the next chapter. See: J. Torras i Bages, "Del Verb Artístic. (Comentari de Sant Tomàs)" (1897), in Estètiques, Barcelona, 1936, pp. 109–61.

[16] Ibid., op. cit., pp. 128–29.

[17] Ibid., p. 127.

[18] Ibid., p. 135.

[19] J. Torras i Bages, "Notes d'art," Estètiques, cit., p. 357.

[20] J. Torras i Bages, "Del Verb Artístic," cit., p. 132.

[21] Ibid., p. 132.

[22] Ibid., "Notes d'art," cit., p. 359.

[23] Ibid., p. 356.

[24] J. Torras i Bages, "Del Verb Artístic," cit., p. 135.

[25] Ibid., p. 131.

[26] J. Torras i Bages, "Notes d'art," cit., p. 359.

[27] J. Tarré, "L'Art i la Liturgia," I Congrés d'Art Cristià a Catalunya. Reseña Eclesiástica, nos. 59–60, November–December 1913, p. 734.

[28] These notes and comments are included in J. Torras i Bages, "Notes d'art," cit., pp. 355–60, and are confessedly based on El arte y la Revolución—in other words, on Wagner's "thought" and not his "music"— and, most improbably, on the librettos of some of the operas. But Torras i Bages, in being more interested in Wagner's personality and the Wagnerian phenomenon than in his music, is not an isolated case among the Catalan intelligentsia of the late nineteenth century: think, for example, of Maragall or Casellas. On this see chapter 2, note 85.

[29] Recall here, for example, Güell's son: "At the age of seventeen I visited Bayreuth with the spirit of a pilgrim of art... Although my father had reserved seats for himself and his children with eight months in advance, we could not sit together" (Vicomte de Güell, op. cit., p. 58).

[30] W. Benjamin, Parigi, capitale del XIX secolo. I "passages" di Parigi, Turin, 1986, p. 308.

[31] C. Baudelaire, "Richard Wagner et Tannhäuser," L'art romantique, cit., pp. 217–18.

[32] Ibid., p. 225.

[33] Ibid., pp. 225–26.

[34] For more on this, see: F. Coblence, Le dandysme, obligation d'incertitude, Paris, 1988, especially pp. 227–31.

[35] For Maragall's attitude to the project for the opera, see: J.Ll. Marfany, *Aspectes del modernisme*, cit., pp. 140–44.

[36] M. Doménech Español, *L'apothéose musicale de la Religion Catholique. Parsifal de Wagner*, Barcelona, 1902. As late as 1924 (and that was not the last edition) the Associació Wagneriana was still publishing a translation of *Parsival*—the substitution of the "v" for the "f" sought to demonstrate the Provençal origin of the name, derived from "per se val"—by Geroni Zanné and Joaquim Pena with Doménech Español's thematic commentary in columns parallel to the libretto. On Doménech Español see: A. Janés i Nadal, *L'obra de Richard Wagner a Barcelona*, cit., pp. 95–105, and his own writings: M. Doménech Español, "Fusió del més pur i seré classicisme y del més fogós romanticisme en l'art de Wagner," *XXV Conférences donades a la Associació Wagneriana*, cit., pp. 47–64; id., "Les grans belleses de l'art wagneriá y sa interpretació," op. cit., pp. 77–98, among others papers in the same volume.

[37] M. Doménech Español, *L'apothéose musicale...*, cit., p. 2.

[38] See for example the three articles of the same title by M. Doménech Español, "Parsifal i Sherlock Holmes," *Revista Musical Catalana*, VI, 1909, pp. 333–38; id., VII, 1910, pp. 196–202, and id., X, 1913, pp. 43–49. On the controversy see, above all, F. Pedrell, "Nuevo comentario sobre el Parsifal," *Musicalerías*, Valencia; Ll. Via, "Quatre paraules i prou," *Joventut*, III, 1902, pp. 483–85; M. Doménech Español, "Moltas paraulas y prou també," id., pp. 501–04. On this polemic: A. Janés i Nadal, op. cit., pp. 100–02.

[39] Much of the polemic with Lluís Via in *Joventut* referred to in the previous note and commented on by A. Janés i Nadal has to do with the role of the critic. While we are on the subject of these "coincidences," it is perhaps worth recalling Baudelaire's remarks to the same effect in "Richard Wagner et Tannhäuser," cit., p. 229.

[40] F. Pujols, *La visió artística i religiosa d'en Gaudí*, Barcelona, 1927; for the comparison with Wagner, see pp. 19–20; on the destiny of Catalonia as the place where Catholicism will meet its end, see p. 28. In his 1929 bibliography of Gaudí, Ràfols glosses the pamphlet by Pujols with the words: "The absolutely Catholic convictions of the authors of the present book would prohibit them even from mentioning this booklet if ... it were not to censure it for the explicit heterodoxy of the principal thesis expounded there" (J.F. Ràfols,

*Gaudí*, cit., p. 295). This is the only work in the bibliography to receive any comment. It was subsequently published in R. Descharnes, C. Prevost, *La vision artistique et religieuse de Gaudí*, Lausanne, 1969, with a foreword by S. Dalí. There are other texts by Pujols on Gaudí, for example: F. Pujols, "In Gaudí," *Revista Nova*, L, 23, May 1914, pp. 3–4; id., *Recull d'articles de crítica artística publicats fins ara*, Barcelona, 1921, pp. 159–72; id., "La obra del nostre Gaudí," *De l'art de la forja*, I, March 1921, pp. 219–20, among others. On Pujols: A. Blade Desumvila, *Francesc Pujols per ell mateix*, Barcelona, 1967; J.Ll. Marfany, "Assagistes i periodistes," *Història de la literatura catalana*, cit., vol. VIII, pp. 172–78; J. Isart, "Les influències noucentistes i wagnerianes de Francesc Pujols als cent anys del seu naixement," *El Mon*, May 1982, p. 18.

[41] J. Sardà, op. cit., p. 3.

[42] Ibid., p. 4.

[43] *Garraf*, cit., p. 14.

[44] Ibid., p. 23.

[45] Ibid., p. 28.

[46] Ibid., p. 102.

[47] Ibid., p. 36.

[48] Ibid., p. 14.

[49] Ibid., p. 14.

[50] It is not surprising that this subject, a recurring presence in the works of the different "symbolisms," should have been interpreted by A. de Riquer, a figure never directly associated with the Gaudí circle, but one of the most international of turn-of-the-century Catalan artists in his "style" and wider relationships. See: (various authors), *Alexandre de Riquer. L'home, l'artista, el poeta*, Calaf, 1978; E. Trenc Ballester and A. Yates, *Alexandre de Riquer. The British Connection in Catalan Modernisme*, Sheffield, 1988.

[51] *Garraf*, cit., p. 123.

[52] There is a classic study of Balmes by H. Auhofer, *La sociología de Jaime Balmes*, Madrid, 1959. With regard to our purposes here, see: E. Valentí, *El primer modernismo literario catalán...*, cit., pp. 85–93.

[53] Balmes' ideas on these questions were fundamentally expounded in a series of articles published in 1843 and 1844 in *La Sociedad*, a magazine affiliated to the *Diario de Barcelona*, and reprinted in J. Balmes, "Cataluña," *Obras Completas*, vol. V, Madrid, 1949, pp. 923–53, and "Barcelona," id., pp. 954–1002.

[54] Among many possible examples, one will serve us here: according to Miquel d'Esplugues, Güell's aim, in his colony, was to realize "the balmesian ideal" (M. d'Es-

plugues, op. cit., p. 98). The importance attached to Balmes had a direct bearing on Eugeni D'Ors' change of attitude towards him (see: E. Valentí, op. cit., pp. 94ff.). But it was above all the Jesuit Ignasi Casanovas who with the founding of the Biblioteca Balmesiana and the editing of his collected works established Balmes as that "necessary philosopher." For more on this, see his *magnum opus*: I. Casanovas, *Balmes. La seva vida, el seu temps, les seves obres*, Barcelona, 1932, 3 vols. On the same subject: M. Batllori, *Balmes y Casanovas*, Barcelona, 1959. Casanovas and Torras i Bages were the principal instigators of the celebration of the Balmes centenary in 1910, for which Gaudí constructed in Vic a group of monumental lampposts, with a base and shaft of rough-dressed blocks of basalt and a virtuoso display of wrought iron in the arms and crown. Josep Canaleta and Josep M. Jujol worked on the execution of the project. The lampposts were demolished in 1924. See: L.B. Nadal, *Crònica de les festes del Centenari d'En Balmes*, Vic, 1911.

[55] H. Auhofer, op. cit., pp. 214–17.

[56] *Garraf*, cit., p. 14.

[57] Transcribed in *Colonia Güell y fábrica de panas y veludillos Güell y Cía. Breve reseña histórica...*, Barcelona, 1910, pp. 125ff.

[58] See: I. Molas, *Lliga Catalana...*, cit., vol. I, pp. 187–90.

[59] E. Prat de la Riba, *Ley jurídica de la industria*, cit., pp. 257–71. See the analysis by I. Terradas Saborit, *La Colònia Industrial com a particularisme històric*, Barcelona, 1979, pp. 29–33. On the industrial colonies in Catalonia in general, see: J.A. Sanz and J. Giner, *L'arquitectura de la indústria a Catalunya en els segles XVIII i XIX*, Sabadell, 1984.

[60] E. Prat de la Riba, op. cit., pp. 258–59.

[61] Ibid., p. 258.

[62] Ibid., p. 257.

[63] Ibid., p. 265.

[64] Ibid., pp. 270–71.

[65] This is the thesis convincingly argued by I. Terradas Saborit, op, cit., p. 88.

[66] E. Prat de la Riba, op. cit., p. 267.

[67] Ibid., p. 267.

[68] Ibid., p. 278.

[69] Ibid., p. 268.

[70] Ibid., pp. 260-261.

[71] Ibid., p. 261.

[72] Ibid., p. 260.

[73] Ibid., p. 262.

[74] Ibid., pp. 266–67.

[75] Ibid., p. 266.

[76] Ibid., p. 259. And further on, addressing the possibility that the employer "*might*

*abuse* his authority" for his own benefit, he proposes the intervention of the State in such cases (pp. 268–69).

[77] I. Terradas Saborit, op. cit., p. 33.

[78] Data and bibliography on this in: J. Bassegoda, *El gran Gaudí*, cit., pp. 365–74. But above all it is worth consulting the publications produced by the company itself: *Colonia Güell y fábrica de panas y veludillos...*, cit.; *Colonia Güell*, Igualada, 1917; P. Rodón, *Els carrers de la Colònia Güell*, Barcelona, 1935.

[79] This is sufficiently borne out by the fundamental part he played in the acts of the Catholic Social Week held in Barcelona in 1910: *Semana Social de España. Quinto Curso*, Barcelona, 1912, pp. 169–71, 180–81, etc. Güell's role is hardly surprising, perhaps, given that the purpose of this Social Week was "the formation of a workers' élite" (p. 45).

[80] *Semana Social de España*, cit., p. 170.

[81] The various associations and their functioning are described in *Colonia Güell*, Igualada, 1917.

[82] Obviously none of this was exclusive to the Colonia Güell; what was remarkable, as we have said, was its exemplary utilization. For a general account of these matters, see: J.A. Sanz and J. Giner, op. cit.

[83] *Semana Social de España*, cit., p. 170.

[84] M. d'Esplugues, op. cit., p. 99.

[85] E. Prat de la Riba, op. cit., p. 269.

[86] The previously cited *Colonia Güell*, Igualada, 1917, whose author, although he is not acknowledged in the book, was Gaspar Vilarrubias, the colony's parish priest (J. Bassegoda, op. cit., p. 372).

[87] *Colonia Güell*, cit., pp. 17–18.

[88] Ibid., p. 17.

[89] See: I. Terradas Saborit, op. cit., p. 32, who in turn cites M. Izard, *Revolució industrial i obrerisme*, Barcelona, 1970.

[90] *Colonia Güell*, cit., p. 19.

[91] Ibid., cit., p. 19.

[92] For a superb analysis of the symbolic and representational value of the *masía* and its elements, see Ll. Prats, *El mite de la tradició popular*, cit., pp. 169–82. In general see: J. Camps i Arboix, *La masia catalana*, Barcelona, 1959, and, from the typological point of view, the monograph issue of *2C. Construcción de la Ciudad*, nos. 17–18, March 1981.

[93] M. d'Esplugues, op. cit., p. 98.

[94] Ibid., p. 98.

[95] Ibid., p. 102.

[96] *Colonia Güell y fábrica de panas...*, cit., pp. 73ff.; *Colonia Güell*, cit., pp. 23ff.

[97] Published as appendices in *Colonia Güell y fábrica de panas...*, cit.

[98] "Curacions extraordinàries ocorregudes

en la Colonia Güell," *Colonia Güell*, cit., pp. 44ff.

[99] M. d'Esplugues, op. cit., p. 99.

[100] *Semana Social de España*, cit., p. 143. In the sermon he delivered at the inaugural ceremony the bishop several times repeated, referring to the workers, the words of St. Mark: "*misereor super turbam*" (pp. 132–33).

[101] J. Torras i Bages, "El espíritu en el problema del trabajo," *Semana Social de España*, cit., p. 214.

[102] J.F. Ràfols, *Gaudí*, cit., p. 153.

[103] On the crypt see the data and bibliography in: J. Bassegoda, *El gran Gaudí*, cit., pp. 365–74. See, too, the monograph studies: I. Puig Boada, *L'Esglèsia de la Colònia Güell*, Barcelona, 1976; E. Rojo, *Antonio Gaudí ese incomprendido: la cripta de la Colonia Güell*, Barcelona, 1988.

[104] It seems that the general plan of the colony was worked out by Francesc Berenguer, possibly under Gaudí's supervision, while the principal buildings were designed by Gaudí and J. Rubió i Bellver. On the attribution of these, however, opinions differ. See: D. Mackay, "Berenguer," *The Architectural Review*, no. 814, December 1964, pp. 411–16; I. Solà-Morales, *Joan Rubió i Bellver y la fortuna del gaudinismo*, cit., p. 40; A. Pabón-Charneco, *The Architectural Collaborators of Antoni Gaudí*, cit., pp. 105–15.

[105] See: J. Bassegoda, op. cit., p. 369. Many of these effects have disappeared as a result of the growth of the colony and the degradation of the area around the crypt over the years.

[106] I. Solà-Morales, *Gaudí*, Barcelona, 1983, p. 26; however, as we shall see, the church was not intended to impose order on the colony in the spatial sense suggested in Solà-Morales' text. The position of the church in the colony is comparable to that which the Chapel with its rose-shaped plan was to have occupied in the Park Güell, on the summit of a low hill. There Sellés justified the site in terms of the "right to be built on the highest points" of both the lord's castle and the church (S. Sellés, op. cit., p. 61). This is exactly what it signifies in the colony: "acropolis," then, in the broader sense of a fortified high point of the city.

[107] *Colonia Güell*, cit., p. 24.

[108] Ibid., p. 51.

[109] On possible interpretations of the signs that appear on this vault and in other parts of the crypt, see: E. Rojo, *Antonio Gaudí ese incomprendido: la cripta de la Colonia Güell*, cit., although the author attaches undue importance to his "own discoveries," embracing these with excessive enthusiasm and a lack of critical distance.

[110] We should not forget here that the crypt is the essential element in a whole "organic" and "expressionist" interpretation of Gaudí and thus the supposed operative precursor of and link with a certain strand of modern architecture. This view was taken by Sert and Swenney (*Gaudí*, cit., pp. 79ff.) and endorsed by O. Bohigas (*Reseña y católogo de la arquitectura modernista*, cit., pp. 157–58), and subsequently by C. Flores (*Gaudí, Jujol y el modernismo catalán*, Madrid, 1983, vol. I, p. 216) and I. Solà-Morales (op. cit., p. 26), who come to the same conclusions by an apparently contrary path. Naturally, a more conventional image of Gaudí has been most in favor in the standard works on contemporary architecture. See the early and pertinent summaries by J.M. Sostres, "Cronología gaudinista en tres tiempos," (1953), "Situación de la obra de Gaudí en relación con su época y trascendencia actual" (1953) and "Interpretación actual de Gaudí" (1958), since reprinted in *Opiniones sobre arquitectura*, cit., pp. 51–56, 57–62 and 107–24 respectively.

[111] On this, see the marvelous lines devoted to the crypt by J.E. Cirlot, *Gaudí*, Barcelona, 1966, pp. 11–12.

[112] See the introduction to the previously cited E.J. Hobsbawm and T. Ranger, *The Invention of Tradition*, cit., and in relation to Catalonia: Ll. Prats, *El mite de la tradició popular…*, cit.

[113] J. Torras i Bages, *La tradició catalana* (1892), Barcelona, 1981, p. 119.

[114] J. Torras i Bages, "El espíritu en el problema del trabajo," *Semana Social de España*, cit., pp. 197–215.

[115] Ibid., p. 203.

[116] Ibid., p. 201.

[117] Ibid., p. 200.

[118] M. d'Esplugues, op. cit., p. 103.

[119] J. Torras i Bages, op. cit., pp. 199–200.

[120] Ibid., p. 200.

[121] See D. Mackay, "Berenguer," *The Architectural Review*, no. 814, December 1964; pp. 411–16; I. Solà-Morales, *Joan Rubió i Bellver y la fortuna del gaudinismo*, cit., pp. 18–19 and 40; A. Pabón-Charneco, *The Architectural Collaborators of Antoni Gaudí*, cit., pp. 105–15. See also: J. Rubió i Bellver, "Construccions de pedra en sec," *Anuario de la Asociación de Arquitectos de Cataluña*, 1914, pp. 33–105.

[122] *I Congrés d'Art Cristià a Catalunya. Reseña eclesiástica*, nos. 59–60, November–December 1913.

[123] J. Tarré, "L'Art i la Liturgia," *I Congrés d'Art Cristià*, cit., pp. 733–34.

[124] Ibid., p. 736.

[125] Ibid., p. 735.

[126] See, for example, the letters that Gaudí wrote to Maragall on November 16, 1906, January 5, 1907, February 16, 1907, March 7, 1908, insistently inviting him to attend the series of lectures given by Father Casanovas. To judge by the friendly but unencouraging tone of his replies, Maragall seems to have felt little enthusiasm for Casanovas' arguments. See: I. Puig Boada, "L'amistat de Gaudí i Maragall," (various authors), *Antoni Gaudí. L'home, l'obra, l'anècdota*, Barcelona, 1964, pp. 88–89.

[127] I. Casanovas, "L'Art en el Temple," *I Congrés d'Art Cristià*, cit., pp. 699–700.

[128] Ibid., p. 700.

[129] Ibid., p. 693.

[130] See chapters 5 and 6.

[131] F. Berenguer, J. Rubió i Bellver and the engineer Eduard Goetz Mauer all helped to calculate and construct the model. On Gaudí's structures, see the description and commentaries in F. Cardellach, *Filosofía de las estructuras*, Barcelona, 1910, and J. Rubió i Bellver, "Dificultats per a arribar a la sintesis arquitectònica," *Anuario de la Asociación de Arquitectos*, 1913, pp. 63–79; and also: F. Ulsamer Puiggari, "Las estructuras funiculares de Gaudí," *Cúpula*, IX, July 1962, pp. 425–28.

[132] See a summary of the available information in: J. Bassegoda, op. cit., pp. 365–74; but see, too, the chronology established by T. Torii, op. cit., vol. I, pp. 276–77 and vol. II, pp. 362–77.

[133] J. Torras i Bages, "El espíritu en el problema del trabajo," cit., p. 215.

## Non Est Hic Locus
Gaudí and the Political Restoration
of the Church in Catalonia and Mallorca

*A Modern and Anti-*Modernista *Art*

"Below the sumptuous baldachin, as new in form as it is exquisite, six large candles illuminated the large, severe crucifix of gilded bronze, in the altar encircled by its three ancient lamps. At the entry to the chapel of the Trinity the seven new lamps were also lit. As the day declined, the temple was enveloped in a mysterious darkness in which the tenuous radiance of the lights was lost, together with the echo of the psalms and sacred canticles. At the back of the choir, among shadows, the bishop appeared, robed as a pontiff in his See, and on either side the figures of the attendant deacons stood out against the rich embroidery of the precious fabrics that draped the wall, forming a picture solemn and monumental in character."[1]

Thus did Mateu Rotger—historian of the origins of Christianity in the Balearic Islands and of their towns, and of the Palma cathedral of which he was canon, but also the author of stilted Latin verse and, most importantly, Bishop Campins' companion on his *Ad Limina* visit in 1901 to the churches of the north of Italy and the south of France, and at his interview with Gaudí in Barcelona on August 19 of that same year, at which the architect accepted the commission to restore Mallorca cathedral—describe the mass held on the eve of the feast of the Immaculate Conception on the afternoon of December 7, 1904 in the now partially restored temple.[2]

Exquisite and rich, its antiquity vaporously discerned by the entranced senses, mysterious darkness, tenuous radiance, echoing canticles: Rotger's language is, in all its conventionality, that of the decadentist aestheticism that, in the Catalonia of the end of the nineteenth century, had been so feared by the vitalist, Nietzschean and Ibsenite young radicals of *L'Avenç*.

Feared because, in its formal modernity, it did nothing but represent—that is to say, to present over again—tradition. As early as 1893 Brossa was warning true modernists to be wary of what this latest symbolism concealed: for example, in *Quimeres contemporànies* he wrote that "the

artistic and literary masquerade of the Rose-Croix is directed towards nothing other than a militant Catholicism."[3] But feared, above all, from the moment when it now no longer had any need to refer to foreign movements: in 1893, in fact, the very year in which *L'Avenç* closed down, the Cercle Artístic de Sant Lluc had been founded in Barcelona at the instigation of a group of Catholic artists that included the Llimona brothers and Alexandre de Riquer— and also Gaudí himself, although not in an active capacity. The Cercle's founders combined a thorough understanding of the latest European literary and artistic developments and their *modern* practice with a conservative and moralistic ideology that they carried to see their art as a form of religious and social restoration: a restoration of art as an expression of collective faith, a restoration of the organic role of the artist and a restoration of the guild. The declarations of the group's founding principles are laden with references to Pope Leo XIII and hasty interpretations of his recent *Rerum novarum*.[4]

So, over and above its—I repeat—scrupulously modern form, and very often in painful conflict with it, what the Cercle promoted in polemical and at first chaotic and visceral opposition to the *Modernista* idea of *art pour l'art* was an objective art; that is to say, a highly ideological and expressly operative art; a thematic art, organically articulated within a society integrated into tradition and religion; an art, in short, that was recognizable not in its own right but as a functional part of a plan: as instrument, as its proponents saw it, of the Divine Plan for society and nature—or of the project for the political restoration of the Catalan Church, as we can see it.

It is hardly surprising, then, that the apologist of that restoration, Josep Torras i Bages—author of *La tradició catalana*, the most effective and influential formulation of Catalan neotraditionalism, and as of 1899, Morgades' successor as bishop of Vic, the most active religious center in Catalonia—should be elected, from the princi-

ple, counselor of the Cercle, or that the director of the religious propaganda section of the Unió Catalanista should be the author of those texts in which the moralistic impulse of the Cercle artists was formulated theoretically, or rather, operatively.[5]

As counselor, Torras i Bages not only ran the Cercle but, in keeping with his skills as a religious apologist and propagandist, effectively directed and systematized the deplorable subjectivism of its membership of modern artists in the service of his project for the political restoration of the Church, creating, with his lectures, his writings, his polemical opinions, an artistic convergence that was to determine the development of the Catalan art of the turn of the century. And it was not only the symbolist aestheticism of Alexandre de Riquer, Joan Llimona or Enric Galwey (that would have been easy enough) and even the decorativism of Homar that were to find in Torras' simplified expositions—constructed on the elementary formulas of Thomist scholasticism, and bearing such significant titles as *De la früició artística, De l'infinit i del límit en l'art, Del verb artístic* and *Llei d'art*[6]—a way of differentiating their work from the style of the modernists, based as both were on the same international models and expressed in the same forms; the tormented and painful art, so driven by its own monsters, of Josep Llimona and Gaudí, also found a source of consolation in those formulas, precisely because they were anti-artistic. It was, paradoxically but inevitably, in Torras' radical negation of the autonomy of art that those extraordinary artists saw their work, so mysterious even to them, made transcendent, just: it was justified. In a society such as Catalonia at the end of the nineteenth century, whose bourgeoisie, having moved on from the *febre d'or* years, had begun to switch the ethic of hard work and saving characteristic of the periods of great accumulation of wealth for an aesthetic of consumption, producing its first generation of modern artists—that is to say, artists with a liberal professional status—

Torras' highly directed utilization of the moral misgivings of those Cercle de Sant Lluc artists thus had a clearly anti-*modernista* orientation.[7] But we can hardly be surprised at the success of the operation, in view of the climate in which it was mounted. On the one hand, these were the years in which, after the demise of *L'Avenç* and, with it, its modernist campaigns, the decadentist currents effectively took control of the Catalan art and literature, to the extent that, as far as the general public was concerned, the term modernism became synonymous with its more external manifestations and thus those most open to parody by its conservative critics; on the other hand these were also, and above all, the years in which a significant part of the modernist intelligentsia was beginning to see in the great decorative-symbolic cycles of European painting—in Puvis de Chavannes, for example, and, even more importantly, in Albert Besnard—the embodiment of the great civil art of their time: an art that was finally integrative, universal, timeless. Thus, as of 1894, Raimon Casellas (Catalonia's leading art critic, the most fully aware of the international situation, and the most incisive and coherent defender of the innovations introduced by artists such as Rusiñol and Casas, for whom he constructed, in long series of articles in the press, a theory of the necessity of the modern) began to champion a painting of great cycles, integrated decoratively with architecture, capable of expressing synthetically the myths and ideals of society; a national art, in other words, that would emulate and translate into a new field what Wagner had already achieved in his music.[8] But the vision championed by Casellas was no less dubious for being energetic, and its fate proved very different from his predictions. On the one hand Casellas was doubtful of the ability of the Catalan artists to develop "an art of such wide horizons and such complex components," although two years later the Exposición General de Bellas Artes of 1896 was to provide him, it seems, with the basis for his reconciliation with them.[9] Above all, however, he had no faith in the

potential of Catalan society to promote such great art: in fact, the very few places in which artists had an opportunity of painting a decorative cycle integrated with the architecture (or simply with a physical setting) in order to pursue its symbolic development were radically private spaces, the preserve of some connoisseur or the self-celebratory space of the artist's own residence: the series of paintings by Aleix Clapés on the walls of the great salon of Gaudí's Palau Güell, the decoration by Rusiñol of the ogival tympana of Cau Ferrat in Sitges, and very little, if anything, more. As has already been noted, on only one occasion did Casellas have the opportunity to comment on a work of decorative-symbolic painting in which the means and the location were of the necessary transcendence: the decoration of the dome of the chapel of the Virgin in the monastery of Montserrat by Joan Llimona. Could the case have been more significant? On the one hand, the founder and principal driving force of the Cercle de Sant Lluc; on the other, the Church restoring the most sacred site of Catalonia, its miracle. Casellas not only acknowledged the value of Llimona's work, but, criticizing the apostolic will with which the artist sought to justify it, attempted to counteract Torras i Bages' influence on Llimona and win him back to true modernism, opening in him, at first polemically and then quite sincerely, a new religious-artistic front for which he advocated an intimate and spiritual—that is to say, anti-ideological—character.[10]

Casellas' endeavor, however, was too personalized to be viable. If Llimona's conviction was great, greater still was the need that the project for the political restoration of the Catalan Church had of an art at once modern and anti-*modernista*, and in this context Llimona's celebrated intervention in Montserrat—or, for example, Gaudí's ever greater freedom of action in the Sagrada Familia—are merely the most eloquent signs of a long and demonstrably effective strategy. Even before Casellas launched his endeavor, the Church had already begun to pro-

mote in Catalonia that great synthetic, timeless art of which, with very different intentions, the critic was concerned, and for a long time to come the Church was to continue to be the only client for such an art.

The program for the Christian reconquest of society proposed by Leo XIII from the moment of his ascending the papal throne found a very coherent translation in the careers of the two successive bishops of Vic we referred to above—Morgades and Torras i Bages—and in the groups of clergy that formed around them—motivated from an early age, as Valentí says, by great political ambition.[11] This is apparent on the one hand in their acceptance of the Liberal constitution of 1876 as the unavoidable context in which to act from within against the progressive secularization of society and their resulting policy of marginalizing the fundamentalists—Leo XIII himself had repudiated the intransigent attitudes of certain sectors of the Spanish Church in his 1882 encyclical *Cum multa*—and on the other, and above all, in their strategy of identifying that restoration of the Church with what we shall call the restoration of Catalonia.[12]

That restoration was, of course, the theme of Torras i Bages' tremendously important book *La tradició catalana*. Its explicitly declared purpose, in response to the radical proposals of Valentí Almirall's *Lo catalanisme*, was to direct Catalanism toward traditionalist positions and to censure its political and secular deviations, and, above all, to implant at the very heart of the Romantic myths of the origins of the Catalan nation and its language constructed by the poets and artists of the Renaixença the necessary and founding presence of the Church. A famous phrase is often attributed to Torras i Bages—a phrase that in fact he never voiced, but one that perfectly sums up his proposed ideology: "Catalonia will be Christian or it will not be." On the other hand, the following phrase does indeed appear, and on more than an occasion, in the pages of *La tradició catalana*: "The Catalan Orpheus was Christ."[13]

But if Torras' theoretical work was fundamental, no less so, and no less directed, was the great constructing action of Josep Morgades. As bishop of Vic from 1882, he initiated the restoration of a series of Romanesque monasteries, most of them located in the Pyrenean valleys of the Ripollès: Sant Joan de les Abadesses, L'Estany, Lluçà, the church of Sant Pere de Mogrony and, above all, the monastery of Santa Maria de Ripoll. The choice, of course, was by no means casual: in fact, the Catalan Romantics placed the origins of the nation in the Pyrenees, and the same period in which the counts of those valleys were becoming politically independent of the Frankish kings saw the birth of a distinct language and the first manifestations of a distinct original art. Romanesque was the language and Romanesque was the style of the churches and monasteries of those first years of Catalonia's foundation. The Catalan language and the Romanesque style were thus identified with one another in the Romantic foundational legends, and it is hardly surprising that while the poets and intellectuals of the Renaixença saw the restoration of Catalan as the primary objective, the Romanesque monuments of the Pyrenees were the principal object of the scientific excursions organized by the Catalanist associations.[14] It is in this context that Morgades' task of restoration takes on its full significance: his actuations are always focused on places with a symbolic value that is not only strong but concrete, on the precise sites that were the sources of many of the epic legends of the reconquest of the country, around which so many of the patriotic and Romantic myths of the origins of Catalonia had been constructed. Santa Maria de Ripoll is the most telling case. Established in the ninth century by Count Guifré el Pilós, the hero of legends of Catalan independence and the creator of the Catalan coat of arms with its four bars, it was from Santa Maria de Ripoll that Montserrat was founded in the early eleventh century, in the time of its great constructor, the abbot Oliva. Santa Maria de Ripoll, considered by Romantic mythology as more than any other place the cradle of Catalonia, had been burned down and its community dispersed in 1835, as a result of the sale of Church lands decreed by the Liberal government, and subjected to continual plunder during the following years. When Morgades was appointed bishop of Vic, Santa Maria was an absolute ruin. Begun in 1885, the restoration of Ripoll—in fact a new construction, which included, in addition to the church and the cloisters of the monastery, the tombs of the counts—was thus a carefully thought-out project, laden with symbolism: the Church restored to Catalonia the cradle that the Liberal state had robbed it of.[15] This was, then, a double-edged gesture, at once conciliatory and authoritarian, by which Catalanism incurred a debt to the Church that political Catalanism would find to weigh heavily on it. And a gesture, too, that was nothing hidden: the holiday of the consecration of Ripoll on July 1, 1893, gathered in the restored basilica virtually all the bishops and chapters of Catalonia, in addition to those of Segorbe and Menorca, representing the other Catalan-speaking lands. In his sermon, the bishop of Urgell, after an uncompromising attack on the Liberalism that had been the cause of Santa Maria's destruction, declared: "May God grant that as Catalonia has paid to the Church the debt of justice it had contracted, restoring to her this basilica, it will also pay the tribute it owes her of love, gratitude and filial submission. May God grant that this renaissance begun some years since with Catalan letters, born each day with greater pride and grace, shall be a true recompense to Catalonia in the fullest meaning of the word. Would that Catalonia may indeed be reborn to its own life, received of the Church, and make her its favorite and pampered daughter!"[16] Could we ask for greater clarity? It will come as no surprise to find bishop Morgades, in that same year of the consecration of Ripoll, presiding over the Jocs Florals, the supreme Romantic institution for the restoration of the language; or that, only apparently in another order of things,

the mosaic of the Virgin in the altar of the Ripoll church should be a gift from Pope Leo XIII; or indeed, to go even further, that a collaborator of Gaudí's, Rubió i Bellver—a modern artist who had been elected fourth president of the Cercle de Sant Lluc in 1904—should have been entrusted, in 1912, with putting the final touch to the decoration of the church, in the form of the sumptuous and controversial baldachin.[17] This is the activity of constructing—or restoring—as the instrument of a very concrete political strategy. It is only a short step from the little Romanesque churches to Ripoll, to the Llimona of Montserrat and the Gaudí of the Colonia Güell or, above all, the Sagrada Familia. A highly conscious step: one that implies the decision to use modern art as the medium for the representation of that policy in its most eloquent moments. The total art demanded by those great symbolic constructions, as Casellas had so clearly seen, could only be modern, and the calculated political utilization that the Church will make of it seems to add something more, only apparently paradoxical: modern as tradition upheld.

### P.J. Campins, Bishop of Mallorca

Mallorca Cathedral, December 7, 1904: we can now perceive further meanings in the description by Rotger with which we began this chapter. The tenuous crepuscular radiance, the echoes of sacred canticles, the precious fabrics and embroidery—despite the slightly ingenuous way in which they are presented and the conventionality of tone we have noted, as befits the author of the Latin *Carmina* that Llorenç Riber translated into Catalan—could easily be seen, for example, "through the blue smoke of the censers, that vomit tongues of fire from their silver urns" of the last mass of the abbot of Croix-Jugan, so described by Barbey D'Aurevilly.[18] Rotger's vision, culminating as it does in the appearance—of course—of the bishop among shadows, at the back of the choir, robed as a pontiff and flanked, as an emblem of the hierarchy, by his deacons, manifests the same pleasure in elaborately

majestic images, the same cult of ritual and the ceremony outside of time, as we find in that "hybrid between dandyism and religion" so perceptively defined by Françoise Coblence: "a secular figure that combines modernity in its 'decadent' version with the reading of the Fathers of the Church, theological debates, solemn processions."[19] Of course Coblence is referring to Huysmans, to Barbey, to the interest that Baudelaire himself felt for the figure of the *catholique dandy* enveloped in the sumptuous settings of the Church. In the evidently modest case of Rotger's description the terms have simply been reversed: this is no longer "modernity in its 'decadent' version" interested in the *mîses-en-scène* of a spectacularly dogmatic ritual Church—a Church that had begun, as of 1870, to compensate for its loss of temporal power by reorganizing the forms of its spiritual power: the grand dramatic ceremonies of the First Vatican Council, the statement of papal infallibility, the renaissance of the liturgy—but, at a slightly later moment, the same Church now interested in the instrument made available to it by the language of that *modernité*. An interest that was highly political, as we have seen. In spite of its evident modesty, I repeat, it seems to me that with regard to Rotger and his description of Mallorca Cathedral restored by Gaudí for the holiday of the Immaculate Conception we are certainly not overstating the case. To appreciate the intention here we need only consider the following excerpt, almost casual in tone, from a letter by Miquel Costa i Llobera, the highly cultured poet of the *Horacianes*, promoter in Mallorca of a Catalanism that has been called aesthetic, intimate collaborator of Bishop Campins and nominator of his appointment, priest and preacher above all: "The new Bishop presents in his person the mark of the renaissance of good taste. Rings, crosier, mitre and pectoral cross, all of the purest style."[20] Only Costa's enthusiasm for these things is more eloquent than the exquisiteness of the liturgical insignia with which the bishop presented himself.

Pere Joan Campins, thirteen years younger than Torras i Bages, thirty-three years younger than Morgades, restorer of the sanctuary of Monti-Sion already in his time as rector of Porreres, masterful canon of the cathedral in Palma, sought from the moment of his appointment as Bishop of Mallorca in 1898 to apply to the Mallorcan Church the same strategy of political restoration that Morgades and Torras, whom he so admired, were undertaking in Catalonia.[21] Highly significant in this respect is his first decision: the reform of the syllabus of the Seminar, instituting two new Chairs, none other than Mallorcan Language and Literature and the History of Mallorca. Even more significant is the fact that he gathered around himself from the outset those members of the Balearic clergy most clearly committed to the cultural and literary concerns of what might loosely be called a Mallorcan *renaixença*. A *renaixença* that, like its Catalan counterpart, based its Romantic ideology of patriotic restoration on the recovery of Catalan as a literary language and the creation of a mythology of origins, essentially grounded in the landscape of the island: However, in contrast to the Catalan *renaixença*, and given that the society in which it developed was not modern and industrialized but agrarian and economically backward, dominated by clannish local power structures, it was never to achieve an effective political organization. It was in the midst of this contradictory Mallorcanism, populist at times, exquisitely elitist at others, that Campins' endeavor assumed its significance: personalities as radically different as Mateu Rotger or Costa i Llobera, together with Salvador Galmés, Llorenç Riber, Joan Quetglas and, above all, Antoni Maria Alcover, who until then had all been involved to a greater or lesser extent and effectiveness, but always in a piecemeal way, in that diffuse Mallorcanism, were to find a point of contact in the apostolic strategy of restoration proposed by the new bishop. Campins' action, then, was a carefully meditated and possibilist interpretation of Torras i Bages' theory, providing a

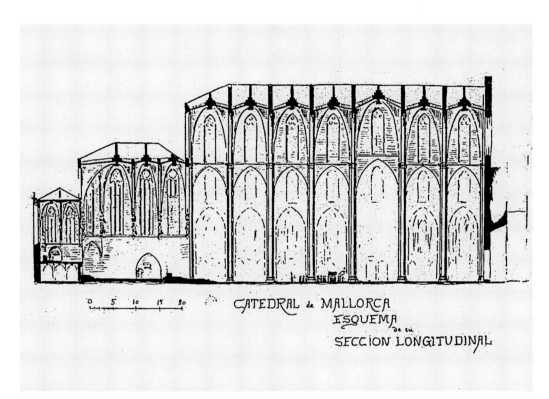

CATEDRAL de MALLORCA
ESQUEMA de su
SECCION LONGITUDINAL

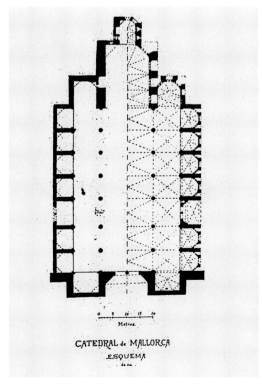

CATEDRAL de MALLORCA
ESQUEMA de su

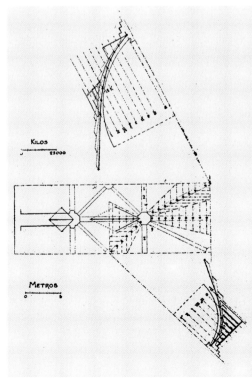

KILOS
25000

METROS

program for the clergy and the Catholic sectors of Mallorcanism as the best way of keeping the fledgling regionalist movement under the wing of the Church and thus guarding against the danger of its political radicalization. In fact this radicalization had not spread outside strictly intellectual circles, but above all after the appearance between 1898 and 1900 of the independent newspapers as *Palma Nova* or *La Veu de Mallorca*, it attracted the attention of conservative sectors. In *La Veu de Mallorca*, in fact, the revolutionary modernist Gabriel Alomar—who, four years later, was to publish his highly important book *El Futurisme*—was already advocating a radical political nationalism as a step beyond regionalism.[22]

Campins' policy of restoration and propaganda assumes its most complex nuances in the remarkable figure of Antoni Maria Alcover, appointed vicar-general of the diocese in 1898. In his personal initiatives—pursued, of course, with the full consent of the bishop, and exploiting to the full the great influence his position enabled him to exercise on the Mallorcan clergy and Mallorcan society—Alcover seems to push to its limits, between the sublime and the grotesque, that strategy of identifying the political restoration of the Church with the restoration of the Catalan language and nation. From 1900 Alcover was, in effect, the principal driving force of the project—so monumental and ambitious, of such transcendent import for Catalanism at a certain moment in time—to compile a general dictionary of the Catalan language. He was also (and this is only a very minor example) the constructor of churches such as Son Carrió and Calonge in Mallorca, in a naïve (in ideological terms) neo-Romanesque style. But, between these extremes, what we must concern ourselves with now is the political operation that made Alcover, until 1917, "Catalonia's man" in Mallorca, and did so much to determine the silent image of the bishop.[23]

The propaganda campaign that Alcover built up around the work of compiling the dictionary had, among its many consequences, the effect of

*Rose window in Mallorca cathedral
and interior view with the choir
in its original position,
in the center of the nave.*

promoting awareness of Alcover himself and his endeavor in Catalonia. The Catalanist political and cultural associations immediately perceived the importance of Alcover's project and gave it their support, culminating in the celebration of the First International Congress of the Catalan Language in Barcelona in 1906. For the Catalanist groups it was a matter of recognizing not only the intrinsic value of the project, but also its idealistic component, its symbolic value: its capacity to evoke a metropolitan Catalonia, a *Catalunya Gran* that reached beyond the bounds of the Principality and extended its program, precisely by virtue of the fact of linguistic identity, to the realms of its former medieval expansion.[24] For Alcover, that symbolism had, furthermore, a politically decisive function: only with the support of the already politically powerful Catalan organizations could Mallorcan regionalism assume an identity and make itself effective. Alcover had always referred to Torras i Bages and his regionalist ideology with evident approval, but from 1904 at least his admiration for Torras was complemented by references to Prat de la Riba, the president of the Lliga Regionalista, the party of the Catalan industrial bourgeoisie, whose *La nacionalitat catalana* had made him the principal theorist of conservative political Catalanism. Alcover's commitment to Prat steadily strengthened, to the point of becoming actively involved in Prat's 1907 election campaign, as the author of a speech of which no fewer than ten thousand copies were printed, tellingly entitled *Conducta política que s'imposa avuy an els católichs.*[25] Alcover's increasing identification with conservative political Catalanism in Catalonia can be seen as a necessary condition of the efficacy of his own program in Mallorca. He gave a series of strongly didactic lectures in Palma in February and March 1908, under the title *Que's el nostre regionalisme?* After explaining the differences between state and nation, and between language and dialect, he identified the restoration of Mallorca with its part in a greater Catalonia. "If we are to

recover our ethnic personality, it will be with Catalonia. To distance ourselves from Catalonia, to attempt to consolidate our tradition without Catalonia, is nothing but childish nonsense, folly."[26] The Mallorcan tradition as such is thus presented as unthinkable, irrecoverable, without that identification. In the course of his talk, Alcover reviewed the orders in which that identity ineffably manifested itself: language, literature, kings, legal system, art. But let us look for a moment at the words he devotes to this. "If we have an art of our own, as proclaimed by the works of our painters and sculptors and, above all, of our architects; as proclaimed by our cathedrals, abbeys, monasteries, churches, exchanges, ancestral houses; as proclaimed by the names of Sagrera and Gaudí…"[27] In the context of the speech as a whole, Alcover seems to attach no more importance to these names than to any others; from our point of view, however, that "above all," assigning as it does a higher value to architects and architecture than to the other arts, is especially eloquent. The reference to Sagrera and Gaudí is clearly not to be understood in the same way as the reference a few lines above, speaking of Catalan literature, to the Catalan, Valencian and Mallorcan writers of the thirteenth to the fifteenth centuries: Ramón Llull, Bernat Metge, Eiximenis, Vicenç Ferrer, Ausías March … Sagrera and Gaudí are not only the two greatest architects of that greater Catalonia: the former, a Mallorcan, the famous architect of Alfons el Magnànim's rebuilding of the Castel Nuovo in Naples and, prior to that, of the extraordinary exchange in Palma and master builder of its cathedral; the latter, a Catalan, the restorer of that same cathedral and the tombs of its kings. A glorious Middle Ages and a restored present, the great Mallorcan and the great Catalan, are thus harmoniously united in the place of their work: the cathedral.

Is it any wonder that it should be as a result of Alcover's dealings with Ramón Picó i Campamar—Count Eusebi Güell's personal secretary, a leading member of the Lliga and himself a Mallor-

can—that Gaudí went to Mallorca?[28] Or that Gaudí, already thought of primarily as the architect of the Sagrada Familia, the temple in process of being born, should have been chosen? The strategies of Bishop Campins' project for the political restoration of the Mallorcan Church and Alcover's Catalanist program find their most eloquent expression in promoting that work of architecture, in which they are also quite deliberately identified. Any possible doubt as to the significance of these connections is dispelled when we read the lines with which, at the end of 1905, Joan Rubió i Bellver, who worked with Gaudí in Mallorca, concluded an article on the cathedral. Referring to its rose window, he wrote: "An opening without comparison in any work raised by human hands, which seems to set the solemn tone on all that harmonious accumulation of stones that constitutes the great work of the Catalan race, begun by a glorious king and restored by Bishop Campins. The latter being one of those bishops who, like Bishop Oliva or Bishop Morgades, in raising new walls or righting those that have fallen, embodies the maxim of another great bishop, Torras, when he affirms that the construction or restoration of monuments is the greatest expansion of a people and its baptismal faith."[29] From the great rose window in which the entire building is summed up, to the building in which a whole race is embodied; from the founding and conquering king to the restoring bishop; from Oliva and Morgades—and thus the history of Ripoll—to Torras' maxim… The political strategy of which the restoration of Mallorca Cathedral set out to form a part seems to leave very little room for doubt. We must now trace its development.

### The Self-Absorbed Cathedral

In Bishop Campins' pastoral letter of August 10, 1904, which deals with the work being done on the cathedral, the architectural and artistic restoration of the temple has an immediate, direct justification in the necessities imposed by the new liturgy.

"Liturgical severity is the only proper ornament of the holy temple":[30] in writing this, Campins is in fact echoing the ideas that Prospère Guéranger—the initiator of the liturgical movement, significantly enough from the recently restored Abbey of Solesmes—had set out to disseminate in his monumental *Année Liturgique*, which had begun to appear in 1841. In the fifteenth volume, in effect, Guéranger put forward his idea of the liturgy as the source of a higher beauty, precisely because of its religious significance. At the same time, Solesmes was also the source of the renewed interest shown by the European Church in the second half of the nineteenth century in Gregorian chant, another of Campins' concerns: an interest that would culminate in Pius X's publication, in 1903, of a *motu proprio* on sacred music, *Tra le sollecitudini*.[31] But it is hardly surprising, perhaps, that a church which under Leo XIII had proposed as its principal objective the reconquest of society should take such an interest in a religiousness that is not personal or private but pastoral. Indeed the hierarchical symbolism contained in the liturgy not only appears to be the best way of interpreting the new relations between laity, local hierarchy and the Vatican created by social action, but its ceremonial practices and its repetitive character imply a concrete idea of continuity with the past, with tradition: these provide, in a changing world, a safe, unalterable haven. In Campins' treatment of them these general themes take on particular accents.[32]

In more than one passage of his pastoral, Bishop Campins insistently affirms—as do his collaborators in other texts—that the operation under way in the cathedral is not a remodeling but the opposite, a restitution, a restoring of things to their place, to their original disposition, a return to a certain first order: "To carry out [the work] it was not a question of improving or innovating but rather of restoring and restituting: it was not a question of destroying tradition but rather of re-establishing it in full; it was not a case of altering the layout of the building but of

*Views of the pulpit constructed
using fragments of the previous
ones, and of the canopy,
the cantoria and the choir after
the repositioning of the presbytery.*

liberating it from the acts of violence committed against it."[33] On the one hand, then, a re-establishing of tradition, and on the other a freeing of the building from the violence of its alterations. But doesn't Campins' declaration contain a paradox? What are these alterations, in fact, but the architectural and decorative interventions that over time, down through the centuries, have served to construct the very cathedral itself as Campins found it when he was made bishop in 1898? If the work of all these centuries is outside of tradition, to what tradition is Campins referring? Above all, in what time does the cathedral exist? A little further on, the same pastoral seems to resolve the paradox in replying to these questions: "Without being initiated in the science of construction, we understood that the clearest, most faithful document for discovering the portentous plan of the architect of the cathedral was without the smallest doubt the cathedral itself."[34]

Campins' words leave very little room for doubt. In his account the cathedral appears to be isolated in some kind of other world, something unique that in its transcendent inalterability speaks of a time with no becoming. The cathedral, needing only itself to say what it is, is not in the time of men but rather manifests itself outside of it. In light of this the adjective used by Campins to refer to its plan is exemplary: the portentous is, in effect, what goes beyond human verification, that which arouses admiration or wonder, that which holds us somewhere beyond reason. This plan, established once and for all by a nameless mythical architect, is something more than a project: it has something of the miraculous. Campins himself, in owning his lack of expertise in the science of construction, seems to assign himself the role of one who can see and hear the message of this portent that goes far beyond the simple physical existence of the building: "it would suffice to listen to the way its very stones cry out,"[35] he goes on to write. I do not believe we are erring on the side of exaggeration in thinking that Campins is implicitly

*Views of the old Gothic reredos
converted into a false gallery
above the Mirador door.*

assuming, in this enterprise of restoration, the role of a visionary. It is exactly in the vision that the necessity of the enterprise is assured beyond all reasonable doubt and, to close the circle, it is in this necessity that the authority of its promoter resides. We are told this, in fact, in another part of the pastoral: "Our cathedral says all things to all of us: its imposing, awful atmosphere, its overpowering austerity, the solemn quiet that neither winds nor waves are sufficient to disturb, speak to our soul."[36] The cathedral, then, an ineffable presence before which there is no place for reflection, is by definition that which remains identical to itself, inalterable in the midst of storms. It is, in short, a perfect, unadulterated image of the Church. The lines we have just quoted are directly preceded by these: "For the children of Mallorca these principles and laws which sit in the same hierarchical order and unfold splendidly in the incomparable ceremonies of worship need neither demonstration nor commentary."[37]

Quite clearly this cathedral, as something invented, does not have to be demonstrated: it needs no other definition than the revindication of its origin, contemporary with, or even prior to—in the sense of being beyond, in another time—that of the island itself. Thus the words of Miquel Costa i Llobera in his inaugural sermon on December 8, 1904, comparing the restoration of the building to the human restoration that follows from the proclamation of the dogma of the Immaculate Conception, present themselves with a significance that goes further than mere metaphor: "The mystery of the Immaculate Conception of Mary is the perfect restoration of the human creature, according to the sublime idea with which the Creator conceived it before the centuries; and the reform of this cathedral, according to the admirable concept of the artist who thought it out, constitutes the most fitting tribute to the glorious festivity that we are celebrating."[38] But Costa i Llobera's words, pronounced at the solemn moment when the temple was literally founded anew, are an extreme case. To arrive at

this extreme he has had to make many other identifications that ensure the efficacy of such a moment, among these, that of landscape. As an exemplary, if rather late, summary of this transcendent vision of the cathedral in the landscape of Mallorca—traditional in the imaginary of Mallorcan Romanticism and used on so many occasions, either by insinuation or clearly, by Campins' collaborators and Campins himself— we have the words of Rubió i Bellver in the aforementioned article from the end of 1905: "The immense silhouette totally dominates the panorama. The whole city is nothing but its pedestal. The whole island is summed up there. From the immense rocks that the boat skirts for hours, from the towering cliffs of living rock, with their heads in the sky and their feet in the depths of the blue abyss that, like a fantastic vision, appear as outpost sentinels of the island, seeming to be its quintessence; it might be said that all of these rough-hewn mountains have given the cathedral its sharper side and we can imagine it as an ideal summary of the beauties of the Mallorcan crags, as a living synthesis of those deepest ravines, of those abrupt cordilleras that, as we sail, from the deck of the boat and in the tenuous light of the nascent dawn, file past us like fantastic visions of Dantesque conception."[39]

The irrationality, the supranatural quality that we have seen Campins assign to the contemplation of the building is extended to the whole landscape, which the cathedral not only crowns but effectively synthesizes and summarizes. The Romantic tradition of creating tradition by attributing significance to the landscape, assigning a historical or mythological interest to every feature, every tree, every rock, is imbued here with the presence of this giant with its bones of rock that, while unable to declare itself a fully divine work is nevertheless unwilling to be a merely human one, the whole island answering its need by becoming its pedestal. With an entire literary tradition having already established that the essence of Mallorca lies in its landscape, springs from its soil, the cathedral is thus its soul, its quintessence.[40]

*Sketches by J.M. Jujol*
*for the second baldachin*
*and for the decoration of*
*the presbytery wall.*

This having been established, however, what are its stones proclaiming, or claiming? In the landscape that Bishop Campins describes, as well as being crowned by the cathedral, there is an ulterior identification: "Erected on the shores of the sea and in the most culminating site of the city, it is as the profession of faith that Mallorca makes before all who come to her; and even the wide bay seems to become a gigantic chamber from whose center springs the cathedral from which, by divine mandate, the bishops preach to all, and without interruption, the invariable Symbol of the Apostles."[41]

The bay, the city, the whole island have now become the image of the cathedral itself, but of the cathedral as a place in which hierarchy reveals itself as the seat of authority. The vision of the cathedral in its original sense of *kathedra* or chair is, above all, the goal of Campins' reform. The bishop's stone seat, hidden away at the far end of the presbytery, becomes, for Campins, the crux on which to base the program of the cathedral's restoration, the point at which the general and the particular meet: "In our renowned cathedral, both general tradition and private tradition are admirably reconciled, and the throne of stone stands as an unchallengeable witness to the one and the other."[42] The primary purpose in moving the choir from the central nave—where it is normally situated in a Spanish cathedral—to the presbytery and in removing the great baroque reredos from the altar was to expose to view once more the cathedral of stone in which authority reveals itself as unalterable and from where the hierarchy transmits its suspended time to the rest of the temple. There is, however, something more that these reforms were to serve to rediscover: also liberated, in fact, at the end of the presbytery, as well as the bishop's stone throne, was the Chapel of the Trinity, the architectural origin of the cathedral, according to Campins and Rotger, and above all the frustrated mausoleum of the kings and queens of Mallorca. At the end of his pastoral, Campins is concerned to make it quite clear that he will not only re-establish the ceremonial and rescue the cathedral "in which the first bishop of this church had his seat" but will also restore to the people their place in the temple and carry out "after five long centuries, the will of our monarchs, setting up their pantheon in the place they had chosen."[43]

The Church restores to Mallorca its kings and queens; we might even say, its origins: an act loaded with symbolism that in fact embodies a radical demand for power. Mallorca Cathedral does indeed have a long history, but who in Campins' circle would have been unaware that, in spite of the fact that it was initiated at the end of the thirteenth century, the last traces of the Arab Mosque it was to replace did not disappear until well into the fifteenth century? Or that the keystone of the last of its vaults was not in place until the end of the sixteenth century? Or that the great portal, in the Roman style, was completed in 1601, not, of course, as an addition to the Gothic temple but rather as a direct continuation of the rest of its construction? Or that its choir, first moved to the center of the cathedral early in the fourteenth century—in other words, as soon as the progress of the work allowed— was merely a reflection, in its changes of style, of the long labor of construction that had gone on continuously for centuries? The erudition displayed by Mateu Rotger in the series of articles devoted to different parts of the cathedral is sufficient to convince us that the stages of this history were well known.[44] But it is one thing for them to be known; another and very different thing was how to interpret them. On the basis of these data Campins invented a tradition, a history that showed in the past the necessity of the present. The mythical architect of the conquering king, the plan established *in illo tempore,* once and for all time, necessarily imply a vision of time as distorting, of the time of man as a time of confusion and disorder. In contrast to the long time of history that stains and besmirches, Campins opposes the single time, always the same, unalterable, of invented tradition. The ex-

*Interior of the church with the second baldachin.*

*Views of the second baldachin.*

tremely violent attacks that both Campins and his collaborators repeatedly directed at the most recent of the reforms carried out on the cathedral—the construction, between 1852 and 1886, of the new neo-Gothic façade by the architect Peyronnet—are thus hardly surprising.[45] It was not so much a question of criticizing its errors of conception, its defects of style or its lack of decorum as of revealing the vast distance between the restoration work then under way and the history of a continuous construction of which that façade was simply the latest chapter and the only one really present in the minds of the people of Mallorca. And it is hardly surprising that Joan Rubió i Bellver, in an extremely important article of 1912 in which he set out the conclusions of the structural studies of Mallorca Cathedral carried out for the restoration work, should argue, against all historical probability, for the Lombard origin of its conception.[46] What was this but an attempt to substitute tradition for history, time the great sculptor being for an instant suspended from the order, identical now and before the centuries?

With their restoration, Bishop Campins and his collaborators were in fact claiming for the Church the history without time in which Mallorcan nationalism was to identify itself: the self-absorbed cathedral, the restored order of which has wiped away the traces of the centuries and the steps of men, is its emblem.

## "Space and Void"

Gaudí visited Mallorca Cathedral for the first time on March 26, 1902; on August 13 of the same year he presented the bishop with a small wooden scale model of his proposed scheme; on April 11, 1903, he made a presentation to the Chapter Committee set up to supervise the work of a practically definitive construction project; on his next trip to Mallorca, on October 31 he installed various pieces of the stained-glass windows he had been working on in Barcelona; on June 19, 1904, with the arrival of Joan Rubió i Bellver to supervise the work on site, the first phase of which was

inaugurated on December 8 that year—the feast of the Immaculate Conception.[47]

From the point of view of its correspondence with Campins' program this first phase of Gaudí's work, effectively carried out on site in just five months, is the most important. It included the major work, which fundamentally consisted of moving the choir-stalls from the central nave to the presbytery, dismantling the baroque reredos with the resulting liberation of the Episcopal throne and the Chapel of the Trinity, bringing the altar nearer to the nave and constructing its baldachin, relocating the pulpits and constructing the cantorias. Literally, then, the liturgical reordering of the temple. The question to be considered now is how exactly this was done. In other words, of all the elements that were to be shifted around, which were to disappear and which were to be conserved; and, above all, how were these to be conserved?

In an article published in the *Gazeta de Mallorca* in April and May 1903, Gaudí is reported as saying that if every monument has a characteristic that makes it what it is, different from others, in the Mallorca Cathedral that characteristic is above all its proportion, its "harmonic correlation of dimensions."[48] Further on, after remarking on the "graceful proportions" of the cathedral and its "elegant lightness of lines," he explains the purpose of its smooth prismatic pillars and its oculi and great windows: to give the cathedral what it needs: that is, "space and void."[49] In another part of the article the journalist comments on the clarity with which Gaudí has understood the physical layout of the building, its naves and chapels, its pillars and vaults… But there is something more that cannot be seen with the eyes, something that is hidden from most mortals: "Gaudí penetrates more profoundly, and goes further."[50] There is more than rhetoric in the phrase. It gives us a fuller understanding of the proportion Gaudí spoke of as the essence, the ideal soul of the building, above and beyond its material presence. *Espay y buit*— space and void—absence of material, transcen-

*Top of the second baldachin
with polychrome decoration
by J.M. Jujol.*

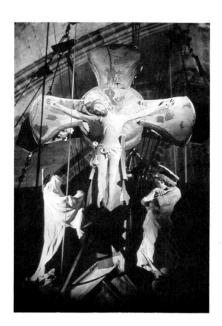

dent air: that is what the cathedral demands, that is what it should contain. There is no need to insist too much on the way this cathedral of Gaudí's, at once immaterial and real—only in its concrete form, understood as characteristic, can his idea be seen—coincides with that original cathedral created by Campins, with the cathedral capable of speaking out to claim a single thing: its own unalterable time. What was to be restored is, in both cases, a vision. Essence as opposed to presence: this is the tension sustained by Gaudí's intervention in Mallorca cathedral. On May 25, 1903, between Gaudí's third and fourth visits to the island, Joan Maragall wrote a letter to Josep Pijoan in which he devoted a long paragraph to Gaudí: "A short while ago, Gaudí invited me to visit the Park Güell with him... We talked a good deal and he managed to convince me of his idea of southern decoration. Afterwards, however, as we went deeper and deeper, we came to a point where it was impossible for us to agree. He sees in work, in struggle, in the material, so to say, the law of punishment... and it gives him pleasure!"[51] With the perspicacity that habitually characterizes his opinions—all the more transparent in this case in being expressed in private, in a letter to a friend—Maragall lays bare what lies at the roots of Gaudí's work, the hidden mainspring of his tensions: the temptation of the material. Among the many phantoms that bedevil Gaudí, the most important is that of the material, the incarnation of sin, and his work can to a great extent be read, especially from the turn of the century onwards, as a struggle against its seductive power: an agony in which sin and atonement are constants and present themselves in tandem. In Gaudí's architecture, in effect, only air seems to be capable of being enclosed in strict concrete forms—capable of being configured. The way in which buildings such as the Palau Güell or the Episcopal Palace in Astorga have been literally voided is eloquent testimony to what we are talking about: it is in this void, in effect, that the building finds its theme, a unity not apparent to the eye or through use, but transcendent and totemic: it is the imaginary axes of the world that traverse these voids,[52] but at the same time the material seems to take on a life of its own precisely in order to reveal itself against its silent, tectonic mission. The always provisional form that the material—marble, stone, ceramics, plaster, wood and iron—assumes in Gaudí's work is the result of the architect's struggle not against that material but against its fascination, against its urgings. The material in Gaudí's work has no solidity; it is not the mythical, opaque, inert block within which is concealed the form that the effort of the artist reveals: rather, as in Genesis, it is the serpent. In Gaudí, in everything from the smallest molding to the building as a whole, the material manifests itself in the most disconcerting forms: like flowing liquid, like escaping lava that cannot be contained by the precarious structures of strings, wires, threads, ironwork and little bags of shotgun pellets that Gaudí opposes to it in an attempt to grasp its tensions. Or like the lustre and color that always survive the chopping up, the fragmentation, the break that Gaudí imposes on it.

"... And it gives him pleasure": Maragall's conclusion is equally transparent. In this struggle with a phantom Gaudí sublimates the apostolic dimension of his work: the drama of the architect who can no longer hold back the material is the sacrifice of the Christian, of the chosen Christian, of the prophet, of the visionary. Can we really be surprised, then, that one of the recurrent themes of Torras i Bages' sermons in the Cercle de Sant Lluc should be precisely that of the material: that is to say, with how the Word was made flesh?[53] And somewhat closer to our concerns here, perhaps we can now understand the apparently ingenuous fact that Rubió i Bellver, in the same article in which he disclosed the Lombard origin of Mallorca cathedral, should also have described it as the only one of all the Gothic cathedrals that enclosed so great a volume of space within such a small quantity of "visible materials."[54]

The voided cathedral that requires no further explanation than its own definition and contains its own time stands there still and unalterable as a solemn vision of the essential. Its imperturbable harmony was to become more visible when, with Gaudí's arrival, the objects that the centuries had deposited in its interior—choir-stalls, altars, pews—began to move, to change places. We shall attempt to follow some of their paths.

No sooner had Rubió arrived in Mallorca than the first operation, the moving of the choir from the center of the nave to the presbytery, was commenced. This was not only the most major work but also the most effective. Once the choir had been removed, in fact, the liberation of the cathedral's space was immediately made apparent. At the same time, however, this was a simple operation: it was only a case of moving the wooden stalls to their new position, against the walls at the back of the presbytery on either side of the Episcopal throne. To take these apart and put them back together again: that is what

Gaudí did. Between the two operations, however, something has changed a little: the corbels, the *candelieri* and the classical frieze on the upper part of the stalls have disappeared. Evidently Gaudí, in eliminating the Roman-style elements from the later stages of the cathedral's long construction, has decided to restore the Gothic language of the choir-stalls, or in other words, to correct their history in order to return them to the new tradition in which the stones of the cathedral were now speaking.

But these elements were not destroyed; they were to find a new place in the cantoria. Let us dwell for a moment on this extraordinary piece of new construction. This is a gallery for lay singers, raised on pillars of colored marble and enclosed by wooden lattices, but it is, in fact, a great collage. From bottom to top: the bench and the marble columns were taken from the baroque presbytery, where the former served to seat the twelve ministers who accompany the bishop at pontifical Masses and the latter were a

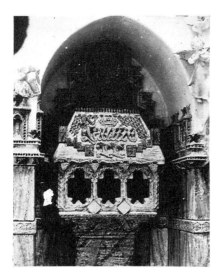

support for the magnificent hangings with which the presbytery was decorated for solemn festivities; on top of these columns the wooden gallery with its screens, little columns, lattices and frieze is constructed from the Renaissance remains of the choir-stalls; finally, the golden crenellation of the finial had originally topped the lintels decorated with the hangings to which we referred in speaking of the marble columns. The result of Gaudí's operation is thus of great complexity. He has constructed a new work, but one whose appropriateness is endorsed by liturgical tradition. This duality is translated, literally, into the immense collage we have been describing: the pieces and the materials used are old, they have come from a long time ago, from the history of the temple, they have the patina of that time and its work, but they have been wrested from their former place and their former use. In this montage they are obliged to represent a tradition that has nothing to do with the custom out of which they had evolved, on which they had been established. In other words, Gaudí has invented a history for them, a past that never existed.

But the choir is not an isolated case: Gaudí carried out this same operation of displacement a number of times. For example, in the new position he assigns to the remains of the ancient Gothic altarpiece—"a jewel as valuable as it is out of proportion,"[55] Campins commented significantly in his pastoral—that was also recovered from the dismantling of the baroque presbytery, and whose two front parts, now superimposed as if they were two levels of galleries, were to be mounted on stone corbels overlooking the interior of the Portal del Mirador; or, for example, the conversion of the ancient columns of the Gothic presbytery—whose original function, like that of the columns used in the cantorias, was to support hangings and tapestries—into candelabras for the new altar.

So, then, what might appear to be a desire to conserve, to retain the memory of the successive interventions in the cathedral down through the centuries, is in reality an act of aggression that tears things out of their own time, which from now on it will only be possible to read archaeologically. In one part of his pastoral Bishop Campins writes: "In order to restore things to their first being it was necessary to allot a new position or a new function to the constructions of different styles that contradicted the original plan: in this way it reappears in all its purest, original beauty."[56] At the same time, then, as these constructions lose their function, they become movable, clearly revealing their contingency and, in the last analysis, their lack of necessity, the plan of the cathedral emerges from the depths of time as necessary and permanent. By demonstrating the interchangeability of these furnishings as far as their use is concerned—preventing them forever more from communicating it—Gaudí is simply confirming the existence of the plan; by giving them a new history he re-establishes "the tradition broadly," just as Campins wanted. There are two points where the inalterability of the plan was to be revealed most convincingly: the altar and the pontifical throne. Both had to be supremely immobile in time and space. So it is no surprise that the top step of the high altar designed by Gaudí should be a great monolithic slab, undressed, weighing more than six tons.[57] Even more noteworthy is the way the first baldachin was constructed.[58] This was a rich canopy, reworked by Gaudí, suspended above the altar from a very slender, almost invisible rod that hung from the vault. Its four corners, decorated with little wrought iron cupolas, established a horizontal plane, but between them the edges of the canopy curved slightly. It was, then, literally, a magic carpet billowed up by an unseen breeze and held eternally in the instant of beginning to move: fixed in a petrified air by the iron of its four corners. The simultaneous vision of the instant and of eternity is what made its appearance solemn, what made its absence of material paradoxically monumental. In effect, Gaudí—following a process that absolutely inverted that of the

displacements we described above—worked here with nothing but air, with essences: an air hardened by the paralyzed flight of the baldachin and fixed to the floor by the immense weight of the stone of the altar.

In due course, after the solemn inauguration in 1904, Gaudí was to intensify still more the hardening of the air at this point, its suspension. On December 8, 1912, in fact, a new baldachin was inaugurated provisionally; it was composed largely of waste materials and as a result of the suspension of the work shortly afterwards has ended up being permanent.[59] The ancient canopy is now slightly inclined, exaggerating with this imbalance the impression of arrested movement. Below it are two crowns: one, heptagonal in form, lifted up at one of its vertices, of wrought iron with colored glass inserts illuminated from the inside, and the other, suspended under the first, consisting of fifty lamps. A series of cables, now necessarily visible, attaches the whole assembly to the vaults. In making its edge evident in the crowns, with the tension that the tautness of the cables seem to charge these with, the air has become even more a prisoner of the force that petrifies it, that holds it immobile over the slab of the altar. But what is it that is allowing itself to be seen there? It is not the materialization of a representative form but the mysterious appearance of the symbol: the fifty lamps are not only fifty lamps but the fifty days of Pentecost; the seven sides of the crown are the gifts of the Holy Spirit; its sharp inclination also turns it into Mount Calvary and its vertex is the summit on which Mary and John wait on either side of the cross, while the spikes that project from it also make it a crown of thorns.

It is clear, then, that the baldachin is not a representation but the form of the symbol. Suspended in the middle of the temple's naves, it is at once as immaterial and as powerful as a blaze of light: it is an immediate totality that demonstrates the transience of things but at the same time reanimates them, causes them to be beyond themselves. In the last analysis, then, the fact that the crown is fashioned from waste materials is of no importance.

Is this not, in effect, what we find in all of Gaudí's work? Whatever they are, the materials of that work are always waste materials: it is the form they take, the words that are superposed on them, that carries them beyond the contingency of the things of this world, beyond precariousness. What else could be allowing itself to be seen in that air, so obsessively a prisoner of the altar of sacrifice, than the crown of thorns and the crown of light announcing the propagation of the Gospel?

Quite a different procedure was adopted for the restoration of the Episcopal throne. Like so many other elements, this too was the result of successive interventions: a screen of delicate tracery had been placed over the semicircular arcosolia that contained it in the earliest period of the cathedral in the nineteenth century, at the same time as the wooden reredos that Gaudí had moved to the Portal del Mirador had been set between it and the nave. At the end of his pastoral Bishop Campins wrote: "We will once again possess the Pontifical Chair on which sat the first bishop of this church."[60] The choice of verb is by no means insignificant: in this having in one's power, in this being master again, lies the whole meaning of the work; with it is established, in the most concrete terms, the equation of the restoration of the cathedral and the refounding of the Church of Mallorca. It is for this reason that there, in contrast to other places, time was not to be corrected on objects but on time itself.

Initially, Gaudí set out to conserve all of the existing elements, even although they were from different periods. Subsequently, in the second phase of the restoration work, he would bring to light those that had been there at one time but for various reasons were no longer extant. Indeed, in the earliest of the records of works kept in the cathedral archives there is an entry, discovered and published by Mateu Rotger, describing what was interpreted, by no means

*Remains of preparatory sketches*
*by J.M. Jujol for the decoration*
*of the Episcopal throne.*

disinterestedly, as the first decoration of the apse of the presbytery: some "tables painted with gold palms."[61] These golden palms were transformed by Gaudí into olive branches with appliqué majolica leaves, in a triangular pattern, set into the wet mortar with which the wall was rendered. By fixing in this way what was no more than the simple evocation of some moveable tables, Gaudí was once again opposing himself to time as becoming. Here, however, it was not a case, as it was on other occasions, of wresting things from it, nor of petrifying the air to bring about the eternal appearance of an instant: time itself is now just another material. By preserving the successive interventions that gave the throne its present form, adding that decoration that had emerged out of the centuries and was now immobilized, Gaudí reveals all the moments of the history of that place, but he does so simultaneously, right there: semicircular arcosolia, Gothic screen, gold palms... The time that Gaudí concentrates around the Episcopal throne

contains no threats: it seems to be the history of the cathedral, but in fact it is nothing but its chronological time. It is hardly surprising, then, that between the olive branches there should be pieces of enameled ceramics by Josep Maria Jujol that reproduce the coats of arms of the successive prelates of the diocese, interpreted on the basis of their tombstones and wax seals, or that Gaudí should make the Episcopal throne speak, perhaps doubting the eloquence of its arrested forms, by means of the bands of wrought iron forming inscriptions on its sides.

However, just as had happened with the construction of the second baldachin, the concentration of force on the sides of the Episcopal throne was to be given a further development that would once again have a transcendent direction. Jujol had already started, in the majolica coats of arms set between the olive branches, to deform the heraldic symbols to the point of illegibility in many cases. This violence that blurred the blazons of the coats of arms and replaced

them with a simple manifestation of shapes and colors was duly transmitted, in amplified form, to the decoration of the backrests of the choir-stalls. Jujol's painting on the dark wood of the Gothic stalls makes the carvings gleam with gold. They literally light up, shining out beyond the material and the work, like apparitions. In the figure of the Crucified Christ, the golden halo is superimposed without distortion on the forms of the figures that flank it: the gold shines and is at the same time the unalterable form of His splendor. The fragmented phrase from the Gospels that Jujol inscribed on the wood of the choir-stalls indicates the continuity that exists between the form of that radiance and the patches of red that drip from a white and gold cloud onto a flower-studded ground: *Su sangre sobre nosotros*—"His blood on us." These patches of red, in effect, dematerialize the opaque wood of the choir-stalls, but do not set out to do so, as has been said so many times, in an illusionistic way, creating a virtual space beyond screens and boards,[62] but transcendentally, so that what is hidden may manifest itself on them. Just as the crowns of the baldachin are crowns, so this is blood. There can be no other reason for the supposed abstraction of Jujol's painting than his own conviction that he was working under inspiration, in the most divine sense of the word. The paint flows directly from his brushes, and for this very reason the casual forms, almost all of them dripping, that come from the simple act of painting admit of no correction or improvement. There is no design because there is only transmission: this is the reason for the state of possession witnesses always describe Jujol as being in when at work. This is not, then, abstract painting but rather the most immediate of concrete forms, also seen in the casual configuration of the clouds or in the knots in the bark of a tree. A form, in short, that is beyond the precariousness of any representation, beyond imitation of the world: bestowed by divinity. It is here that the famous anecdote recounted by Sagristà takes on its significance: as Jujol was applying

his paint to the wood, Gaudí observed him in silence from a few steps back, only occasionally exclaiming "Very good, Jujol, very good."[63] And also the way that Gaudí himself direct instructed the blacksmith on site as to the shape of a handrail, or the way he modeled with his fingers the strips of lead that were transformed into the wrought iron inscriptions on the throne. This movement of Gaudí's and Jujol's hands and fingers admits no intermediaries; it comes from an essential quality that is in them, that makes the artist God's stylus. All observers concur in their accounts of the enthusiasm with which Gaudí and Jujol worked on this second phase of the restoration work, but isn't this the classic description of the artist as *alter deus*? What better example could there be than these patches of paint, these gleams of gold, these letters, these illegible blazons, these crowns zigzagging in the void, of an art based on inner vision, the enemy of representation, of imitation? Gaudí and Jujol worked directly, transfiguring material and form. The cult of genius, the sin of pride of which they were accused by a cathedral chapter increasingly opposed to their work,[64] was exorcized by Torras i Bages' advice to the artists: "Carry out with the greatest ingenuity, with all of the perfection, as skillfully as you can, what your heart tells you and you will realize the great thought and admirable expression of Saint Thomas: *Verbum cordis.*"[65] Could any advice be more ambiguously integrative, that is to say, more politically effective?

## Our Delos

Shortly after the first phase of the work commenced in 1904, the pace slackened considerably. On the one hand it is clear that the essence of Bishop Campins' program had already been made reality; on the other, the spontaneity of Gaudí and Jujol's intervention in the second phase served only to increase the misgivings of the conservative Chapter, who openly declared their opposition to continuing with the reform. In fact, once the objective of the liturgical restoration of the cathedral had been achieved, the whole exercise became increasingly hard to justify: the coincidence between Campins' program and Gaudí's work had reached its limit. Campins died in 1915; Mateu Rotger in 1916. But Gaudí had already abandoned the work in 1914, in a climate of considerable hostility. As far as we know, neither Campins nor Rotger did anything to prevent this.[66] At the same time it is surely significant that one of Campins' staunchest supporters from the first moment, his chaplain Llorenç Riber, also seems to have left Mallorca in 1913 to establish himself in Barcelona. Within Campins' group, Riber was not only one of the most committed Catalanists, but a close friend of Gaudí's, on whose death he wrote one of the most beautiful obituary tributes.[67] Also significant is the fact that during the latter stages of Gaudí's sojourn in Mallorca, King Alfonso XIII offered to finance the construction of the royal tombs, but was opposed to their being built according to Gaudí's project.[68] It would be naïve to imagine that Gaudí and Jujol were driven out of Mallorca by mistrust, misunderstanding or envy.[69] Evidently, something else had changed. We have already seen how the Lliga Regionalista had—above all after its great success in the 1905 municipal elections—set about defining itself as the hegemonic party in Catalonia, commencing a process of assuming control of provincial and local institutions that was to culminate in the creation, in 1914, of the Mancomunitat de Catalunya, a first attempt at Catalan self-government. At the same time the Lliga was developing a broad-based program of normalization of Catalan culture: on the one hand, through the institutionalizing of the sites of that culture, setting up institutes, academies, libraries, museums and so on,[70] and on the other, through the designing—and it was literally that: design from power—of a generation of intellectuals directly committed to its political program. Eugeni D'Ors, in his column in *La Veu de Catalunya*, the influential mouthpiece of the Lliga, defined this generation in

*Study by Gaudí for the remodeling
of the roofs and bell towers drawn
over a photograph.*

aggressively polemical opposition to modernism as the *noucentista* generation, but in fact the confrontation was not generational or even aesthetic but ideological. D'Ors *noucentisme*—and we have seen clear proof of this in his attitude to the Park Güell—is nothing but a decanting of *modernisme* in strictly political terms:[71] a refined artistic taste, urban and cosmopolitan, complacently contemplating itself in the mirror of a mythologized classical Mediterranean, which D'Ors himself was to define by contrast to modernist spontaneity as Arbitrary Aesthetics (the *noucentista* articulation in opposition to the modernist interjection),[72] it was far from new. Indeed its origins lie in the controversies and disputes that had developed within the *modernista* camp in the years around the turn of the century. Determined, as we know, by the success of the *École Romane*, it was revived in 1905—at the beginning of D'Ors' definition—by the awarding of the Nobel Prize to Carducci. But we have seen enough of all this. All we need to do now is to stress the programmatic and exclusionary way in which that sector of the Catalan intelligentsia was to impose itself by marginalizing (in some cases to the point of exile) the most radical figures of *modernisme*, the artists who refused to align their work with the political program of the Lliga; and when those figures were too great to be silenced, as in the case of Maragall or Gaudí, by launching against them the anathema of the exceptional, the monstrous. In 1906, with malicious ambiguity, Eugeni D'Ors wrote the following lines—lines that were to become famous, and which we shall consider at length in the next chapter: "At times, I must confess, I cannot think without terror of the destiny of our people, obliged to support on their poor, precarious normality the weight, the greatness and the glory of these sublime abnormalities: the Sagrada Familia, the poetry of Maragall..."[73] The political break and the ideological and aesthetic tyranny that *noucentisme* imposed on the Catalan intelligentsia were to have very serious consequences for Mallorcan Catalanism, whose

*J.M. Jujol, remodeling
of the windows and railings for
the Episcopal Palace in Palma
de Mallorca.*

difficulties in articulating itself politically—and whose resulting weakness—we have already noted: a Catalanism reduced—with one or two exceptions, such as Gabriel Alomar—to the heterogeneous group of intellectuals Campins so fragilely assembled around his program, and, above all, increasingly dependent on Catalonia. The definitive break-up of that precarious conjunction of individuals inevitably led to their pursuing one of two possible paths: that of integration into the program of *noucentisme* or opposition to that program; in other words, marginalization. The most significant instance of the first case is Costa i Llobera; of the second, Antonio Maria Alcover. Both, as we have seen, had worked with Campins from the beginning and both were, in one way or another, defenders of Gaudí; they also represent the two extremes of the new situation.

Costa i Llobera was to become, for the Catalan *noucentistes*, the supreme representative of what came to be called the Mallorcan School. The history of this concept is highly significant. It had been created in 1903 by Eugeni D'Ors as a further element of his incipient program: the defining of regional schools was a very direct way both of normalizing—establishing norms, models, styles, provable and transmissible methods—and of culturally integrating the former realms of Catalan expansion into a Catalonia that was once again metropolitan, imperialist in the most political sense of the word.[74] D'Ors, always selective, as befits one elaborating a project, identified the concept of the Mallorcan School with the refined and artistic, cosmopolitan and arbitrary work of Gabriel Alomar, who in an article published in that same year of 1903 had written: "The artistic ideal of Mallorca should be, without a doubt, to make of our island the Delos of Catalanism."[75] In legend, Delos was covered in gold after Apollo was born there, but the abiding presence of the Greek spirit, so instrumental a part of D'Ors' program, had already been associated with Mallorca by Costa i Llobera in *La deixa del geni grec*, a great epic poem on the Greek origins of Mallorca. Indeed, Costa i Llobera had a great advantage over Alomar: while Alomar's work had a strong ideological and political content linked to the more radical sectors of Catalanism, Costa's presented itself as a formal literary model, the most elegant example of the poet's craft. In 1904, a number of leading Mallorcan speakers were invited to address the Ateneo in Barcelona: Alomar, who read his enormously important *El Futurisme*,[76] was deliberately marginalized, while Costa i Llobera, whose talk was entitled "La forma poètica," was hailed as the new symbol of the Mallorcan School and, above all, a model of Christian classicism.[77] From this point on Catalan cultural circles were to identify Mallorca and its landscape with that Homeric myth: an identification designed by, and due to, the *noucentistes*.

Alcover's fortunes could hardly offer a starker contrast. We have already looked in some detail at the way he had associated himself with the program of the Lliga. Prime mover of the work of compiling the Dictionary, undoubtedly one of the most interesting aspects of the normalization of the Catalan language, in 1911 Alcover was appointed director of the newly formed philological section of the Institut d'Estudis Catalans, the Catalan academy founded in 1907 by Prat de la Riba, president of the Lliga. The aim here was evidently to incorporate into the orderly scientific program of the Institut not only a popular man but, above all, a project of the first importance that had emerged somewhat tangentially, as a private initiative. From the start, however, Alcover was in conflict with the ideas and interests of the other members of the Institut. The history of Alcover's progressive marginalization, of which his appointment to the Institut was merely a subtle beginning, came to a stormy close in 1918, with the series of manifestos he directed against the Lliga, the Catalanist policy and Puig i Cadafalch, who by that time was president of the Mancomunitat de Catalunya. From then on he was literally declared a traitor and deliberately ignored, while he himself, in his Mallorcan retreat, became a ferocious anti-Catalanist, gathering around him, to some extent by default, the island's most reactionary political sectors.[78]

In 1921, Costa i Llobera, whom Miquel Ferrà had consulted about the possibility of holding a Congress of the Catalan Language in Mallorca, wrote: "I believe that, however opportune the Congress may be, *non est hic locus*. Mgr. Alcover would be very displeased, and we all know he has no limits... You think he has no supporters in Mallorca; but I can assure you that, while he may not have many direct supporters, they would immediately appear from all the centralist parties, from the official circles, from the neutral classes and from under the very stones... It is necessary to recognize that Mallorca, in general, is fundamentally anti-Catalanist."[79] This opinion, although late, is enormously meaningful. It bears witness to the abnormality that Alcover has slowly but surely come to assume in the reasonable eyes of his former companions, and to the position of detachment, *au dessus de la melée*, that the exemplary Costa i Llobera adopts towards events. But what it reveals above all is the precariousness, the extreme

fragility of the program that had briefly yoked together such different personalities, and against which, at the slightest opportunity, all its enemies were ready to rise up in unison. But if Campins' project seems fragile in relation to what it might have been, it is not at all so in relation to what it was: a very effective way of ensuring that, in the crucial years near the turn of the century, Mallorcan Catalanism did not take a different course.

In 1936, on the tenth anniversary of Gaudí's death, Guillem Forteza wrote in *El Matí*, with regard to Gaudí's intervention in Mallorca Cathedral: "Gaudí's coming to Mallorca was considered more extraordinary because he was a Catalan than because he was an architect."[80] Within a short time, however, Gaudí had become an abnormality—albeit a sublime one—that Catalonia had to support with terror on its back. Catalonia saw Mallorca as the pure landscape of Delos; Mallorca saw itself as profoundly anti-Catalanist. With Campins' program already achieved, what need could either of these Mallorcas have for Gaudí's now useless work?

[1] M. Rotger y Capllonch, *Restauración de la Catedral de Mallorca*, Palma de Mallorca, 1907, pp. 54–55. The book is a compilation of a series of articles written by Rotger in 1904, with a chronology of the work carried out until that date and a select anthology of other material from the Mallorcan press. The article that concerns us here is dated December 15, 1904.

[2] On Rotger see: F. Bonnín Aguiló and M. Bota Totxo, "Mateo Rotger y Capllonch, historiador de Pollensa," *Mateu Rotger y Capllonch, Juan Guiraud y Rotger, Lorenzo Cerdá y Bisbal, ilustres hijos de Pollensa*, Palma de Mallorca, 1962, pp. 5–15; J. Massot i Muntaner, *Església i societat a la Mallorca del segle XIX*, Barcelona, 1977, p. 26. On Gaudí being commissioned to carry out the work, see: E. Sagristà, *Gaudí en la Catedral de Mallorca. Anécdotas y recuerdos*, Castellón de la Plana, 1962, especially pp. 7–9.

[3] J. Brossa, "Quimeres contemporànies,"

*L'Avenç*, 2nd epoch, V, 1893, p. 14. Quoted and discussed by J.Ll. Marfany, "El modernisme," in *Història de la literatura catalana*, cit., vol. VIII, p. 97.

[4] On the Cercle Artístic de Sant Lluc see: J.F. Ràfols, *Modernismo i modernistas*, Barcelona, 1949, pp. 265–75; E. Valentí, *El primer modernismo literario catalán y sus fundamentos ideológicos*, cit., pp. 289–95; E. Jardi, *Història del Cercle Artístic de Sant Lluc*, Barcelona, 1976; and, above all: J. Castellanos, *Raimon Casellas i el modernisme*, cit., vol. I, pp. 173–218. There is a clear reference to the *Rerum novarum* in the following excerpt from its statutes: the Cercle was founded "with the desire of interpreting the intentions of our Holy Father Pope Leo XIII, of re-establishing the old Catholic guilds that do so much to foment the development of the arts and help to affirm mutual charity among the unfortunate" (cit. in E. Jardi, op. cit., p. 9). An inexpensive edition of Leo

XIII's encyclical had been published by the bishop of Vic, Josep Morgades, in 1891, and that same year it was translated into Mallorcan by Bartomeu Ferrà and published in pamphlet form (see J. Massot, op. cit., p. 343); it was also published as a pamphlet in Spanish by Tipografía Católica in Barcelona and the Sociedad Editora San Francisco de Sales in Madrid, among others.

[5] On Torras i Bages, to whom we have already referred on so many occasions, see contemporary accounts such as: I. Casanovas, *L'Ilm. Sr. Bisbe de Vich Dr. Torras i Bages de santa memòria*, Barcelona, 1916; id., *Exemplaritat de l'Ilm. Dr. Josep Torras i Bages, bisbe de Vich*, Barcelona, 1928; and, above all: J. Collell, *Dulcis Amicitia*, Vic, 1926. See, too: *El Episcopado Español ante la obra apologética del Dr. Torras i Bages. Colección de pensamientos de todos los obispos de España alrededor del Dr. Torras con motivo de su centenario*, Vilafranca del

Panadés, 1948. A classic biography is: F. Sola, "Biografía," Torras i Bages, *Obres Completes*, vols. I–IV, Barcelona, 1935. Another classic, on Torras and the arts: C. Cardo, *Doctrina estètica del Dr. Torras i Bages*, Barcelona, 1919. On Torras and modernism, see the fundamental: E. Valentí, op. cit., pp. 243–62. For a reply to Valentí, see: J. Massot i Muntaner, *L'Església catalana al segle XX*, Barcelona, 1975, pp. 193–97. See, too: J. Castellanos, op. cit., vol. I, pp. 173–218.

[6] Torras gave his lectures in 1894, 1896, 1897 and 1905. They were published with other writings on art and aesthetics in J. Torras i Bages, *Obres Completes. Estètiques*, vol. XV, cit.

[7] On the changing customs of Catalan society at the turn of the century see: J.Ll. Marfany, "Estetes i menestrals," cit., pp. 36–41; id., "La cultura de la burgesía barcelonina en la fi de segle," cit., pp. 54–63; id., "El modernisme," cit., pp. 87–93; id., "Gaudí i el modernisme," *Gaudí i el seu temps*, cit., pp. 69 ff. On the antimodernism of Torras and of the Círculo: E. Valentí, op. cit., pp. 243–62, 289–95. See, too: J. Castellanos, op. cit., vol. I, pp. 173–218, and id., "Un arte al servicio de la edificación social," *La Vanguardia. Cultura y arte*, October 17, 1989, p. 4; id., "Torras i Bages i Gaudí," cit.

[8] See the articles by Raimon Casellas on the Exposición General de Bellas Artes in *La Vanguardia* on April 22, May 1, May 14 and May 24, 1984. Of major importance on this subject is: J. Castellanos, *Raimon Casellas...*, cit., vol. I, pp. 150–55.

[9] R. Casellas, "Exposición General de Bellas Artes. II: La pintura religiosa é histórica," *La Vanguardia*, May 1, 1894 (cit. in J. Castellanos, , op. cit., p. 154). See the articles by Casellas on the III Exposición General de Bellas Artes published in *La Vanguardia* April 22, April 29, May 12 and June 4, 1896. Once again: J. Castellanos, op. cit., vol. I, pp. 155–59.

[10] J. Castellanos, op. cit., vol. I, pp. 155 ff. and 214 ff.

[11] E. Valentí, op. cit., pp. 244–45. On the Vic group see the memoir in: J. Collell, op. cit.; id., *Memòries d'un noy de Vich*, Vic, 1908. See, too: A. Pérez, *El canónigo Collell*, Barcelona, 1933; J. Anglada, *El canonge Jaume Collell*, Vic, 1983; and M. Ramisa, *Els orígens del catalanisme conservador i "La Veu del Montserrat." 1878–1900*, Vic, 1985.

[12] On the strategy of the Spanish Church in the nineteenth century see: J. Connell and Ullman, *La Semana Trágica. Estudio sobre las causas del anticlericalismo en España, 1898–1912*, Barcelona, 1972, especially pp. 29–109. For different reasons see, too: J.A. Gallego, *La política religiosa en España. 1889–1913*, Madrid, 1975; J.M. Gómez-Heras, *Cultura burguesa y restauración católica*, Salamanca, 1975; M.F. Núñez-Muñoz, *La Iglesia y la Restauración*, Santa Cruz de Tenerife, 1976; J.M. Cuenca, "El catolicismo español en la Restauración. 1875–1931," *Historia de la Iglesia en España*, vol. V, Madrid, 1979, pp. 277–329; A. Yetano, *La enseñanza religiosa en la España de la Restauración*, Barcelona, 1988, pp. 19–46. Much more rewarding than the title might suggest is: M. Revuelta, *La Compañía de Jesús en la España contemporánea. Supresión y reinstalación*, vol. I, Santander-Bilbao, 1984. With regard to Catalonia and Mallorca, it is worth consulting the books by J. Massot i Muntaner cited above. The encyclical *Cum Multa*, of December 8, 1882, is included in: M. de Castro Alonso, *Colección completa de las encíclicas de S.S. León XIII*, vol. I, Valladolid, 1892, pp. 199 ff. See, too: *Carta de S.S. el Papa León XIII al Obispo de Urgel sobre las actuales contiendas entre católicos*, Tarragona. The submission of the Catalan Church to the authority of Leo XIII was also manifested in apparently secondary matters. See: *Homenaje a S.S. León XIII. Fiesta científico-literal-musical celebrada en la iglesia de San Agustín de Barcelona en conmemoración del XXV aniversario de su exaltación*, Barcelona, 1902; or the publication of *La Ilustració Catalana: Lleó XIII. Poesies. Traducció catalana*, Barcelona, 1903.

[13] J. Torras i Bages, *La tradició catalana* cit., p. 35. Also, for example, on p. 110: "We said at first that Christ was the Orpheus of the Catalan nation..."

[14] On Morgades see: J.I. Gatell, *Lo Dr. D. Josep Morgades y Gili, Bisbe de Barcelona*, Barcelona, 1901; J. Collell, *Lo Bisbe Morgades. Oració fúnebre*, Barcelona, 1901. The ideological operation that made Romanesque the original style of Catalonia is clearly apparent in the fundamental texts of conservative Catalanism. For example: "This timbre with which the Catalan people mark things to make them their own ... can also be perceived in architecture ... It appears that the Romanesque style was closest to us ... presenting a truly just balance or proportion of the parts, a comprehensible whole, and in the case of churches leading the soul to ascetic concentration more than to mystic exaltation ... Romanesque architecture seemed to be identified in great measure with our practical race, legislative, reflective and moderate in spirit. No in vain ... did it have a long and fruitful existence in Catalonia, and even in supplanting it its successor, ogival architecture, received from it a powerful influence" (J. Torras i Bages, op. cit., pp. 140–42). This was written many years before the "invention" of Catalan Gothic, which did not take place until the 1930s. Another example: "The unity of the artistic ideal of our nation is embodied in the simple and well-proportioned naturalism and severity of Romanesque art, which is the art of our people, that which has flourished best in the Catalan-speaking lands: just as is also apparent in that special atmosphere, in our highly distinctive Gothic architecture, which, come from the lands of the north, did not take root among us until it had been molded to the needs of the genius of our race" (E. Prat de la Riba, *La nacionalitat catalana*, cit., p. 91): it is important to note that Prat identifies Romanesque with all of the Catalan-speaking lands when there are, of course, no examples south of the Ebro or in the Balearic Islands. Among the scientific study visits to Catalan Romanesque constructions it is worth recalling the excursions organized by the Asociación de Arquitectos de Catalunya, regularly recorded in its Bulletin and written up in the numerous series of short monographs by Jaume Gustà i Bondia, Joaquim Bassegoda, Elías Rogent, Antoni de Falguera and Puig i Cadafalch, among others. Torras i Bages referred to Bassegoda, recalling that he described Romanesque as the "national style" (op. cit., p. 142). Out all of this was to come the monumental work by J. Puig i Cadafalch and A. Falguera, *L'arquitectura romànica a Catalunya*, 4 vols., Barcelona, 1909–18.

[15] On the ceremony of restoration of Ripoll see: *Nova Consagració de Santa Maria de Ripoll*, Vic, 1893, which includes the speeches by Morgades and the bishops of Urgell and Segorbe, as well as the letter from Leo XIII and descriptions of the acts; see also: F. Carreras Candi, *Crónica de la traslació de les despulles de Ramón Berenguer III lo Gran, Comte Sobterà de Barcelona*, Barcelona, 1893. Especially interesting here is: J. Franquesa i Gomis, "Lo Monastir de Ripoll y'l Renaxement català," *Lo Moviment Regionalista*, July 1, 1893, a monograph published by the Associació de Propaganda Catalanista. See, too: *Corona poètica a Nostra Senyora Santa Maria de Ripoll*, Vic, 1895. The symbolic significance of Ripoll was generally acknowledged: "All say that Ripoll is the cradle of Catalonia" (J. Torras i Bages, op. cit., p. 33). At the same time, a dense ideological web was woven around the figure of the restoring Morgades that identified him with the abbot Oliva and the very origins of the nation: we must remember that in 1886 Verdaguer had dedicated canto XI of his *Canigó*, "Oliva," to Morgades: "To the most worthy successor...." Evidently Verdaguer's poem is absolutely involved in this ideological exercise: at the consecration of the monastery, Verdaguer was crowned "poet of Catalonia" by Morgades, whom he recalls with bitterness in his "Llorers espinosos" (J. Verdaguer, *Obres Completes. Edició popular. En defensa propia*, vol. XVII, cit., pp. 44–46). The great monograph study of Ripoll written in this period, J.M. Pellicer y Pages, *Santa Maria del Monasterio de Ripoll*, Mataró, 1888, is also dedicated to Morgades, "successor to Godmaro, Jorge, Froilán and Oliva." For the strictly architectural aspects of the restoration see: E. Rogent, *Santa Maria de Ripoll. Informe sobre las obras realizadas...*, Barcelona, 1887; P. Hereu Payet, *Vers una arquitectura nacional*, Barcelona, 1987, pp. 110–28.

[16] *Nova consagració de Santa Maria...*, cit., p. 77. The speech by the bishop of Urgell, the future Cardinal Casañas, is perhaps the crudest expression of the ideological aims of the operation. For example: "A great people such as ours must not abandon its traditions to serve as the fawning lackeys of sectarian men, enemies of God and disturbers of the social order, following the baneful fashions that have come from abroad ... I would like to refer to these modern liberties of perdition that are preached at us on all sides ... the restoration and consecration of this basilica of Ripoll must signify a protest by Catalonia against such baneful negations; because we have not come here merely to celebrate the restoration of an artistic monument, but ... an essentially religious monument, with all of the historical and political meanings that this entails" (p. 73). And a little later: "May God grant that the State be not stricken with new calamities for the indifference with which it treats the Church" (p. 77). Setting aside the references to the state, the foreign and the modern are clearly identified with one another.

[17] On the controversy surrounding the baldachin see: J. Rubió i Bellver, "El baldaquí de Ripoll," *La Veu de Catalunya*, May 2, 1912; id., "Carta oberta al Sr. Just Cassador," *La Veu de Catalunya*, May 16, 1912; id., "Més ciència y menys contorsions," *La Gazeta Montanyesa*, May 30, 1912. See, too: I. Solà-Morales , *Joan Ru-*

bió i Bellver y la fortuna del gaudinismo, cit., pp. 46–47. Significantly, he designed it in collaboration with Joan Llimona.

[18] J. Barbey D'Aurevilly, L'ensorcelée, in id., Oeuvres romanesques complètes, Paris, 1964, vol. I, p. 728.

[19] F. Coblence, Le dandysme. Obligation d'incertitude, cit., pp. 229–30.

[20] M. Costa i Llobera, "Epistolari," Obres Completes, Barcelona, 1947, p. 1067. The letter is from 1898. Campins' taste for refinement in objects and insignia should be seen in the light of the "incident" occasioned by the "modernista" crosier by Josep Llimona that the Cercle de Sant Lluc presented to Bishop Torras i Bages, which ultimately required a justification from Mgr. Rivera in Montserrat. See: R., "Quatre mots a propòsit del bàcul regalat al Dr. Torras," Montserrat, no. 7, July 1900, pp. 98–100. The story is explained by J. Castellanos, "Un arte al servicio de la edificación social," cit.

[21] On Campins see: El Ilmo. Sr. D. Pedro Juan Campins Barceló, Obispo de Mallorca, Palma de Mallorca, 1915; A.M. Alcover, Vida del Rdm. i Ilm. Sr. D. Pere Joan Campins i Barceló, Bisbe de Mallorca, Palma de Mallorca, 1915. See, too: J. Massot i Muntaner, Església i societat a la Mallorca del segle XIX, Barcelona, 1977, especially pp. 311–16. In fact, before being appointed bishop, Campins had links with the most progressive Mallorcan literary circles as a participant in the regular Sunday discussions that Joan Alcover hosted in his house, at which A.M. Alcover and M. Rotger were also frequently present. See: M. S. Oliver, La literatura en Mallorca, (1903), ed. J.Ll. Marfany, Montserrat, 1988, p. 202. I am indebted to Marfany for drawing this to my attention.

[22] In addition to the book by M.S. Oliver cited above, see: J.M. Llompart, La literatura catalana a les Balears, Palma de Mallorca, 1964; id., "Literatura mallorquina contemporánea," Historia de Mallorca, Palma de Mallorca, 1973; J. Pons i Marqués, "Cent anys de poesia a Mallorca i l'escola mallorquina," Crítica literaria, vol. I, Palma de Mallorca, 1975, pp. 57–73; G. Mir, Els mallorquins i la modernitat, Palma de Mallorca, 1981; and the excellent synthesis by J. Castellanos, "L'escola mallorquina," Història de la literatura catalana, vol. VIII, cit., pp. 325–77. On Alomar in particular: J.Ll. Marfany, Aspectes del modernisme, cit., pp. 253–65. In general: G. Mir, El mallorquinismo político (1975), Mallorca, 1990, 2 vols.

[23] On Alcover see the very complete F. de

B. Moll, Un home de combat. Mossén Alcover, Palma de Mallorca, 1962; also: J. Massot i Muntaner, op. cit., pp. 21–45. Moll discusses Alcover's interest in drawing (reproducing some of his sketches), archaeology and architecture, and—of course—his admiration for the Romanesque (F. de B. Moll, op. cit., pp. 35–37, 133–35 and 276). Alcover is presented here as the architect of churches, chapels and oratories such as those mentioned, and also Mendia, Son Negre and Pedra Sagrada de Santa Ponça (associated with the landing of King Jaume on the island), among others, all of them neo-Romanesque. In the construction of the ideological argument for the Christian and Catalan origins of Mallorca, the absence of Romanesque architecture was always a "problem." Note, for example that Guillem Forteza could write, as late as 1929: "One of the dreams that has given me the greatest poetical delight, is that of considering Mallorca as forming part of the old Romanesque Catalonia of the eleventh and twelfth centuries and imagining our montainous landscapes, and that of the plain, glorified with authentic Romanesque chapels and towers, and, dotted here and there, some few monasteries of pre-Gothic austerity" (G. Forteza, "Estat de l'arquitectura catalana en temps de Jaume I. Les determinants gòtiques de la catedral de Mallorca," La Nostra Terra, no. 24, December 1929, p. 497, since reprinted in id., Estudis sobre arquitectura i urbanisme, M. Seguí Aznar, ed., vol. II, Montserrat, 1984, p. 5).

[24] On the Congress see: Primer Congrés Internacional de la Llengua Catalana, Barcelona, 1908, a collection of descriptions, speeches, etc.; see, too, for example, La Veu de Catalunya for the day of the inauguration, October 13, 1906, which carried an important article by E. Prat de la Riba, and the special issue of La Ilustració Catalana, no. 177, October 21, 1906. On the idea of an imperialist Catalonia and the role of the language in this, see E. Prat de la Riba, La nacionalitat catalana, cit., especially pp. 81–89 and 107–18; his own contribution to the Congrés de la Llengua: "Importància de la llengua dins el concepte de nacionalitat," Primer Congrés Internacional…, cit., and the famous "Greater Catalonia," cit. The same issue in relation to Mallorca is very clearly addressed in A.M. Alcover, Conferencias sobre el regionalisme ditas en la sala del Centre (Català de Mallorca) els dias 28 de febrer y 7, 14, 21 y 28 de mars, Palma de Mallorca, 1908, pp. 9–40, since reprinted in J. Massot i Muntaner, op. cit., pp. 79–100.

[25] A.M. Alcover, Conducta política que s'imposa avuy an els católichs. Conferència en el Comité de Defensa Social de Barcelona, Barcelona, 1907. There is some doubt as to Alcover's authorship of the whole of this 30-page pamphlet. Moll and Massot both make case for seeing here the hand of the Jesuit Ignacio Casanovas (F. de B. Moll, op. cit., pp. 123–25; J. Massot i Muntaner pp. 35–36). Whatever the truth may be, Alcover allowed it to be published under his name. Alcover's Catalanism gave rise to a fundamentalist reaction in Mallorca. See the attack on him by J. Tuesta, D. Antonio María Alcover. Algunos datos para su biografía, Palma de Mallorca, 1911. He was subsequently defended from an anti-Catalanist position: J. Rotger, Don Antonio María, Palma de Mallorca, 1928.

[26] Conferencias sobre el regionalisme ditas en la sala del Centre els dias 28 de febrer y 7, 14, 21 y 28 de mars, cit., p. 98.

[27] Ibid., p. 86.

[28] Sagristà explains, in words he attributes to Rotger without citing the reference, the circumstances of the interviews between Gaudí and Campins in the Sagrada Familia. At the second of these, Campins was accompanied by Mateu Rotger, and Gaudí by Picó i Campamar. This is highly significant: given his position in the Güell household, it is likely that Picó was a major influence on Gaudí's decision to accept the commission. No less important was the part played by Alcover, who, in view of his other activities, features prominently in all of the contemporary accounts (E. Sagristà, op. cit., pp. 7–8). The meeting in question took place on August 19, 1901 (M. Rotger, op. cit., pp. 45–46).

[29] J. Rubió i Bellver, "La Seu de Mallorca," La Veu de Catalunya, January 12, 1906, also published in Diario de Mallorca, January 18, 1906, and in M. Rotger, op. cit., pp. 84–90. I quote from the latter, p. 90.

[30] P.J. Campins i Barceló, "Carta pastoral sobre la restauración de la Santa Iglesia Catedral de Mallorca," Boletín oficial del obispado de Mallorca, no. 15, August 16, 1904, p. 262.

[31] The Motu proprio of Pius X is of November 22. See: J. Portas, Breves comentarios a la carta que S.S. Pio X ha dirigido […] al Emmo. Cardenal Respighi […] sobre la música religiosa, Barcelona, 1904. Tra le sollecitudini on pp. 23–31. The influence of Dom Guéranger and the Solesmes reforms in Catalonia is amply borne out by the numerous references to Vida Cristiana and other publications in J. Massot i Muntaner, L'església catalana al segle XX, Barcelona, 1975, pp. 36–46. In

addition to the very important influence of L'Anné Liturgique on the Catalan clergy, there were more "popular" presentations of Guéranger's works, such as: P. Guéranger, La Santa Misa explicada. Sus oraciones y ceremonias, Barcelona, 1907. On the problems of the restoration of the liturgy in relation to art, see: I. Casanovas, "L'art en el Temple," cit.; J. Tarré, "L'Art i la Liturgia," cit.: both texts were delivered to the I Congrés d'Art Cristià a Catalunya, in 1913. 1915 saw the I Congrés Litúrgic de Montserrat, for the conclusions of which, see: Reseña Eclesiástica, VII, 1915, pp. 581ff. See, too: J. Torras i Bages, Dignitat i popularitat de la liturgia católica, Vic, 1915; I. Goma, El valor educativo de la liturgia católica, Barcelona, 1918, especially pp. 461ff. in the chapter "Liturgia y arte." On sacred music, see: D. Pothier, Les métodes grégoriennes, Tournai, 1880; or the pamphlet: Solesmes y la restauración gregoriana, Tournai, 1905. In Catalonia the propaganda activity of G.M. Suñol was especially important. See, for example: G.M. Suñol, Método completo de solfeo, teoría y práctica de canto gregoriano según la escuela de Solesmes, Tournai, 1907; id., La interpretación tradicional y artística del canto gregoriano, Tournai, 1909. See, too: Crónica del Tercer Congreso Nacional de Música Sagrada celebrado en Barcelona del 21 al 24 de noviembre de 1912, Barcelona, 1913, with lectures by Suñol, Pedrell, Millet, etc. For various other aspects, see the earlier: M. Rue y Rubió, La reforma de la música religiosa, Gerona, 1901. Gaudí attended some at least of G.M. Suñol's classes in Gregorian chant in 1916 (see C. Martinell, Gaudí. Su vida, su teoría, su obra, Barcelona, 1967, p. 193) and, as we have suggested, was greatly concerned with the liturgy (cf. I. Puig-Boada, El pensamiento de Gaudí, Barcelona, 1981, pp. 216ff.); this and the fact that he had very little else in his library other than a set of L'Anné Liturgique have become commonplaces in almost all of the biographies. In less strictly ecclesiastical circles, there was considerable interest in religious music in Catalonia: it was one of the preferred themes of Amadeu Vives, while the Orfeó Català generally included some polyphonic religious music in its concerts, as well as masses by Palestrina or Victoria, for example. If Campins' concern with the restoration of the liturgy is reflected in the pastoral letter, with regard to Gregorian chant it is worth recalling that F. Clop was in Mallorca, teaching at the Seminary, where he wrote a Breve método de canto

*gregoriano* dedicated to Campins and published at the latter's expense (*El Ilmo. Sr. D. Pedro Juan Campins...*, cit., p. 66); with the idea of establishing a standard for the whole diocese, in 1909 Campins made a grant to the Seminary's professor of Gregorian chant to take part in a course being run on the Isle of Wight by A. Mocquereau, subsequently prior of Solesmes. Also in 1909 he set up a *Schola Cantorum* in the Seminary (op. cit., p. 68). At the same time his efforts at cultural normalization led him to launch the weekly *Bolletí Dominical* in 1910, with a print run of 12,000 copies (op. cit., p. 70). Even before he was proclaimed bishop Campins' love of music was the basis for his involvement with Antoni Noguera's Salón Beethoven, out of which grew the Sociedad de Conciertos de Palma. Alcover was also associated with Noguera and the Chapel of Manacor, in which he took a special interest. And it is worth recalling that Father Eustoquio de Uriarte, one of Spain's foremost specialists in Gregorian chant, spent his latter years on the island, where he died in 1900. (I am indebted to J.Ll. Marfany for these points.) Costa i Llobera also took an interest in Manacor: M. Costa i Llobera, "Santa Cecília, patrona de la Capilla de Manacor," in id., *Sermons panegírics*, Barcelona, 1916, pp. 77–84. The program that Campins set out in his pastoral letter and his ideas of restoration thus tied in to a clearly structured system. This being so, there can be no justification for such recent claims as those to the effect that "it is important to see how valuable the thoroughly modern [sic] position of the bishop was" ("A. Gaudí i J.M. Jujol a La Seu," *D'A*, no. 1, 1989, p. 42).
[32] On the role of tradition in contemporary social systems and power structures, see: E.J. Hobsbawm and T. Ranger, *The Invention of Tradition*, cit.
[33] P.J. Campins, op. cit., pp. 251–52.
[34] Ibid., p. 252.
[35] Ibid., p. 261.
[36] Ibid., p. 250.
[37] Ibid., p. 250.
[38] Cit. in A. Kerrigan, "Gaudí restaurador o la historia de Cabrit y Bassa," *Papeles de Son Armadans*, XIV bis, December 1959, p. 126. In adapting the article for publication as one of the *Panorama Balear* monographs (A. Kerrigan, *Gaudí en la catedral de Mallorca*, Palma de Mallorca, 1960), the author dispensed with this quote. Costa i Llobera wrote about the Virgin a number of times: M. Costa i Llobera, "La Concepció Immaculada," in id., *Sermons Panegírics*,

cit., 1916, pp. 35–58; id., *Novenari de la Puríssima. Sermons dogmàtic-morals sobre el misteri de la Concepció Immaculada de la Mare de Déu*, Barcelona, 1918.
[39] J. Rubió i Bellver, op. cit., p. 85.
[40] Rubió referred to the cathedral as "the giant with bones of rock" (op. cit., p. 85).
[41] P.J. Campins, op. cit., pp. 250–51.
[42] Ibid., p. 254.
[43] Ibid., p. 265.
[44] M. Rotger, *Restauración de la Catedral de Mallorca*, cit.; the book by E. Sagristà, *Gaudí en la catedral de Mallorca*, cit., not only attacks Gaudí's work but devotes great deal of space to refuting Rotger's archaeological theses. Mallorca Cathedral and its historical and architectural origins were at the center of controversy and debate for a number of years. In addition to the sources cited above, Rubió i Bellver, as part of his ongoing efforts to establish the Romanesque style in Mallorca, invented an implausible Lombard origin for the cathedral: J. Rubió i Bellver, "Conferencia acerca de los conceptos orgánicos, mecánicos y constructivos de la Catedral de Mallorca," *Anuario de la Asociación de Arquitectos de Cataluña*, 1912, pp. 87–140. See, too: G. Forteza, "Estat de l'arquitectura catalana en temps de...," cit. It is still worth consulting the classics: R.A. Cram, *The Cathedral of Palma de Mallorca: an Architectural Study*, Cambridge, Mass., 1932; P. Lavedan, *L'architecture gothique religieuse en Catalogne, Valence et Baléares*, Paris, 1935, pp. 162–68, a book of fundamental importance in the "invention" of Catalan Gothic, dedicated to Puig i Cadafalch.
[45] See: C. Cantarellas Camps, *La intervención del arquitecto Peyronnet en la Catedral de Palma*, Palma de Mallorca, 1975. The façade by Peyronnet attracted criticism from all sides, but above all as a result of the campaigns mounted by Rotger and Campins. Consider, for example, the following highly suspect lines picked out almost at random: "The Academia de San Fernando entrusted the restoration to the architect, a member of the said Academia, D. Juan Bautista Perronnet [sic], who being absolutely unfortunate in his plans, designed a façade that earned the severest censure, which even after being reformed as far as was possible by another architect who directed the work, Sr. Pavía, has not ceased to be a most lamentable mistake" (D. Fernández y González, *Las grandes catedrales de Europa*, vol. I, Barcelona, c. 1905, pp. 138–39).
[46] J. Rubió i Bellver, "Conferencia acerca

de los conceptos orgánicos...," cit.
[47] The essential data on Gaudí's intervention in Mallorca is found in: M. Rotger, *Restauración de la Catedral de Mallorca*, cit.; E. Sagristà, *Gaudí en la catedral de Mallorca. Anécdotas y recuerdos*, cit.
[48] Quoted in M. Rotger, op. cit., pp. 78–83. Cit. p. 80.
[49] M. Rotger, op. cit., p. 81.
[50] Ibid., p. 79.
[51] J. Maragall, *Obres Completes*, cit., vol. I, p. 1017. On the relations between Gaudí and Maragall: I. Puig-Boada, "L'amistat de Gaudí i Maragall," cit.
[52] On the Palau Güell see chapter 2. The Episcopal Palace in Astorga, constructed between 1887 and 1893 but left unfinished by Gaudí, is dealt with in chapter VI below. See: L. Alonso Luengo, *Gaudí en Astorga*, Astorga, 1954; M.J. Alonso Gavela, *Gaudí en Astorga*, León, 1972; J. Rivera *El palacio Episcopal de Gaudí y el Museo de los Caminos de Astorga*, Valladolid, 1985. According to all of the contemporary sources, Gaudí's interest in the Catholic liturgy developed out of his acquaintance with the bishop of Astorga, Joan Grau Vallespinós, who was from Gaudí's home town of Reus, and with whom he came into contact on other commissions (the Torre Bellesguard, for example). See: *Homenaje al Obispo Grau*, Reus, 1916.
[53] For example: "*I així com el Verb etern deïficà la carn, la bellesa embelleix la matèria*" (J. Torras i Bages, "De la fruïció artística," *Estètiques*, cit., p. 25).
[54] J. Rubió i Bellver, "Conferencia acerca de los conceptos orgánicos, mecánicos y constructivos de la Catedral de Mallorca," cit., pp. 6–7.
[55] P.J. Campins, "Carta pastoral sobre la restauración...," cit., p. 255.
[56] Ibid., p. 258.
[57] M. Rotger, *Restauración de la Catedral de Mallorca ...*, cit., p. 72.
[58] E. Sagristà, *Gaudí en la catedral de Mallorca*, cit., pp. 36–37.
[59] E. Sagristà, op. cit., pp. 53–67. For an interesting interpretation of the baldachin see: A. Kerrigan, "Gaudí restaurador o la historia de Cabrit y Bassa," cit.
[60] P.J. Campins, op. cit., p. 265.
[61] On this interpretation of Rotger and the origin of the document: E. Sagristà, op. cit., pp. 15–18.
[62] See, for example: J. Quetglas, "Comentario núm. 4," *D'A*, no. 1, nos. 179–80, February–March 1989, pp. 97–100.
[63] E. Sagristà, op. cit., pp. 35–36.
[64] This is the accusation, based on Gaudí's reputed disregard for other people's opin-

ion of his work, made by E. Sagristà, op. cit., especially pp. 58–60.
[65] E. Torras i Bages, "Del Verb artístic," *Estètiques*, cit., p. 161.
[66] E. Sagristà, op. cit., p. 60. According to Sagristà it was Antoni M. Alcover in person who "dismissed" Gaudí.
[67] Published in *La Veu de Catalunya* and reprinted in the miscellany of tributes to the architect: *Antoni Gaudí. La seva vida, les seves obres, la seva mort*, Barcelona, 1926, pp. 12–15.
[68] E. Sagristà, *La Catedral de Mallorca*, Castellón de la Plana, 1948, p. 41.
[69] J. Quetglas expresses this opinion in relation to Rubió i Bellver in: "A. Gaudí i J.M. Jujol a la Seu," *D'A*, no. 1, winter 1989, p. 42; id. "Pintado con su sangre," cit., p. 97.
[70] We have already referred to this several times, but see especially: J.Ll. Marfany, "Modernisme i noucentisme, amb algunes consideracions sobre el concepte de moviment cultural," cit.; J. Cassasas Ymbert, *Intellectuals, professionals i polítics a la Catalunya contemporània (1850–1920)*, cit.
[71] J.Ll. Marfany, *Aspectes del modernisme*, cit., pp. 76–77.
[72] For the full political significance of this distinction see D'Ors' 1906 texts "Dos llibres," "*La Nacionalitat Catalana* i la generació noucentista," "*Enllà* i la generació noucentista" and "En resum...," E. D'Ors, *Obra completa catalana*, cit., pp. 182–86.
[73] E. D'Ors, "*Enllà* i la generació noucentista," cit., p. 184. We shall comment on these lines in greater detail in chapter 6.
[74] On all of this: J. Castellanos, "L'Escola Mallorquina," *Història de la literatura catalana*, cit.
[75] G. Alomar, "L'aspiració de Mallorca," *La Veu de Catalunya*, August 30, October 1, and November 7, 1903, cit. in J. Castellanos, op. cit., p. 328.
[76] G. Alomar, *El Futurisme*, Barcelona, 1905. On Alomar and this extraordinary text: A. Ll. Ferrer, "Pròleg," *El futurisme i altres assigs*, Barcelona, 1970; J.Ll. Marfany, *Aspectes del modernisme*, cit., pp. 253–65; J.J. Lahuerta, "El nombre del futurismo," *Buades. Periódico de Arte*, nos. 8–9, February–March, 1987, pp. 55–58
[77] J. Castellanos, op. cit., p. 328.
[78] See: F.B. de Moll, *Un home de combat...*, cit., pp. 108–13, 161–227.
[79] M. Gaya, *Contribució a l'epistolari de Miquel Costa i Llobera*, Barcelona, 1956, p. 133.
[80] G. Forteza, "Gaudí i la restauració de la Seu de Mallorca," *El Matí*, June 21, 1936, since reprinted in *Estudis sobre arquitectura i urbanisme*, cit., vol. II, pp. 150–55.

**Temple and Time**
The Sagrada Familia in the Formation
of the Myths of Conservative Catalanism

*Expiatory Temple, "Sublime Abnormality"*
On November 8, 1871, Pope Pius IX received a group of devotees of St. Joseph from Barcelona in the Council Chamber of the Vatican.[1] Laid out on a table in front of the papal throne were a number of gifts: religious prints and medals and a small silver sculpture by Francesc Pagès. This sculpture was a not entirely successful attempt to reproduce a large painting, itself utterly mediocre, that presided over the altar in the chapel of St. Joseph in the Basilica of Montserrat, depicting the Holy Family accompanied by an angel bearing the flowering staff—others hover among clouds with flowers of different kinds and an iris—resting, against a background of pyramids and obelisks, on their flight into Egypt. Only the figure of Joseph introduces a slight note of singularity into the extreme conventionality of the composition: the grave elder of traditional iconography is here a young man, and it is he rather than Mary who supports the sleeping Christ-child in his lap. It is evident that the painter of the Montserrat picture (apparently Antoni Ferrán, *circa* 1830) had to bring Joseph forward from the middle ground and place him with full honors—as we have noted, an angel carries his staff—in the center of the composition, as befitted Jesus' putative father in such a scene: after all, the altar was devoted to St. Joseph. Joseph, then, is no longer a half-fascinated, half-doubtful observer of the miracle, but a protagonist and central axis of the family group. This exaltation is no doubt the result of an error of calculation, a lack of decorum on the part of Ferrán or his clients, in having chosen to honor Joseph here with a theme typical of another iconography, that of the Holy Family. However, in the eyes of the fervent Josephists who had been granted the honor of an audience by Pius IX, the pope who only a year before had instituted the universal patronage of Joseph on the Church, the thematic content of the image would have been perfectly clear.
In reproducing it for them, Pagès increased the conventionality of the figures, but more impor-

tantly he stressed the most ambiguous aspects of the composition. It is still Joseph, taller than Mary, who holds the Christ-child, while the setting is indicated only by a sign: a palm tree. He thus converts what had formerly been a scene—and, in iconological terms, a well established scene—from a story into an isolated and static image of the Family. Separated from circumstance, the figure of Joseph gains, generically, in importance: the group is now ordered around him, and not only in a strictly formal sense. In effect, while the Child sleeps and Mary, with drooping head and closed eyes, languidly plays with his hand, Joseph appears erect, contemplating the other two in their unconsciousness—of sleep, of play—as he who knows. Evidently this is not the role that the Gospels assign to Joseph, but what in Ferrán's painting was simply a lack of propriety has here, in Pagès' interpretation, been loaded with intentionality. Joseph is now visibly the head of the family, and it is only through the exaltation of his figure that the Family becomes precisely that: the minimum identifiable cell of a hierarchically ordered society, and at the same time, circularly, its image. It mattered little that to achieve this it was necessary to inflate the importance that Holy Scripture attributed to Joseph: his worship was, by definition, worship of the Holy Family. In the course of the nineteenth century, and above all in the second half, this previously unimportant cult grew to a spectacular extent to become one of the most popular. The support that the official Church gave to the propagation of the cult was prompted, of course, by its virtual social content: its potential as an example and its service value make this quite clear. So, in proclaiming the patronage of Joseph on December 8, 1870, Pius IX was being perfectly consistent with his other gestures of political intransigence: his proclamation of the dogma of the Immaculate Conception in 1854, his publication of the *Syllabus* ten years later, his declaration of papal infallibility and primacy at the First Vatican Council in 1869 and 1870, and so on.

The history of the choice of those figures, and of the signs that the devotees of Joseph saw in them, were the subject of the grandiloquent discourse read to Pius IX at the audience. To quote an excerpt: "The Association of Spanish devotees of St. Joseph wishing to take part in the exhibition of artistic and precious objects… proposed by the Society of Catholic Youth of Bologna, it was felt that its contribution should be none other appliance than the image of its sublime Patron, in the company of Jesus and Mary, in that the privileged Patriarch was never to be seen separate from his virginal Wife and divine Son. The choice of the scriptural passage referring to the flight of the Holy Family into Egypt was purely casual. Taking refuge in the mountain and sanctuary of Montserrat, because of the plague that was raging in Barcelona, some of the members commissioned to carry out this intention had a sculpture made as a copy of the picture there that represents this event. But in this choice there shines, Holy Father, something providential that is related to present circumstances. Pursued by an ambitious king and his corrupt courtiers, Mary and Joseph ventured forth with their sweet Jesus on a path of privation and suffering, sown with thorns and encircled with dangers. So, too, the great of the earth have driven Your Holiness on an unknown path of tribulation and bitterness, of hardship and poverty. Under the friendly shade of the palm the Holy Family rests on its hard journey… To Your Holiness a most manifest and special divine assistance has served as a rest and consoling respite in the long series of afflictions you have endured."[2] So, then, for the devotees from Barcelona, Joseph is accompanied—simply that—by the other two members of the Family, while the choice of subject, the flight into Egypt, was quite random. The figure of Joseph is significantly singled out from the accidents of circumstance, and the words we have quoted merely corroborate what we have already noted in relation to the silver statuette. What we must consider now, however, is the other part of the discourse, that in which chance is interpreted as Providence, and the flight into Egypt as an image of the sufferings of the Pope occasioned by the loss of his temporal power, his States. This is an obvious reference, if we bear in mind that only a few months earlier the celebration of the First Vatican Council had had to be broken off because Piedmontese troops were besieging Rome. Just as clear, and equally natural, is the ultramontane spirit that underlies the interpretation of the image. The audience, at which members of the Roman nobility were also present, concluded with a cry of "Long live the Pope-King!," and it is not hard to see "the ambitious king and his corrupt courtiers" of the speech as a direct allusion to Victor Emmanuel and his ministers and, in effect, to the liberal State that had already been condemned by the *Syllabus* several years before.[3]

All of this is perfectly evident, almost schematic. However, another reference adds a further nuance. The idea of making a sculpture of the Montserrat painting, the speech says, occurred to the Josephists when the plague that was ravaging Barcelona drove them to take refuge in the monastery. This was also, then, a flight from a calamity, in this case a natural one: the icteric typhus outbreak of 1870.[4] Once again the signs were, to devout eyes, providential. Without too much effort, the Josephists sheltering on Montserrat could relate their own flight—which found refuge on sacred ground—with the image in the picture, as they explicitly did with the flight of the beleaguered pope. What is more, in 1870 the country was still in the period of political interregnum that followed on the Liberal revolution of September 1868 and the dethronement and exile of Isabella II. At the same time, all through the autumn of 1869 there had been the federal uprisings, especially significant in Catalonia. Meanwhile General Prim y Serrano, representing the provisional government created after the revolution, concluded the negotiations to establish a new dynasty in the person of Amadeus of Savoy—the son of none other than

Victor Emmanuel—that were to culminate in Amadeus's election by the Cortes in November 1870 and his proclamation as constitutional monarch in January of the following year. In the face of all this the Spanish Church adopted a posture of absolute intransigence: specifically, the Catalan bishops had already been involved, in 1869, in the organization of a great plebiscite "for Catholic unity," officially declaring their opposition to the new constitution, and attending en bloc the ceremonies of the First Vatican Council.[5] But these were also the years in which that reaction began to assume more immediate, less official forms: 1871, for example, saw the launch in Barcelona of *La Revista Popular*, one of the principal and most constant platforms of fundamentalist propaganda, founded and edited by Sardà i Salvany, who went on to write a widely read book, entitled *El liberalismo es pecado*— "Liberalism is Sin."[6]

Revolutionary interregnum and uncompromising and catastrophic reaction by the Church in Spain, on the one hand; annexation of the Papal States on the other. On top of this already sufficiently explicit groundwork we have the specific circumstance in which our devotees found themselves: flight from an epidemic. It is hardly surprising, then, that a strong social sense of catastrophe, both religious and natural, should have assailed them. That all of this was a sign of a divine punishment seemed perfectly clear, and as such it was expressed. It was by no means difficult, in fact, to see this state of affairs as the palpable fulfillment of the most providentialist interpretations of ultramontane ideology. A single, but extremely concrete and immediate, example will suffice: in his famous and influential *Ensayo sobre el catolicismo, el liberalismo y el socialismo*—which came to be the principal theoretical mainstay of Carlism, and whose mystical and irrationalist tone was a feature of Spanish Catholic literature, and not only the most reactionary, for many years to come—Juan Donoso Cortés explained the increasing secularization of society as a result of the unbelieving arrogance of the times, as a sin of pride, and interpreted the revolutionary processes as a punishment sent by God. He called, in short, for the absolute submission of the State to the Church.[7] In this atmosphere, so laden with signs, one of those who took refuge from the Barcelona plague of 1870 on Montserrat was the bookseller Josep Maria Bocabella.[8] In fact, it was Bocabella who had, in 1866 (after a very similar experience as the result of another epidemic, in this case of cholera, in Barcelona in the summer of 1865 and the subsequent isolation on Montserrat), founded the Asociación Espiritual de Devotos de San José, whose journal, *El Propagador de la Devoción a San José*, was launched the following year.[9] And it was Bocabella, together with Father José María Rodríguez,[10] director of the Asociación and General of the Mercedarians, who organized the pilgrimage to Rome to which we referred above. Both men were of course present at the audience with the Pope, and after the audience the pilgrims extended their trip with a tour of other sanctuaries in Italy. Apparently it was on this trip that the decision to construct a temple to the Holy Family in Barcelona was made. Undoubtedly, the idea had been thought over before this: we need only think of the very close links between Bocabella and Father Josep Mañanet,[11] a great propagandist and founder of schools, whose *El Espíritu de la Sagrada Familia* the bookseller had edited, and who had been lobbying for the construction of a temple dedicated to the Holy Family since 1869.

It is hardly surprising that these men should fill their account of events with meaning, presenting the decision as having been taken in Loreto, on a visit to the relic of the Holy House. At the same time, the temple was to have a very clear mission, in keeping with the sense of social and religious catastrophe that had motivated the pilgrimage and informed the speech. It was to be an expiatory temple; its construction, financed entirely by charitable donations, would be an explicit act of social purification. On his return to

Barcelona, Bocabella set in motion a series of mechanisms for commencing his project—shares, draws, subscriptions—and tried to obtain a plot in the old part of the city. Finally, after several disappointments, he managed to purchase an outlying block in the Eixample towards the end of 1881, and the diocesan architect Francesc de Paula del Villar drew up a highly conventional neo-Gothic project.[12] The first stone was laid on St. Joseph's day, 1882. The following lines from the inaugural speech, delivered before the bishop of Barcelona, indicate that the concerns and desires of the Devotos had not changed in the slightest in the intervening ten years: "may this expiatory church … intercede with the Lord to have mercy on the country [and] ease the distress of the Holy See…"[13] Work on the temple began at its unhurried pace: a year later, the first stone was still the only one. Around the end of 1883 Villar abandoned the work as a result of differences with the board. Villar suggested Joan Martorell as his successor, and Martorell, in turn, suggested Antoni Gaudí. On March 28, 1884, in the thirty-first of his seventy-four years of life, Gaudí's signature appeared for the first time on a document relating to the Sagrada Familia.[14]

From the pilgrimage to Rome to the first stone of the temple: very little seems to have changed for the Asociación Espiritual de Devotos de San José. However, those ten years had seen the Restoration of the Bourbons in the person of Alfonso XII and the definitive military defeat of Carlism; Leo XIII ascended the papal throne and wrote, in that same year of 1882, his encyclical *Cum Multa*,[15] calling for unity among Spanish Catholics and criticizing the most uncompromising sectors: none of this was to be in vain. We need only consider the absolutely conventional terms in which the Barcelona press reported those events that, to judge by the information in *El Propagador*, were not only important for the construction of the Sagrada Familia but represented a major propaganda effort. Consider, for example, the inauguration in 1885 of the chapel of St. Joseph, Gaudí's plans for which the magazine of the Devotos had described and published. Only *El Correo Catalán*, a newspaper aligned with the Carlists and fundamentalists, went beyond a brief outline in its general news pages. Its headline was significant: "This will be the first religious monument of Catholic Spain in this century."[16]

Pilgrimages, magazines disseminating religious propaganda, popular devotions, the collection of donations, expiatory sentiments, images, medals, prints: the fundamentalist climate in which the Sagrada Familia was born and in which reflect its long formative years did not, perhaps, require much comment. But we must now jump forward in time.

1906: Xénius—pseudonym of Eugeni D'Ors—pontificates from his column in *La Veu de Catalunya*, the newspaper of the Lliga Regionalista; he distributes warranties of *noucentisme*, and where necessary issues anathemas against intellectuals and artists who have failed to identify themselves with the Lliga's political project, effectively determining—this is in, that is out—the culture of Catalonia.[17]

In June, the article he devoted to Maragall's latest volume of poems, entitled *Enllà i la generació noucentista*, included the following lines that, as we noted in the last chapter, have become especially famous: "At times, I must confess, I cannot think without terror of the destiny of our people, obliged to support on their poor, precarious normality the weight, the greatness and the glory of these sublime abnormalities: the Sagrada Familia, the poetry of Maragall…"[18] The malicious ambiguity of these words is inescapable: by insisting on their enormity, Xénius is clearly seeking to detach those works from their present, their reality, effectively consigning them to the pantheon, to that place where the most illustrious things can be manipulated precisely because they must arrive there dead, alienated.

What is of interest here is not the success or failure of D'Ors' attempt—we will consider this

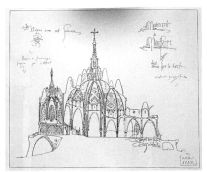

in due course—but the specific mention he makes of the Sagrada Familia. Gaudí scholars have always interpreted this as Xénius' judgment of the whole of the architect's work, of Gaudí himself, putting forward an imaginary vision of *noucentisme* in which Maragall and Gaudí possess the same glorious eccentricity.[19] But it is enough to scan the rest of the *Glosari* to see that, in contrast to his admiration for Maragall, Eugeni D'Ors was profoundly unimpressed by Antoni Gaudí. In what is perhaps his most representative period—the five years from 1906 to 1910—D'Ors wrote a daily column. In these hundreds of printed pages, the name of Maragall, to whom several "glosses" are specifically devoted, is by far the most frequently cited. Gaudí's name appears only three times, and each time as the butt of a piercing irony.[20] It is solely and exclusively with the Sagrada Familia that Xénius is concerned in the lines quoted above: with the construction, the temple. This, and not Gaudí the man or his work as a whole, shares that definitive glory with Maragall. Its presence terrifies a D'Ors engaged in a rigorous project of normalization: in that same project, Gaudí's work—the rest of his works—does not merit even the most minimal attention.

Having said all this, a question presents itself: how is it that a building that came into being as a result of a private initiative, inspired by the most uncompromising and most deeply conventional fundamentalism, should in just a few years have come to constitute a symbol of Catalonia? And how is it that Xénius could envisage it as such, in isolation from—indeed, in spite of—his disdain for the work of its architect?

D'Ors' admiration, perhaps *malgré lui*, for Maragall has a great deal to do with the association he makes between the poet and the temple, because it was Maragall and no one else who "invented" this building that filled him with terror, that monument worthy as few others have been of waiting, in glory, to be used. It is at how and why Maragall did this that we must look now.

## In Time, Outside of Time

In 1953 Columbano Cucurella published a book of spiritual exercises in Barcelona of which there is certainly nothing remarkable other than the title and the form in which this is represented on the front cover: *El Montserrat del espíritu.*[21] In effect, the title is depicted by a very eloquent image: a mountain, vaguely reminiscent of the strangely shaped rocks and hallucinatory landscape of Montserrat, is repeated three times in vertical sequence. The lowest of these images, with a broad horizontal development, is a kind of very distant panoramic view from Manresa, as the guidebooks would say. The second, intermediate image seems to be simply an enlarged section of those same rocks, the inaccessibility of which is emphasized, none too successfully, by the nervous quality of the drawing in India ink with its exaggerated chiaroscuro; it also contains the first panoramic stratum, as if it were a cave. The third image rests on the platform in which the second seems to conclude: this time the mountain has been transformed into an extraterrestrial fusiform temple articulated in small domes around a larger, gilded central dome, surrounded by a luminous ethereal halo rose of pink, white and yellow…

"Fundamenta ejus in montibus sanctis": the same line from Psalm 86 that Alexander VII chose as the motto for the foundational medal of the Bernini colonnade in St. Peter's has been adopted as the book's emblem. In the case of a book of spiritual exercises, the meaning could hardly be clearer. The ascent of the mountain is a symbol of the road to perfection, and it almost goes without saying that the book starts by reminding us that Ignatius of Loyola first practiced his spiritual exercises in Montserrat and Manresa. It is obvious, too, that the structure of the drawing on the cover is intended to represent the various strata of an axis of the world, of the *axis mundi*: that, simply, is the traditional significance of a sacred mountain. The cave of the lowest realm contains, according to legend, the material Montserrat, shown pertinently as a

simple panorama, a pure landscape that calls out to the eyes, to the senses; the intermediate Montserrat, more mysterious and difficult, more rugged, reveals the difficulty of this life, the difficulty of the path, and represents, with the ostentation of its rocks converted into watchful sentinels, the Church militant; finally, the gilded temple floats in the heaven of the Church triumphant. However, the kitsch drawing on the cover of Columbano Cucurella's book is not only an immediate figure of the eschatology of the Church. We have already said that the three images represented here, one above the other and containing one another, are all of the same mountain. It is quite clear, then, that Montserrat is also represented in the highest of the three, where we find, of course, the Montserrat of the spirit. But at the same time it is a temple. This total identification, this perfect match between temple and mountain requires an explanation.

In the first place it is worth noting that the temple not only crowns the mountain, but seems to spring from it. Its peaks have been converted into a soft platform, something like a crater all but overflowing with lava, thus determining the sense of the hollowness of that mountain, whose interior is now in touch with the primeval magma, with the center of the earth. It is exactly that, the center of the earth transmuted into precious gold what seems to spring forth from the mountain in the form of a temple. What we have here is not, then, simply a temple built on the mountain: in effect, the temple is the mountain and the mountain a temple, and the two things are the earth itself.

From a generic point of view, every religious tradition accords the temple that symbolic sense of being the mountain whose ascent marks the passage from one time to another, from the profane time of change and becoming, to the sacred time of the absolute and eternal, to Time without temporality. But what is of interest in this particular case is that temple and mountain are configured in their representation here on a real form, the specific form of a real mountain. In other words,

an orographic configuration is presented here as a temple. This direct formal identification, as we shall see, is imbued with a symbolism that goes beyond the generic.

In the first place, the occasions on which the system depicted on the cover of *El Montserrat del espíritu* was actually constructed in the Catalonia of the early twentieth century are more numerous than the hallucinatory character of the image might suggest. The following is perhaps the most minor example: late in 1925, on a hill some fifty meters high near Montferri in the province of Tarragona, Josep Maria Jujol commenced construction of a sanctuary dedicated, precisely, to the Virgin of Montserrat, although the work was halted around 1930.[22] The shrine—built by "volunteers," with a very meagre budget, using surplus and recycled materials—twice recreates (in the bay of the church and even more clearly in the side-chapel of the Virgin, which rises up from the slope of the hill on top of a "cave" of parabolic arches) the eschatological sequence we referred to above: from the cave, its ostensibly natural vaults conflated with those of the body of the Church, to the tallest of the spires, which represents the temple erected on the mountain top. What is more, the little domes ranged around the central spire, each topped with a cross, are quite literally naïf reproductions of the cliffs of Montserrat. Even the partially built enclosing wall around the precinct was to reproduce the profile of the mountain. And another example, without doubt the greatest: on the summit of Tibidabo, in Barcelona, isn't the Temple of the Sacred Heart, also expiatory, begun in 1902, with its neo-Romantic crypt, and its small spires arranged around the central and much higher spire terminating in the great statue, once again a direct formal allusion to the mountain?[23] Indeed an official history of the temple describes it in the following terms: "The architect has given great height to the general lines of the building, as if coming as a continuation of the hillside, so that the mountain, the temple and the sky are in proportion, the first

two constituting a single monumental mass of which the former is the base and the latter the continuation, and both the magnificent pedestal of the statue of the Saviour."[24] What concerns us here is not so much the political significance of this other great expiatory temple in Barcelona in relation to the Sagrada Familia as to note how in this case the symbolic meanings can be extended almost to the point of hallucination. In effect, at the foot of the church is a sizeable fun fair, construction of which began at the same time, which was a front for a large-scale piece of property speculation.[25] In this exemplary case, then, the sacred *tempus* of the temple-mountain was in fact erected on the place where the automatic time of the metropolis, the discontinuous and unconnected time of shock, is expressed in its fullest, most quintessential form. On it time in the temple is fixed and stopped.

Montferri and Tibidabo are merely two examples, extreme in terms of their size, time and circumstances, but they are not the only ones: it would be easy to cite others.[26] In all of them we find the same formal framework: a compact plan and a decidedly vertical development grounded on a crypt that is always expressed on the exterior, culminating in a great spire surrounded by other smaller spires and a realistic evocation of the mountain. The model of this premise is none other than the Sagrada Familia designed by Antoni Gaudí. In these cases, then, the mountain is evoked, albeit by means of an interpretation. However, to say this here is to go too far. We must first go back a little.

The basis of the identification thus established in immediate and purely formal terms between sacred mountain and temple, that deliberate conflation, is not only symbolic but mythical. When the mountain is invested with significance by its actual orographic configuration, to the point of being a direct model for architecture, it is the land itself—a land represented synthetically by a mountain—that is being presented to us: a land that is characteristic and identifiable and, above all, sacred and configuring. Of course it is

well known that Montserrat has been a sacred mountain since the earliest times, but that it is the sacred mountain of Catalonia in the strict sense that its very form as such expresses a supposed essence of Catalonia—something that thus goes beyond religion—is a relatively recent ideological construct. And this construct bears a far from negligible relation to the identification of temple and mountain we have been considering here, and in its diffuseness goes far beyond facts such as the celebration of the millennium in 1881,[27] which in their undoubted importance had a more immediately operative political significance, more closely linked to a specific moment. If we open *El Montserrat del espíritu* at the first page we find: "It is the round [of spiritual exercises] that was performed on this Miracle Mountain at the end of December of the year 1929." Miracle Mountain: this is very different from holy mountain or sacred mountain. The qualifiers holy and sacred seem to be terms added to the mountain; miracle, on the other hand, envelops it with a greater power, endows it with the special life of the wonderful, invests it with a radiant quality out of which the physical mountain emerges, because its physical appearance has become its very essence. But like the cover illustration (that extreme, almost grotesque interpretation of the models we have been considering), so, too, the term Miracle Mountain was not coined by Cucurella. They are the words of the poet Joan Maragall.

In 1905 Maragall published an article entitled "Montserrat" in the conservative *Diario de Barcelona*, to which he was a regular collaborator. The piece commences with these words: "Montserrat is the miracle of Catalonia."[28] It is as if the terms of the merely sacred were being displaced elsewhere. Let us attempt to identify them. "The miracle of Catalonia" itself speaks, in effect, of the quality of the wonderful associated with a land. But there is more. At the end of the article we read: "And the image reigns in [our] hearts, and its mountain reigns in the lands, and in the views of the distant seas, and in

*The Nativity façade under construction, in a series of photographs from 1897–1908.*

*Nativity façade and bell towers.*

the end mountain and land, image and soul of the people, come to form a sublime amalgam, a single thing, a great spirit."[29] Maragall thus starts off by speaking of the miracle mountain, but the meaning contained in those two words is at once extended to lands and seas, to a whole geography, to a soil, strictly, to a land. That land is placed in relation with the mountain once again by a connecting "and": mountain and land. But this identity is immediately made synonymous with another identity: image and soul of the people. The circle, then, is perfectly closed. The geography of a country, its orographic configuration, and the soul of the people that inhabit it, the spirit of that people, do not merely determine one another; Maragall tells us, they are a single thing. It is easy to deduce that this single thing, this great spirit, has a name, a word much in circulation in certain intellectual circles of the Europe in which Maragall wrote his articles, the Europe that was experiencing a new imperialist expansion: race. But we must not run too far ahead.

The theme of the miracle mountain, or rather, of Montserrat as miracle, is a very important component—a leit-motiv, Marfany calls it[30]—of the problems dealt with in the *Visions*, a series Maragall wrote in the last years of the nineteenth century, and on which he spent a good deal of time. There are five poems in *Visions*: *El Mal Caçador*, *Joan Garí*, *L'estimada de Don Jaume*, *La fi d'En Serralonga* and *Compte Arnau*.[31] These are Catalan legends already elaborated and rewritten—and largely invented—by the Romantic poets of the Renaixença.[32] They had added to the schematic basis of each of these legends a whole series of fragments, elements borrowed from other legends and other traditions, together with historical details with which they attempted to situate the stories in a specific place and time. Operations of this kind are, of course, a characteristic feature of Romantic culture in general: the effect of historicizing legend is to make history legendary; to construct, in other words, a tradition, a memory stocked with

*Trumpeting angels in photographs from 1904 and 1915.*

myths that serves to justify people in its own eyes as a nation. Romantic nationalism, in effect, has a marked slant, and the means of its identification are historicist. Only the ideology of Romanticism could revive an epic in the strict sense of the term: that, quite simply, is the result of the impassioned retelling of the legend.

At the same time, in a much-cited letter to the musician Felip Pedrell, Maragall speaks of his *Visions* in the following terms: "figures of legendary Catalan personages as seen by a poet today."[33] What Maragall means by "today" here could hardly be clearer: he is distancing himself from yesterday, from the Romantics, from their epic narrative tradition. In effect, his is a project not of narration but, as the title of the series tells us, of vision, and vision is transfigured contemplation, revelation. The vision illuminates the legend, goes beyond it, reveals its essence. It is not now a matter of making history legendary: the legend has become valuable in itself, and is superior to the history in being the essential—not physical; not determined by events and chronology—creation of a people. It is outside of history and of time because it is the expression of the soul of that people, not the mere sequence of their deeds in time. In turning to legend, Maragall is engaged not in reconstructing history in mythical terms but in constructing the myths demanded by the present. In other words, in turning his visionary gaze on Catalan legends already recounted by the Romantics—by none other than the Romantics—Maragall is criticizing the historicist conception of nation and proposing—in perfect harmony, as we saw above, with the mood elsewhere in Europe—a new elaboration of nationalism in supremely irrational terms.

Of course, Maragall was not alone in this project. During this same period, if not before, writers such as Brossa, Pompeu Gener and Casas-Carbó were shaping a nationalist ideology in their books and "current affairs" articles. This was based not on political theory or law, but on the pure manifestation of idealized images—the soul of a people, the spirit of a people, etc.—that were, however, put forward in a supposedly scientific context.[34] Above all, the positivist concept of the "medium" as the set of physical, geographical, climatic and other phenomena that shape the character of the people that inhabit it is transformed into the irrational image of the soul of the land, the spirit that is transferred from the land itself to the people that dwell in it. It is hardly surprising that Renan—not so remote, of course, as the chronology might lead us to suppose—and Taine are always at the origin of such theories, nor that writers such as Maurras, for example, should be involved in their latest elaboration. Maragall did not take part directly in the pseudo-scientific debates which that nationalist ideology orchestrated around the concept of race—one extreme example of which we have seen in our analysis of the work of Miquel d'Esplugues—but he did provide the most powerful formulation of the "myths of the land" that such a nationalism needed.

Clearly, then, in this set of myths Montserrat has an essential role as representation of the land and, above all, the miraculous quality of that land. Thus, *Joan Garí*, the very origin of which is a legend traditionally associated with Montserrat, opens with these lines: "On the mountain, miracle, / a legend has blossomed."

We have already said enough about what it means to call the mountain "miracle," but note that here the legend blossoms on the mountain, springs from the land itself.[35] However, let us return to Maragall's 1905 article "Montserrat." The last lines are crowded with images: "See the mountain in a new vision, that now figures itself to me definitively; it is not a mountain that strives to make itself a temple, but like the great ruin of some enormous temple that nature recovers and vests with her perpetual renewal. All of the dome has fallen in and there stand the stunned columns raising their thousand arms, that no longer have anything to support, towards the blue vault of the sky they cannot reach… And everything has been flooded with

light; in the joints between the stones of the broken columns herbs and flowers have rooted; thus seem to me now the naked rocks of Montserrat haloed with verdure. And in the heaping up of the demolished mass, the precipices have opened their throats, springs have bubbled forth from them, birds have sung, paths have been opened to the renewal of all piety, all strength. And this, heed it well, is ours, it is the symbol to which our soul has given itself, it is the miracle of Catalonia, Montserrat."[36]

Temple and mountain, identical. The temple has become a ruin, a gigantic ruin, but not to provoke a nostalgic sense of the power of time over the works of man, the nostalgia of the perishable, but precisely in order to manifest itself as the abolition of time, as the work of nature outside of time and of history, as origin. Mountain and temple have become unmistakable, they are the same thing, equally eternal, springing in the same way from the land and from the soul of the people. This gigantic ruin does not "re-mortalize" time, it immortalizes the land with which it is absolutely conflated.

The temple is there, made mountain, as it always has been and always will be, so that the people can no longer recall the time of its construction. However, the idea that this is a work, a construction, although clearly in conflict with the idea of flowering, with the idea of the fruit of the people, is essential to the effect of Maragall's text. The admonitory and ineffable quality of Maragall's prose, the origin of which we shall consider in due course, allows it to glide without a pause over its own paradoxes. Maragall himself tells us that before the vision of the mountain we should recall, first and foremost, that it was a temple. Of course it goes without saying that in this temple there is something much more profound than a merely religious sentiment. It is, as we have said, the place where the soul of the land and the spirit of the people identify with one another. What is more, the image of the temple evidently contains an implicit reference to the myth of the medieval cathedral and

its construction over the centuries, to its power as the work of a people, to its organizational relationship with the body and the spirit of that constructing people. It is perhaps superfluous to recall here that the continual evocation of a harmonious and integrated Middle Ages was essential to the elaboration of conservative Catalanist ideology. If this seems to follow logically from its Romantic origins, in the work of Torras i Bages or Prat de la Riba the evocation is deployed without the least trace of naïvety, with a highly operative purpose. That course—its direction, its meaning—is exemplified in almost strident terms in the last lines of a speech delivered by Prat himself in 1897: "The Middle Ages are the age of the autonomous communities. The advent of the Renaissance, the reinstating of autocracy and of classical forms, which for the Romantics were equivalent to death, blighted all the liberties of medieval times. The new era is called Romanticism, and with it the Middle Ages return."[37] Maragall was merely describing the crown of that return: its cathedral. Much as he had done with Catalan legends, Maragall pursues to its logical conclusion the Romantic myth of the medieval cathedral as communal phenomenon: the temple of which he writes is an immense ruin that at the same time buds and blossoms, is filled with verdure; lives, in fact. This is what Maragall seems to be doing here: putting forward a living myth, physically alive, a tangible myth, we might almost call it. Something that in effect is being made, something in and with whose construction everyone identifies; something that does away with differences, that smooths over the contradictions of reality. An endeavor, in fact, an enterprise. The temple of which Maragall speaks is at the same time, without exclusion, the product of the work of men and of nature, of the time of the land. That collective enterprise is itself the life and, in the most transcendent sense of the word, the art of a people. Art, in effect, as expression of the genius—of the spirit, of the character—of a people; but, above all, art as a place of con-

vergence of all their interests and efforts. Art, then, as a unique work, without an artist: cathedral, temple.

Here is another excerpt from Maragall, also from 1905: "There was a time when every great Barcelona burgess, in disposing of his property in his will, felt obliged to leave a legacy in favor of the hospital of the Santa Cruz. The hospital was a private foundation, as the temple is today, and so each citizen felt it to be in some way his, because inside himself he felt the whole city; because that old city had its citizens, and the new city does not yet have citizens who feel the great new citizenship; those citizens in the past felt the pious usefulness of the general hospital, and do these not feel the usefulness of the Temple? Well, I say to them that the Temple is more useful than a hospital, and more than an asylum and more than a convent; because in the action of erecting it there lies the virtue that makes all the hospitals and all the asylums and all first convents, and I say to them that the temple is as urgent as succouring the greatest material need. Think that in classical Athens a lot of people lived and died very poorly, and it will pain you; but think that the Parthenon had never been built, and you will not know what ails you. What did the Greek people need more? What did the human spirit need more?"[38]

There is no need to insist on the aristocratism and elitism that underpins the idea of need here, or on what lies behind that spirit that is so far above and beyond the miseries and contingencies of human life: the text speaks for itself. But it also sheds a new light on Maragall's image of the temple. It comes from an article entitled "Una gràcia de caritat…!," on the Sagrada Familia by Antoni Gaudí.

The article begins with these lines: "I often feel as proud to be from Barcelona as an ancient Roman could be of his citizenship; but there are other times that I feel ashamed of being from here; and this is one of those times." And a little further on: "The day that work on the Sagrada Familia is halted for want of resources will be for

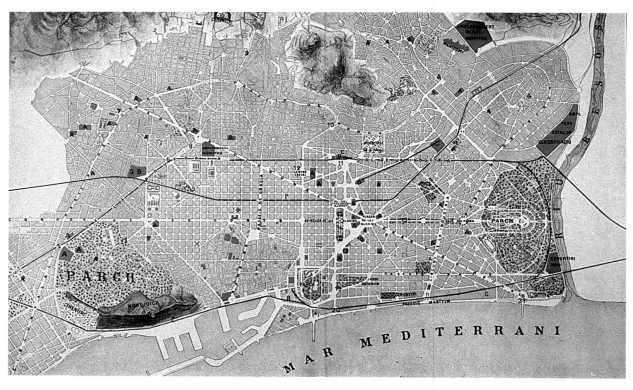

Barcelona and for all of Catalonia, a more ill-fated day than that on which a bomb explodes in the public thoroughfare, or that on which a hundred factories are closed."[39] As we know, Maragall's references are not generic but very specific: 1902 had seen the first general strike in Barcelona,[40] which ended in failure for the workers but "justified" a terrible repression on the part of government and employers that continued for years, with very far-reaching consequences. In effect, the workers' movement was to take a long time to recover and reorganize effectively, and its place was filled in part by anarchist terrorism, which made Barcelona one of its principal European bases in the early years of the twentieth century. Of note among the bombings and shootings that marked those years in the city were the attempt on the life of Antonio Maura, the president of the government, in 1904, and the attack against Cardinal Casañas, in the very cloister of the cathedral, in 1905. In addition Maragall, like the rest of the Catalanist

right, saw the rise of the Republican Alejandro Lerroux—anti-Catalanist, anticlerical and demagogically pro-labor—as a sign of disorder no less disturbing than the bombs.[41] But why so clear a reference to that disorder, to the violence, and, in short, to the absence of social cohesion, to the absence of what Maragall most dearly wished to encourage: the people?

Perhaps we can better understand the context in which Maragall's words were written by considering two other interpretations of that disorder, located in time symmetrically before and after his article, which represents—and not only chronologically—two extremes. The first is a painting, *La Càrrega* [*The Charge*] by Ramón Casas. Everything about this great work is in some way false, and if it has been more or less specifically associated with the 1902 general strike to which we referred above, that is because Casas himself saw to it that this occurred. He had painted the picture for presentation to the International Exhibition of Paris in 1900, but

*Projects for the integration
of the Sagrada Familia into
the Jaussely plan.*

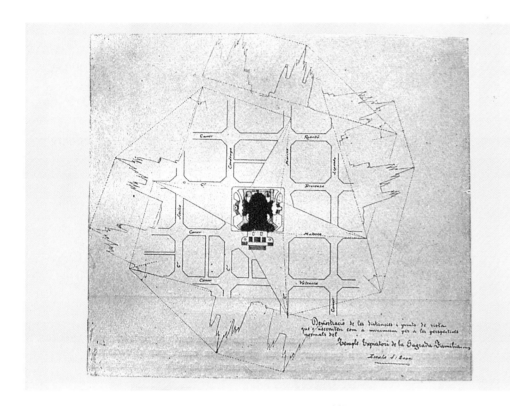

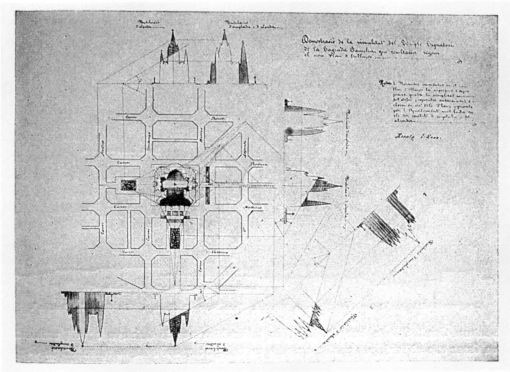

after being turned down by the selection committee there he tried his luck again at the Exposición General de Bellas Artes de Madrid in 1903, retitling the picture *Barcelona 1902* in order to give it an immediate topicality and the living, instant value of present reality. However, the fact that the painting was not intended to—indeed, could not—arouse anxiety is amply demonstrated by its being awarded the gold medal and purchased by the State.[42] In everybody's eyes, then, it was a historical painting. This clearly helps us to understand it better, and to appreciate, above all, its picturesqueness. The crowd, in effect, has been converted into a kind of great animal, a serpentine wave whose presence is exorcized, rendered inexpressive, by the way in which the concrete, anecdotal fact is detained by the power of the artist: that fallen worker is beaten by that mounted Civil Guard. The action is shown in isolation, detached from the background, unmistakable, so as to make it precisely the place of the observer's generic attention to the story being told there. A very different image of disorder struck the eyes of Barcelona a few years after, in July 1909, in the famous photograph of the city from Montjuich showing columns of smoke rising from the burning churches during the Semana Trágica.[43] Strictly speaking this is not a representation but a presentation. The city is presented not to the concentrated gaze of the person looking at a painting but, published in the newspapers, to thousands of eyes simultaneously, the bewildered eyes of people who thought they knew the city and now no longer recognize it. The panorama of Barcelona, formerly so familiar, becomes sinister when the only points of reference are columns of smoke, signs of what no longer exists, of what has been burnt. In the photographs there are no people; even the eye of the camera, an objective mechanism, establishes distances in relation to what it shows. This anonymity, which is the other side of the Casas anecdote, is what makes the situation so profoundly terrible, because it excludes the consolation that the indi-

vidual case contains. The disorder represented by Casas is only an exception to a state of order; that of the photographs is diffuse, spectral: it has no body, no head on which to load responsibilities, it spreads and appears on all sides, as ungraspable as the smoke in the image. The savage repression that followed the revolt is the most pathetic demonstration of all this: the executions by firing squad of Ferrer i Guàrdia and so many unknown workers were arbitrary because the forces of order were seeking only to reinstate the concrete—concrete death, in this case.

The photograph, however, could hardly be more eloquent: its buildings replaced by columns of smoke, it is the qualities of the city that disappeared, and it reveals itself as simply the privileged territory of class struggle. In this way, then, Casas' representation and the presentation of the photograph are two faces of a single thing: the disappearance of the city as such, of the city of the citizens to which Maragall was referring.

The events of the Tragic Week left a deep impression on the poet and on his work. In 1909, a few weeks before the start of the violence, Maragall had begun to write a great poem of epic scope: the *Oda nova a Barcelona*.[44] Its opening lines are strongly landscapist, descriptive, addressed to an ideal Barcelona in which all of Catalonia is embodied: "Where are you going, Barcelona, Catalan spirit / who have crossed the mountain chain and leapt the wall? … / There I see the Pyrenees with their blushing snows, / and below Catalonia spread out at their feet, / and I go … It is love that impels me, / and I go raving with open arms."[45]

Then the Tragic Week radically changed Maragall's vision. What is important, however, is that Maragall did not rework what he had already written, but simply carried on in a very different tone, hitching the two parts together, the before and the after.

Thus, for example: "… Run far, Barcelona, / you must be other to be what you should be; /

because you are high and graceful and of good stature, / though yet you lack much more than what you have. / You are cowardly, cruel and coarse…"[46]

Or this, below: "Death comes down your smiling roads / in the soft air: / explodes unsuspected, sure and treacherous / like another blasphemous guffaw … / Guffaws of blood! / The mud of your streets, Oh, Barcelona! / is smeared with blood."[47] And at the end of the poem: "Even as you are, I love you, wicked city: / you are like a contagious evil that oozes: / you are vain and mean, treacherous and coarse, / you make us lower our eyes / Barcelona! in spite of your sins, ours! ours! / Our Barcelona! the great enchantress!"[48]

Maragall, then, recognizes that disorder and recognizes in it the city, the whole city. Making a juxtaposition imposed by circumstances the thematic core of his poem, he manages to overcome his bewilderment at events that had left the city looking like a disaster zone, left it looking no longer familiar, while at the same time turning his back on the comforting representation of the historical painting. Explanations of the causes of the Tragic Week, from almost every shade of opinion, were fundamentally of two types. One, that the disturbances had been provoked by outsiders, professional agitators: this was the official version endorsed by the government and the institutions of Catalanism. The other, that they were nothing other than a manifestation of the eternal struggle between Good and Evil, once again in the form of persecution suffered by the Church: this was the Church's view, as voiced by Bishop Torras i Bages. Maragall, on the other hand, both in the verses of his *Oda Nova* and, much more directly, in the difficult and controversial newspaper articles he wrote in response to events, recognized what he had called the "city of the bombs," the city of disorder, as the only city.[49] That was the totality to which an enterprise had to be offered. The life, the energy that the disorder had simply brought to the fore needed to be channeled, made to coincide in a collective effort, so that the city might recognize

itself as such and those who dwelt in it might be a people. We should not be surprised at Maragall's response, a response so at odds with the prevailing mood that one of his articles attracted the censure of Prat de la Riba and was not published: what else could he do, this poet who had tried to bring the myth of the land to the city? He devoted years to the idea that the mountain was to spring forth in the very heart of the city, that the temple was to be born in it to draw together the life that, amid all the contradictions, fills it. Before going on to consider this, however, a final quote from the *Oda Nova*: "To the East, mystic example, / like a gigantic flower blossoms a temple / wondering at having been born here, / among such grim and wicked people … / Yet amid misery, rage and smoke, / the temple (what does it matter?) rises up and grows / awaiting the faithful that are to come."[50]

It seems, then, that the temple is rising up not in the midst of desolation and the desert, but in the midst of all the feelings, turbulence and contradiction of life, wondering at this and waiting, in its enchantment, for what is to come. The sacred mountain and the temple served to bring those who ascended them closer to heaven, so as to speak with God: the mountain that Maragall has spring up in the heart of the city, the temple that is born there, serves precisely the opposite purpose: to be closer to the land so that, in it, the spirit of the people can speak to itself.

But this image that is presented in exemplary form in the *Oda Nova* is the product, as we have seen in part, of a long elaboration. Let us consider it more closely. We have already spoken of the 1905 newspaper article "Montserrat" and the way that the mountain was conflated there with the temple in ruins. We have also seen how, again in 1905, Maragall declared the construction of Antoni Gaudí's Sagrada Familia an urgent need. This, of course, is the temple referred to in the *Oda Nova*: not a mere image, then, but an actual temple, a specific construction, a real enterprise. This is the myth in the city; and indeed even the image of Montserrat as a temple

*J. Mir,* A extramurs, *a drawing*
*published in* Hispania *in 1899,*
*and* La catedral dels pobres, *1897.*

in ruins, the idea of that conflation, derives from Gaudí's work. In fact, Maragall devoted four articles to the Sagrada Familia, the first in 1900, five years earlier than "Montserrat," and nine years earlier than the *Oda Nova;*[51] its title was, precisely, "El templo que nace" ["The Temple that is Born"], and in it we find all of the ideas we have been considering here. The images of the mountain as the work both of nature and of man, of the temple that is not built but springs forth, blossoms, the product of telluric forces, are found here for the first time. Maragall calls the Sagrada Familia "stony flowering," and writes: "That portal is something wonderful. It is not architecture: it is the poetry of architecture. It does not seem constructed by men. It is like the earth, the rocks striving upward as they lose their inertia…"[52] In a previous paragraph, that "flowering" is revealed as the time of the temple: "It seems to be rising up by itself, like a tree that grows with slow majesty. Like some colossal tree no doubt it seems to the birds that nest and flutter singing among its spires … like a tree that has sheltered many generations of birds past and are yet to be seen in their passing by many generations of men…"[53] This reference to time, a time that is entirely of the earth and halts the passage of the everyday, the long, long time of generations—generations of birds and of men that inhabit it—is fundamental, because it is not simply the time needed for the slow formation of the temple, but the time of the endless. Maragall writes: "The temple that shall not be completed, that is in everlasting formation, that never finally closes its roof to the blue sky, or its walls to the winds, or its doors to the chance steps of men… The temple that constantly awaits its altars."[54] For Maragall, then, this is not an uncompleted but an endless work. Only what is in the process of becoming can exercise a mythical function. It is hardly surprising that the myths Maragall reworks in his *Visions* should so often refer to an eternally errant soul that, unable to die, wanders forever: Joan Garí, Comte Arnau…[55] Similarly, the Sagrada Familia, if it is to be myth and

symbol, must wait forever, nurture for all time the hope of an unattainable conclusion, because to arrive at it would be to die. Maragall exclaims: "What a beautiful symbol for the centuries to pass down to one another!."[56]

In "Una gràcia de caritat…!," the 1905 article to which we referred above, Maragall is even more explicit in his identification. Here he writes: "Away over there the temple would be rising by itself, the stones blossoming stones, the columns sending out arches like branches, the vault curving gently, the vision would be because the people would be."[57]

But, above all, the Sagrada Familia has become a magical apparition surrounded by providential signs: "When the sense of the Catalan character commenced its material expansion, out of the obscure depths of the ancient population there emerged a little man with a big idea: to build a new cathedral … the city was still far off and he knew nothing of it … years pass … and at the moment when the germinated seed lifts the clod and the plant is about to appear above ground to raise itself to the light there emerges, as God's envoy, another man, a visionary with the same vision as the first."[58] It is hardly necessary to point out how Maragall has idealized the story we recounted above; nevertheless, these lines contain a number of new elements that we must appraise in detail. On the one hand, the seed germinates in a city that, wrapped up in its material progress, knows nothing of the miracle that is taking place in its bowels; on the other, that necessary miracle is a matter for the initiated, for the visionary. The second of the two men is obviously Gaudí. And with the very mention of the architect, the significance of Maragall's temple changes. It might seem as if Maragall is contradicting himself once again here: was it not precisely the cathedral as a collective work, without an artist, that he sought to offer as an enterprise to his fellow citizens? Indeed it was, but this is not so much a contradiction as an extreme case. Maragall is referring not to the individualistic modern artist, the artist of *art pour l'art,* but to

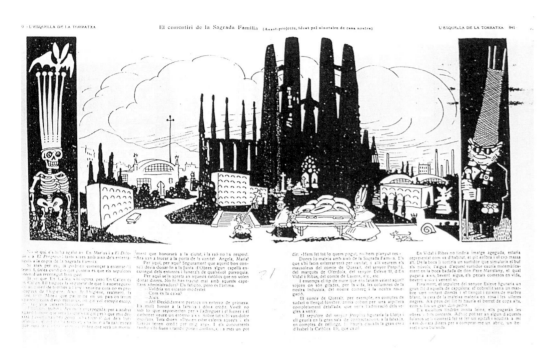

an artist whose flashes of genius are simply the essence of the spirit of his people; an artist whose genius is not that of the free man but, on the contrary, that of one predestined, who has a transcendent, because collective, mission to fullfill. Here again Maragall transforms a Romantic image into a vision: the cathedral has been pervaded by a providencialist irrationalism that, as we shall see, becomes increasingly pronounced. The demiurgic architect is the key to this rarefaction of matter that manifests itself in the flowering stones of the temple. What he is constructing, as Maragall says in his article, is not a work of architecture, but poetry in the transcendent sense in which Maragall understood it: disturbed contemplation, emotion. In this exchange between initiates, in which Maragall's role is that of revealer of the mystery, the temple that is born is the place—although the city does not yet know this—where the symbolic union of culture and nature is to be effected. The visionaries messianically signal the place of hope; in other words, the place where the material city, liberated from its slavery, released from its contradictions and conflicts—or, to put it more explicitly, from the division of labor—will construct the sublime cathedral of the future. In opposition to the crowd as background in Casas' historical painting, the crowd as invisible presence, only sinisterly intuited in the pillars of smoke of the Tragic Week, Maragall offers us the mystical union of the visionary poet—the demiurgic architect—with the disalienated people in the long, endless time, the Time without temporality, of the construction of the temple.

In 1899, in the second of the articles he devoted to Richard Wagner, "Wagner fuera de Alemania" ["Wagner outside Germany"],[59] Maragall made it perfectly clear what interested him in the German composer. It was certainly not the music, still less the poetry (in private, Maragall remarked that "As a poet, Wagner is a blockhead"),[60] but the way his operas fashioned a great system of myth based on the transmission of legend, expressed in an overwhelming, total

art. Specifically, he ended the article by saying: "And this is the one way for us to understand Wagnerism: as the interpenetration of the art and the life of each people."[61] If this idea is fundamental to the elaboration of Maragall's *Visions*, his pieces on the Sagrada Familia constitute, as we have suggested, a kind of extreme case, and extremes, of course—as we shall see—tend to cancel each other out.

The third article to deal with Gaudí's temple, in 1906, is simply entitled "En la Sagrada Familia" ["In the Sagrada Familia"].[62] There are no references to the visionary architect here, and Maragall's attention is focused now on the work, as if he felt a need for one or two clarifications at this point. The first has to do with the way the temple embodies in its form a polyphonic world. "And the temple appeared to me, as always, as it has to so many, like a great ruin … knowing that this ruin is a birth redeems me from the sadness of all ruins; and ever since I have known this construction that seems like a destruction, all

destruction can seem like constructions to me."[63] The power of the temple, then, is a redeeming power. At one and the same time it is uncompromisingly construction and destruction, it wipes away the pain of all differences. Not by annulling them, but embracing them in its sublime growth, in its form, which is the highest expression of all forms. Another phrase makes this quite clear: "Our spirit is wholly committed in the work of that temple." And again: "What is a temple but a place in which everything is filled with meaning, from the stones and the fire to the bread, the wine and the words?"[64] That is the temple: the enterprise that makes things eloquent, that imbues them with value once again.

The fourth and last article Maragall devoted to the Sagrada Familia dates from 1907, and has a meaningful title: "Fuera del tiempo" ["Outside of time"]. This is how it begins: "Every time I pass through the gates of the Sagrada Familia, I experience the same sensation of stepping out of time… From that moment I see myself enter the

precinct in which there appears only one half-formed wing, that has unwontedly emerged from the bosom of the earth where there lies what is lacking of the colossal proportion of the whole."[65] It could be said that Maragall is inventing here new images for the same ideas that we have already seen him express elsewhere, but this simile of the immense wing rising from the earth—which Maragall had already hinted at in the previous article in the delightful metaphor of something taking to the air—has a monstrous quality that we have not seen before. What we have here is no longer a tree or a budding flower but an immense animal that has lain buried and is now awaking. At the same time, in this last article, the architect himself has been made the protagonist, and this has been done in a highly characteristic way. Thus, about half way through his piece, Maragall writes: "What can Gaudí have been like?—people will ask who sleep as yet and still have long to sleep, waiting in the mystery of a distant future. I have that Gaudí now before my eyes, speaking to me intensely stirred by his monstrous conception. —'And with whom would he have spoken?'—And here am I, living also, with him who speaks to me. One of those with whom Gaudí spoke was myself…"[66] The poet, then, not only insists on Gaudí's presence, on the mysterious power the architect has of giving form to—of transforming—the spirit of a whole people, of building the crown of the city, but uniting himself with him, with his strange time, he also insists on an idea he has already suggested: that this place of hope is, for the time being, only accessible to the initiated. Visionary architect and visionary poet await the necessary coming of the people to the place of integration. This waiting of those marked out by destiny, the predestined, makes them feel terribly alone: "The day ended ruddily, away off in the distance, further all the time, and around us all was already darkness, and he told us that at the summit of the Temple, through the open tracery there would enter rays that bathed everything in brilliant light without it being apparent where

they came from. Exactly as in a forest. As in a forest, he repeated with the serene and smiling exaltation of the seer. But to think that neither he nor we will be able to see this wonder with mortal eyes! And I believe that this heightened our delight. Between the vision and ourselves we felt all the gravity of death."[67] The time of the temple is no longer only that of the endless, that of the simultaneous construction and destruction that makes life spring forth forever and finds its consummation in the symbol of earth and spirit, of nature and culture, that is precisely the temple that waits eternally. Now is also a time outside of time, and the awesome black time of death is superimposed on it. The elaboration of the myth seems have given way, almost imperceptibly, to the greatest of nostalgias: the nostalgia for the time of men. Only two years before, in 1905, the images of the mountain as a temple in ruins in "Montserrat" served to exorcize that nostalgia by abolishing time. Now, those images, in being imbued with the "gravity of death," in making mortal the time in which the vision can be contemplated, are filled with nostalgia. Maragall himself makes this apparent: "Those who will see with their own eyes the day on which the wonderful temple shines forth… will be able to envy the vision of these four men who in centuries gone by have thought with melancholy on the same site, but beneath the night, without the cover of any vault." At the end of the article, the twilight in which both the day and the men bid farewell causes the presence of death to be felt also in the monstrous birth that is painfully and silently taking place there: "We departed. In the night air our voices drifted away as if in conversation with spirits outside of time; and the great wing of the now commenced temple, innocent as yet of the sublime proportions to which it will be subjected, stretched out behind us a long time, all bathed in the moonlight, and open, skeletal, monstrous…"[68]

The temple, I insist, has ceased to be a flower to become a monstrous skeletal wing. It is not the blue sky of day but the spectral light of the moon that bathes it. Seven years on from "El templo que nace," its absence has metamorphosed into monstrosity. And, most important of all, the visionaries are alone. Certainly, Maragall had made of some of his personae, condemned to an eternal wandering, solitary, Nietzschean heroes,[69] but the loneliness of which he speaks now is a terrible, melancholy loneliness, a loneliness outside of time; in a word, anachronic. Regarded from this perspective, his last reference to the temple, in the *Oda Nova* two years later, has to be seen in a new light; it fills us with a certain pathos, the result not now of a vision but of a great effort, the effort to believe. Maragall's mythical tree, that enterprise unveiled by a messianic artist, could not take root in the metropolis, which is no longer a city but a commodity, a place of indifference.

But while all this is true, it is not all. Let us not deceive ourselves: Maragall's anachronism, in which Gaudí is absolutely involved, pervaded by a melancholy that he himself acknowledges in his text, should not be thought of as a surrender, as a retreat. If it is an anachronism brought about by force of circumstances, it is also willed, looked for. To be anachronistic is the last role, perhaps the greatest, of the visionary, the supreme expression of the sacrifice that his mission demands of the predestined. Such is the servitude of myth: the initiated heroically undertakes to bear on his own shoulders the faults of society. *Vox clamantis in deserto*: is there any other sign of the true prophet?

### *"The Dream Realized"*

The Sagrada Familia, that temple born amid signs of religious and social catastrophe as an initiative of the most recalcitrant fundamentalism, had been transformed by Maragall's elaboration into Catalonia's great enterprise. That transformation, in spite of the autobiographical nuances with which it is ultimately invested, has, as we have seen, a strongly ideological slant. We must investigate its various strata.

In the first place, the political stratum. In 1898,

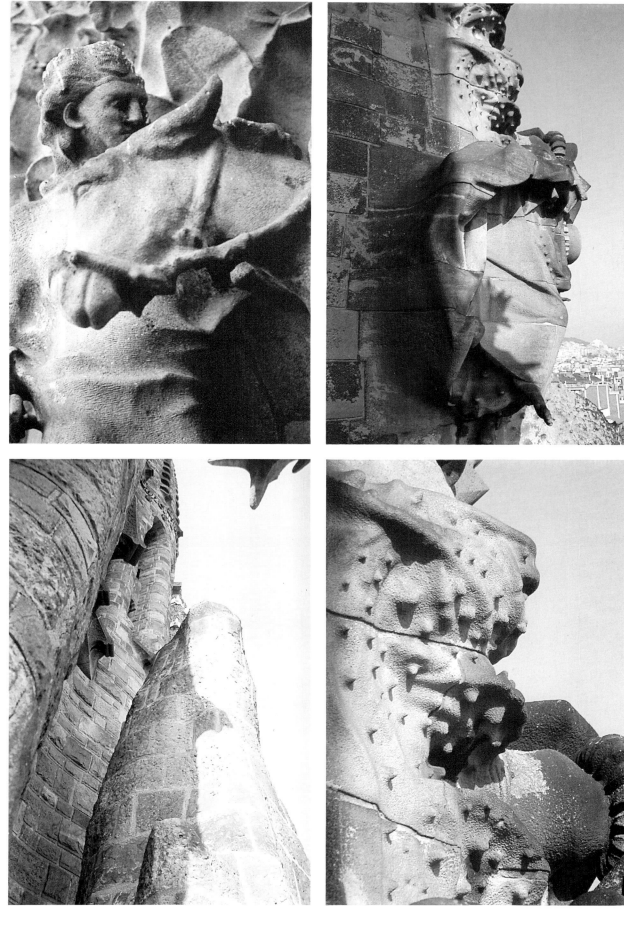

279

*Details of the decoration
of the interior of the Nativity
façade.*

the disastrous war against the United States and the loss of Cuba and the Philippines had immersed Spanish society in a major crisis—political, cultural and economic—that in Catalonia assumed its own distinctive features. The Barcelona bourgeoisie, after failing in their attempt to play a last card—certainly, *manu militari*—within the system of the Restoration by their support for General Polavieja, began to seek new forms of identification. The attempt at intervening in specific affairs of State by means of pressure groups and one-off actions that had been the norm in the 1880s and 1890s now gradually gave way to the adoption of a concrete ideology and a concrete strategic program, developed by professional politicians grouped together in an effective modern party. In the last years of the nineteenth century a number of young nationalists had broken away from the still, in many respects, Romantic Catalanism of the Unió Catalanista to create new and thoroughly pragmatic platforms for action. From these—and especially from the newspaper *La Veu de Catalunya*, of which Prat de la Riba, as we have seen, was editor-in-chief—they had begun to propagate a very concrete political ideology in step with the circumstances: a Catalan nationalism proposed, in the last analysis, as a means of regenerating the Spanish State.[70] That the middle classes who had sought a solution to their problems in General Polavieja should find it now in the nationalist intellectuals of *La Veu* is hardly surprising, and has been studied in depth. The party to emerge from this compromise was the Lliga Regionalista, and in 1901, newly founded, it won its first election victory and put a permanent end in Catalonia to the turn-and-turn-about two-party system instituted by the Restoration. But the Lliga was not the only party from outside the regime to obtain good election results; the Republicans also did well, and what is more, from then until the municipal elections in 1905 they systematically beat the Lliga in every contest. This was to have a decisive influence on the definitive orientation of the Lliga. On the one

*F. de P. del Villar, first project
for the Sagrada Familia, published
in 1882, and general plan
of the final version of 1883.*

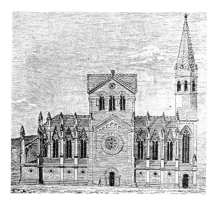

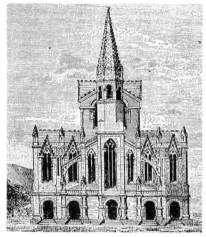

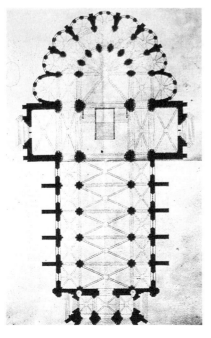

hand, the most radical sector of *La Veu* nationalists, unhappy from the outset at the compromise with the Polaviejist bourgeoisie, blamed the Lliga's poor election results on its increasing shift to the right, the outcome being a breakaway by a dissident minority on the left in 1904, following Alfonso XIII's visit to Barcelona; on the other hand, the fact that the Lliga had emerged in such a short time as the only organized force capable of standing up to the ascendant Unión Republicana caused that swing to the right to become even more marked and irreversible as the Lliga attracted not only groups and organizations from the commercial and industrial bourgeoisie, but also broad sectors of the rural land owning class and the Church. In 1905, after a major propaganda effort, the Lliga once again obtained a good electoral result, winning the Barcelona municipal elections; in the wake of this victory, army officers in uniform attacked and ransacked the offices of the party's two newspapers, *La Veu de Catalunya* and the satirical weekly *Cu-cut*.[71] The Spanish government not only failed to condemn the soldiers' action, it decreed a Law of Jurisdictions that placed under martial law any supposed offense to the Spanish nation or its symbols. All of this provoked a strong reaction in Catalonia, and gave rise to the formation in 1906 of a great coalition of forces ranging from the Carlists on the extreme right to Federal Republican groups: Solidaritat Catalana, which won forty of the forty-four Catalan seats in the general election of April 1907.[72] The Lliga, which in fact led the coalition, was able to place its leader, Prat de la Riba, at the head of Barcelona County Council. From that moment on all of the Lliga's policies were directed towards the single objective of obtaining an institutional platform in Catalonia that would ensure their hegemony to act from that power base at the Spanish level. This was already, in all of its aspects, a State policy that, particularly in the cultural field, was to manifest itself in an unmitigated *dirigisme*. The Lliga developed ever closer links with Maura's central government in Madrid, and in 1909, after the Tragic Week, gave its unconditional support to the brutal and arbitrary repression unleashed by that government: what was at stake, among other things, was a Law of Local Administration that was to allow the union of the four Catalan County Councils and with it a first attempt at regional autonomy. The Maura government fell, however, a few weeks later, and the potential autonomous government of the Mancomunitat was not constituted until 1914.[73] Prat de la Riba became the first president of the Mancomunitat, and the Lliga effectively dominated Catalan politics unchallenged until 1923. But that part of the story need not concern us for the time being.

The rise of the Lliga to political hegemony in Catalonia took place amid strong internal contradictions, shaped fundamentally by the tension between two opposing impulses: on the one hand, the desire to be independent of a Spanish State whose artificiality was seen as the source of all Catalonia's ills, and towards which it manifested a sense of superiority that had distinctly racist overtones; on the other, the need to remain part of that State with which Catalonia was united by so many interests—not the least of these, of course, being that Spain was its principal market—and, consequently, the desire to take control of it, to regenerate it. That tension—at bottom the tension between a radical nationalism of an intellectual cast and the needs of the conservative sectors that saw this as a path to political power—was to find its resolution in Prat de la Riba's pragmatic synthesis: as we have said, the creation in Catalonia of a system of autonomous government that would ensure the hegemony of the new groupings of power as a platform from which they could then impose their influence on the rest of Spain.

Maragall occupies a fundamental place in the ideological elaboration of that specific form of Catalanism, and this is the second stratum we must investigate.[74] Having positioned himself at the opposite extreme from concrete political

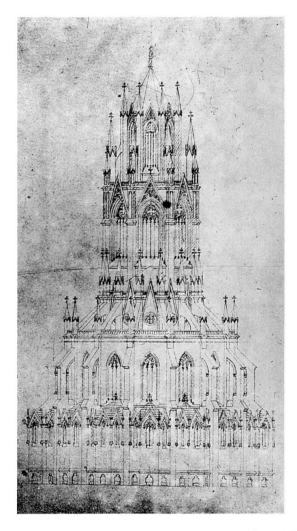

action, Maragall's work represents the most sentimental and irrational aspects of this ideology. His role—at once deliberately adopted by him and bestowed on him by society—is that of its inner voice: the voice that speaks, that sometimes thunders, from beyond the everyday, beyond the contingent, far from any commitment that is not the transcendent commitment to watching over and safeguarding the Catalan values. We looked in the last section at the ineffable quality of his language. But if Maragall's poetry—sublimating the landscape of Catalonia, its people and its things or imbuing the Romantic legends with his vision in an essential search

for the soul of the land—provides an ideal crystallization of the myths that Catalanism called for, his newspaper articles—which were simply another means of expounding the same ideas and, in many cases, prose versions of his poems—gave his voice a far more constant social presence than his poetry did, as well as being more ideologically and politically identifiable.

In 1897 Maragall wrote an article entitled "La independencia de Catalunya." At the height of the colonial war he explicitly outlined the need for Catalonia to be separate from Spain. "Spanish thought is dead," he began, and a few lines further on, "we must quickly rid ourselves of

any relationship to a dead thing."[75] In fact this article was never published, but one which did appear a few months later had a no less eloquent title: "La regeneración política."[76] The tone here is much more prudent, and even the premise has changed: not only does regeneration now seem possible to Maragall, but in some of his insinuations it is not hard to discern an implicit support for the Polaviejist strategy of certain sectors of the Barcelona bourgeoisie.

Only a few months later, however, comes another article, "Hamlet." "The *Hamlet* of whom I wish to speak is the Spanish people," he says.[77] Catalonia, meanwhile, is Fortinbras: "The renovation has begun; let us accept it by fomenting it, and soon Hamlet will start to feel the effects of the transfusion of life from Fortinbras." Finally, "Fortinbras must be lord of Hamlet's Kingdom." Maragall's ideas, then, although expressed in the elliptical manner that comes naturally to the poet, are already perfectly in step with those of the Catalanists on *La Veu* who were soon to go on to launch the Lliga Regionalista. His political articles from the turn of the century all address the same subject: Catalanism is the force that is to renew the Spanish State, and will do so in spite of the fact that, as he wrote in 1902 in "La patria nueva" (a text that almost earned him a spell in prison), to do so it must "vanquish itself."[78] Slowly but surely, Maragall's tone finds itself, becoming increasingly ineffable. It is no longer Maragall but his voice that signs his articles. His attitude becomes considerably more committed from 1904 on, in direct proportion to the strength of his ideological identification with the dominant group emerging from the split in the Lliga, and 1905 and 1906 were to see this dual process come to a climax. On the one hand, Maragall, who had penetrated the legends of Catalonia with his initiate's eyes, sees into the depths of all politics in his articles: he is concerned now not with giving transcendent form to a political program, but with revealing to Catalanism its essential goals, its essential enterprises, situated entirely on the spiritual plane; on the other, Prat de la Riba—who had told Maragall in a letter that the Lliga was not a party but "a people being born"[79]—was attempting to include him—and apparently Gaudí, too, which makes the whole thing even more significant— on the list of Lliga candidates for the 1905 elections.[80] Maragall, however, was by now too convinced of his vocation as a prophet to accept such a concrete political commitment. Thus, just as the emergence of Solidaritat Catalana raised the oracular tone of his writing to a new intensity, the institutionalizing of the strategy of the Lliga on the strength of its electoral success marked the beginning of Maragall's isolation, a process that finally culminated in 1909. In effect, the cultural model designed by the party intellectuals—which was conceived above all as a model of normalization—no longer had any place for Maragall's individualism and irrationalism. At the same time, however, the enterprises of mythic definition that Maragall had undertaken, now dissociated from him, were now established as indispensable ideological objects: the Sagrada Familia would not be the least of these.

I do not believe it is necessary to comment on the close relationship between the subtle evolution of the images, the tone and the aims of the four articles on the Sagrada Familia that we looked at in the last section and the unfolding of the twin paths—that of the political situation and that of Maragall's own activities—we have been considering here. In that jigsaw puzzle, however, we will have to deal with other pieces. The internal circumstances of the construction of the Sagrada Familia had been changing slowly but surely during the last years of the nineteenth century. After the death of Bocabella, in 1892, the supervision of the work was handled in various different ways before being normalized in 1895, when the bishop of Barcelona appointed a Board of Construction for the Works of the Temple. This was to mean, strictly speaking, a despersonalization of the enterprise, responsibility for which was now to be spread more widely, so that the project's identification with partic-

*F. de P. del Villar, project
for the Chapel of the Virgin
in the monastery of Montserrat,
1876.*

ular fundamentalist sectors was on the way to becoming a thing of the past. Thus, while the *Propagador* began timidly to cast its net beyond the ranks of the devotees, the diocese started to take a more than merely formal interest in the significance of the temple. What is more, this had begun to be something more than an idea: as of 1892—by no means fortuitously, the year of Bocabella's death—Gaudí had been deliberately concentrating all of the resources on a single point of the project, the Nativity façade, and in 1899, with the trumpeting angels that crown it already in place, work commenced on the spires.[81] That same year Josep Morgades was appointed bishop of Barcelona. How could the restorer of Ripoll fail to recognize the extraordinary ideological potential of the Sagrada Familia, of that immense portal that already towered more than thirty meters above the empty fields of the Eixample? It is hardly surprising that Morgades should have been the first to press Gaudí to draw up an all-embracing project for the temple, which until then had not even been considered: only the death of the bishop in 1901 released Gaudí from that obligation.[82]

The details, scattered here and there, thus began to take on significance. But there is another important factor to be considered in relation to this change in meaning of the image of the Sagrada Familia, and that is the attitude of Gaudí himself. In 1899, unusually for him, Gaudí made two gestures of a public nature: he joined the Cercle Artístic de Sant Lluc and the Lliga Espiritual de la Mare de Déu de Montserrat.[83] We have already spoken at sufficient length about the first of these institutions. The second, also founded that same year, under the watchful eye of Torras i Bages, undertook in its statutes "to ask of God through the Virgin of Montserrat the total temporal and spiritual reconstitution of the Catalan people."[84] The Church, then, was at the very core of the restoration of Catalonia; we have also examined this in depth, but it is worth adding that, almost inevitably, this strategy started to be expressed in the form of an organized intervention

A. Gaudí, Sagrada Familia,
first sketch.

The project for the crypt
by F. de P. del Villar, of 1883,
and Gaudí's project of 1885.

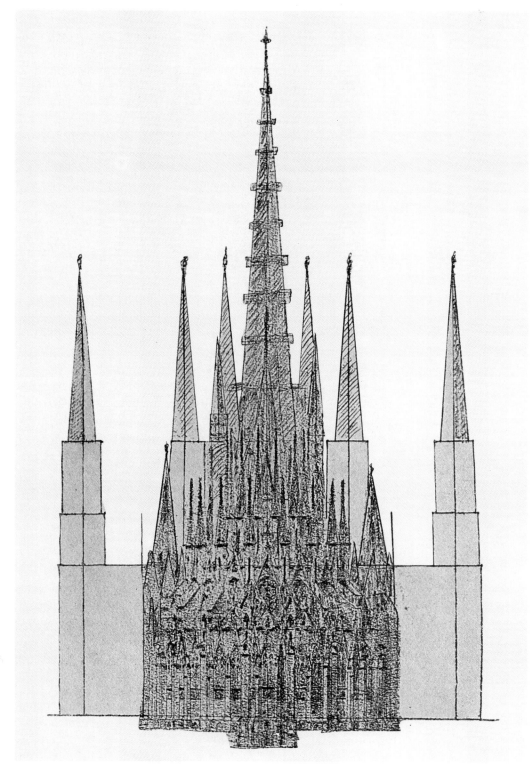

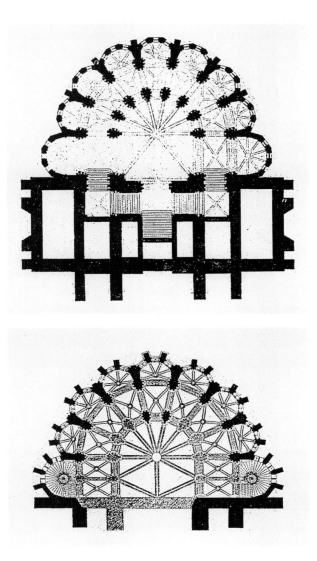

in the public sphere (hence the founding of the Lliga Espiritual, for example) at the very moment that a certain Catalanism, by means of a certain political organization, began its rise to hegemonic dominance. Gaudí, like many other Catalan artists and intellectuals of the day, literally put himself at the service of that Catalanism, and did so, as we have seen, by way of Christian associations that made religion their founding principle. We might also note that the Lliga Espiritual was an important source of clients for Catalan Catholic artists around the turn of the century. In the case of Gaudí these were to include the Figueras family, Lluís Graner, the Lliga itself… Catalanism and a restored Church came together in individuals, places and, to a great extent, works.

But there is yet another factor, impossible to separate from those we have just been considering. If one of the essential conditions for the successful political restoration of the Catalan Church was the marginalizing of the fundamentalist sectors, this strategy did not begin to show tangible results until these very years. Sardà i Salvany, who in 1884 had published the very widely-read *El liberalismo es pecado* and in 1888 had been one of the founders of the Partido Integrista, began to moderate his attitudes; in his 1896 book *Alto al fuego* [*Ceasefire*] he still sought some compromise with the reforming hierarchies, while by the 1899 *Integristas?* [*Fundamentalists?*] he was already resigned, albeit implicitly, to their more radical positions.[85] This situation has a corollary that very clearly reveals its significance: Catalan Catholics were initially divided in their attitude to Solidaritat Catalana. While figures such as Antoni Maria Alcover or Miquel d'Esplugues (both already familiar to us) declared in favor of Solidaritat, in which they saw not a political coalition but the transcendent union of the Catalan people, other sectors, grouped behind Sardà i Salvany, came out against it, accusing Solidaritat of harboring Republicans and liberals and as such casting doubt on its orthodoxy. The attitude of the hier-

*The crypt under construction in an etching published in 1884 and section of the Chapel of Saint Joseph.*

archy, represented by Cardinal Casañas, was to reserve judgment; under the circumstances, this could only be interpreted as implicit support. The most conservative faction then played its last card, inviting Pope Pius X to rule on the legitimacy of that support. His response was elliptical, but it contained an important eulogy to Catalan union: the political interests of the Church, which Solidaritat could defend in the Parliament in Madrid, were at stake.[86] The Church, in other words, needed a Solidaritat Catalana directed by the Lliga Regionalista—and was not Solidaritat the most effective instrument in the Lliga's bid for power?—as much as the Lliga needed the support of the Catholics. That tacit agreement left the fundamentalist groups no alternative but submissive acceptance.

It is not surprising that in such a situation the significance of the Sagrada Familia should change. The coincidence of interests and strate-gies between Catalanism and the Church, the appointment of Morgades as bishop and his desire to see a complete project for the temple, Gaudí's public affiliations and, of course, a construction that imposed on the people of Barcelona both its unexpected size and its eccentric forms… All of these are discrete circumstances, and the extent of their influence varies considerably: no one alone would have been sufficient to change the significance of the temple. What is indeed important, what demands our attention, is that they all presented at the same time, at that particular moment in time: 1898, 1899, 1900. If the Sagrada Familia was becoming an ineffable presence, in 1900 Maragall was beginning to mark out its future course.

In 1906, coinciding with the foundation of Solidaritat Catalana, and with the tension that the new coalition created in Catholic circles, *La Veu de Catalunya* devoted—most unusually—a page

to Gaudí's temple.[87] In the center of the page was a drawing by Rubió i Bellver in which the temple as a whole can be seen for the first time, with its cluster of towers grouped about the great central spire, crowned with a beacon that radiates its beams of light to the four cardinal points. The title could hardly be more eloquent: *El somni realisat* [*The Dream Realized*]. The caption to the illustration makes it clear that the execution of the drawing has been authorized by Gaudí; what Morgades failed to achieve seems to have been effected by the integrating imperatives of Lliga policy. The "prodigious temple" comes, without a doubt, from Maragall, but only in the pages of *La Veu* and only in 1906 could it make its appearance "once completed."

*Style and Order*
In the first section of this chapter we mentioned the 1906 article in which D'Ors accorded to Maragall and the Sagrada Familia, and shared between them, a dreadful but definitive glory.

Definitive, indeed; in that same article, D'Ors returned to a subject he had already touched on in his two or three previous articles: the comparison of the latest collection of poems by Joan Maragall, *Enllà*, with the recently published book by Enric Prat de la Riba, *La nacionalitat catalana*, and the relationship of each with the "generació noucentista." D'Ors makes it very clear that he sees Prat's book as the supreme expression of the political will of the new generation, and, yet more, an indispensable lesson, a guide, while Maragall's book is "the most acute note ... of Romanticism anywhere in the world";[88] in other words, the climactic expression, yes, but of a past time. The science of a political ideal and the irrationality of an aesthetic ideal: that is what these two works, respectively, represent for D'Ors. Prat is great, and Maragall is, too, but while the former is the first of the new era, the latter is the last of the old one, all the more anachronistic the more he strives to inhabit the present. D'Ors affirms this quite explicitly

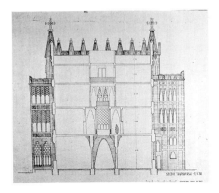

in his conclusion: "A new cycle has now appeared. The era of Romanticism is close to exhausting its meaning among us…"[89] From his pontiff's throne he thus consigns Maragall to the pantheon of history. It is hardly surprising that the Sagrada Familia should go with him: Gaudí's temple, as we have seen, was not itself but what the poet had made of it. Of all the myths he had created, no other had such a great popular impact: it was the only one taken in directly by the eyes, understood by all; it was also the only one to which not only the soul but the hands of each and every one could be effectively applied: a tangible structure.

The Sagrada Familia: Maragall had created a myth that, like the solitary personae of his *Visions*, was obliged to wander forever if was to be a myth. The temple that had constantly to await its altars: this was the only reason for its diffuse existence; this was what raised it to the status of a collective endeavor, beyond time, belonging to the generations of men that in the effort of constructing it over the centuries would be identified as a people. But what we are shown in the January 1906 issue of *La Veu* to which we referred at the end of the last section is the *somni realisat*, the temple completed. In short, a political object and a political objective. How was Maragall's vision to be transformed into such a thing? How could it be made to coincide with the image of tightly clustered domes and spires drawn by "an admirer of Gaudí" that appeared in *La Veu*?

The artist Joan Llimona, the *noucentista* intellectuals Josep Carner and Joan Pijoan and the prestigious engineer Félix Cardellach all contributed short texts to the feature in *La Veu*. All of them issue the same summons, urging people to contribute, regardless of class, regardless of condition, to the construction of the temple, which is not so much a religious enterprise as a patriotic one. This summons is essentially based on two ideas: first, on the genius of a visionary Gaudí directly inspired by God, whose mere ineffable existence would itself suffice to justify it,

to make any sacrifice worthwhile; second, on the optimistic vision of a growing Barcelona, a new city for which the Sagrada Familia is to be, precisely, the new cathedral.[90] Maragall's invention had not fallen on barren ground: Llimona's crude rhetoric and the simplistic parables of Pijoan and Carner are merely versions of it, reduced to immediate, operative terms. But what seems particularly important is the subtle change that these writers have made in the temple's relationship to the city. For Maragall, the temple, wondering at its own growth, was waiting for a different city with the miracle that was taking shape inside it; for the contributors to *La Veu*, on the other hand, the temple is a monument—the greatest of all in terms of divine purpose, no doubt, but when all is said and done a monument—of the new city: such is the scale of the reduction that has been made between the two interpretations. Thus Carner—for whom the Sagrada Familia is "God who desires to live with our prosperity": less a comparison or an image than a simple identification—can describe the city only by means of the formal figure (*malgré lui*, the thoroughly Romantic figure) of "houses around a temple," while Llimona is even more immediate in proposing, amid transcendent allusions to genius and invocations of the divine, the construction of a very concrete system of gardens and squares around Gaudí's building; quite simply, its integration into the city in urban-design terms.[91]

Here, then, for all the mystic overtones with which the *La Veu* writers invest their texts—a mysticism that from this point on unfailingly pervades the greater part of the literature on Gaudí—we are a long way from the diffuse oracular voice of Maragall. And not by chance: we do not go to believe, in effect, that all of this was being written in the air. Since their first election victory in 1901, the leaders of the Lliga had begun to concentrate much of their efforts on a project for the urban renewal of Barcelona.[92] Ideological, political and economic reasons came together in that strategy. In effect, it was not

A. Gaudí, Botines house in Leon,
ground floor plan and view
in its original condition.

A. Gaudí, Episcopal Palace
in Astorga, section of the original
project that was never executed
and present view, with the wall
in the foreground and the cathedral
in the distance.

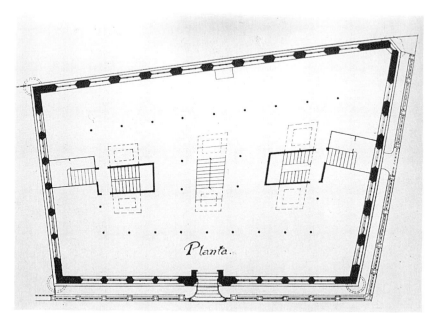

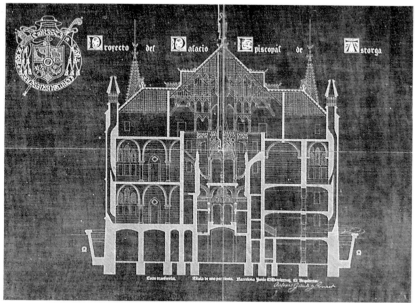

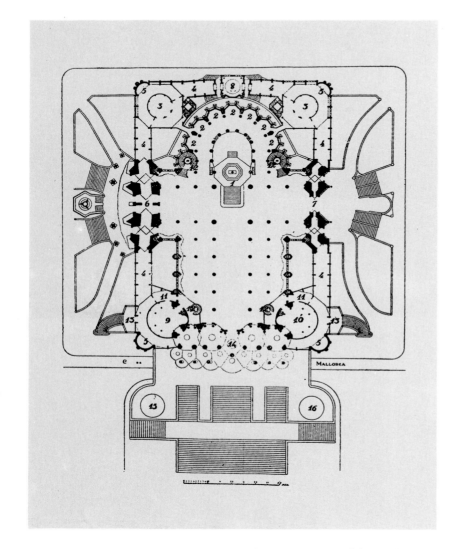

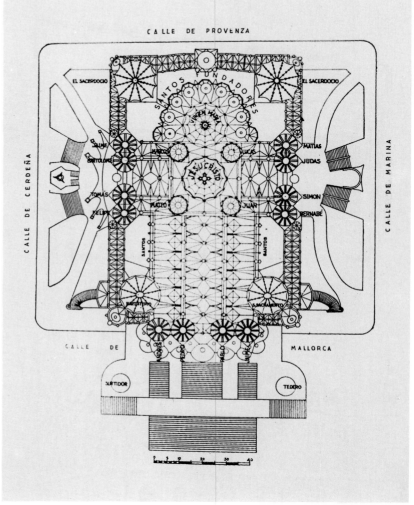

only a question of formally transfiguring a city that, according to the party ideologues, the isotropy of the Cerdà Plan had de-monumentalized and prevented from establishing its image as a capital, but of creating an urban or, more precisely, a metropolitan system that would forge a new kind of relationship between city and capital. In 1903 an international design competition was announced for a new general plan for Barcelona. Of the three members of the competition jury, two—Cambó and Puig i Cadafalch, both city counselors—were leading figures in the Lliga. The first prize was awarded to the

Languedoc architect Leon Jaussely. In May 1905 the City Council accepted the plan, and in August Jaussely received the definitive commission. He finally submitted his project in August 1906, and it was approved the following year.[93] Large urban parks, new railway lines, a new city center, wide avenues cutting across the regular Cerdà grid to create monumental perspectives on public buildings (existing or to be constructed): these were the principal elements of Jaussely's plan, greeted with lavish praise by the Lliga leaders and party intellectuals; a plan that was to be the basis of what came to be known in

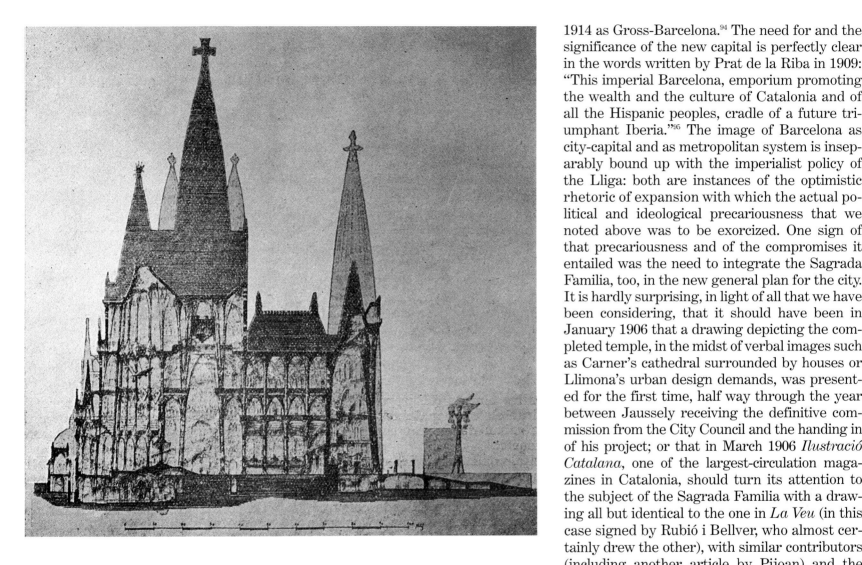

1914 as Gross-Barcelona.[94] The need for and the significance of the new capital is perfectly clear in the words written by Prat de la Riba in 1909: "This imperial Barcelona, emporium promoting the wealth and the culture of Catalonia and of all the Hispanic peoples, cradle of a future triumphant Iberia."[95] The image of Barcelona as city-capital and as metropolitan system is inseparably bound up with the imperialist policy of the Lliga: both are instances of the optimistic rhetoric of expansion with which the actual political and ideological precariousness that we noted above was to be exorcized. One sign of that precariousness and of the compromises it entailed was the need to integrate the Sagrada Familia, too, in the new general plan for the city. It is hardly surprising, in light of all that we have been considering, that it should have been in January 1906 that a drawing depicting the completed temple, in the midst of verbal images such as Carner's cathedral surrounded by houses or Llimona's urban design demands, was presented for the first time, half way through the year between Jaussely receiving the definitive commission from the City Council and the handing in of his project; or that in March 1906 *Ilustració Catalana*, one of the largest-circulation magazines in Catalonia, should turn its attention to the subject of the Sagrada Familia with a drawing all but identical to the one in *La Veu* (in this case signed by Rubió i Bellver, who almost certainly drew the other), with similar contributors (including another article by Pijoan) and the same tone.[96] But what is even more important is to note the extent to which Gaudí himself had become involved: not only did he endorse the drawings of Rubió, but between 1905 and 1907 he drew up a series of projects for the laying out of the area around the temple, evidently with the intention that these should be included in the Jaussely plan.[97] Gaudí initially proposed to create around his built mass an open space in the form of an eight-pointed star, so that the whole of the central spire could be seen from the tip of each point, together with at least two façades at

*Positioning of the column bearing
the genealogy of Christ in 1893,
and a view of the construction
of the façade.*

the same time. A second version of this scheme maintains the basic idea but reduces the number of points to four. Quite apart from the ingenuous technical justifications for this solution put forward by Gaudí's collaborators (it was determined, they said, by the minimal angle necessary for those sightlines), the symbolic aspects of the solution could hardly be more evident; as if radiating a halo, the temple would be in the middle of a star, enclosed within it, but at the same time converted by its virtual isolation into the center of the city. Jaussely accepted the substance of Gaudí's proposal, but replaced two of the star points with a more effective diagonal avenue that monumentally connected the apse of the church with the main façade of the Hospital de Sant Pau, designed by Lluís Domènech i Montaner; another of the great architectural achievements of the Barcelona bourgeoisie, this was a private initiative loaded with ideological significance, also subsumed within the overall strategy of the Lliga.[98] For Jaussely, then, the Sagrada Familia was not to be the center of the city in the symbolic, transcendent sense in which Gaudí imagined it, but it was one of the most important landmarks in his system of perspectives. Indeed Gaudí's temple is shown on Jaussely's definitive plan very close to the new City Hall, next to the buildings of the projected Social Center, in a sector of the Eixample containing numerous public buildings and railway stations; this was in fact to be the future metropolitan center, in which the temple would be the new cathedral. What we have here, then, are two simultaneous and parallel processes, each of which is the formal image of the other, as the Sagrada Familia was integrated, with a well defined role, into the urban structure of the city while at the same time, and for no less concrete motives, as we have seen, it took its place in the political strategy of conservative Catalanism.

However, in this dual process the Sagrada Familia presented a serious problem, namely its style. Right from the start the intellectuals of *noucentisme*, from D'Ors and Carner to Puig i

Cadafalch, had called for a return to classicism in architecture.[99] On the one hand, because for them classicism was synonymous with the order and clarity of an ideal Mediterranean, Greek and Roman, from which Catalonia could trace its roots; it is no accident that these were the years of the discovery—more ideological than archaeological—of the ancient town of Empúries, whose marble columns and mosaic pavements were on more than one occasion to replace Catalonia's Romanesque stones in the construction of a mythology of origins. On the other, because the universal and cosmopolitan value that attaches to classicism is the best line of opposition to Romantic particularism; it is no accident either that these were also the years in which Puig i Cadafalch launched the slogan, perfectly in tune with the metropolitan and imperialist policy of the Lliga, of making Barcelona the Paris of the south.[100] Can we wonder at Eugeni D'Ors' distaste for Gaudí's excessive forms—a distaste he never concealed, as we have seen? Can we doubt that the Sagrada Familia is mentioned in his column only because it is implicitly recognized, as I have tried to show, as Maragall's creation? Or, only apparently in another order of things, that Gaudí and his architecture were to become, from more or less the fifth year of the century, one of the favorite targets of Barcelona's satirical press?[101] Certainly, short of Maragall's metaphors, images and poetic license, it was no easy task to accommodate the actual architecture of the Sagrada Familia within those political and ideological programs. The task was attempted in two ways: the first, inaugurated by Rubió i Bellver and endorsed by the impartial and authoritative opinion of Félix Cardellach, was that of justifying the temple in terms of Gaudí's technical originality in the matter of structures. Gaudí's "deformed forms," parabolic sections and striated surfaces were presented as the culmination of the essential course followed by architecture down through the centuries.[102] Thus in 1915, in the *Album de la Sagrada Familia*, published by the Asociación

Espiritual de Devotos de San José in five languages, a text evidently supervised by Gaudí
himself detailed the technical achievements of
the architecture of the temple, which "has dispensed with flying buttresses and arches, the
two great and constant concerns of architecture
since its origins, accentuated in the construction
of the magnificent medieval cathedrals."[103] This
culmination of architecture, then, was being
achieved in a field that, however unique and
essential—and thus definitive in its structural
innovations—it was in the eyes of the master
and his acolytes, must have seemed very limited
to the *noucentista* intellectuals: that of construction in stone and, even more specifically, the construction in stone of religious buildings. What
was more, quite apart from its anachronism, this

justification was too specialized, of little impact
in a popular campaign such as the one being
built up around the temple on the basis of the
reduction of Maragall's fantasy. It is hardly surprising that it has always been architects—and
architects of Gaudí's circle, who worked with
him on the temple—that have defended it so
tenaciously over the years. What was needed
was a less partial interpretation, one more directly related to the style of the work, to that
viscous exuberance that the people of Barcelona
saw each day, flowing like lava on the Nativity
façade: this was what had to be exorcized. It was
Joaquim Folch i Torres—without doubt the principal and most official mouthpiece of what we
might call the artistic ideology of *noucentisme*,
initially by way of his articles on the arts page of

*La Veu de Catalunya* and then from his position as director general of Barcelona's museums—who took on the mission of constructing a new and equally totalizing interpretation of the Sagrada Familia: the second way.

As early as 1906 there was a short article in the issue of *Ilustració Catalana* devoted to the Sagrada Familia, signed by J.F.: I do not believe there can be much doubt, taking into account the content and the style, that its author was Joaquim Folch.[104] In any case, this article sets out for the first time to provide a justification of the Sagrada Familia both in its own right, as a style, and as part of the urban development of Barcelona, and to do this in some kind of a systematic way, equally remote from the religious mystifications of Llimona and from the fervor of Carner or Pijoan. The article starts with an image of a Barcelona that is not growing or being developed in a material sense so much as rising up out of its own ashes: "the flight of the revived eagle that, after a long time unnerved and sick, launches itself into the spaces it had not yet mastered." That great revitalized Barcelona that in its renewed ambition aspires to being everything is bubbling with projects, "the hot spring of our concerns."[105] The Sagrada Familia is one of these, or rather, is the culmination, the material synthesis of them all. The form in which J.F. expresses this idea could hardly be more meaningful: "Let us suppose, then, that this fever for glory, this desire for greatness, this set of aspirations, are gathered together in a concretion of forms so as to offer themselves sculpturally to our eyes, and there suddenly springs forth an immense, colossal monument, a gigantic temple that could cover under its spans the most daring Cathedral in the world, a poem in stone, twin brother of the most wonderful constructions, in which we could read on each pillar an eternal song to immortality."[106] The images—the temple that springs forth, the poem in stone—clearly come from Maragall, but the meaning here is quite different. On the one hand, Maragall's spiritual dimension has been reduced here to a

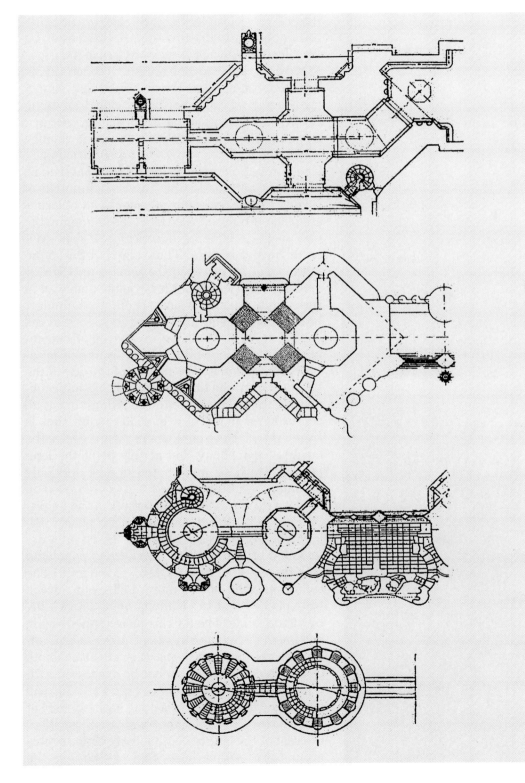

description of specific plastic forms that are presented as such to the physical eye of the body rather than to the eye of the soul: J.F. speaks quite explicitly of a concretion. On the other hand, and this is especially important, the Sagrada Familia comes into being as a result and natural conclusion of the aspirations and desires of the city that grows unceasingly: the true origin of the temple is thus obscured, and Gaudí's work is now shown as organically linked to the new history of Barcelona, without a past of its own. Setting on one side the terms in which the author refers to the architect (God's envoy, a mystic and a visionary),—terms that, thanks to Maragall, had become commonplace—and the no less explicit account he gives of the destiny of the temple as the work of the "great Catalan family" of "rich and poor, old and young," what this natural monument of the resuscitated city needed was, as we have said, an explanation of its style, above all from the moment that J.F. presented it so stridently to his readers' eyes. The disorderly cascade of forms of the Nativity façade is subtly but insistently conflated in the text with the disorder of the unfinished work itself, of the fabric in construction. However, it is the architect who has the mission of putting an end to all this confusion: "And yet no one doubts that the person responsible for dispelling the shadows from that chaos has on his brow the light that dissipates them and in his arm the strength sufficient to raise the incomparable building." What is more, it is in that very chaos in which Gaudí's infinite forms merge with the elements of the work still in construction that the secret of its ultimate order is found, an order that has a very precise aspect: "there throb the inspired notes of a composition destined to astonish men."[107] For the first time a solution is suggested, then, to Gaudí's apparent disorder, to the infinite dispersal of the elements and the forms of his architecture, to the luxuriant irreducibility of his style: its order is that which is conjugated beyond variety, it is the order of the polyphonic.

Interior view of the oculus
of the lantern and the rose window
on the Nativity façade.

Several years later, in 1910, having recently been appointed editor of the arts section of *La Veu*, Joaquim Folch i Torres was to use the pages of the newspaper to give definitive concretion to this suggestion. The article is entitled simply "L'ordre":[108] it could hardly be called anything else when its purpose was to normalize, once and for all, the architecture of the Sagrada Familia within the confines of a *dirigista* cultural policy. The starting point of Folch i Torres' article is, of course, scholastic: the Thomist definition of Beauty as the "splendor of order" and of Order as "place of repose." Also from the beginning the text seeks to adhere, didactically, to very concrete formal images. Thus the rhythm of the universal order is set by "the arms of the Creator open on the Cross," but it is visible above all in the infinite variety of life: "From the humblest to the most elevated…; from the waters to the stones, by way of all the mysteries of decompositions and crystallizations; from the creatures that populate the depths of the sea to the birds …; from the tiny insect to the gigantic animals … from the reptile to the flying bird … all are ordered notes of a glorious hymn that is raised up …" Here once again, then, we have the image of polyphony, and at this point the long passage we have just quoted in part suddenly becomes concretely focused: "… as are raised up in glory these stones of the temple of the Sagrada Familia."[109] What, then, have we been reading: a joyful representation of nature or a description of the Nativity façade, also populated with insects, fish, reptiles, birds and plants? The confusion could not be more deliberate: "it will be explained that the Nativity door is as if Life, by virtue of her love for this most glorious man, had given birth to her symbol." After such a conclusion, the rhetorical question about order in Gaudí's work cannot help but be expressed with a certain defiant, admonitory fury: "Who will dare to say that Order is lacking in the symbol of all ordering?"[110] Consistent with that question, the rest of the article does no more than revolve around an ineffable idea, that of Gaudí as the

*Details of the bell towers and view
of the apse from the interior
of one of the towers.*

arm of God, and a demand, that of giving an extended, non-restrictive interpretation to the concept of order: in this context the references to Ruskin or to the spiritual elevation and the social organicism of the Gothic are nothing but expected clichés. Only in the last paragraph does the educational slant of the article take on a concrete form once more. Folch compares the attitude of the Greek architects who built the Parthenon with that of Gaudí. With the forms of their architecture the Greeks, Folch says, strove to pronounce these words: "Everything rests here for eternity." Although the words pronounced by his work are different—"Everything is resurrected with the birth of the Lord"—what Gaudí has done is no different from what those architects did: ordering the forms so that they may speak. The last lines of the article read: "The diversity between the forms of the Parthenon and those of the Sagrada Familia is found not in the elements that they had at their disposal and those that our architect has at his, but in these two words.[111] There could not be a more insidious ending. The difference between the two temples, Folch tells us, is in their dedication, pagan or Christian, more than in their actual forms or in the attitude of their architects: an implausible classical or, rather, Mediterranean—in the mythologized sense, charged with resonances, that *noucentisme* gave to the word—Gaudí is thus invoked. Only with difficulty can subsequent interpretations shake off the persistent idea that Folch introduces here almost without being noticed, in the most unobtrusive way. The idea's effectiveness down through the years, however, is beyond doubt. Another article by Folch, written many years later on the occasion of Gaudí's death, expresses the matter very plainly, reducing it, once again, to the formal image.[112] Folch compares the Greek temples, dedicated to the gods, but having as their point of departure "the human eye and the human intellect," with the Gothic cathedrals, full of details inaccessible to the eyes of men that "only the angels can see," and concludes: "They are two concepts, but the

Greek is the more fitting, and to this Gaudí turned."[113] The paradox of making Gaudí more Greek than Gothic is necessary to give a concrete conclusion to the old insinuation: "The temple is a homage to God, and is the man who must understand the expression of this act of homage. As a result, the order, the measure, the proportion, the part describing historical figures, must be related to man. Let us flee from the monstrous to move on the only base possible in this world: human reason."[114] What else was Folch doing here, in effect, but bringing reason—political reason—into Gaudí's work? The Sagrada Familia has thus been definitely trivialized. But is not Maragall's vision the one real victim of this trivialization? Perhaps the possibility of such processes was present in Gaudí's work from the start, and it is there that we must look for it.

### The Great Cathedral and the Architect's Little Hut

Certainly, as we have seen, Gaudí was not unaware of the different ways in which the Sagrada Familia was being incorporated into the system of myth and even more into the politics of turn-of-the-century conservative Catalanism. The drawings by Rubió i Bellver in *La Veu* and in *Ilustració Catalana* were done, as we specifically remarked, under Gaudí's supervision, and Gaudí himself drew up the various urban design proposals for the area around the temple that were presented to Jaussely. Gaudí essentially arrived at that interest and that commitment by the path of religion, following the guidance of a Church that, as we have seen, established as the principal strategy in its program for the Christian reconquest of society the original identification between its own restoration and that of the Catalan nation. In such circumstances the temple can only have, for Gaudí, an apologetic, pastoral significance, and in it—even more rigorously, if possible, that in other works—the seamless, uncompromising identification between architectural order and liturgical system

*Decoration of the walls
and the lantern of the Rosary
chapel.*

is the end pursued. This was for Gaudí the only full synthesis, truly reached: any other would be an illusion, a phantom.[115] At the same time, however, the myth of the temple as Maragall had outlined it in his articles had, as we have seen, made Gaudí's genius a commonplace of all the subsequent interested interpretations. The ineffable, necessary quality of the temple as collective work has been established by God Himself through Gaudí, who is a visionary, a mystic, a prophet. We have seen time and again how those words came to be used, slowly but surely, and with ever greater insistence from 1905 on, to refer to Gaudí. This was, of course, not only one of the means of sublimating the work in political and religious terms but a way of justifying, in a time of order and normalization, its strident and extravagant aspects. Gaudí was also slowly but surely convincing himself of that transcendent role: of being God's envoy, His chosen one among his people. For a person who, as we have seen, had always had a strong sense of his own exceptional qualities it could not have been too difficult to arrive at such a conviction, which by 1910 or so had taken the form of an exemplary renunciation of the world. But if in the writings of the *noucentista* intellectuals and the propagandists of the Church the genius of the architect, his touch of the divine, was the surest guarantee of the transcendent and necessary significance of the temple, for the architect himself this would obviously be a source of conflict, the contradiction that fed his own bedeviling ghosts. Let us try, then, to look at the work from close up.

When, late in 1883, Gaudí was put in charge of the Sagrada Familia it was already more than a year since construction of the crypt had commenced. The foundations had been dug and, to judge by contemporary drawings and photographs, the construction of pillars and walls had almost reached the height of the capitals. The project had been designed by the diocesan architect, Francisco de Paula del Villar. There is no denying the conventionality of its neo-Gothic

303

language, ingenuously overlaid with ideologically inspired Romanesque or Byzantine touches, but it was not without a certain grandeur. In effect, in the successive phases of the elaboration of his project—drawn up in the brief period of little more than a year—Villar had moved from a bad, smaller-scale imitation of the basilica of Loreto to a great temple whose apse, bristling with pinnacles almost forty meters high, served as the base for a great lantern rising more than eighty-five meters above the crossing and a spire on the façade that in some versions reached a height of a hundred and twenty-five meters. That, at least, is what Gaudí found: a euphoric project that grew with each successive elaboration, apparently without limits. The optimism of the project, however, was not matched by the reality: the crypt, to which Gaudí devoted himself almost exclusively after taking on the direction of the work, was not completed until four years later. However, so long a period gave him time to outline an alteration of Villar's project—and of the parts already constructed—that was absolutely exemplary, definitive: that moderately-sized crypt was to become an authentic laboratory, not only for the Sagrada Familia, but for all of Gaudí's architecture of these early years.

In Villar's project the crypt coincided exactly with the chancel of the temple, reproducing its form: a central space under a vault whose ribs converged on a single keystone, surrounded by an ambulatory with side-chapels. There was to be direct access to the crypt from the temple by way of a great flight of steps that occupied practically the whole width of the central nave. From the nave, then, both altar and crypt, one on top of the other, were visible at the same time. This was evidently a plan based on a traditional model—a model found in several Gothic churches in Barcelona, notably in the cathedral. Considered in this light, Gaudí's intervention is surprisingly heterodox. In the first place he eliminates the great flight of steps in favor of two lateral accesses set in the place of the first two chapels of the ambulatory, while the place of the flight of

steps is taken by five chapels, those in the center containing the main altar. The crypt has thus been oriented in a direction contrary to the temple: a far from negligible inversion of meaning that is simply a herald and a symbol of those that were to follow, the first and most important with respect to the virtual space that the crypt occupies. In Villar's project, in keeping with an almost unvarying tradition, it opened, as we have seen, into the interior of the temple, but remained closed and concealed from the exterior; in Gaudí's project we have exactly the opposite: a wall and five chapels are interposed between the nave and the crypt, which at the same time literally turns its back on the temple, while making itself quite remarkably visible on the exterior. In effect, Gaudí excavated a deep moat around the crypt that allowed the total height of its walls to be appreciated from the outside; what is more, he cambered its vault to create a ring of arches that, rising above the ambulatory, let abundant light into the central space. The specific treatment of these arches is especially significant: springing directly from the capitals of the pillars, with the moldings that frame them virtually superposed on the walls of the ambulatory, they demonstrate their structural independence of the walls, which are suddenly interrupted by a vertical line, without moldings, pierced by the luminous opening of the large window. The ribs of the vault thus have the fleshless appearance of a skeleton standing in the midst of a remarkable luminosity; the ambulatory, on the other hand, remains dark under the weight of a wall that seems to be there for no other purpose, behind the small openings between the pillars.

There is no need to recall that at the same time as he was constructing the crypt of the Sagrada Familia, Gaudí was also working on the pavilions for the Güell estate. We have seen there how the discontinuous procedure, the paratactic montage of elements that Gaudí deploys in his composition, gives rise to points of radical dematerialization: on the corners, in effect (in other

words, where the tectonic tension of the building is virtually at its greatest), the walls do not articulate with one another, do not turn, but are split by deep vertical breaks. The material has literally disappeared from these points. We need only observe the exfoliation to which the walls of the Casa Vicens are subjected or the way the heavy inverted Mudéjar crown floats above the tower of El Capricho on its slender metal supports to perceive that the dematerialization to which Gaudí submits his architecture is not entirely unforeseen or sporadic, but lies at the very heart of all his work. But we have already spoken of all this at some length. What is of interest to us here is the change in degree that this operation underwent in the laboratory of the crypt. What, in effect, was the result of Gaudí's alterations to Villar's project? This might be described as a paradoxical concentric system in which each ring is not an expanded version of the one before but, in a sense, its annulment.[116] We have, in the first place, a central area in which the replacement of the walls by the void between the cambered ribs lays bare the structure of the vault, whose single keystone is thus left floating in a strangely luminous air; a little below this, however, ten thick fasciculated pillars seem to support not the vault, which sustains itself, but the gloom of the ambulatory, from which the barely glimpsed space resembles a courtyard; finally, on the exterior, a deep moat prevents contact between the walls of the crypt and the earth in which it is buried. Dematerialization, then, of an interior transformed into mere air, a void radically separated from the darkness, the dense and heavy darkness that surrounds it like a ring; dematerialization, too, on the exterior, where the void of the moat establishes a protective distance with respect to some walls that we do not see as rising from the earth we walk, but from some lower stratum, harder and deeper.

Dematerialization, void, protective distance: in the obsessive concentricity of the crypt Gaudí seems to pursue something that, ghost-like, constantly escapes his grasp, or disappears before his hand can even touch it. The moat allows us to see but not to touch the walls; the dark mass of the ambulatory surrounds the radically voided central space: an Annunciation, sculpted in the single keystone of its vault, has made it disappear as stone; the gilded stars that seem to have spangled the robes of Mary and the Angel are the last resonance, so paradoxically silent, of that air.

Gaudí's space is a void space. It is no longer merely a question of making the material disappear from the corners, but of dematerializing the very core of the architecture.

Gaudí's crypt is in fact a void center surrounded by another void: the moat that protects it. Between the two, only the ambulatory—where the people walk—has gravity and matter. Gaudí seems to want to protect the air from human hands: the center is void because, as a center—in other words, as an immobile, transcendently interior unity—it must not be trodden.

But over and above the character of the crypt itself, it seems to be this sense of the sacred condition of the architecture, manifested in the ineffable necessity of its form, that directly determines all the projects Gaudí carried out before the end of the century. The laboratory for the Palau Güell, begun in 1886; for the Episcopal Palace in Astorga, in 1887; for the Theresan convent school, in 1888, and even for the Casa de los Botines in León, designed in 1891, was undoubtedly the crypt of the Sagrada Familia.

We can set aside the Santa Teresa convent school,[117] with its interior voids, like contracted cloisters, exhibiting in their obsessive sequences of diaphragmatic parabolic arches the solitude of walls that are simply superimposed in perspective, but can never articulate with one another, and with its exterior corners, topped by schematic towers with no base, that have been voided to accommodate the floating presence of the emblems of the order: disappearances enough to make us think that the traditional explanation of this disturbing building as an interpretation of Theresan interiority can only be a simplification. We can also set aside the Botines house,[118] the compactness of whose presence is given the lie by the way the walls disappear in the sharpest corner, beneath the highest of the four towers that delimit these, and, above all, in the surrounding moat and the grilles that prevent its being approached, fortifying it and paradoxically transforming it into an untouchable apparition emerging out of the depths of the earth. What is presented in these projects as the fragmentary application (at times mechanical and to a certain degree adulterated) of the problems and themes of the crypt of the Sagrada Familia is brought in the Palau Güell and the Episcopal Palace in Astorga to paroxysmal resolution. We have already commented sufficiently, in considering the Palau Güell, on that *axis mundi* that literally voids the whole building from the ground up, pregnantly converting it into a sacred foundation; let us look briefly now at the Episcopal Palace in Astorga.[119] Standing by the cathedral and the city wall, it seeks, first of all, to match their weighty antiquity: the passage of time that has not only stained the stones of these two constructions but also, especially in the case of the wall, conferred on them the density of that which has survived and overcome it. A defeated temporality that has managed only to scar but not to cast down their stones: this is what the cathedral and the wall present, and what the Episcopal Palace seeks to represent. The moat that surrounds it, revealing the great socle, below the earth trodden by men, on which the rest of the building is supported, is the principal mechanism of that representation. It ensures that the angular towers and the corners of the Palace's volumes are seen as something that emerges from deep inside the earth and thus manifests its complicity with that earth. So much does the building weigh that it has had to thrust down into the ground to find a place for its foundations: like the Palau Güell, so too the Episcopal Palace will remain forever immobile, set fast in the earth of an instantaneous eternity. And

also like the Palau Güell the whole building has been voided internally, from the entrance hall with the staircase to the immense space beneath the roofs, where the walls have ceased to be opaque and, replaced by a great system of wooden lattices, simply reveal the air that passes through them. However, the perfect identification that the Palau Güell establishes between the axis of the building and the *axis mundi*, that contraction of physical strata and cosmic strata concluding in the star-studded vault and the sun of its oculus, is not repeated in Astorga: the section shows that the building does not emerge from the depths of the earth but is supported on its own walls, making the moat a mere artifice. What is more, the void axis of the Episcopal Palace takes the opposite road to that of the Palau Güell: while the latter concludes in the luminous *unicum* of the oculus, the former is dispersed in the multiple filters of the lattices of the roof; while the latter is voided in order to reveal itself, the former suddenly materializes in the strange cylinder on the exterior supporting the figure of the angel, solidifying to let itself be seen. But, how are we to compare the situation of the Palau Güell with that of the Episcopal Palace in Astorga? In the first, as we have seen, ideological project and architectural project are quite uncompromisingly one: a single thing. We are well aware, on the other hand, of the endless obstacles, misunderstandings and difficulties of all kinds that Gaudí had to deal with in constructing the second, which was in addition so physically distant. And this, above all, is what Gaudí's architecture cannot overcome: physical distance between itself and its architect. The Episcopal Palace in Astorga is, in this sense, merely architecture: lacking flesh and blood, it is dead, and, indeed, will never be born.

But precisely for this reason it reveals better than the Palau Güell the ghosts that the laboratory of the Sagrada Familia crypt has let loose. That obsession with creating concentric rings of pure air, in which the material always disappears in favor of the mysterious hardening of the air,

clearly reveals the two directions in which Gaudí's architecture moves. One of these directions stems from its conviction of the existence of the sacred, expressed in the empty core of its architecture: walls and moats are, in this case, veils that hide from the eye what must not be profaned; the other direction, that of the temptation of the center, the pursuit of which discovers, in each wall and each moat, an end that is always postponed. The architecture, then, although it produces effects, cannot summon up truths.

But the crypt of the Sagrada Familia is more than just the laboratory in which Gaudí would have tested the effect of certain mechanisms later applied in part in the Theresan convent school or the Botines house, or amplified with the truth in the foundation of Eusebi Güell, or frustrated in the paradoxical stripping away of the Episcopal Palace in Astorga: it is also the model for the functioning of the whole temple.

In 1893 Gaudí seems to have begun to give definitive form to an overall scheme for the plan of the Sagrada Familia, although in fact a complete plan was not published—in the *Propagador de la Devoción a San José*—until April 1917. A series of changes, some of them minor and others not so minor, gave rise to the definitive plan published by the Asociación Espiritual in 1929—more than two years after Gaudí's death—drawn up on the basis of his last sketches and the great plaster model whose construction he had patiently directed in the workshop in the temple. What was the result of so long a process of elaboration? A Latin cross structure of five naves, completed by an ambulatory which in contrast to the naves has side-chapels opening off it. Only when it began to grow—in the form of the plaster model, for example—did the conventionality of the plan begin to be lost. In effect, the arborescent pillars, the tremendously elevated parabolic sections and, above all, the vertiginous voids created by the lanterns devoted to the Evangelists, to Mary and to Jesus, towering above the crossing and the presbytery in very high, narrow sections and

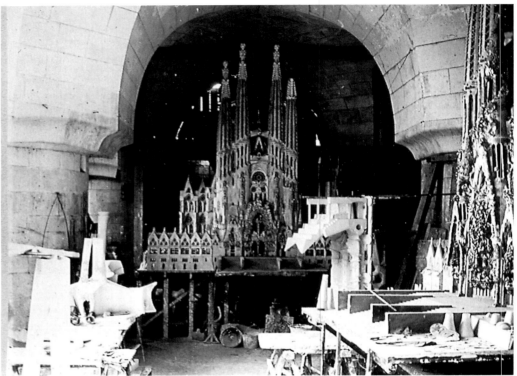

concluding the system of bell towers on the façades, seem not to belong to the diagrammatical plan we have just described. It is evident that while this embodies the model of the Gothic plan that the books of Viollet-le-Duc had established as canonical, as the very category of style, the section, with its series of domes and its piling up of volumes on the exterior, is based—for all that it transcends these with a much greater lack of inhibition than we find in the plan—on Byzantine models.

A very concrete, paradigmatic longitudinal type—a *schema*, in fact—and a delirious amplification of a diffusely sensed centralized model over which there lingers, on the crossing itself, the shadow of the quincunx; right from the start, probably in accordance with the architect's own intentions, this result was interpreted as the achieving of a synthesis, that of the centralized plan and the longitudinal plan: a synthesis that, having been obtained in the temple, could only be seen by Gaudí and his collaborators as literally the conclusion of something that the architecture had been pursuing for centuries—the elimination of the contradictions between the world and its representation, its symbol, and the absolute coincidence of those three things in one: the temple.

In the *Album* of the Sagrada Familia to which we referred above we read: "All this makes the Temple of the Sagrada Familia the first Christian temple whose project develops in an integral organization within the most complete unity the symbolic and artistically representative thought of the spiritual content of our religion. It is developed integrally and organically because Gaudí makes his architecture symbolic through the similarity of the representations he confers on the major components of the Temple: through the structuring, in other words, of the theological concepts and the doctrinal body; integral because all the other arts help and serve the same ideology of the symbolisms. It has unity because it follows a complete plan in its doctrinal exposition and neither mixes thought or concepts nor distorts or twists these. On the exterior is distributed the catechismal and apologetic imagery that without our noting it raises us to the Christian truths in order to lead us into the contemplation of the supernatural world we will see in the interior."[120] There is no need to insist here on liturgical issues—that liturgy understood as being in itself the finest, the highest of artistic expressions—or on the theory of the submission of the arts to the liturgy: these are subjects we have discussed at sufficient length elsewhere. In any case, the text of the *Album*, drafted in large part under Gaudí's personal supervision, marks no more than an increase of degree in the intensity with which these matters are treated: that provided by the concrete example of the work itself, so purposively directed, so identifiable. The Jesuit Ignasi Casanovas, in his speech on "L'art en el temple" delivered to the Congrés d'Art Cristià in 1913, referred to the "universal mirror of Life, of Death and of Eternity" that are the medieval cathedrals, clearly affirmed this amid references to and quotations from Huysmans: "those of us who, with our own eyes, see reborn all the ancient splendors, enhanced with a new luminosity, in this wonder of the spirit that is the triumphal arch of the Sagrada Familia, seem to have the right, and even the duty, of perceiving this great synthesis of the Christian temple."[121] The world, its representation and its symbol, I must repeat, find their synthesis in the temple, but this occurs, according to the passage we have just quoted, not as the product of a will—that of the architect—but ineffably: the temple cannot help but represent a world that is necessarily symbolic. Everything in the temple serves a single ideology: it is hardly necessary to recall here how Casanovas, at that same congress, generically defined the temples as "monuments of dogma, supremely rich in ideology."[122] In other words the architect is not a will, but the third element in a catalysis: only thus the results can be identical to themselves,

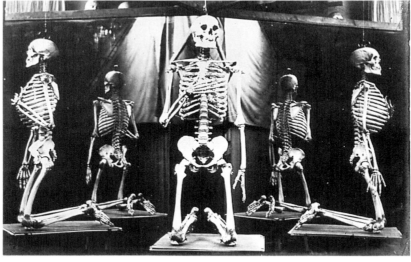

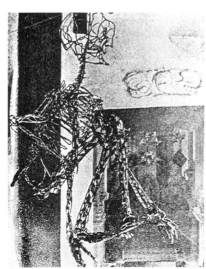

without adulterations, without dilution; and only thus is the architect transformed into a visionary, a prophet.

To the ideological unity we have seen described in the passage from the *Album* cited above merges seamlessly with an architectural unity now envisaged in its more formal aspects. A little further on we read: "Gaudí achieves architectural unity. The basilica form gives the interior of the temple of the Sagrada Familia the elegance of its alignments and the grandeur of its space, and the cupular structure of the crossing and the apse gives it the unity of volume that the basilica plan of itself would not have achieved: the combination of the cupular structure governed by the proportion and the coordinated connection between the vaults, without distortion to the volumes, confers the perfect structural solution. To this interior architectural unity there corresponds on the exterior the ordered agglomeration and distribution of masses, governed by the verticality that, as a law of internal equilibrium, moves within the most perfect mechanical truth and unity, since the real result of

the various mechanical projects—that is to say, the flection—does not distance it from the desired truth."[123] "The desired truth": those last words may perhaps mean something more than their writer intended. A desire is not, in fact, the achievement that has been so insistently described. Architecture—and Gaudí knew this well, as we have seen—for all that it creates effects, cannot summon up truths. In that desire the ghosts reappear. Because despite the obsessive manifestations we have transcribed here, this explanation of Gaudí's project for the temple looks more like an addition, a summing, than a synthesis. Between the schematic, conventional basilica plan and its dense upward development in vertiginous towers, domes and spires there is no correspondence; we have already suggested this, but it is easy to deduce even from the description quoted from the *Album*. The cupular structure, this tells us there, gives the whole the unity that the plan alone would have been unable to confer. The exaggerated Byzantine development of the fabric does not, then, stem from the plan, but is obsessively oriented at remedying its impotence. It is there, in the formal excesses that the prolonged time of the project seems to carry to the utmost extremes, that the silenced will of the architect, his resolve as much as his servitudes, emerges. In other words, his pathetic desire for truth.

We have already noted the paratactic character, the summation of surpassed quotations, of Gaudí's architecture: it is, precisely, its will to interpret the truth that surpasses them. We will not be surprised, then, at the vertical overlapping that takes place in the general plan of the temple, nor that the architect's obsessive revising of this should come to be the principal theme of the project: what else could we expect of a work that sought to meet so many demands? The absence of synthesis effectively engenders its own undoing, prejudicing unity, prejudicing the center. Thus, using the same mechanism we have seen him apply in the project for the Palau Güell, in the project for Astorga and, indeed, in the crypt itself, Gaudí surrounds the temple with an exterior processional cloister that constitutes the bounds of the sacred precinct. The resulting image is absolutely spectacular: the ceremony itself. The processions would circle around the temple, the immobile center whose complexity seems thus contracted into a nodal, totemic immediacy. At the same time, however, that concentricity, converted by the processions into radiant ritual splendor, also has a profound impact on the materiality of the plan, in which the mass of the façades is, in effect, divided longitudinally: a void has been created between the interior and the exterior that renders their difference unbridgeable, all the more so because this is only intelligible as a path opposed to that of the façade itself, to its identification as such. In passing through the façades the cloister is transformed into a moat that once again separates us from the center, the center that here more than in any other work by Gaudí allows itself to be seen even as it shows itself to be unreachable: to go round it is, literally, a penance.

On the Nativity façade, the only one constructed, this division is revealed in its most terrible, its most physical, aspects. On the exterior, covered with figures of animals, birds, plants and trees, the stone, as in Maragall's description, seems to blossom. We might scrape at it and find roots under the plants. The effect does not, however, run very deep. In the interior everything seems to have contracted in a diagrammatic geometrical crystallization. If these are two facets of the same world, they are also an image of the impossibility of that world being one in the transcendent, creational sense of the word. Here, in effect, as if denying the order that Folch i Torres invoked, we find not polyphony, not even variety, but simply parallelism, duplicity. A double world, with two faces: could there be a more immediate image of the absence of synthesis? Its immediacy, however, is bound up with its excess, with the quantity of stone that represents it: the irreconcilable doubleness thus fails to be what it might have been—terrible—to re-

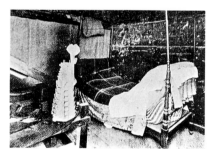

veal itself instead as something simply elemental or even conventional. The great manger cannot be, however much its hagiographers might wish it, *biblia pauperum*: in a strange vicious circle, its very quantity, inflated to compensate for its insignificance, prevents this. It is merely an unconvincing piling up of empty symbols, whose vacuity has to be exorcized by the letters, the words and the fragments of Holy Scriptures that cover the façade. The immense slab of the Nativity façade, rising up in the absence of the rest of the temple, in the middle of a still half-deserted Eixample, lifts up its two faces as an unexpected emblem of silence, but, as we can now see, of a banal silence. And, as we have already suggested, it is that immense banality that, beyond all its dramas, makes the temple usable.

In the interior, however, these traces take on a different tonality: that of the intensely private pain of wounds. It is only the architect who sees himself in them through his own architecture, always missing: the oculus that opens onto the window of the crossing, barely glimpsed but present, amid so much abundance, as the most paradoxical image of what is missing; the spiral stairs that ascend the towers, without a shaft, turning in an obsessive helix around the void they themselves have created; the stripping away of the upper parts of the bell towers, in which everything seems to have been expelled from the center to the skin, which, converted into ribs and scales, has proved similarly incapable of retaining the material; and finally the mullion, in which the column that bears the fillet with the genealogy of Christ has had to be surrounded by a thick wrought-iron grille. The most profound of origins, although simply written, is also out of reach: could there be any better image of Gaudí's architecture as a whole?

It has always been said that the Sagrada Familia was the goal of all of Gaudí's work; that everything he did was an experiment directed towards finding solutions to the problems of the temple; that in it those solutions attained their own transcendent value.[124] However, what there is of meaning in Gaudí's work—or rather, what has a *raison d'être* in the concrete drama of his own terrible vision—seems to be lost in the excessive quantity of the Sagrada Familia; and, vice versa, while the material liquefies and the things of the world—of this world and the next—disappear from his work, leaving terrifying voids, in the Sagrada Familia the liquid is contained within molds of the reality and the voids are filled with symbols—also empty, but present. It is hardly surprising that Gaudí should have ended up concerning himself solely with that great manger, devoting to it a will that time would slowly but surely transform into something sinisterly ingenuous: in the edifying commitment of the Nativity façade, art ceremoniously represents its own renunciation.

It is not the material that is lost there—on the contrary, in spite of the wounds that we have already mentioned, it flourishes and manifests itself in incontinent profusion—but its substance: that is the trivialization. But in the paradox of that anodyne transcendency, might not Gaudí have felt free, at last, of his ghosts?

From Maragall's mythical interpretation to the political, ideological and urbanistic commitments of the Lliga, to the re-established representation of the Church, to the normalizing order of Folch i Torres' representation, to the continuous interpretation of its excessive presence in a new city: in the midst of all this, in the midst of so many demands, the architecture of the Sagrada Familia must, necessarily, be irrelevant, insignificant in itself. Size is not in this case greatness but, I repeat, need. For this reason the autobiographical material so present in all of Gaudí's work seems here to have stopped just short of giving form to the stone, or, more accurately, of dissolving it. Only in those places we have mentioned—the oculus on the great window, the non-existent shaft of the spiral staircase, the stripping away of the upper part of the towers, the column bearing Christ's genealogy—does the hand of the architect manifest itself, erecting barriers between

*Front cover and inside page
of the pamphlet printed in tribute
to Gaudí in 1926, and the architect's
funeral on June 12 of the same year.*

*En Gaudí combregava cada dia...*

itself and what it strives to reach or, when it reaches it, making what it touches disappear. Gaudí, however, seems to have wanted to replace that autobiographical absence that the temple as political object imposes on his architecture with his own presence, with the presence of the architect. From 1914 on Gaudí began to interpret radically the road that Maragall had predicted for him—and that he had counseled. He turned down every private commission, slowly but surely, even physically, shutting himself inside the temple. The photographs of his workshop, its walls lined with papers, with plans and prints, with those models of the details of the façade scattered on the floor, with the great models on the tables, with the plaster casts of the sculptures—heads, legs, arms, whole bodies—hanging from the ceilings: those images are, quite simply, terrifying. Terrifying, too, are his methods: methods that begin with the photograph of a man, an animal, a plant, a form, surrounded by mirrors—converted into the impotent center of their own images and penetrated by the most terrible of eyes, the mechanically inquisitive eye of the camera—and continue with an embodying—strips of cloth soaked in plaster draped on wires—that, detained in its own mold, has also foregone being incarnation. And terrifying, too, at last, is the image of his bed, photographed after his death, still giving a sensation of the impression of his body, in the middle of that studio, in the middle of all of that. But what makes these pictures terrifying? Without a doubt, the image they offer us of a life of mortification. What other way out was left to Gaudí? If the Sagrada Familia was a symbol, so was he. He symbolized the architect of the temple, and as such he lived and died in the little hut under the great cathedral. As guardian of the temple and its secrets Gaudí revised the banal quantity and the disappearance—finally so real—of his own architecture. That is what, until his death on June 10, 1926, two days after being knocked down by a tramcar, his poverty represented.[125]

[1] For all that follows on the chapel of St. Joseph and the Josephists of Montserrat: J. de C. Laplana, "La capilla de Sant Josep de la Basílica de Montserrat. Notes històriques i artístiques," *Montserrat. Boletín del Santuari*, no. 9, May–August 1984, pp. 34–40.

[2] *El Propagador de la Devoción a San José*, VI, 1872, pp. 16–17, cit. in J. de C. Laplana, op. cit., pp. 39–40.

[3] Ibid., p. 40.

[4] Ibid., p. 39.

[5] For a rapid overview of the Catalan Church in the nineteenth century, see: J. Massot i Muntaner, *Aproximació a la història religiosa de la Catalunya contemporània*, cit., pp. 11–13; id., *L'Església catalana al segle XX*, cit., pp. 13–23, both with bibliography. On the relations of the Spanish Church to the policy of the Restoration see the bibliography cited in chapter 5, note 12. See, too: F. Lannon, *Privilege, Persecution and Prophecy. The Catholic Church in Spain*, Oxford, 1987; W.J. Callahan, *Iglesia, poder y sociedad en España*, (1984), Madrid, 1989. See, too: J. Bonet, C. Marti, *L'integrisme a Catalunya. Les grans polèmiques (1881–1888)*, Barcelona, 1990.

[6] Published in 1884. On Sardà i Salvany: R. Rucabado, *Sardà i Salvany, apóstol social*, Sabadell, 1944.

[7] Published in Spanish and French in 1851. E. Valentí comments on D'Ors' reaction against Balmes with the presence in the background of Donoso Cortés (*El primer modernismo literario catalán y sus fundamentos ideológicos*, cit., p. 93, no. 33).

[8] On Bocabella see: A. Masriera, "De la Barcelona ochocentista: D. José María Bocabella," *La Vanguardia*, September 2, 1921; F. Ratera, "Aspectos de nuestro Templo: D. José María Bocabella y Verdaguer, notas bibliográficas," *Templo*, no. 89, September 1954, pp. 6–11; id., "Biografía del fundador, II," *Templo*, no. 90, June 1955, pp. 2–11. See, too the data offered by J. de C. Laplana, op. cit.

[9] This is the basic source for the data on this work by Gaudí and on the people associated with him. It was published from 1867 to 1936 and from 1943 to 1948 as *El Propagador de la Devoción a San José*, and after 1948 as *Templo*.

[10] On J.M. Rodríguez see the obituary published in *El Propagador...*, no. 3, February 1879, pp. 67–74, and also: L.A. Beltrán, "El culto a San José, el P. José M. Rodríguez Mercedario, y la génesis del templo de la Sagrada Familia de Barcelona," *Obra Mercedaria*, no. 41, January–March 1955, p. 3; F. Ratera, "Fray José M. Rodríguez Mercedario," *Templo*, no. 94, March 1959, pp. 10–11; R. Rucabado, "Nuestro primer director, P. José M. Rodríguez, padre del Concilio Vaticano I," *Templo*, no. 97, January 1963, pp. 8–9.

[11] On Father Mañanet and J.M. Rodríguez: F. Ratera, "Dos grandes josefinos," *Templo*, no. 98, March 1964, p. 10.

[12] Classic general studies of the Sagrada Familia are: I. Puig-Boada, *El temple de la Sagrada Familia*, Barcelona, 1929, and new edition, Barcelona, 1979; C. Martinell, *La Sagrada Familia*, Barcelona, 1952. Gaudí had worked with F. de Paula del Villar as his assistant in 1876, on the project for the side-chapel of the Virgin of Montserrat. For the

range of opinions concerning this collaboration see data and bibliography in: J. Bassegoda, *El gran Gaudí*, op. cit., pp. 115–16; also: T. Torii, *El mundo enigmático de Gaudí*, cit., vol. II, pp. 23–25. On Villar: J. Bassegoda Amigo, "Francisco de P. del Villar y Lozano," *Anuario de la Asociación de Arquitectos*, Barcelona, 1903, pp. 443–46.

[13] Cit. in I. Puig-Boada, op. cit., p. 10.

[14] Data, transcriptions of documents and bibliography in: J. Bassegoda, *El gran Gaudí*, pp. 209–45.

[15] M. de Castro Alonso, *Colección completa de las Encíclicas de S.S. León XIII*, vol. I, Valladolid, 1892, pp. 109ff. See, too, chapter 5, note 12.

[16] *El Correo Catalán*, March 17, 1885, pp. 1–2.

[17] On all of this see chapter 2, note 58; chapter 3, note 86.

[18] E. D'Ors, cit., in *Obra Catalana Completa*, cit., p. 184. We referred to this text at the end of the last chapter.

[19] A late instance of this interpretation: I. Solà-Morales, "Una arquitectura abierta a la especulación," *La Vanguardia. Cultura y Arte*, October 17, 1989, p. 2.

[20] The three cases in which D'Ors cites Gaudí by name are: "Palmons al balcó," (1909), *Obra Catalana Completa*, cit., pp. 1004–05: "It is strange that Gaudí should not yet have thought of exhibiting the palms in some unexpected form, and more logical than usual"; "Ocasió única," (1909), cit., pp. 1161–63, where referring to the bar Els Quatre Gats, D'Ors mentions a whole series of *fin-de-siècle* artists and architects, including Gaudí and Puig i Cadafalch, and a series of literary "fashions," in a note that "attempts" modernism in the same essential terms in which it was interpreted many years after, with enduring historiographic fortune, by J.F. Ràfols, *Modernismo y modernistas*, cit.; and "Gener," (1910), cit., pp. 1233–35: "They say that don Antoni Gaudí, our famous architect, believes in the principle that it is impossible to draw up plans, and that it is far better to trust to the inspiration of each night. But if Gaudí has his own particular methods, we have ours."

[21] C. Cucurella, *El Montserrat del espíritu*, vol. I (sole), Barcelona, 1953.

[22] On this work by Jujol, see: *El Santuari de Montferri. Nostra Moreneta al Camp de Tarragona*, Montferri, 1929; (various authors), *La arquitectura de J.M. Jujol*, Barcelona, 1974, pp. 101–03; "Josep M. Jujol, arquitecte. 1879–1949," *Quaderns*, cit., pp. 183–87.

[23] The origins of this expiatory temple on the summit of Tibidabo, overlooking the city, date from the visit to Barcelona by Don Bosco in 1886. It was begun by replacing a small chapel in 1902, and the crypt was inaugurated in 1911, the same year in which the Eucharistic Congress in Madrid declared it a National Expiatory Temple. It is worth studying the possible "Spanish centralist" significance of this temple in relation to the also expiatory Sagrada Familia, which by that time was totally integrated into the mythology of political Catalanism. See: *Templo Nacional Expiatorio al Corazón de Jesús en la cumbre del Tibidabo. Su historia, prodigio del amor*, Barcelona, 1943.

[24] *Templo Nacional Expiatorio...*, cit., pp. 6–7. The architect was Enric Sagnier (1858–1931), the elegant but sober designer of some major official buildings (the Customs House and the Palace of Justice in Barcelona, for example) and religious buildings (the college of Jesus and Mary and the Salesian college) who was ennobled by Pope Pius XI in 1923.

[25] See: S. Rubió i Tudurí, *El funicular del Tibidabo*, cit.; J. Mínguez, *Salvador Andreu*, cit.

[26] We need only think of churches such as the impressive Vistabella, by Josep M. Jujol, built between 1918 and 1923—(various authors), *La arquitectura de J.M. Jujol*, cit., pp. 94–96; "Josep M. Jujol, arquitecte. 1879–1949," cit., pp. 158–68, which includes a memoir by Jujol himself)—or his side-chapel of the Carmelite order in Tarragona, built around 1919 *(La arquitectura de J.M. Jujol*, cit., pp. 96–97), or other far more discreet works such as the church of Sant Miquel de la Roqueta, built in 1912 by Joan Rubió i Bellver, or, of the same, the project of the *templo* of Santa Eulàlia de Provençals, around 1925 (I. Solà-Morales, *Joan Rubió i Bellver i la fortuna del gaudinismo*, cit.).

[27] We have already referred to the millennium of Montserrat on various occasions. See chapter 1, note 101.

[28] Now in J. Maragall, *Obres Completes*, cit., vol. II, pp. 685–87. This article was translated into Catalan with some minor changes and published in a book of selected reading for children: *Tria*, Girona, 1909 (*Obres Completes*, cit., vol. I, pp. 750–51).

[29] J. Maragall, op. cit., p. 686.

[30] J.Ll. Marfany, *Aspectes del modernisme*, cit., p. 115. I base my analysis on these lines by Marfany, cited above.

[31] See chapter 3, note 46.

[32] J.Ll. Marfany, op. cit., p. 113.

[33] Ibid., p. 111, who refers in turn to A. Terry, *La poesía de Joan Maragall*, Barcelona, 1963, pp. 87–106.

[34] J.Ll. Marfany, op. cit., pp. 113–14. We have already referred to these issues. See chapter 3, note 23.

[35] Ibid., p. 115.

[36] J. Maragall, op. cit., p. 687.

[37] Cit. in M. Esteve, *Biografía d'Enric Prat de la Riba*, Barcelona, 1917, p. 33, and by J. Solé-Tura, op. cit., p. 215.

[38] J. Maragall, "Una gràcia de caritat...!," *Obres Completes*, cit., vol. I, p. 706.

[39] Ibid., p. 705.

[40] See: A. Colodron, "La huelga general de Barcelona de 1902," *Revista de Trabajo*, no. 33, 1972, pp. 67–119.

[41] See: J. Romero-Maura, "*La Rosa de Fuego.*" *El obrerismo barcelonés de 1899 a 1909*, (1974), Madrid, 1989; J.B. Culla, *El republicanisme lerrouxista a Catalunya (1901–1923)*, Barcelona, 1986.

[42] On this painting by R. Casas see: F. Fontbona, "Es pot parlar de pintura social en el cas de Ramón Casas?," *Actes del Colloqui Internacional sobre Modernisme*, cit., pp. 79–92, with the reply by J. Castellanos, pp. 100–02.

[43] On the Semana Trágica the basic source is still: J. Connelly Ullman, *La Semana Trágica. Estudio sobre las causas socioeconómicas del anticlericalismo en España*, cit.; and in relation to Maragall: J. Benet, *Maragall davant la Semana Trágica*, Barcelona, 1964.

[44] Maragall's initial project for this "new" ode to Barcelona must be seen in relation to the Verdaguer ode: the changes were to come later. In *Obres Completes*, cit., vol. I, pp. 175–77. On the poem, see: A. Terry, *La poesía de Joan Maragall*, cit., pp. 164–70, but above all for the links with the Semana Trágica, see: J. Benet, op. cit., pp. 95–99.

[45] J. Maragall, op. cit., p. 175.

[46] Ibid., p. 176.

[47] Ibid., p. 176.

[48] Ibid., p. 177.

[49] The articles were: "Ah! Barcelona...," *La Veu de Catalunya*, October 1, 1909, and "La iglésia cremada," id., December 18, 1909, although between the two there was another article, "La ciutat del perdó," censored by *La Veu de Catalunya* with the direct intervention of Prat de la Riba and not published. On the history of these articles and Maragall's relations with Prat and with Torras i

Bages on this matter see: J. Benet, op. cit., pp. 95–217; but also: J.Ll. Marfany, foreword to J. Maragall *Articles polítics*, cit., pp. XXI–XXIII. The three articles are in *Obres Completes*, cit., vol. I, pp. 775–82.

[50] J. Maragall, *Oda nova...*, cit., p. 177.

[51] In *Obres Completes*, cit., vol. II, pp. 614–15.

[52] J. Maragall, op. cit., p. 614.

[53] Ibid., p. 614.

[54] Ibid., p. 615.

[55] In relation to this, see: J.Ll. Marfany, *Aspectes del modernisme*, cit., pp. 135–38.

[56] J. Maragall, op. cit., p. 615.

[57] J. Maragall, "Una gràcia de caritat...!," cit., p. 707.

[58] Ibid., p. 705.

[59] In *Obres Completes*, cit., vol. II, pp. 114–16. The other article devoted to Wagner the same year is "Una malla inteligencia," id., pp. 112–14.

[60] Cit. in J.Ll. Marfany, *Aspectes del modernisme*, cit., p. 144.

[61] J. Maragall, op. cit., p. 116.

[62] In *Obres Completes*, cit., vol. II, pp. 726–28.

[63] J. Maragall, op. cit., p. 727.

[64] Ibid., pp. 727 and 728.

[65] In *Obres Completes*, cit., vol. II, pp. 768–69.

[66] J. Maragall, op. cit., p. 769.

[67] Ibid., p. 769.

[68] Ibid., p. 769.

[69] In relation to this, see: E. Valentí, "Joan Maragall, modernista i nietzscheà," *Els clàssics i la literatura catalana moderna*, cit., pp. 123–51, and J.Ll. Marfany, *Aspectes del modernisme*, cit., pp. 135–38, in addition to the articles on Nietzsche that Maragall wrote in 1893 and 1900, since reprinted in *Obres Completes*, cit., vol. II, pp. 136–39.

[70] See especially: I. Molas, *Lliga Catalana...*, cit., pp. 27–45; B. de Riquer, *Lliga Regionalista: la burgesia catalana i el nacionalisme (1898–1904)*, cit.; id., *Regionalistes i nacionalistes (1898–1931)*, Barcelona, 1979.

[71] See: R. Lezcano, *La ley de jurisdicciones, 1905–1906*, Madrid, 1978; and, in general: S.G. Payne, *Los militares y la política en la España contemporánea*, Paris, 1968.

[72] On Solidaritat Catalana: J. Camps i Arboix, *Història de Solidaritat Catalana (1905–1910)*, Barcelona, 1970; B. de Riquer, "Les eleccions de Solidaritat Catalana a Barcelona," *Recerques*, no. 2, 1972, pp. 93–140.

[73] See: J. Camps i Arboix, *La Mancomu-

*nitat de Catalunya*, Barcelona, 1968; (various authors), "La Mancomunitat de Catalunya," *L'Avenç*, no. 3, June 1977.

[74] On Maragall's ideological development, see: J.Ll. Marfany, *Aspectes del modernisme*, cit., pp. 122–85, and above all the already cited foreword by Marfany to J. Maragall, *Articles polítics*, cit., drawn on here.

[75] In *Obres Completes*, cit., vol. I, pp. 739–41.

[76] Ibid., vol. II, pp. 575–78.

[77] Ibid., vol. II, pp. 580–82.

[78] Ibid., vol. II, pp. 653–55.

[79] Cit. in R. Olivar Bertrand, *Prat de la Riba*, Barcelona, 1964, p. 409.

[80] This proposal made to Gaudí, and his supposed friendship with Prat and Cambó, are discussed in J.F. Ràfols, *Gaudí*, cit., p. 142.

[81] All of the data in the bibliography on the Sagrada Familia already cited and in the successive issues of the *Propagador…*; see, too: id., *Album del Temple Expiatori de la Sagrada Familia*, Barcelona, 1915 and various subsequent editions, published in five languages; and id., *Album record a Gaudí i al Temple Expiatori de la Sagrada Familia*, Barcelona, 1936.

[82] Explained in this way by F. de P. Quintana, "Les formes guerxes del Temple de la Sagrada Familia," in *Album record a Gaudí i al Temple Expiatori de la Sagrada Familia*, cit., p. 112.

[83] The significance of this has been judiciously commented on by J. Castellanos, "Un arte al servicio de la edificación social," cit.; id., "Torras i Bages i Gaudí," *Gaudí i el seu temps*, Barcelona, cit. On the *Lliga Espiritual*, see J. Massot i Muntaner, *L'Església catalana al segle XX*, cit., pp. 137–49.

[84] J. Massot i Muntaner, op. cit., p. 137.

[85] On Sardà i Salvany see note 6 above.

[86] This controversy can be followed in a series of contemporary pamphlets arguing for and against the active participation of Catholics in Solidaritat Catalana. Among the former: A.M. Alcover, *Conducta política que s'imposa vauy en els catòlichs*, cit. Among the latter: G. Soler, *La Solidaridad Catalana y la conciencia católica*, Barcelona, 1907; L. de Cuenca, *Pro Aris et Focis. Puntos negros de la Solidaridad Catalana. El catalanismo y los partidos políticos católicos españoles*, Lérida, 1909. See F. de B. Moll, *Un home de combat…*, cit., pp. 123–25; J.A. González Casanova, *Federalismo y autonomía en Cataluña*, cit., pp. 185–202; and above all: G. Mir,

"Una polémica sobre catolicisme i catalanisme. A propòsit de Miquel dels Sants Oliver i la crisi de direcció del *Diario de Barcelona*, 1906," *Recerques*, no. 6, 1976, pp. 93–118. See, too: M. Batllori, "El pare Ignasi Casanovas a favor de la llengua i la cultura catalanes," *A través de la història i la cultura*, Montserrat, 1979, pp. 333–50

[87] *La Veu de Catalunya*, January 20, 1906, p. 3.

[88] E. D'Ors, "*Enllà* i la generació noucentista," cit., p. 184.

[89] E. D'Ors, "En resum…," cit., p. 186.

[90] The idea of the Sagrada Familia as another cathedral had taken shape over the change of the century, albeit with a variety of implications and significations. We might recall the title of an 1897 painting by Joaquim Mir in which the poor are depicted against the background of the Sagrada Familia in construction: *La catedral dels pobres*. Mir published other drawings on the same theme, such as *A extramurs*, in *Hispania*, April 15, 1899 (see: E. Jardi, *Joaquim Mir*, Barcelona, 1975; F. Fontbona, *La crisi del modernisme artístic*, Barcelona, 1975, pp. 119–27); and see Sunyol's assessment of the Sagrada Familia as a monument no less indispensable for the city than the cathedral: E. Sunyol, "El Orféo Català," *Hispania*, February 15, 1990, pp. 40–47. See: J. Rohrer, "Una visió apropiada. El Temple de la Sagrada Familia de Gaudí i la política arquitectònica de la Lliga Regionalista," *Gaudí i el seu temps*, cit., pp. 191ff.

[91] J. Carner, "Per a la Sagrada Familia," and J. Llimona, "Manifestacions divines," *La Veu de Catalunya*, cit., both reprinted in *Album record a Gaudí i al Temple Expiatori de la Sagrada Familia*, cit., pp. 162 and 148–51 respectively.

[92] In relation to this, see: F. Roca, *Política econòmica i territori a Catalunya, 1901–1939*, Barcelona, 1979; M. de Torres Capell, *El planejament urbà i la crisi de 1917 a Barcelona*, Barcelona, 1987.

[93] L. Jaussely, *Memoria del proyecto de enlace de la zona Ensanche de Barcelona*, 2 vols., Barcelona, 1903. See, too, the special Jaussely issue of *La Ilustració Catalana*, January 1, 1911.

[94] See: J. Maluquer i Nicolau, "Gross-Barcelona," *La Veu de Catalunya*, March 1, 1914. See, too: F. Roca, op. cit, pp. 27–35, and I. Solà-Morales, "L'Exposició Internacional de Barcelona (1914–1929) com a instrument de políti-

ca urbana," *Recerques*, no. 6, pp. 137–47.

[95] E. Prat de la Riba, "Nosaltres," *La Veu de Catalunya*, April 24, 1909.

[96] *La Ilustració Catalana*, March 18, 1906.

[97] I. Puig-Boada, *El Temple de la Sagrada Familia*, cit., pp. 20–22.

[98] See: *Hospital de la Santa Cruz y San Pablo*, Barcelona, 1930; *L'Hospital de la Santa Creu i Sant Pau, hospital de Barcelona*, Barcelona, 1971; as well as the bibliography on Domènech i Montaner cited above: chapter 1, note 28.

[99] See: I. Solà-Morales , "Sobre *noucentisme* y arquitectura. Notas para una historia de la arquitectura moderna en Cataluña (1909–1917)," *Cuadernos de Arquitectura y Urbanismo*, no. 113, March 1976, pp. 19–34; J.M. Rovira, *La arquitectura catalana de la modernidad*, Barcelona, 1987; J.M. Rovira, *La arquitectura noucentista*, Barcelona, 1983; id., "Architecture and Ideology in Catalonia, 1901–1951," *AA Files*, no. 14, pp. 62–68.

[100] In fact the expression had already been used by Prat de la Riba and by Verdaguer before him. See chapter 3, note 153.

[101] See: J.M. Garrut, "Gaudí en la caricatura," *San Jorge*, no. 37, January 1960, pp. 18–24.

[102] J. Rubió i Bellver, "Dificultats per a arribar a la síntessis arquitectònica," cit., on which we have already commented at length; F. Cardellach, "La mecànica d'en Gaudí," *La Veu de Catalunya*, January 20, 1906, p. 3; and also, for example, D. Sugrañes, "Disposició estàtica del Temple de la Sagrada Familia," *Album record a Gaudí i al Temple Expiatori de la Sagrada Familia*, cit., pp. 100–09; F. de P. Quintana, "Les formes guerxes del Temple de la Sagrada Familia," cit.

[103] *Album del Temple Expiatori de la Sagrada Familia*, cit., p. 25.

[104] J.F., "La Sagrada Familia," reprinted in *Album record a Gaudí i al Temple Expiatori de la Sagrada Familia*, cit., pp. 137–41, from which I quote.

[105] Ibid., p. 137.

[106] Ibid., p. 139.

[107] Ibid., p. 139.

[108] J. Folch i Torres, "L'ordre," *La Veu de Catalunya*, April 7, 1910, reprinted in *Album record a Gaudí i al Temple Expiatori de la Sagrada Familia*, cit., pp. 168–72, from which I quote.

[109] Ibid., p. 168.

[110] Ibid., p. 168.

[111] Ibid., p. 172.

[112] J. Folch i Torres, "L'arquitecte Gaudí,"

*Gasetá de les Arts*, July 1, 1926, reprinted in *Album record a Gaudí i al Temple Expiatori de la Sagrada Familia*, cit., pp. 50–60, from which I quote. See, too, as a minor example that nevertheless contains all of the commonplaces of the interpretations we have commented on: J.M. Casas de Muller, "Del Temple exemplar," *Pindàriques modernes*, Barcelona, 1926, pp. 81–84.

[113] Ibid., p. 58.

[114] Ibid., p. 58.

[115] Ignasi Casanovas wrote: "The artist will always feel the temptation to linger over the facile aesthetic elements of religion … The Christian religion is a way of life, and as such it is either lived in its entirety or it is a pure phantasmagoria" ("L'Art en el Temple," cit., pp. 699–700). The symbolic and liturgical ordering of the Sagrada Familia is explained in: I. Puig-Boada, *El Temple de la Sagrada Familia*, cit.

[116] See chapter 4 for the way this anular system was repeated in the Crypt of the Colonia Güell.

[117] On the Theresan convent school see data and bibliography in: J. Bassegoda, *El gran Gaudí*, cit., pp. 319–25.

[118] On the Casa de los Botines see data and bibliography in: J. Bassegoda, *El gran Gaudí*, cit., pp. 327–32.

[119] See chapter 5, note 52.

[120] *Album record a Gaudí i al Temple Expiatori de la Sagrada Familia*, cit., p. 27.

[121] I. Casanovas, "L'Art en el Temple," cit., pp. 706–07.

[122] I. Casanovas, op. cit., p. 697.

[123] *Album record a Gaudí i al Temple Expiatori de la Sagrada Familia*, cit., p. 27.

[124] This is the thesis put forward by J.F. Ràfols, *Gaudí*, cit., pp. 160ff.

[125] In relation to Gaudí's death see the book published as an obituary tribute: *Antoni Gaudí. La seva vida, les seves obres, la seva mort*, Barcelona, 1926.

## Vanitas and Flight
A "Terrifying and Edible" Architecture

Of all the furniture designed by Gaudí for the Palau Güell, none is so interesting as the small dressing-table.[1] And not only on its own account. It embodies the form and the theme of Gaudí's architecture, or, at least, of almost all of his architecture: in some sense, its scheme.

The form, in the first place. Or perhaps we ought to say, the style. Nothing could be more absurd than to see the curves of this piece of furniture, as some writers have insisted on doing, as a remarkably early antecedent of the *coups de fouet* that characterize Art Nouveau.[2] In fact, Gaudí was not anticipating that hysterical decoration that in Paris or Brussels was to replace the *pompier* style whose obsession with continuity had set the tone of the fin-de-siècle bourgeoisie with a sublimating synthesis pursued exclusively in the forms, with no other break than that between generations. On the contrary, he was taking *pompier* to its limits.

What, in effect, do that divided angled frame, those ballerina legs and that flowing mirror, with their grotesque deformations and rhetorical striving after eccentricity, signify but the last interpretation of those cartouches that did indeed frame mirrors or, more usually, titles and emblems?

There were whole catalogues of such cartouches: those by Babel, by Cuvilliés, by Mondon and by Meissonnier had a very wide circulation, and were drawn and made up in silver by craftsmen such as Josep Albarado of Reus.[3] It is hardly surprising that the tiny, meticulously crafted volutes produced by Albarado, his little angels with palm fronds, his richly gleaming silver banderoles, his painstaking craftsmanship, should resound in the work of two other famous sons of Reus who belong to consecutive generations united, among many other things, by their shared interest in what the Rococo represented: Fortuny and Gaudí.[4]

A representation of the Rococo: at the end of the nineteenth century the Goncourts made that eighteenth-century style the aristocratic style par excellence, the ultimate style, and Goupil,

thanks to the meticulous paintings of his artists—of whom Fortuny was not the least important[5]—placed it in the hands and hung it on the salon walls of the European and American upper middle classes who were eager to purchase a Versaillesque past.

The dressing-table we have been considering looks strange, in some ways, in that great house in which, as we have already noted, the representation is of a different order: that of private property and private wealth converted by myth and symbol into an incarnation of the country itself, and above all, of a property and a just and inalienable wealth: the representation, in short, of a gift condensed in the heat of Renan's ideas into a princely rather than a bourgeois gesture. It does not seem so strange, however, if we remember that it formed part of one very specific place in the Palau Güell; the most intimate space: the boudoir. We are in the presence, then, of a convention. We have already noted in the second chapter that the last of the rooms on the *piano nobile* aligned along the façade was decorated in the *pompier* style: this was precisely the one set aside as a dressing-room for the ladies. Gaudí's furniture thus exercises, together with the Güells' bedroom, a role that is only paradoxically social: like the Hôtel Chanac de Pompadour, for example, so, too, the Palau Güell has cartouches of implausible mirrors in its *petite chambre à coucher*. The public intimacy of the fin-de-siècle bourgeoisie was, without doubt, *ancien régime*: some of Eusebi Güell's children were born in Versailles, and there Picó i Campamar wrote several of the poems with which he celebrated their births for the family.[6] At the same time, what else but that same convention could account for certain of Eusebi Güell's celebrated artistic tastes, as that felt for Francesc Plà "el Vigatà," without doubt the most interesting of the eighteenth-century Catalan painters. Significantly, he painted the frescoes in the Palau Moja, in which the marquises of Comillas, as we know, had their Barcelona residence; a taste that, for example, led Güell to buy and in-

*Dressing-table from the Palau Güell, designed by Gaudí around 1889.*

stall in his house in the Park Güell the pictures from the Sala d'Estat of the Ribera's old *palau*.[7] A celebrated taste, in effect: those pictures, with their stories of Apollo and Daphne, of Adonis and Venus and Mars, had previously been exhibited by Eusebi Güell at the Exposició d'Art Antic in 1902. Joaquim Folch i Torres was still lauding them in 1914 in the pages of *La Veu de Catalunya*: "If the gentlemen of the past called for 'el Vigatà' to paint their principal drawing rooms, it is beautiful that there is at present one such as the Comte de Güell who collects that work with devotion and love."[8] Still later, Miquel d'Esplugues was to write: "With the room by 'el Vigatà' alone ... the Park is transformed into a princely mansion."[9] There can be little doubt, then, of the social value of that style: we need only recall the long series of articles on *L'estil imperi a Barcelona* [*The Empire Style in Barcelona*] published by Raimon Casellas in *La Veu* in 1910, and greeted by the paper's readers as an authentic discovery.[10]

But if the Rococo spirit of Madame Güell's dressing-table is at the origin of many of Gaudí's forms, it is where the princely project does not establish limits that will find its best road to expression. In the town houses of the Calvets, the Batllós and the Milàs, in their façades, in their hallways, in their staircases: it is there that the public anonymity that is the irremediable condition of the bourgeosie must be sublimated at all costs in the excessive form of the ancient baroque. The recourse to the aristocratic style par excellence is nothing other than an attempt to remedy that anonymity. Nothing could be more evident than the fact that it was in Gaudí's urban houses—in those subleased houses constructed on the streets of the Eixample, in buildings that in contrast to his usual practice are secular rather than being elaborated on an essentially religious brief, and not princely, but fatally bourgeois—where the style we are considering here, and Gaudí's own style, takes on its most mundane tonalities. Or, at least, it does so at first, because—not surprisingly—in time

Gaudí's gesture slowly but surely came to oppose itself to that sin of mundaneness. As I say, this is hardly surprising: we have already seen how Gaudí was inclined by nature to disdain all things bourgeois, and it will be well to recall Miquel d'Esplugues' admonition: "In modern Barcelona [... we have] too many bourgeois villas and a shortage of lordly palaces."[11] Here we have one of the keys to the evolution of Gaudí's architecture from the Calvet house to the Batlló house to the Milà house.

Let us begin, then, with the first: the Casa Calvet, designed and built during 1898 and 1899 for the textile manufacturing sons of Pedro Mártir Calvet.[12] In the entrance hall we are greeted by mirrors that do not attempt to conceal with deformations, as the little dressing-table in the Palau Güell does, the conventional disposition of their quadrilobular cartouches. Positioned directly opposite one another, hanging slightly out from the wall and reflecting one another, they reproduce to infinity the rich detail of the lamps mounted on their frames and the sheen of the volutes and wreaths that, as in a small sacrarium by Albarado, crown them. This same model determines the forms: both outward, as in a reverberation, whether in the plan of the balconies and the line of the railings or in the whole crown of the building, topped by two orbs; and inward, in the little columns of the second entrance hall: not only the more conventionally Solomonic but those other, faceted columns with lance-tip motifs that support Ionic capitals whose volutes are duly repeated in the ends of the handrails of the smooth balustrades. Even more precisely, developed around an elevator whose ironwork makes it a tour de force of manual skill there is an authentic baroque baldachin whose formal connection with eighteenth-century Catalan altarpieces, and especially with the work produced by Lluís Bonifas in Gaudí's native Camp de Tarragona, goes beyond what would conventionally be called inspiration.[13] We need only look at the decoration of the side-chapel of the Virgin of Mercy in Reus or the Victory and Sorrows altarpieces

*A. Gaudí, the Casa Calvet*
*in a photograph from 1901,*
*and the mirror in the first vestibule.*

in Valls, all of which date from the 1750s,[14] and compare some of their details with other very specific details developed by Gaudí—for example, the Ionic capitals with inverted volutes,[15] or the penchant for crowns with very tight spirals—to understand how closely the architect had studied that style. A style that pervades every element of the project and culminates, like a wave that breaks and returns to the center, in the rocaille of the miniature garden in the courtyard. Gaudí's faith in those bombastic formal gestures that have their origins in the gilded baroque leads him directly to solutions of an extraordinary immediacy that are quite different from those model treatments we have been considering so far: for example, the way that, according to tradition, he designed—although it would be better to say shaped—the handles and peepholes of the apartment doors by working with his fingers in a mass of soft clay has a great deal of the demiurgic, of the pregnant consciousness of the power to create that only authentic style, overflowing with its own forms, confers. It is hardly surprising that alongside this evocation of the act of the Creator the religious allusions in this building should be, perhaps for the only time in all of Gaudí's work, not exactly light, but certainly superficial: added on rather than integrated into the building. On the one hand, the busts of martyrs that crown the building have a direct and obvious relation with the client: they are his holy patrons; on the other, details such as the cross-shaped door-knocker that beats on a bug are enclosed inside their own ingenuity and, in this particular case, their opulence. But underlying that confidence there are the larvae of crisis: perhaps the place where the constant formal correspondence of the building is most evidently interrupted is in the composition of the façade. In effect, the two gables of the crown determine two axes that nevertheless seem to dissolve when they come down to the first floor; in which everything is structured on a single axis of symmetry determined by the decorative and symbolic concentration of the glazed bal-

cony, and vice versa. It would be naïve and anachronistic to imagine that in doing this Gaudí was seeking honestly to express the interior distribution of the building. We have seen time and again in the previous chapters that this was never one of the postulates of his architecture. On the contrary, we find ourselves once again with that fragmentation determined by an architecture of continuous movements. Here the interruption serves as a warning against a momentary over-confidence that was simply a surrender to the opulence of the style.

A spectacular change begins to take place with the Casa Batlló, built on the Passeig de Gracia in Barcelona between 1904 and 1906 for another important manufacturer, José Batlló Casanovas.[16] The façade of this building, which in reality is based on the remodeling of an existing building, has many points that derive from the Casa Calvet. Some of these, above all the ones that refer to particular details and aspects, reveal a very direct correspondence between the two projects. Thus, for example, the balconies of the Casa Batlló are designed on the same trilobular plan as those of the Calvet house, while the famous balustrades in the form of masks have an immediate precedent in those cast iron balustrades that protect the openings in the Calvet's gables, although these are more faithful to the cartouche that determines their disposition. And again, the little columns of the glazed balcony on the façade of the Batlló house, with those soft palms that divide their shafts, derive from the same formal plan as the shafts with Solomonic facets and lance-tip motifs in the entrance hall of the Calvet house; and finally, at the foot of the staircase that leads to the main floor of the Casa Batlló, the balustrade twists in a spiral around a shaft ending in a ball of glass and a gilded wreath that once again invites us to see in its forms the scepter of a baroque Infant Jesus or the grille of a reliquary. Of course we are speaking only of isolated details, but it is not only these that draw on a Rococo model. A single reference will suffice: the preparatory

*Details of the interior and exterior of the Casa Calvet.*

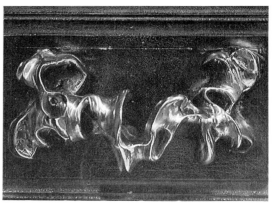

*A. Gaudí, the Casa Batlló, foot
of the staircase and sketch
of the façade.*

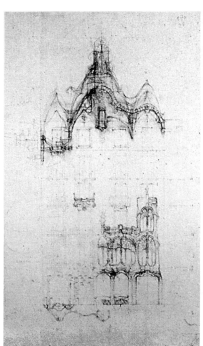

drawing made by Gaudí and his assistants for the remodeling of that façade, the only one to have—miraculously—survived. Here the small baroque forms—balustrades, balls, volutes, rocailles—are manifestly present, not yet subjected to the process of "softening" that, it need hardly be said, was to make them all but unrecognizable in the completed work. We can see, for example, how one of the iron railings on the third floor is perfectly drawn in every detail: in place of the disturbing mask of the definitive work we have a decorative system of leaves and tendrils formally supported by symmetrical volutes. The same thing occurs with the jointing expressed on the ground floor, which alludes to a constructive strength already suggested in the baroque stonework of the Calvet house but that is not present in the Batlló house; with the balusters that crown the glazed balcony, here perfectly drawn and at the same time distorted by the undulating forms of the built work; with the little columns of this same glazed balcony, which in the drawing meticulously conserve their constituent parts or, last but not least, with the stone banderoles that zigzag down its sides, an ornament that links the form of these openings to those of the quadrilobular mirrors of the Calvet house and the mirror of the dressing-table in the Palau Güell, and, indeed, to the model from which they derive: the cartouche and the Rococo *forme rocquaille*. The fine pencil that drew this sketch seems to have delighted in establishing a great number of continuous forms, undulating lines that always conclude in spirals, and although these are still present in the built work they have been reduced to mere vestiges. At this point it is particularly interesting to consider the crown. In effect, in order to remedy the confusion between the axes originating in the gables and the principal axis of symmetry determined by the glazed balcony, which in the Calvet house finally dissolved the hierarchy of the façade, in the Casa Batlló Gaudí extended the glazed balcony the full width of the façade, and crowned it with a pair of smaller glazed balconies on either side of the floor above, this emphatic symmetry effectively focusing attention on the center. He also set a small balcony in the center of the highest part of the façade, above the top floor. Just above this, the undulating roof is basically composed of three symmetrical domes, with the highest in the center cut off horizontally. As yet we see no sign of the bulbous tower that, with a concentrated plasticity similar to that of the right-hand pavilion in the Park Güell or the Torre Bellesguard, was to displace the symmetrical balance; what we do see, on the other hand, is the fine trace of two volutes that, like a great Ionic capital, crown the whole composition on the axis itself. At the same time, the very beautiful coloring of the skin of the façade and its slight but striking undulation can be seen as the extreme form of those stone curtains that, in so many baroque monuments, open onto the great theater of the world. This, of course, brings us to the Milà house: built between 1906 and 1910, also on the Passeig de Gracia and also, like the two previous houses, for a textile manufacturer, Pere Milà i Camps.[17] Here the very long ripples of the façade, or the folds of the capitals of the columns, or the undulating surfaces of the chimneys, nearly always culminate in an obsessive spiral, the final indication that the origin, however remote it may now seem, is in every case the same: that style. We should not run on too far: we are still dealing with details, but precisely with this in mind, we must note one last point here. The source of the undulating arrises that traverse the very long façade of the Milà house from one side to the other is surely the Japanese wave, emblematic of what was held to be the most elegant and refined of exoticisms—and also the most persistent, since unlike those others that were merely picturesque, it profoundly transformed European artistic sensibility—already present, of course, in the eighteenth-century *chinoiseries* and also introduced into the aristocratic and would-be aristocratic circles of Europe by the Goncourts.[18] Certainly, what immediately strikes us in the

*Details of the balconies of the Casa Batlló.*

*The Casa Batlló and on the left*
*the Casa Amatller, by Puig*
*i Cadafalch, between 1898 and 1900.*

Calvet house—something the scholars have tended to marginalize as reflecting a supposedly historicist moment in Gaudí's work, a certain Neo-Baroque—is, in the Casa Batlló and above all in the Casa Milà, flattened and concealed, at times dilating, at times withdrawing into disturbing forms in which volutes and rocailles survive only as a distant impression, albeit as a still noticeable larva, exactly as we find in the fluid mirror and frame of the Palau Güell dressing-table, which is, without a doubt, the contraction into a single image of the extended time of these three houses. In many parts of the Casa Batlló, but above all in the Casa Milà, a layer of soft material has covered everything, only reflecting, here and there, moldings and wrinkles buried under a paste that has flowed over them and suddenly hardened. We have already referred at sufficient length to Gaudí's difficulty with a tempting material. Gaudí had at least two reasons for spreading that viscous mass over the meticulously detailed luxuriance of the Rococo ornamentation: both to expiate his own surrender to the opulence of the style—in other words, to confront the besetting ghost of his artist's vainglory, which we have already considered at length elsewhere; and to castigate a richness that, in the discontinuities of the Calvet house, he found to be different from the gift of God that made the patrician palace a synthesis. Otherwise, why should that richness be so adverse to integrating the sacred symbols into its expression? It was a case, in fact, of castigating that public anonymity that is the fatal concomitant of bourgeois opulence. There is, in the way that Gaudí spreads his flowing material on top of a style transformed into larva, the symbolic resonance of the death of Pompeii. But, let us be quite clear: like nineteenth-century moralism in general (the famous novel by Bulwer-Lytton was read in Spain in a version amended by an anonymous French Catholic, J.R.),[19] Gaudí, too, interpreted the lava as God's punishment of the pagans, not because they were pagan but because turn-of-the-century bourgeois morality

had represented to itself a facet of Antiquity in which Antiquity was a paradise of the senses.[20] They had only to travel close to Pompeii, to the place where many of the treasures unearthed there were kept, to confirm their comforting prejudices about the morality of their own time, and visit the rooms of the *raccolta pornografica* in the Museum of Naples, for example. Pompeii was, in other words, a Sodom, all the more exemplary in that the petrified molds of its inhabitants, contorted by the most sudden agony, were there to be seen with the eyes: this was no fabrication. But this takes us into the very theme of Gaudí's architecture: a few words more, first, on the subject of its style.

It is surely no exaggeration to see a Rococo model in nearly all of these forms of Gaudí's to which we have referred. It is precisely this style, underlying the material in hidden, larval forms, that would have been seen by many of his contemporaries. We shall attempt to demonstrate this with a concrete example: the Comalat house, an apartment building constructed by Salvador Valeri between 1909 and 1911, also in the Barcelona Eixample.[21] It has often been said that Valeri was interpreting Gaudí's forms here, and, in effect, it is striking to see how far the façade on the Diagonal recreates not only the glazed balcony of the Calvet house but, above all, the bone-like columns and the curvature of the balconies of the Batlló house, as well as its crown of greenish scales. These things are obvious: what is surprising, however, is to note how much more closely the form and the detailing of Valeri's Comalat façade reflect the preparatory drawing for the Casa Batlló, discussed above, in which the Rococo molding of the decoration had not been yet obscured and was still clearly visible, than they do the finished result, the house as built, since it was this rather than the preparatory drawing that was Valeri's model. Historians of Barcelona architecture have always concluded this inevitable comparison with the disparaging comment that the Comalat house is "more Neo-Baroque" than the Batlló, and certainly in

*Details of the decoration*
*of the parapet of the Casa Milà.*

the former the volutes, the rocailles and the flowered cartouches that frame letters, shields and openings seem to be directly copied from the drawings of those catalogues we have mentioned—from Meissonnier, above all. Or they can be directly identified with the decoration of those gilded interiors that pseudo-eighteenth-century "frock-coat" domestic painting—by Fortuny, for example—delights in representing. And not only because they derive from these, but also because Valeri, with his eye on Gaudí, stops short of subjecting the ornaments of the style to such punishment in the form of lava, the material liquefied. The borders, the festoons, the banderoles and even the large Ionic volutes that crown the roof were also present in Gaudí's preparatory drawing, in the form of all that the punishment must banish from sight, but Valeri, like so many of his contemporaries (note, for example, the Rococo quality of the details of the Milà house in most of the period cartoons), would quite naturally have seen in the façade of

the Casa Batlló those rocailles that we now, tainted by our prejudiced view of a modern Gaudí, find it so hard to make out. From this point of view, a number of details of the Comalat house could hardly be more eloquent. Thus, in comparison to Gaudí's disturbing, massive and terrible sinuosity, the borders that Valeri draws on the base of the glazed balcony of the extraordinary rear façade are blue waves that in their wake have left ceramic shells on the unexpected mosaic beach. Then there are the drops that fall from the stone, also on that rear façade, dripping and sliding in a joyful representation of water from the smooth rocks on which mosaic butterflies are about to settle, while in Gaudí it is the stone itself that is liquefied, covering the trusting forms it contained with its sinister pasty coating.[22] As we have already said, this is the theme of much of Gaudí's architecture. We can verify this by going back to Mme. Güell's dressing-table. The mirror, like crystal or glass, is the very embodiment of hardness, of that which cannot

*Ceramic and marble* trencadís *on the roof accesses.*

be deformed or molded without being broken or scored, yet in Gaudí's furniture, as if it had returned to a state prior to its cooling, seems to have been converted into viscous liquid. The mirror drips onto the table from the tilted broken frame, forming a puddle that spreads out slowly, with difficulty, as any liquid will do on a flat surface, in all directions, forming a curving globular outline. From its spiraling support the mirror simply falls until it finds a second support on which to rest. The two legs on this side seem to be dancing, trying to shake off the liquid as quickly as possible. The mirror literally pours out of its frame onto the wood of the dressing-table, prompting us to wonder whether this is not another very baroque symbol. That unconscious mirror, overflowing its frame, necessarily undermines the consistency of the face reflected in it, too. It is surely no accident that it should do so when the person reflected is shaving, or applying make-up; is absorbed, in other words, in complacent contemplation of the beauty of a face. And what is such complacency, reflected in the dripping mirror, but a vain and idle emotion? If all mirrors symbolize vanity, none does so better, or more terribly, than this one.

We have seen, then, how the style of Gaudí's urban houses was condensed in Mme. Güell's dressing-table; we shall see now how it also condenses its theme, the theme of his architecture. Liquefaction of the material as symbol of vanity and, in short, of death and the sin it punishes. The theme of this dressing-table is none other than that which informs a baroque *Vanitas*: the *memento mori*. It stands at the same time at the heart of Gaudí's problematic relations with the material, with an untenable material that constantly escapes him, like liquid, slipping through his fingers, or between the folds of his style, leaving nothing behind when it is gone. Certain details of the Milà house may provide us with a very material illustration of this. One of the stone pillars of the main floor is decorated with soft bas-reliefs of Marian symbols such as roses and shells, set among volutes and spirals.

The larva of a rocaille, or, more exactly, of a very naturalistic grotesque, seems to lie just beneath the surface of the stone. The pleasure that the sight of these sweet ornaments gives is curtailed, however, by an invocation carved in their midst: "*oblida... perdona... tot*"—"forget... forgive... everything." And there is more: Gaudí and Jujol inscribed on Mme. Milà's dressing-table the motto "*memento homo qui pulvis eris et in pulvis reverteris*" [sic].[23] Can there be any doubt that this motto had already been represented, and even more effectively, in the little dressing-table in the Palau Güell? We might recall here the lines from the letter that Joan Maragall wrote to Josep Pijoan on May 25, 1903, which we have already cited: "A short while ago, Gaudí invited me to visit the Park Güell with him... We talked a good deal and he managed to convince me of his idea of southern decoration. Afterwards, however, as we went deeper and deeper, we came to a point where it was impossible for us to agree. He sees in work, in struggle, in the material, so to say, the law of punishment... and it gives him pleasure!"[24] We have already seen how the temptation of the material constitutes the core of the tensions in Gaudí's architecture, and how the architecture can in large part be understood, above all from the turn of the century, as his struggle against that serpent. But we must not forget that Maragall also refers with evident distaste to the pleasure that Gaudí takes in this. In that struggle with a ghost, in effect, Gaudí sublimates his work in an apostolic dimension. The model of the Colony Güell church with its strings and little bags of lead pellets, constituted the moment when that sublimation arrived at its own limits: in the precariousness of the elements used, in the almost total absence of material, in the profound void it contained inside it and, above all, in its impossible evolution. That realization was, finally, all that the construction could represent. But there is another place where, lacking the grandeur of the limit, all of this takes on, if possible, an even more sinister resonance: in the

procedure Gaudí followed as a sculptor.[25] As we know, Gaudí himself designed the figures for the façade of the Sagrada Familia, and the sculptors and carvers who worked for him only intervened in the final stage of the execution. For this, in addition to a human skeleton which he surrounded with mirrors and photographed to study poses, he constructed wire mannequins, which he then built up in a painstaking process of materialization. Once he had obtained the pose he wanted he swathed his models in very fine metallic fabric, rolled up like muscles, and as this contracted it took on the form of living sinew; a fine layer of plaster then transformed the fabric into flesh. On top of this, canvas sacking soaked in plaster gave form, as it hardened, to the clothing, and similarly hardened strips of hemp were used for the hair. The whole process of fleshly incarnation was photographed in great detail: the series of images that have survived create a profoundly sinister impression of something that can only be known in part, or rather, of something that while seeming familiar is unknowable. The figures finally resulting from this process are not plastic forms extracted from or found in the material, but the result of waiting for the liquid, retained by the most precarious structures, to harden. In these photographs Gaudí's workshop, full of plaster models hanging from the roof and the walls, has the air of a miraculous chapel filled with *ex votos*. The sheer quantity perhaps compensates for the insignificance of each offering in relation to the grace received: the tragic pleasure— "… and it gives him pleasure!"—of waiting for the unattainable, the pleasure of impotence.

It is in the Batlló house and, above all, in the Milà house that the material is made most intangible, where it most clearly reveals the impotence of the architect's efforts to arrest it and configure it. In its wake it leaves in some places folds and wrinkles, and in others, such as the plasterwork on some of the ceilings, terrifying holes. Through these, as in the *memento mori* we referred to above, the skeleton appears. But

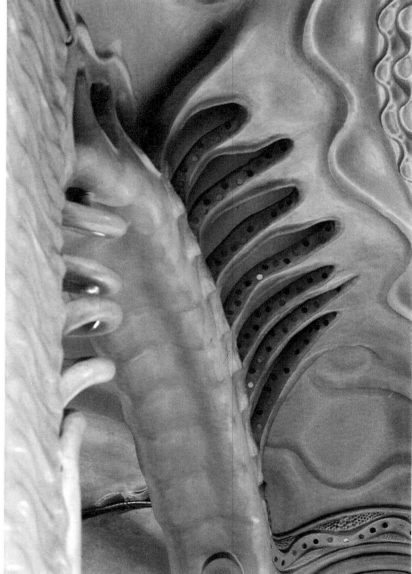

the bones that we see under the liquefied material of Gaudí's architecture are not bare and clean: they still have on them something slippery. Gaudí's architecture thus becomes a baroque reflection on death, expressed, as in those exemplary paintings, in the most terrible aspects of putrefaction.

We have mentioned the example of the Gaudíesque house by Valeri: in focusing on the style he saw, as we have said, what it is difficult for us to see in Gaudí's work, but at the same time he made it banal. So too, albeit in a different way, did Jujol, throughout his career, because in imitating the forms created by his master and transposing them with his skill in enclosing voids with lines, Jujol's obsession was not with death but with an impossible rural life that makes his work the dying breath of the most artful ingenuousness and the most sought-after anachronism. For Jujol the city was sin, and therefore he denied it in a ruralism imbued with the primordial quality that Torras i Bages had described. The whole thrust of this endeavor leads to the most traditional of fragmentations, the unconscious; how was it ever possible to see in Jujol's work an anticipation of the techniques of displacement of modern art?[26] The sin and death of which Gaudí was so conscious, the decomposition of the material, gluey rather than fragmentary, in which it is reflected, are at the same time absolutely urban. There is no flight from their social origin, since they depend on the public anonymity of the bourgeosie, and therefore their forms go hand in hand with the urban crowd.

Perhaps only one architect captured the terrible, sinister facet of Gaudí's architecture that Maragall had described with such precision: Manuel Sayrach.[27] In his building on the corner of the Diagonal and Carrer Enric Granados the turret that crowns the corner seems to split into strands that lay bare, at their top, strange, hard bones, while in the decorative redundancy of the entrance hall, marked as in Gaudí by a tenacious Rococo model, everything seems to decompose like dead flesh, suddenly revealing, here and

there, hard spirals that look like ribs. At either end of the balustrade on the main balcony of the much more modest neighboring building on Carrer Enric Granados, also by Sayrach, we find little stumps of soft, dripping material, almost naturalistic in form. In the spectacular entrance hall great plaster curtains are drawn back to expose bones, like those shrouds that Death lifts up in baroque sepulchres, or the proscenium arch of the great theater of the world.

"And it gives him pleasure!": what in Gaudí was always sublimated by his consciousness, in Sayrach is all the more disturbing and sinister in that it is a direct representation, rather than a reflection, of death.

But if Sayrach understood that terrible aspect of Gaudí's art, others saw it and used it to greater advantage. It is perhaps not surprising that Gaudí's first appearance in the realm of modern art, in the magazine *Minotaure* in 1933, was thanks to Man Ray and Dalí. Alongside Man Ray's photographs—of the Park Güell and the Batlló and Milà houses—Dalí published his famous essay "De la beauté terrifiante et comestible de l'architecture modern style."[28] A terrifying and edible Beauty: this is what Dalí makes of the softening that the material is subjected to in Gaudí's work, a softening that is also obsessively present in his own paintings of this period, where it is always an image of the decomposition of the flesh: those bodies reduced to stumps in which the navel manifests its soft presence and the hair announces its revolting life, and, a little later, those soft and dripping lumps of flesh propped up on sticks and crutches on desolate plains scattered with bones. Dalí's meditations on putrefaction have the same origin as Gaudí's: on the one hand original sin and the punishment of work and death, and on the other a loathing of bourgeois pomposity that, going beyond the political jargon of Surrealism, Dalí reflected in his little drawings of *putrefactos*: bureaucrats, academics... Worms, flies and ants are frequently present in Dalí's paintings of the late twenties and thirties. Without a doubt it is they who hear the

*Cartoon of Gaudí trying to place
a large statue of the Virgin
on the roof of the Casa Milà
and other cartoons published
in Republican newspapers, 1910–11.*

material say "eat me," as the ants on the hand and the rotting mules on the grand piano had already done in *Un chien andalou*. And, in *L'âge d'or*, those skeletons of bishops with their mitres and staffs and gold embroidered chasubles sticking to their bones, stretched out on the stones of an island beach, confused with them like pirate treasure. What is their origin but, like that mirror on the dressing-table, the *memento mori*, the last things?

Gaudí and Dalí share the same mentality, the same background: it is not a question, then, of influences, but of the fact that Dalí was so able, operatively, to recognize and express it. In one scene in *Un chien andalou* Batcheff drags with evident difficulty those Christian Brothers who also appear, with a violin, in *L'âge d'or*: such presences provide the key to a reflection on sin,

death and the decomposition of the material that had been suddenly condensed, in exemplary form, in that dripping mirror that seems to want drag down with it the flesh of the face it reflects, like the commentaries to Loyola's exercises in which he recommends first closing the windows and sitting down alone in front of a skull. This is what Gaudí did in his own unique way, and it is hardly surprising that Dalí should have seen in him a reflection of Surrealism; a subtly distorted reflection, of course, because Dalí's work is all about style and vanity. And at the same time, in spite of all the efforts to rationalize Gaudí's work in the official histories of contemporary architecture, how else, other than through the sacred formality of Surrealism, could Gaudí find a place—equally officially, endorsed by magazines and museums—in modern art?

[1] On Gaudí's furniture there is a very general monograph: R. Dalisi, *Gaudí, mobili e oggetti*, Milan, 1979, and also the catalogue *Gaudí diseñador*, Barcelona, 1978. See, too: J.J. Lahuerta, "La silla del comedor de la casa Batlló," *Barcelona. Metrópolis Mediterránea*, no. 16, Barcelona, 1990, pp. 61–64. Many of the originals are now in the Casa-Museu Gaudí in Barcelona: *Guía de la Casa-Museu Gaudí*, Barcelona, 1989. There is a general overview and bibliography on modernism in the decorative and applied arts in: M. Freixa, *El modernismo en España*, Madrid, 1986, pp. 129–50.

[2] See, for example, the following, in a classic monograph: "Dressing-table for the Palau Güell that anticipates modernist forms" (C. Martinell, *Gaudí. Su vida, su teoría, su obra*, cit., p. 148). Or the following, in a characteristic overview: "Gaudí designed furniture for the Palau Güell, of which the most notable are a dressing-table and a *chaise-longue*. In the elegant and appropriate curvature of the *chaise-longue* modernism can already be seen in full; nor should we overlook, in spite of its small size, the truly heterogeneous formal language of the dressing-table" (R. Schmutzler, *Art Nouveau-Jugendstil*, Stuttgart, 1977, pp. 150–51 of the Spanish translation, Madrid, 1980). This kind of "pioneering" innovation has often been seen in the Palau Güell: "In the first instance we must see here a firm adaptation to a formal repertoire that anticipates Art Nouveau..." (O. Bohigas, *Reseña y catálogo de la arquitectura modernista*, cit., pp. 147–48).

[3] See in general: F. Kimball, *The Creation of the Rococo Decorative Style* (1943), New York, 1980. Carlos Flores very perceptively relates Gaudí's designs with these Rococo cartouches, but restricts his scope to details of the Calvet house, insisting on Gaudí's personal interpretation, and equating his baroque inspiration with that of other Art Nouveau architects: C. Flores, *Gaudí, Jujol y el modernismo catalán*, cit., vol. I, p. 313. But see the very early: J. Cassou, "Gaudí et le baroque," *Les Formes*, no. 32, 1933, pp. 364–66.

[4] On Gaudí's ideal relation to Fortuny, on the basis of the mythologized Camp de Tarragona where both were born, see the supposed opinion of the former: "Els dots de situació i la gent del Camp de Tarragona," in I. Puig-Boada, *El pensament de Gaudí*, cit., p. 138, which, apocryphal or not, clearly reflects a widespread ideological restoration of the importance of origins.

[5] On Fortuny's fortunes in turn-of-the-century Catalonia and on the Rococo that so delighted his dealers and clients, see chapter 1, note 76.

[6] See for example: "Recort de Versailles," in R. Picó i Campamar, *Obra poètica*, cit., pp. 173ff., or: "Versailles," id., pp. 192–93. See, too the memoirs of the Vicomte de Güell, *D'Alphonse XII a Tut-Ank-Ammon*, cit., pp. 60ff. A late but significant example of the fashion is: C. Bosch, *En las cataratas de lo barroco*, Madrid-Barcelona, 1932, with a foreword by E. D'Ors.

[7] On F. Plà "el Vigatà" see: S. Alcolea, "Francisco Plà, El Vigatà (1741–1805)," *Ausa*, no. 9, 1954, pp. 404–06; id., "La pintura en Barcelona durante el siglo XVIII," *Anales y Boletín de los Museos de Arte de Barcelona*, vols. XIV and XV, 1969; id., *Sobre la pintura catalana del segle XVIII. Un cicle de Francesc Plà el Vigatà*, Barcelona, 1987. Specifically on the cycle for Eusebi Güell, see: J. Folch i Torres, "La sala de El Viguetà a casa del comte de Güell," *La Veu de Catalunya*, June 25, 1914. See, too: J. Folch i Torres, "La sala de El Viguetà a can Serra," *La Veu de Catalunya*, February 6, 1913; id., "Una pintura de El Viguetà al Museu de Barcelona," id., November 27, 1916.

[8] J. Folch i Torres, "La sala de El Viguetà a casa del comte de Güell," cit.

[9] M. d'Esplugues, op. cit., p. 107.

[10] This was a series of eight articles centered on Flaugier's work published in the *Pàgina artística de la Veu de Catalunya* in 1910: January 6 and 19, February 3 and 17, March 3, 17, and 31 and April 14.

[11] M. d'Esplugues, op. cit., p. 104.

[12] On the Calvet house see contemporary accounts such as: M. Vega y March, "Arquitectura Española Contemporánea: casa de alquiler en la calle de Caspe, núm. 52, Barcelona," *Arquitectura y Construcción*, no. 81, July 8, 1900, pp. 200–01 and no. 82, July 23, 1900, pp. 215–17; J. de Vignola, "La casa de los sres. Calvet," *Hispania*, no. 68, December 15, 1901, pp. 439–41; J. Martorell, "Arquitectura moderna: casa de los sres. Calvet en la calle de Caspe. Barcelona," *La Hormiga de Oro*, no. 35, September 1, 1906, pp. 556–59.

[13] On Gaudí's relationship to the baroque in the Camp de Tarragona: C. Martinell, *Gaudí i la Sagrada Familia comentada per ell mateix*, Barcelona, 1951, p. 88; id., *La raíz reusense en la obra de Gaudí*, Reus, 1952; id., *Gaudí. Su vida, su teoría, su obra*, cit., pp. 16–17. Martinell was a pioneer in the study of the baroque in Catalonia. See: C. Martinell, *L'Art català sota la unitat espanyola*, Barcelona, 1933; and his great work: id., *Arquitectura i escultura barroques a Catalunya*, Barcelona, 1959 (vol. I), 1961 (vol. II), 1963 (vol. III).

[14] Especially on Lluís Bonifàs, see: C. Martinell, *Llibre de notes de Lluís Bonifàs Massó, escultor de Valls*, Valls, 1917; id., *Homenaje a los escultores Bonifàs*, Doldellops, 1944; id., *El escultor Luis Bonifás y Massó (1730–1786)*, Barcelona, 1948.

[15] Nevertheless, Lily Litvak devotes a couple of very perceptive lines to these volutes: she feels that too much has been made of the Neo-Baroque association and suggests a Graeco-archaic inspiration for certain details (*El sendero del tigre. Exotismo en la literatura española de finales del siglo XIX*, cit., p. 219).

[16] On the Casa Batlló, see contemporary accounts such as: "Arquitectura Española Contemporánea: Casa de Alquiler en el Paseo de Gracia. Barcelona," *Arquitectura y Construcción* no. 183, 1907; "La casa Batlló al Passeig de Gràcia, projectada i dirigida por Gaudí," *La Ilustració Catalana*, no. 197, March 10, 1907. See, too, such characteristic interpretations as: J. Elías, "Gaudí y la Casa de los Huesos," *Diario Español*, January 3–4, 1953; A. Martorell, "Un monu-

ment a Sant Jordi," *Cavall Fort*, no. 65, April 1965.

[17] On the Pedrera, see contemporary accounts such as: "Arquitectura moderna. Detalls de la casa que està dirigint l'arquitecte sr. Gaudí al Passeig de Gràcia cantonada Provensa," *La Ilustració Catalana*, no. 236, December 8, 1907, p. 793. There are various characteristic interpretations of the symbols and the circumstances of the building's construction: J. Elías, "Gaudí y la Pedrera del sr. Milà," *Recull*, December 24, 1952, January 10, 1953, February 7, 1953. See, too: M. Tapie, *La Pedrera*, Barcelona, 1971; J. Bassegoda, *La Pedrera de Gaudí*, Barcelona, 1980. Pere Milà i Camps was also the developer of other important "modernista" buildings in Barcelona such as the Monumental bull-ring, constructed by Ignasi Mas i Morell. See: J.J. Lahuerta, "El arquitecto Ignasi Mas (1881–1953)," *Carrer de la Ciutat*, no. 2, March 1978, pp. 3–7.

[18] The fashion for Japonaiserie was formed by books such as R. Alcock, *Art and Art Industries in Japan*, London, 1878; L. Gonse, *L'Art Japonais*, Paris, 1883; and, above all: E. de Goncourt, *Outamaro, le peintre des maisons vertes*, Paris, 1891; id., *Hokousaï, l'art japonais au dix-huitième siècle*, Paris, 1896, which draw together elements Goncourt had begun writing and publishing as early as 1861. More contemporary with the Pedrera is: W. Crane, *Line and Form*, London, 1900. On this theme in general see: S. Wichmann, *Japonisme*, New York, 1981, and the catalogue *Le Japonisme*, Paris, 1988. Japonaiserie was in vogue among Barcelona artists from an early date and inspired many very fine pieces. See, for example, the work of artists such as Apel.les Mestres or Alexandre de Riquer, jewelers such as Josep Masriera and architects such as Josep Vilaseca, to name only a few. On this early and conscious reception of the style see: J. Masriera, "Influencias del estilo japonés en las artes europeas," *Memoria de la real Academia de Ciencias y Artes de Barcelona*, vol. II, no. 1, pp. 97–104. There are no published studies of the subject in Spain or Catalonia, but see the panoramic overview in L. Litvak, *El sendero del tigre…*, cit., pp. 109–45.

[19] The popularity of *The Last Days of Pompeii* can be seen from the numerous editions of the translated version only in the years around the turn of the century: 1883, 1898, 1900, 1909, 1912… On the

censoring of the book, see: P. Ladrón de Guevara, *Novelistas malos y buenos*, Bilbao, 1910, p. 86. The edition corrected by J.R. was published in Barcelona in 1892.

[20] Another novel containing this interpretation of Antiquity that met with extraordinary editorial success in Europe at the end of the century was: *Quo Vadis?* by Sienkievicz. See: M. Kosko, *Un best seller 1900: Quo Vadis?*, Paris, 1960. On his popularity in Spain and on that "fascination with Roman orgies, with the spectacle of the virgins thrown to the lions," see L. Litvak, op. cit., p. 224.

[21] See: L. Cantallops, "Salvador Valeri i Pupurull, 1873–1954," *Cuadernos de Arquitectura y Urbanismo*, no. 63, 1966, pp. 15–19.

[22] The undulations of the rear façade of this building by Salvador Valeri have been seen as an interpretation of those of the Pedrera. This is perfectly plausible, but in that case Valeri was also interpreting, no doubt *malgré lui*, the precariousness of the Gaudí construction: Valeri's undulations are not of stone, but lightweight glazed galleries of glass and wood with movable shutters. Something similar can be seen in the Planells house by Josep M. Jujol, a good deal later (1923). On this last, see: (various authors), *La arquitectura de Josep Maria Jujol*, cit., pp. 98–99.

[23] J. Bassegoda, *El gran Gaudí*, cit., p. 520.

[24] In *Obres Completes*, cit., vol. I, p. 1017.

[25] On Gaudí the sculptor: J. Folch i Torres, "L'arquitecte Gaudí," cit., pp. 58–60; R. Descharnes and C. Prevost, *La vision artistique et religieuse de Gaudí*, Lausanne, 1969.

[26] This interpretation stems from the view put forward by authors such as Sert and Swenney, Collins and Cirlot, who have seen Gaudí as a precursor not only of contemporary architecture but of many of the techniques of modern art: collage, abstraction, etc. (see chapter 2, note 119). Slowly but surely Gaudí scholars (see above all the in many ways interesting study by C. Flores, *Gaudí, Jujol y el modernismo catalán*, cit.) have clarified the attribution to Jujol of the most emblematic elements of that interpretation, such as the ceramic cladding of the undulating bench and the soffits of the hypostyle hall in the Park Güell, or the paintings in Mallorca Cathedral, establishing him as a "free artist" and the true precursor—an interpretation that

is pertinently manifested in the latest crop of publications on Jujol, in which this view is definitively stereotyped: (various authors), "Gaudí i Jujol a la Seu," *D'A*, no. 1, winter 1989, pp. 40–71; (various authors), "Josep Maria Jujol, arquitecte. 1879–1949," *Quaderns*, cit.; Perejaume, *Ludwig Jujol. Què és el collage sino acostar soledats?*, Barcelona, 1989; I. Solà-Morales, *Jujol*, Barcelona, 1990, etc.

[27] Manuel Sayrach (1886–1937), architect and writer, is a little-known figure. As an architect he produced few built works, most of them for himself or his family: the "House of the Demons" just outside Barcelona, since demolished, with a fantastic garden and a great mural allegory of the Creation; the house on the Avenida Diagonal discussed in the text (1917) and the neighboring building on Carrer Enric Granados (1926), the family tomb in Barcelona's main cemetery (1934) and little else, in addition to a few unbuilt projects. In 1909 he wrote a short architectural manifesto, *L'arquitectura nova*, in which he advocated the development of an "*estil catalàunic*." He also published a book of poems, *L'idili del poeta* (1904), and a major dramatic cycle under the generic title *Drames de la llum*, of which only the first two of the seven envisaged plays were published: *Abelard i Eloïsa* (1919) and *Reigzel, l'íntim amic* (1920), which he refused to have staged. See: F. Fontbona, "Notícia del Manuel Sayrach escriptor," *Miscel.lania Aramon i Serra*, Barcelona, 1979; C. Borbonet, "L'arquitectura filosófica de Manuel Sayrach," *Serra d'Or*, no. 332, May 1987, pp. 57–61.

[28] S. Dalí, "De la beauté terrifiante et comestible de l'architecture modern style," *Minotaure*, nos. 3–4, June–October 1933, pp. 69–76. But Dalí had already championed the "modern style": S. Dalí, "L'âne pourri," *Le surréalisme au service de la révolution*, no. 1, 1930, p. 12, precisely as "*architecture ornementale*." On his fascination with Gaudí see, for example, his recommendations to Paul Éluard concerning the Pedrera and the Sagrada Familia when Éluard was to visit Barcelona to give a series of lectures late in 1935; his advice did not fall on deaf ears: Éluard hailed the buildings as "integral surrealism." See: R. Santos Torroella, *Salvador Dalí corresponsal de J.V. Foix. 1932–1936*, Barcelona, 1986, pp. 204–06. See, too, the numerous references to Gaudí in: *The Secret Life of Salvador Dalí*, New York, 1941, as well as the foreword to R. Descharnes and C. Prevost, op. cit.

*A+U*, no. 86, December 1977 (special monographic issue).

"A. Gaudí i J.M. Jujol a la Seu," *D'A*, no. 1, 1989, (special issue).

J.B. Ache, "Les précurseurs de la révolution architecturale. L'empirisme et le rêve: Gaudí," *Architecture d'Aujourd'hui*, April–May 1964, p. 4.

A. Albanesi, "Divagazioni su Antonio Gaudí: un tempio come vaso spaziale," *L'architettura*, no. 23, September 1957, pp. 319–22.

*Album del Temple Expiatori de la Sagrada Familia*, Barcelona 1915, (several editions).

*Album record a Gaudí i al Temple Expiatori de la Sagrada Familia*, Barcelona 1936.

G. Alomar, "Sobre les estades a Mallorca dels arquitectes Gaudí i Le Corbusier," *Estudis Baleàrics*, no. 27, December 1987, pp. 25–74.

M.J. Alonso Gavela, *Gaudí en Astorga*, León 1972.

L. Alonso Luengo, *Gaudí en Astorga*, Astorga 1954.

*Antoni Gaudí. La seva vida, les seves obres, la seva mort*, Barcelona 1926.

*Antoni Gaudí. L'home, l'obra, l'anècdota*, Barcelona 1964.

M. Armengol, *El jardí dels guerrers*, Barcelona 1987.

R. Artigas Amat, "Gaudí creador d'estructures," *La Veu de Catalunya*, June 11, 1928, p. 4.

D. Ashton, "Antonio Gaudí," *Craft Horizons*, no. 17, November–December 1957, pp. 35–41.

F. de P. Baldello, *Petites biografies des grans barcelonins*, Barcelona 1965, pp. 67–116.

R. Banham, "The Return Curve," *Motif*, no. 6, 1961, pp. 82–88; id., "The Last of the Goths," *New Statesman*, April 7, 1961, pp. 556–57.

G. Barbe Coquelin de Lisle, "El teatro mercado del Park Güell de Gaudí y el mito del Mediterráneo en el arte catalán de 1900," *Fragmentos*, nos. 15–16, 1989, pp. 123–29.

J. Bardier Pardo, "Gaudí y el Par-

que Güell," *Destino*, nos. 25, 28, January 1961, p. 11.

D. Baroni, "Il maestro di un medioevo prossimo venturo. Gaudí e l'ambiente domestico," *Ottagono*, no. 87, December 1987, pp. 38–49.

J.M. Bartrina, "La Sociedad Cooperativa Mataronense: su origen, vicisitudes y actual estado," *Obras en prosa y verso escogidas y seleccionadas por J. Sardà*, Barcelona-Madrid 1881, pp. 219–58.

B. Bassegoda Amigó, "Cuestiones artísticas: el Parque Güell," *Diario de Barcelona*, January 14, 1903, pp. 567–569; id., "Antonio Gaudí: el Dante de la arquitectura," *La Vanguardia*, June 23, 1926, p. 5.

J. Bassegoda Nonell, J. Garrut Roma, *"Guía de Gaudí,"* Barcelona 1970.

J. Bassegoda Nonell, "Los muebles de Gaudí," Barcelona 1975; id., "Antonio Gaudí. Vida y arquitectura," Barcelona–Tarragona 1977; id., "La Pedrera de Gaudí," Barcelona 1980; id., "Gaudí," Barcelona 1985; id., "The Inscriptions on the Bench at Park Güell as Transcribed by J. Matamala i Flotats in 1967," *Sites*, no. 15, 1986, pp. 12–14; id., "Verdaguer, els Güell i Gaudí," *Anuari Verdaguer 1986*, Vic 1987, pp. 215–19; id., *El gran Gaudí*, Sabadell 1989.

D. Bayón, "Gaudí: 1852–1926," in P. Francostels, *Les architectes célébres*, Paris 1958–59.

T.G. Beddall, "Gaudí y el gótico catalán," *Hogar y Arquitectura*, no. 112, May–June 1974, pp. 32–68.

J. Belle, "A New Interest in Gaudí," *Painter and Sculptor*, no. 1, 1958, pp. 16–20.

R. Bellmunt, F. Maña, "Aproximación a la patología en la obra de Gaudí," *CAU*, no. 70, March 1981, pp. 66–73.

R. Benet, "Fent coneixença amb Le Corbusier," *La Veu de Catalunya*, May 21, 1928, p. 4; id., "El gust de Gaudí," *La Veu de Catalunya*, June 11, 1928, p. 4.

E. Bentivoglio, "Come Mahler nella musica Gaudí nell'architettura,"

*L'Architettura*, no. 277, November 1978, pp. 395–400.

J. Bergós Masso, *Antoni Gaudí. L'home i l'obra*, Barcelona 1954; id., *Antoni Gaudí i el Comte de Güell*, Barcelona 1969; id., *Gaudí*, Madrid 1971; id., *Antoni Gaudí, arquitecte genial*, Barcelona 1972.

A. Boada, "Verdaguer i Gaudí," *Igualada*, June 22, 1968.

O. Bohigas, "Carta a una amiga muy poco gaudinista: Parque Güell, Casa Batlló, Casa Milà," *Cúpula*, no. 39, January 1953, pp. 740–44; id., "Gaudí y el gaudinismo," *San Jorge*, no. 15, July 1954, pp. 22–26; id., *Arquitectura modernista*, Barcelona 1968; id., *Reseña y catálogo de la arquitectura modernista*, Barcelona 1973.

J. Boix, "Las chimeneas de Gaudí," *Cúpula*, no. 26, August 1971, pp. 472–76.

A. Bonet, *Antonio Gaudí*, Buenos Aires 1960.

L. Bonet Gari, "El arquitecto D. Antonio Gaudí," *El Propagador de la Devoción a San José*, no. 61, June 1, 1927, pp. 186–203; id., "El estudio de Gaudí," *Templo*, no. 83, May 1948, pp. 4–5; id., "El funcionalismo y el sentido decorativo de la obra arquitectónica de Gaudí," *Proyectos y Materiales*, no. 5, September–October 1949, pp. 26–29; id., "Arquitectura en el Palacio Güell," *San Jorge*, July 1954, pp. 61–66; id., "Los modelos y maquetas del Templo," *Templo*, no. 91, April 1956, pp. 8–9.

O. Brachfeld, "Psicoanàlisi i decepció: una patografia d'Antoni Gaudí," *Mirador*, April 6, 1933.

I. Buckmann, "Antoni Gaudí. Ein pathographischer Versuch, zugleich ein Beitrag zur Genese des Genieruhms," *Zeitschrift für die Gesamte Neurologie und Psychiatrie*, no. 139, 1932, pp. 133–57.

C. Buxade, J. Margarit, "Otra visita al Palau Güell," *Arquitecturas Bis*, no. 45, December 1983, pp. 23–31.

A. Campanya, *Gaudí*, Barcelona 1980.

P.J. Campins i Barceló, "Carta pastoral sobre la restauración de la Santa Iglesia Catedral de Mallorca," *Boletín Oficial del Obispado de Mallorca*, nos. 15–16, August 1904, pp. 247–66.

F. Camprubi Alemany, *Die Kirche der Heiligen Familie*, Barcelona 1960.

M. Canela, *La fantasía inacabable de Gaudí*, Barcelona 1980.

J.M. Carandell, "Elsinor a la Pedrera," *El País. Quadern*, July 19, 1990, p. 8.

F. de P. Cardoner Blanch, *El Gaudí marià i el pessebre gegant*, Barcelona 1987.

F. de P. Cardoner Blanch, *Casa Güell*, n.d. (Barcelona 1910).

E. Casanelles, "Gaudí ante Montserrat," *Destino*, May 26, 1972, pp. 54–55.

J.M. Casas de Muller, "Del temple exemplar," *Pindàriques Modernes*, Barcelona 1926, pp. 81–84.

J. Cassou, "Gaudí et le baroque," *Les Formes*, no. 32, 1933, pp. 364–66.

M.L. Caturla, *Arte de épocas inciertas*, Madrid 1944.

F. Chueca Goitia, *Gaudí: interpretación de una vida*, Madrid 1983.

A. Cirici Pellicer, *Picasso antes de Picasso*, Barcelona 1946; id., *El arte modernista catalán*, Barcelona 1951; id., *La Sagrada Familia de Antonio Gaudí*, Barcelona 1952; id., *Gaudí dissenyador*, Barcelona 1984.

J.E. Cirlot, "El arte de Gaudí," Barcelona 1950; id., "El sufrimiento de Antonio Gaudí," *Templo*, no. 90, May 1955, pp. 6–10; id., "La plástica de Antonio Gaudí," in Goya, no. 9, November–December 1955, pp. 176–82; id., *Introducción a la arquitectura de Gaudí*, Barcelona 1966.

L. Cirlot, "Una aproximació a la iconografía gaudiniana," *Quaderns de l'obra social. Fundació Caixa de Pensions*, no. 25, October 1984, pp. 15–18.

"Civis," "La ciudades jardines de España. Barcelona: el Parque Güell," *Civitas*, no. 1, July 1914, pp. 55–59.

G.R. Collins, *Antonio Gaudí*, New York 1960; id., "Antonio Gaudí: Stucture and Form," *Perspecta*, no. 8, 1963, pp. 63–90; id., M.E. Farinas, *The American Ass. of Architectural Bibliographers. Papers X. Antonio Gaudí and the Catalan Movement. 1870–1930*, Charlottesville 1973; id., *The Drawings of Antonio Gaudí*, New York 1977; id., J. Bassegoda, *The Designs and Drawings of Antonio Gaudí*, Princeton 1983.

*Colonia Güell y Fábrica de panas y veludillos de Güell y Cía. Breve reseña histórica...*, Barcelona 1910. *Colonia Güell*, Igualada 1917.

U. Conrads, H.G. Sperlich, *Phantastische Architektur*, Stuttgart 1960.

S. Dalí, "L'âne pourri," *Le surréalisme au service de la révolution*, vol. I, no. 1, 1930, p. 12; id., "De la beauté terrifiante et comestible de l'architecture Modern Style," Minotaure, nos. 3–4, June–October 1933, pp. 69–76; id., R. Descharnes, C. Prevost, *La vision artistique et religieuse de Gaudí*, Lausanne 1969.

R. Dalisi, *Gaudí, mobili e oggetti*, Milan 1979.

E. D'Ors, *Obra catalana completa. Glosari 1906–1910*, Barcelona 1950, pp. 184; 1004–5; 1161–63; 1233–35.

*El Templo Expiatorio de la Sagrada Familia que erige en Barcelona la Asociación de Devotos de San José*, Barcelona 1947.

J. Elías, "Gaudí y la Pedrera del sr. Milà," *Recull*, December 24, 1952, January 10, 1953, February 7, 1953; id., "Gaudí y la Casa de los Huesos," *Diario Español*, January 3–4, 1953; id., "Gaudí en Montserrat," *Templo*, XCI, February 1956, pp. 8–11; id., *Gaudí. Assaig biogràfic*, Barcelona 1961.

F. Escalas, "Gaudí," *Hispania*, January 15, 1903, pp. 10–16.

*Exposición Gaudí*, (catalogue), Barcelona, June 1956.

*Exposición Gaudí 1967*, (catalogue), Barcelona May–June 1967.

C. Flores, *Arquitectura española contemporánea*, Madrid 1961; id., *Gaudí, Jujol y el modernismo catalán*, Madrid 1982.

J. Folch i Torres, "L'ordre," *La Veu de Catalunya*, April 7, 1910; id., "L'arquitecte Gaudí," *Gaseta de les Arts*, no. 1, July 1926.

E. Fort i Cogul, *Gaudí i la restauració de Poblet*, Barcelona 1976.

G. Forteza, *Estudis sobre arquitectura i urbanisme*, Montserrat 1984.

R. Fradera, *Antonio Gaudí: teorías y sistemas constructivos*, Barcelona 1968.

J.(osep) F.(ranquesa), "Una vetillada memorable," *La Renaixença*, November 4, 1894; id., "La Sagrada Familia," *Ilustració Catalana*, March 18, 1906.

M. Freixa, *El modernismo en España*, Madrid 1986.

J.M. Garrut Roma, "Gaudí en la caricatura," *San Jorge*, no. 37, January 1960, pp. 18–24.

*Gaudí*, (catalogue), New York, February–March 1957.

*Gaudí*, Barcelona 1960.

*Gaudí: Colonia Güell*, Santa Coloma de Cervelló 1962.

*Gaudí: Exposición 1964*, (catalogue), Madrid 1964.

*Gaudí diseñador*, (catalogue), Barcelona 1978.

*Gaudí the Visionary*, New York 1971.

*Gaudí*, (catalogue), Florence, July–September 1979.

A. Gaudí, *Manifiestos, artículos, conversaciones y dibujos*, (edited by M. Cocinachs), Murcia 1982.

*Gaudí (1852–1926)*, (catalogue), Barcelona, December 1984–January 1985; Madrid, May–June 1985.

*Gaudí dibuixat pels estudiants de l'Escola Tècnica Superior d'Arquitectura*, Barcelona 1985.

*Gaudí and Modernism Catalan. Human Love and Design* (catalogue), Nagoya, July–November 1989.

"Gaudí y su tiempo," *La Vanguardia. Cultura y Arte*, October 17, 1989.

V.M. Gibert, "Gaudí, músico poten-

cial," *La Vanguardia*, June 17, 1926, p. 7.

C. Giedion-Welcker, "Bildhafte Kachel-Kompositen von Antonio Gaudí," *Werk*, no. 42, April 1955, pp. 126–37; id., *Park Güell*, Barcelona 1966.

V. Girardi, "Alla ricerca di Antonio Gaudí," *L'Architettura*, January 1969, pp. 688–694; February 1969, pp. 760–64; March 1969, pp. 830–34; April 1969, pp. 900–04; June 1969, pp. 130–34; July 1969, pp. 200–04; August 1969, pp. 270–74; September 1969, pp. 342–44.

A. González Moreno-Navarro, R.R. Lacuesta, "Resumen histórico de la evolución del entorno urbano de la Sagrada Familia," *CAU*, no. 40, 1976, pp. 20–34.

A. González Moreno-Navarro, J. Isern, *El Palau Güell d'Antoni Gaudí. Centenari de l'inici de les obres*, Barcelona 1986.

B. Gravagnuolo, "Gaudí o dell'architettura incommestibile,"*Modo*, no. 40, June 1981, pp. 53–55.

X. Güell, *Antoni Gaudí*, Barcelona 1986.

*Guía de la Casa-Museu Gaudí*, Barcelona 1989.

J.M. Guix Sugrañes, *Gaudí, l'arquitecte de l'empremta divina*, Reus 1952; id., *Defensa de Gaudí*, Reus 1960.

H.R. Hitchcock, "Gaudí Today," *Ark*, no. 17, ver. 1956, pp. 14–18; id., "The Work of Antoni Gaudí i Cornet," *Architectural Association Journal*, no. 74, November 1958, pp. 86–98.

E. Hosoe, *Gaudí*, Tokyo 1984.

F. Huerta, *La arquitectura de Antoni Gaudí*, Barcelona 1986.

*Ilustració Catalana*, March 18, 1906 (partially dedicated to the Sagrada Familia).

J. Joedicke, "Antonio Gaudí," *Architecture d'Aujourd'hui*, no. 33, June–July 1962, pp. 16–21.

*Jornadas internacionales de estudios gaudinistas*, Barcelona 1970.

C. Kent, "The Park Güell Bench in Context," *Sites*, no. 19, 1988, pp. 66–76; id., "Gaudí's Capricho in Context: Barcelona on the Atlantic," *Sites*, no. 20, 1988, pp. 48–56.

A. Kerrigan, "Gaudianism in Catalonia," *Arts*, no. 32, December 1957, pp. 20–25; id., *Gaudí en la Catedral de Mallorca*, Palma de Mallorca 1960.

U. Kultermann, "Une architecture autre: Ein neugeknüpfter Faden der architektonischen Entwicklung," *Baukunst und Werkform*, vol. XI, no. 8, 1958, pp. 425–41.

I. Kurita, *Antonio Gaudí*, Tokyo 1978.

J.J. Lahuerta (edited by), *Gaudí i el seu temps*, Barcelona 1990; id., "La silla del comedor de la casa Batlló," *Barcelona. Metrópolis Mediterránea*, no. 16, 1990, pp. 61–64.

J. de C. Laplana, "La capilla de Sant Josep de la Basílica de Montserrat. Notes històriques i artístiques," *Montserrat. Butlletí del Santuari*, no. 9, May–August 1984, pp. 34–40. *La Veu de Catalunya*, January 20, 1906 (page dedicated to the Sagrada Familia).

M.A. Leblond, "Gaudí et l'architecture méditerranéenne," *L'Art et les Artistes*, no. 11, 1910, pp. 69–76.

Le Corbusier, *Gaudí*, Barcelona 1958.

J. Llarch, *Gaudí, biografía mágica*, Barcelona 1982.

T. Llorens, "Gaudí Diseñador o El Crepúsculo de los Gaudinismos," *Arquitecturas Bis*, no. 19, November 1977, pp. 27–29.

F. Loyer, "La Chapelle Güell: laboratoire d'un nouveau langage plastique," *L'Oeil*, no. 198, June 1971, pp. 13–21.

D. Mackay, "Tres escriptors estrangers encarats amb Gaudí," *Serra d'Or*, vol. III, March 1961, pp. 26–28; id., "Berenguer," *Cuadernos de Arquitectura y Urbanismo*, no. 58, 1964, pp. 45–47.

J. Maragall, *Obres Completes*, Barcelona 1981, vol. I, p. 1017; vol. II,

pp. 614–15, 705–07, 726–28, 768–69.

C. Martinell, *Gaudí i la Sagrada Familia comentada per ell mateix*, Barcelona 1951; id., *La Sagrada Familia*, Barcelona 1952; id., *La raíz reusense en la obra de Gaudí*, Reus 1952; id., *Gaudinismo*, Barcelona 1954; id., *Antonio Gaudí*, Milan 1955; id., "Las farolas de la Plaza Real," *Destino*, XXVIII, September 25, 1965, pp. 26–28; id., *Gaudí. Su vida, su teoría, su obra*, Barcelona 1967; id., *Conversaciones con Gaudí*, Barcelona 1969.

A. Martorell, "Un monument a Sant Jordi," *Cavall Fort*, no. 65, April 1965.

J. Martorell, "Arquitectura moderna: la casa de los sres. Calvet en la calle de Caspe. Barcelona," *La Hormiga de Oro*, no. 35, September 1, 1906, pp. 556–59; id., "En Gaudí a París," *La Veu de Catalunya*, June 23, 1910, p. 3.

L.V. Masini, *Antonio Gaudí*, Florence 1969.

J. Matamala, *Mi itinerario con el arquitecto*, Barcelona 1965 (unpublished in Catédra Gaudí); id., *Album de las inscripciones*, Barcelona 1967 (unpublished Catédra Gaudí).

*Memoria de la Cátedra Gaudí. Curso 1967–68*, Barcelona 1969.

*Memoria de la Cátedra Gaudí. Curso 1968–69*, Barcelona 1970.

*Modernismo en España, El*, (catalogue), Madrid, October–December 1969.

A. Moravanski, *Antonio Gaudí*, Budapest 1980.

G. Morrione, *Gaudí. Immagine e architettura*, Rome 1979.

D. Mower, *Gaudí*, London 1977.

C.A. Müller, *On ne badine pas avec Gaudí*, Geneva 1986.

A. Oriol i Anguera, "Epoques de transició: a l'entorn del modernisme," *Ariel*, III, July 1948, pp. 75–76.

A. Pabón-Charneco, *The Architectural Collaborators of Antoni Gaudí*, Ann Arbor, Michigan 1983.

R. Pane, *Antoni Gaudí*, Milan 1964; id., *Antoni Gaudí*, Milan 1982.

*Papeles de Son Armadans*, IV, vol. XV, December 1959 (monographic issue on Gaudí).

I. Paricio, "El Park Güell de Barcelona: una lección de construcción," *CAU*, no. 70, March 1981, pp. 54–62.

J. Perucho, *Gaudí, una arquitectura de anticipación*, Barcelona 1967.

N. Pevsner, "The Strange architecture of A. Gaudí," *Listener*, August 7, 1952, pp. 213–14; id., "Gaudí. Pioneer or Outsider?," *Architects' Journal*, December 15, 1960, p. 852.

J.M. Pi i Suñer, *Gaudí y la familia Güell*, Barcelona 1958.

*Pionniers du XXe siècle: Gaudí*, (catalogue), Paris, June–September 1971.

J. Plà, "Gaudí: la Sagrada Familia," *Grandes Tipos*, Barcelona 1959, pp. 43–58; id., *Homenots. Antoni Gaudí*, Barcelona 1960.

A. Plana, "El ferro i l'estil de l'arquitecte Gaudí," *De l'art de la forja*, no. 1, March 1921, pp. 214–18.

J.M. Poblet, *Gaudí, l'home i el geni*, Barcelona 1973.

*Propagador de la Devoción a San José, El*, 1867–1936 and 1943–48.

I. Puig Boada, *El temple de la Sagrada Familia*, Barcelona 1929; id., "El palacio Güell en la calle Conde del Asalto de Barcelona," *Cuadernos de Arquitectura*, no. 2, November 1944, pp. 25–34; id., *El templo de la Sagrada Familia: síntesis del arte de Gaudí*, Barcelona 1952; id., *El temple de la Sagrada Familia*, Barcelona 1975; id., *L'església de la Colonia Güell*, Barcelona 1976; id., *El pensament de Gaudí*, Barcelona 1981.

J. Puiggarí, *Monografía de la Casa Palau y Museu del Excm. Sr. D. Eusebi Güell y Bacigalupi*, Barcelona 1894.

F. Pujols, *Recull d'articles de crítica artística publicats fins ara, referents a les arts plàstiques i dedicats als artistes i a les exposicions*, Barcelona 1921; id., *La visió artística i religiosa d'En Gaudí*, Barcelona 1927.

F. de P. Quintana, "Les formes guerxes del temple de la Sagrada Familia," *La Ciutat i la Casa*, no. 6, 1927, pp. 16–29, and in *Album record a Gaudí*, Barcelona 1936, pp. 112–19.

J.F. Ràfols, F. Folguera, *Gaudí*, Barcelona 1928; id., *El arte modernista en Barcelona*, Barcelona 1943; id., *Modernismo y modernistas*, Barcelona 1949; id., *Gaudí 1852–1926*, Barcelona 1952.

F. Rahola, "Palacio Güell de Barcelona. Planeado y construido por Gaudí," *La Vanguardia*, August 3, 1890, pp. 4–5.

E. Raillard, "Le Parc Güell de Gaudí: une école au hasard," *Techniques & Architecture*, no. 344, November 1982, pp. 121–23.

S. Rasigade, *Antonio Gaudí: la structure d'un rêve*, Barcelona 1972.

M. Ribas Piera, "Consideraciones sobre Gaudí a través de sus obras urbanísticas," *Cuadernos de arquitectura y urbanismo*, no. 63, 1966, pp. 20–33.

J. Rivera, *El palacio episcopal de Gaudí y el Museo de los Caminos de Astorga*, Valladolid 1985.

J. Rohrer, *Artistic Regionalism and Architectural Politics in Barcelona, 1880–1910*, Ann Arbor, Michigan 1984.

E. Rojo, *Antoni Gaudí aquest desconegut: el Park Güell*, Barcelona 1986; id., *Antonio Gaudí: ese incomprendido. La Cripta de la Colonia Güell*, Barcelona 1988.

M. Rotger Capllonch, *Restauració de la Catedral de Mallorca*, Palma de Mallorca 1907.

S. Rubio, *Cálculo funicular del hormigón armado. Generalización de los métodos... del arquitecto Gaudí...*, Buenos Aires 1952.

J. Rubió i Bellver, "La Seu de Mallorca," *La Veu de Catalunya*, January 12, 1906; id., "Conferencia acerca de los conceptos orgánicos, mecánicos y constructivos de la Catedral de Mallorca," *Anuario de la Asociación de Arquitectos,*

Barcelona 1912, pp. 87–114; id., "Dificultats per a arribar a la síntessis arquitectònica," *Anuario de la Asociación de Arquitectos*, Barcelona 1913, pp. 63–79.
N.M. Rubio i Tuduri, "A propos de Gaudí," *Cahiers d'Art*, IV, 1929, sup., p. XXII.
R. Rucabado, "José Llimona y Antonio Gaudí," *Templo*, June 1965, pp. 6–7.
S. Rusiñol et al, "Notas locales," *La Vanguardia*, December 28, 1889, p. 8.

E. Sagristà, *La catedral de Mallorca*, Castellón de la Plana 1948; id., *Gaudí en la Catedral de Mallorca. Anécdotas y recuerdos*, Castellón de la Plana 1962.
A. Salvador i Carreras, "Gaudí. Impresión de viaje," *Pequeñas monografías*, November 1, 1907, pp. 1–4.
H.G. Scheffauer, "Barcelona Builds with Bold Fantasy," *New York Times Magazine*, November 21, 1926, pp. 5–17.
A. Schweitzer, *Aus meinem Leben und Denken*, Leipzig 1932, pp. 84–86.
S. Sellés, "Park Güell," *Anuario de la Asociación de Arquitectos*, Barcelona 1903, pp. 47–67.
J.L. Sert, "Gaudí: visionnaire et précurseur," *L'Oeil*, no. 2, February 15, 1955, pp. 26–35; id., *Cripta de la Colonia Güell de A. Gaudí*, Barcelona 1968.
P.E. Skriver, "Gaudí," *Architekten*, no. 18, 1959, pp. 317–30.
I. Solà-Morales, *Joan Rubió i Bellver y la fortuna del gaudinismo*, Barcelona 1975; id., *Gaudí*, Barcelona 1983.
J. Sola Toroella, *Técnica de Gaudí*, Vilanova y la Geltrú, 1954.
A. Soler y March, "En Gaudí a la Seu de Manresa," *Ciutat*, June 1, 1926, pp. 93–100.
J.M. Sostres, *Opiniones sobre arquitectura*, Murcia 1983.
G. Steiner, *Gaudí*, Cologne 1979.
G. Steiner, *Antoni Gaudí. Architecture in Barcelona*, New York 1985.

D. Sugrañes, "Disposició estática del Temple de la Sagrada Familia," *Anuario de la Asociación de Arquitectos*, Barcelona 1923, pp. 16–36.
J.J. Swenney, J.L. Sert, *Antoni Gaudí*, New York 1960.

S. Tanaka, *Gaudí. Architectural works. Drawing of actual measurement*, Tokyo 1987.
M. Tapie, *La Pedrera*, Barcelona 1971.
S. Tarragó, *Gaudí*, Barcelona 1974; id., "Antonio Gaudí: la construcción de una arquitectura. Entre la estructura y la forma," *CAU*, no. 69, February 1981, pp. 50–68.
Technische Hogeschool Delft, *Gaudí, rationalist met perfecte materiaalbe-heersing*, Delft 1979.
*Temple Expiatori de la Sagrada Familia*, Barcelona 1952.
*Templo*, 1948 and following years.
J.J. Tharrats, "El Arte Otro comienza en Gaudí," *Revista*, May 9, 1956, p. 4.
J. Tomlow, *Das Modell*, Stuttgart 1989; id., "El modelo colgante de Gaudí y su reconstrucción. Nuevos conocimientos para el diseño de la iglesia de la Colonia Güell," *Informes de la Construcción*, no. 404, November–December 1989, pp. 57–72.
T. Torii, *El mundo enigmático de Gaudí*, Madrid 1983.
E. Torno, "Antonio Gaudí," *Dau al Set*, December 1948.
J. Torres-García, "Mestre Antoni Gaudí," *Universalismo Constructivo*, Buenos Aires, 1944, pp. 560–66.
"23 opiniones sobre Gaudí," *Revista*, May 21–June 6, 1956, p. 13.

F. Ulsamer, "Las estructuras funiculares de Gaudí," *Cúpula*, IX, July 1962, pp. 425–28.

E. Valentí, *El primer modernismo literario catalán y sus fundamentos ideológicos*, Barcelona 1973.
M. Vega y March, "Arquitectura española contemporánea: casa de alquiler en la calle de Caspe n. 52. Barcelona," *Arquitectura y Construcción*, no. 81, July 8, 1900, pp. 200–01 and no. 82, July 23, 1900, pp. 215–17.
J. de Vignola, "La casa de los sres. Calvet," *Hispania*, no. 68, December 15, 1901, pp. 439–41.
P. Voltes Bou, "Cómo imaginaron Rusiñol y otros humoristas que sería la Barcelona de 1889," *La Vanguardia*, June 24, 1964, p. 27.

M. Whiffen, "Catalan Surreal," *Architectural Review*, CVIII, November 1950, pp. 322–25.

R. Zerbst, *Antoni Gaudí i Cornet. Ein Leben in der Architektur*, Cologne 1987.
C. Zervos, "Gaudí, Editorial Canosa, Barcelone," *Cahiers d'Art*, IV, 1929, suppl., p. XVII.
B. Zevi, "Un genio catalano: A. Gaudí," *Metron*, XXXVIII, October 1950, pp. 26–53.

**Analytical Index**

*The numbers in italics refer
to the pages of the illustrations.
The letter "n" following page
numbers refers to note entries.*